INUYASHA

VOL. 46　Shonen Sunday Edition

STORY AND ART BY
RUMIKO TAKAHASHI

CONTENTS

THE STORY THUS FAR

Long ago, in the "Warring States" era of Japan's Muromachi period, dog-like half demon Inuyasha attempted to steal the Shikon Jewel—or "Jewel of Four Souls"—from a village. The village priestess, Kikyo, put a stop to his thievery with an enchanted arrow. Pinned to a tree, Inuyasha fell into a deep sleep, while mortally wounded Kikyo took the jewel with her into her funeral pyre. Years passed...

In the present day, Kagome, a Japanese high school girl, is pulled down into a well and transported into the past. There she discovers trapped Inuyasha—and frees him.

When the Shikon Jewel mysteriously reappears, demons attack. In the ensuing battle, the jewel *shatters*!

Now Inuyasha is bound to Kagome with a powerful spell, and the grudging companions must battle to reclaim the shattered shards of the Shikon Jewel to keep them out of evil hands...

LAST VOLUME Inuyasha's archenemy Naraku absorbs Yomeiju, a demonic tree, then attacks Moryomaru, who carries Naraku's heart inside his being. Moryomaru appears to absorb Naraku. Elsewhere, reincarnated Kikyo tries to force wolf demon Koga to relinquish the Shikon shards in his legs, but he refuses. Then Koga attacks Moryomaru. Naraku reappears from inside Moryomaru and, using the abilities he gained from Yomeiju, penetrates the barriers around his own heart. Inuyasha's ally Miroku is injured while attempting to suck Naraku's heart into his Wind Tunnel, and Kikyo warns him he must stop using this technique or perish...

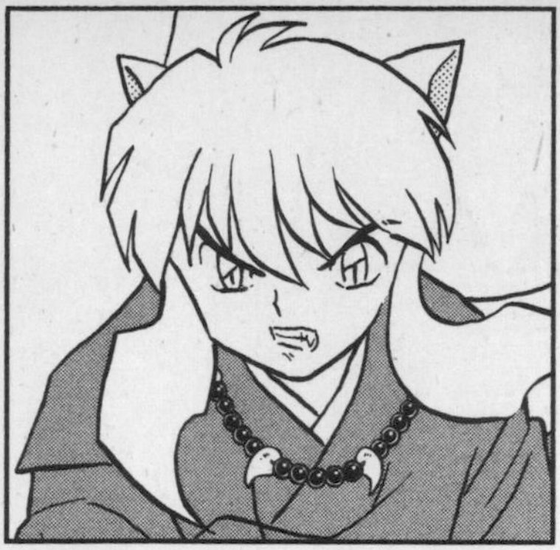

INUYASHA
Half-demon hybrid, son of a human mother and demon father. His necklace is enchanted, allowing Kagome to control him with a word.

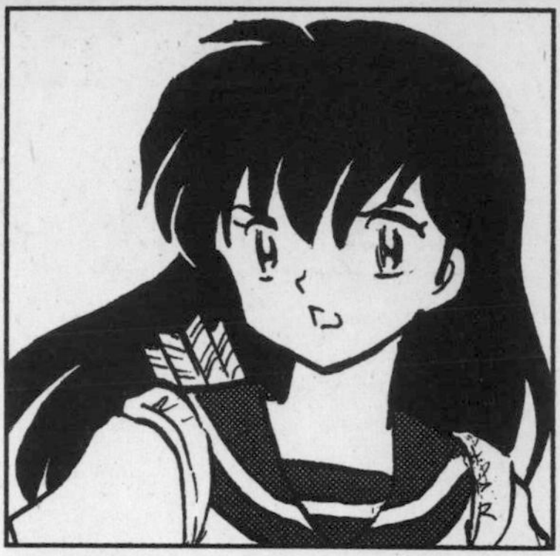

KAGOME
Modern-day Japanese schoolgirl who can travel back and forth between the past and present through an enchanted well.

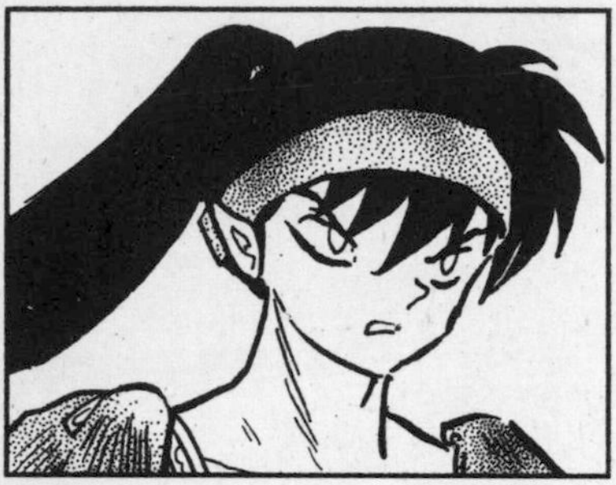

KOGA
The leader of a wolf demon clan. A Shikon shard in each of his legs imbues him with super speed. Enamored of Kagome, Koga quarrels with Inuyasha frequently.

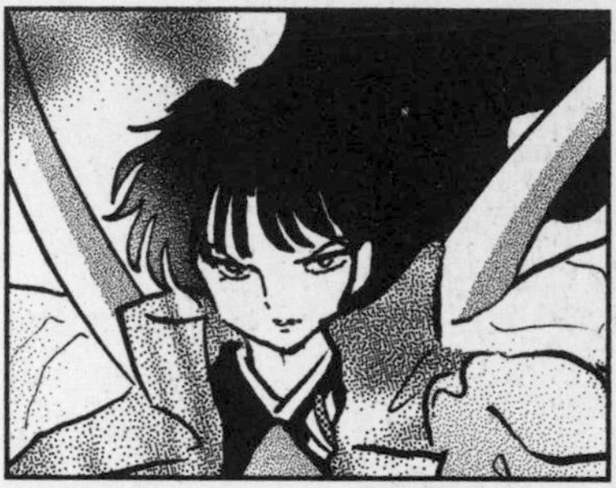

NARAKU
Enigmatic demon mastermind behind the miseries of nearly everyone in the story. He has the power to create multiple incarnations of himself from his body.

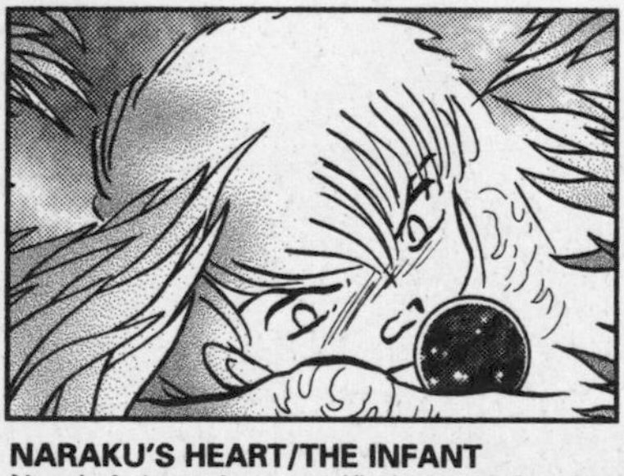

NARAKU'S HEART/THE INFANT
Naraku's heart is personified as an infant hidden inside Moryomaru, a being Naraku created to house it. As long as Naraku's actual heart is alive inside Moryomaru, Naraku cannot be killed.

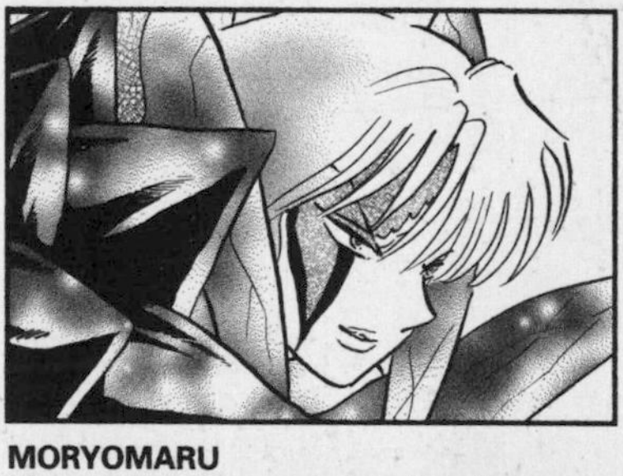

MORYOMARU
Moryomaru was created by Naraku to serve him, but now he has ambitions of his own. He is immune to energy-based attacks.

SCROLL 1
YAMA'ARASHI

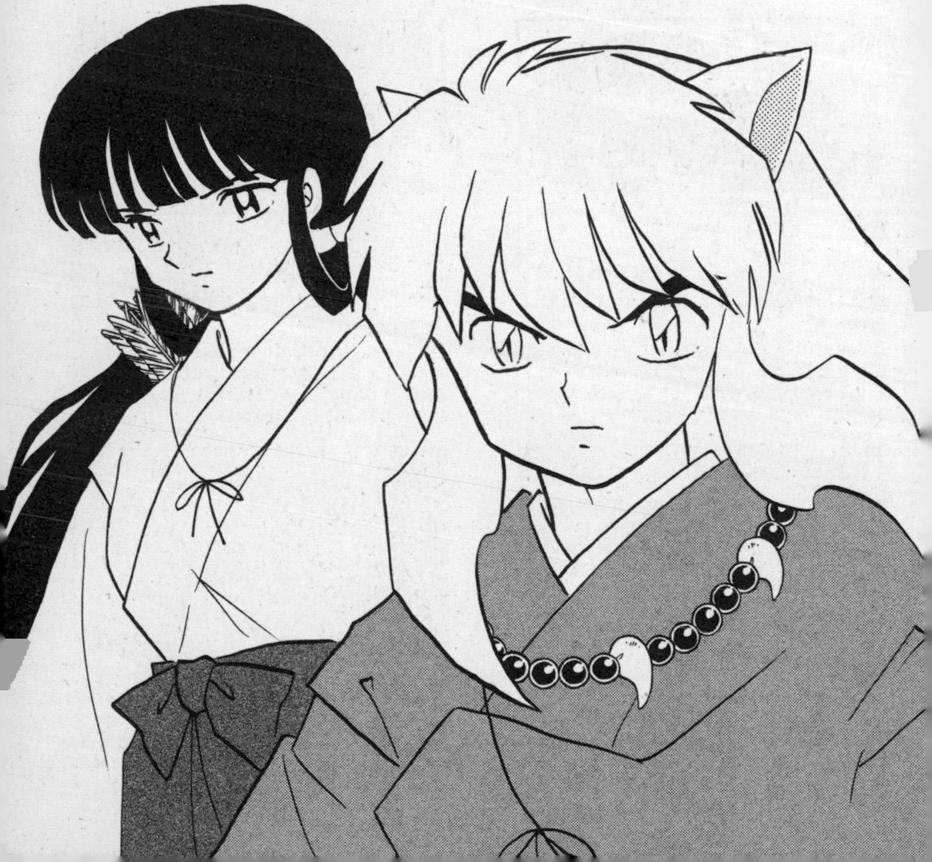

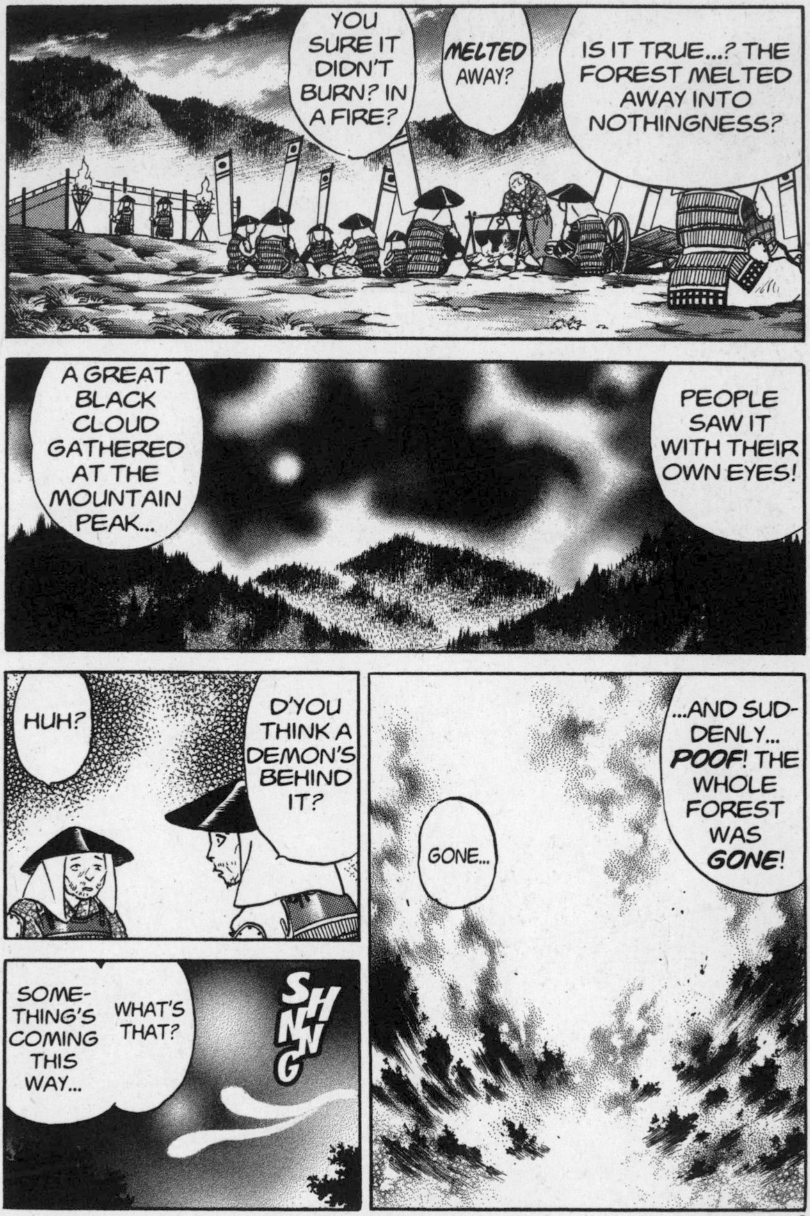
IS IT TRUE...? THE FOREST MELTED AWAY INTO NOTHINGNESS?
MELTED AWAY?
YOU SURE IT DIDN'T BURN? IN A FIRE?
PEOPLE SAW IT WITH THEIR OWN EYES!
A GREAT BLACK CLOUD GATHERED AT THE MOUNTAIN PEAK...
...AND SUDDENLY... POOF! THE WHOLE FOREST WAS GONE!
GONE...
D'YOU THINK A DEMON'S BEHIND IT?
HUH?
SHNNG
WHAT'S THAT?
SOMETHING'S COMING THIS WAY...

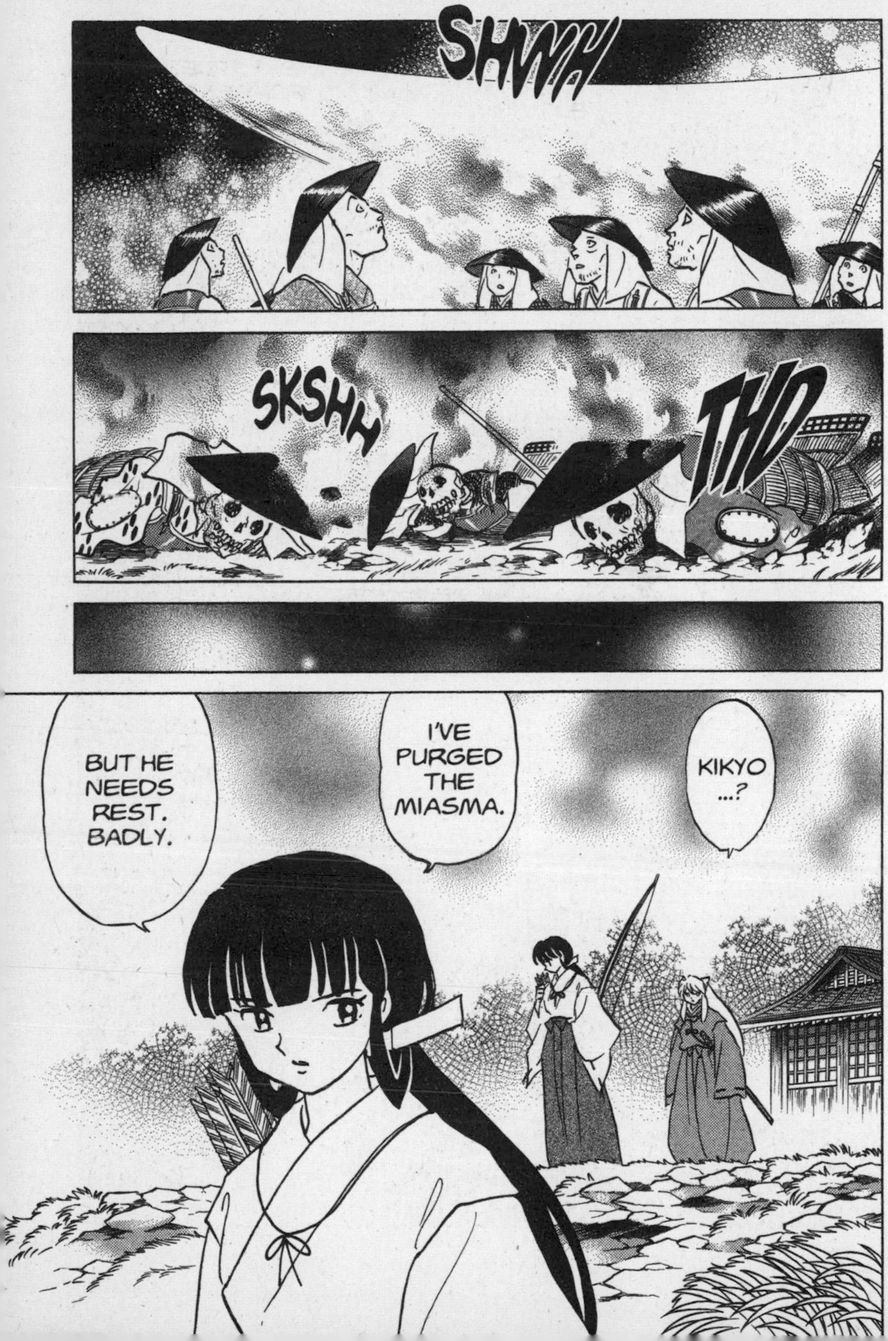
SHWWH
THD
SKSHH
KIKYO ...?
I'VE PURGED THE MIASMA.
BUT HE NEEDS REST. BADLY.

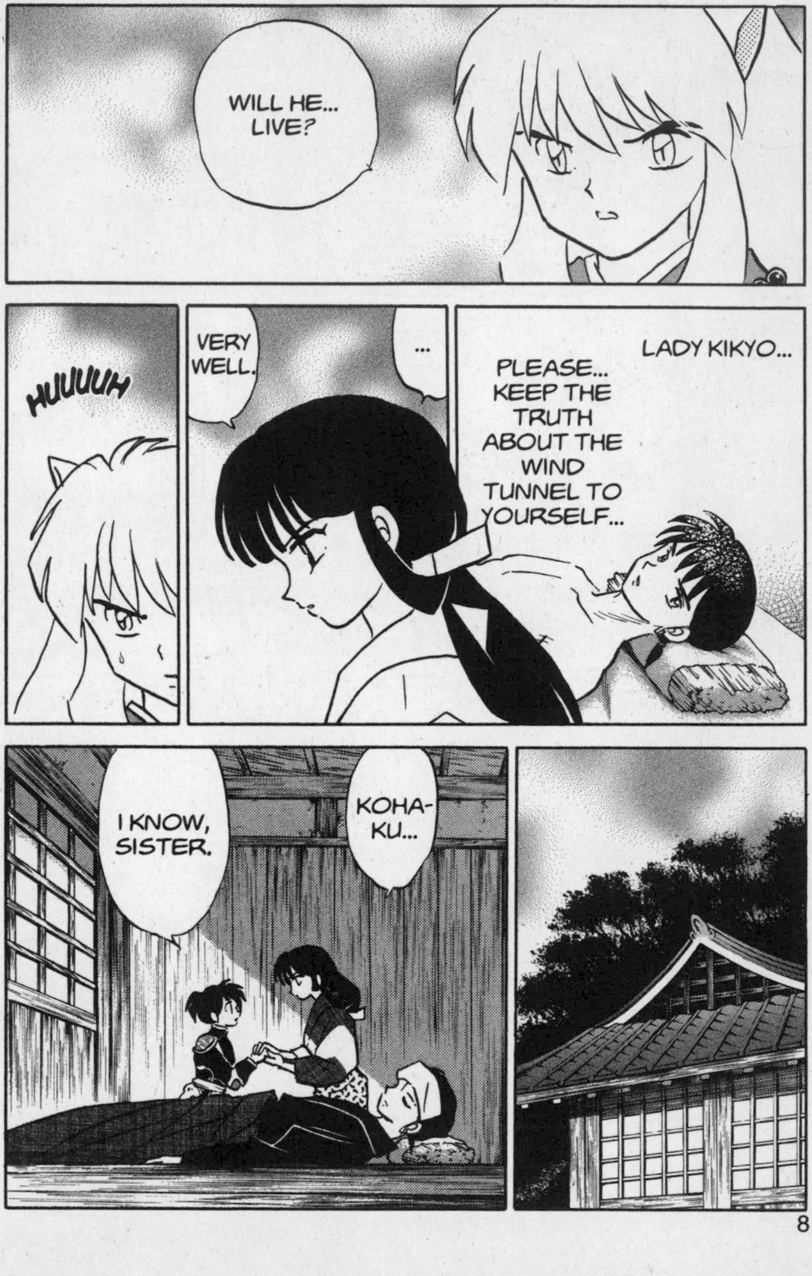
WILL HE... LIVE?
LADY KIKYO...
PLEASE... KEEP THE TRUTH ABOUT THE WIND TUNNEL TO YOURSELF...
...
VERY WELL.
HUUUUH
KOHA-KU...
I KNOW, SISTER.

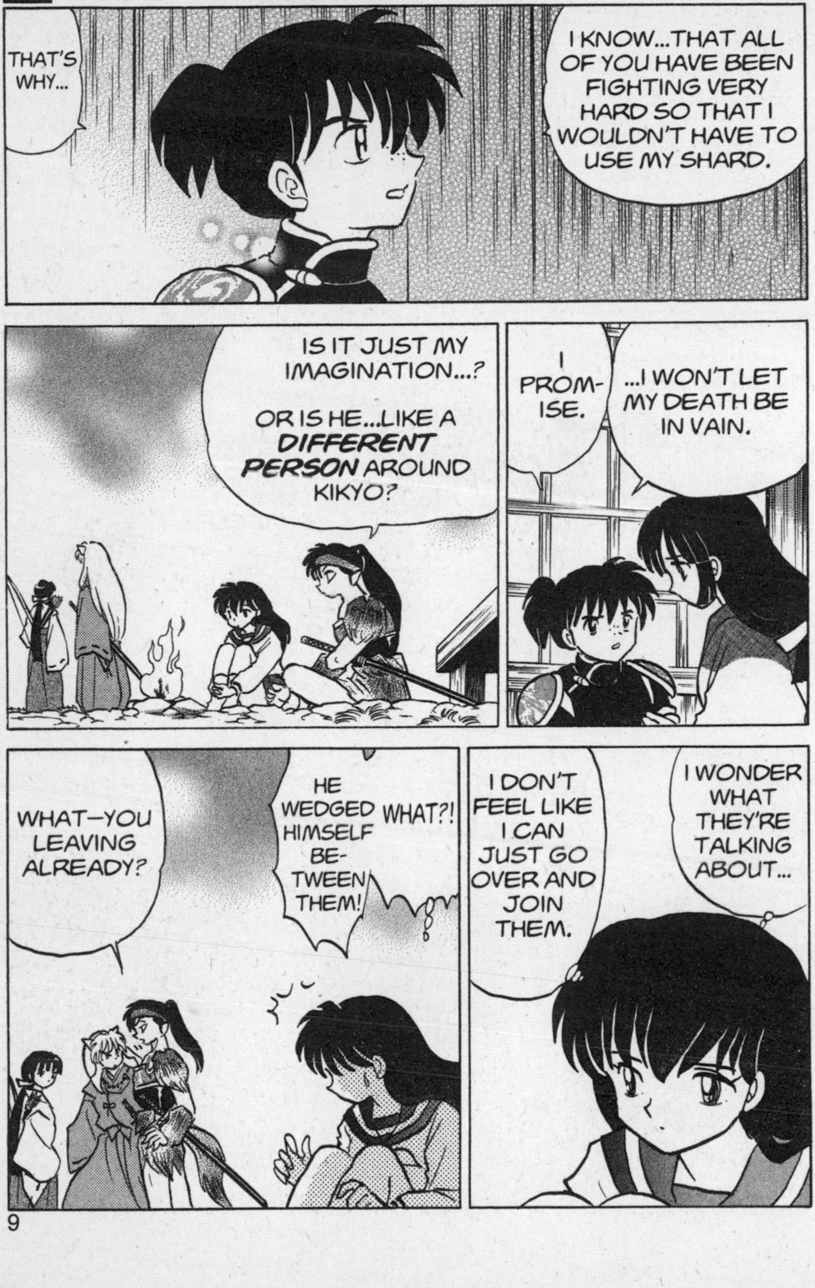
I KNOW...THAT ALL OF YOU HAVE BEEN FIGHTING VERY HARD SO THAT I WOULDN'T HAVE TO USE MY SHARD.
THAT'S WHY...
...I WON'T LET MY DEATH BE IN VAIN.
I PROMISE.
IS IT JUST MY IMAGINATION...?
OR IS HE...LIKE A DIFFERENT PERSON AROUND KIKYO?
I WONDER WHAT THEY'RE TALKING ABOUT...
I DON'T FEEL LIKE I CAN JUST GO OVER AND JOIN THEM.
WHAT?!
HE WEDGED HIMSELF BETWEEN THEM!
WHAT—YOU LEAVING ALREADY?

I AM.
I HAVE SOME TIDYING UP TO DO.
TIDYING UP?
THERE’S SOMETHING OUT THERE... LIKE TRACES OF MIASMA...
I SENSE THEM... MOVING ABOUT.
I CANNOT LET THEM ROAM FREE.
YOU’RE GOING...
...WITH KIKYO?
...
IT’S HARD TO EXPLAIN, BUT...
...WHEN I’M AT KIKYO’S SIDE...
...I FEEL MORE AND MORE SERENE...
...AS IF SHE’S CLEANSING MY SOUL.

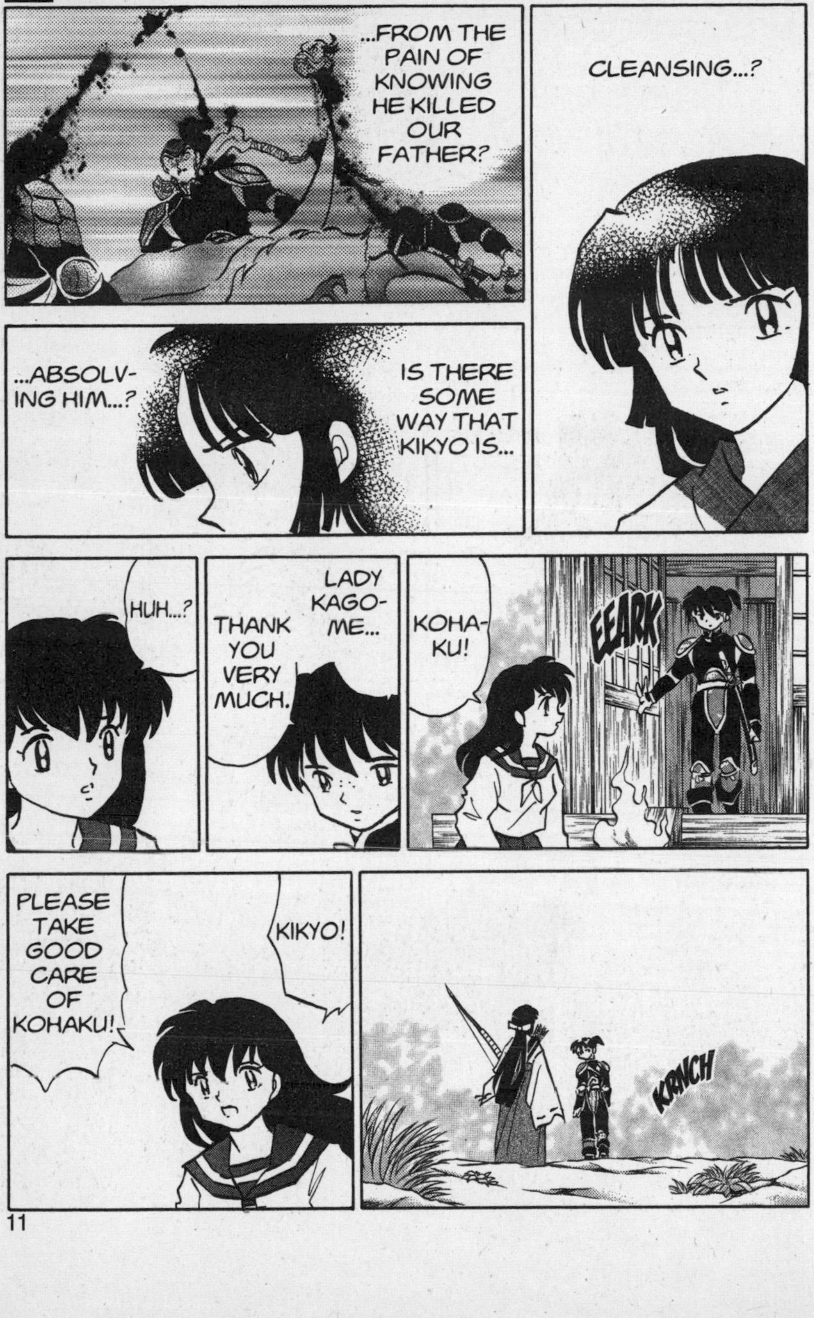
CLEANSING...?
...FROM THE PAIN OF KNOWING HE KILLED OUR FATHER?
IS THERE SOME WAY THAT KIKYO IS...
...ABSOLV-ING HIM...?
KOHA-KU!
EEARK
LADY KAGO-ME...
THANK YOU VERY MUCH.
HUH...?
KRNCH
KIKYO!
PLEASE TAKE GOOD CARE OF KOHAKU!

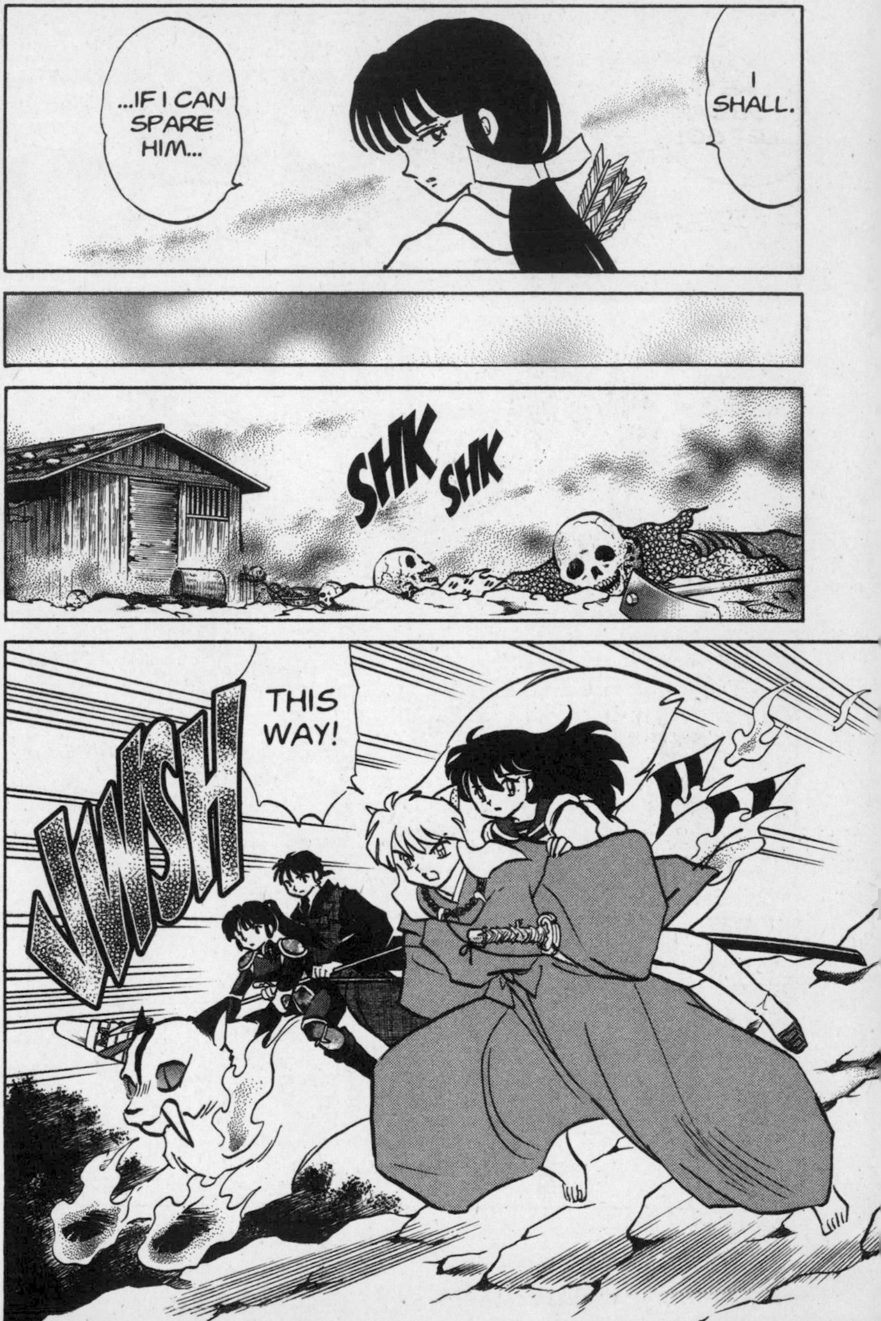
I SHALL.
...IF I CAN SPARE HIM...
SHK
SHK
THIS WAY!
WHSH

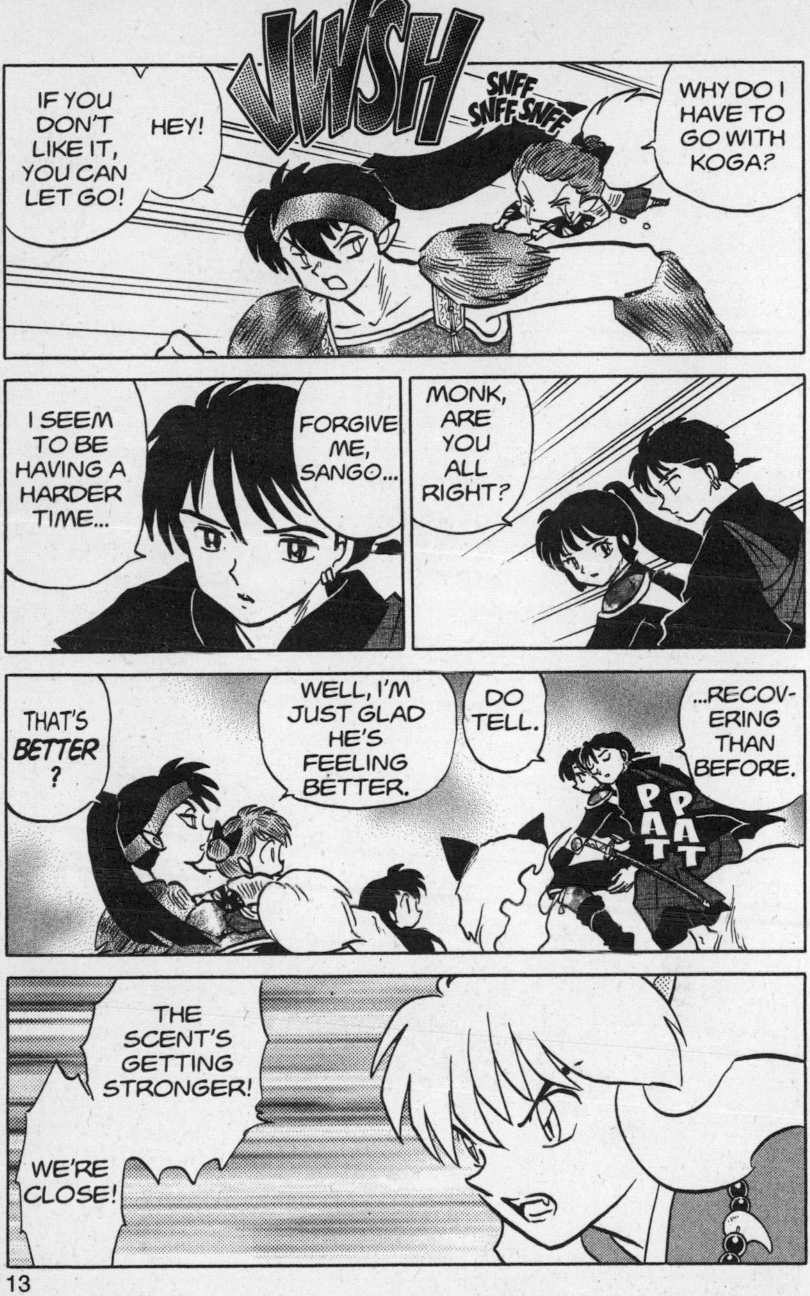
WHY DO I HAVE TO GO WITH KOGA?
SNFF SNFF SNFF
VWSH
HEY!
IF YOU DON'T LIKE IT, YOU CAN LET GO!
MONK, ARE YOU ALL RIGHT?
FORGIVE ME, SANGO...
I SEEM TO BE HAVING A HARDER TIME...
...RECOV-ERING THAN BEFORE.
PAT PAT
DO TELL.
WELL, I'M JUST GLAD HE'S FEELING BETTER.
THAT'S *BETTER*?
THE SCENT'S GETTING STRONGER!
WE'RE CLOSE!

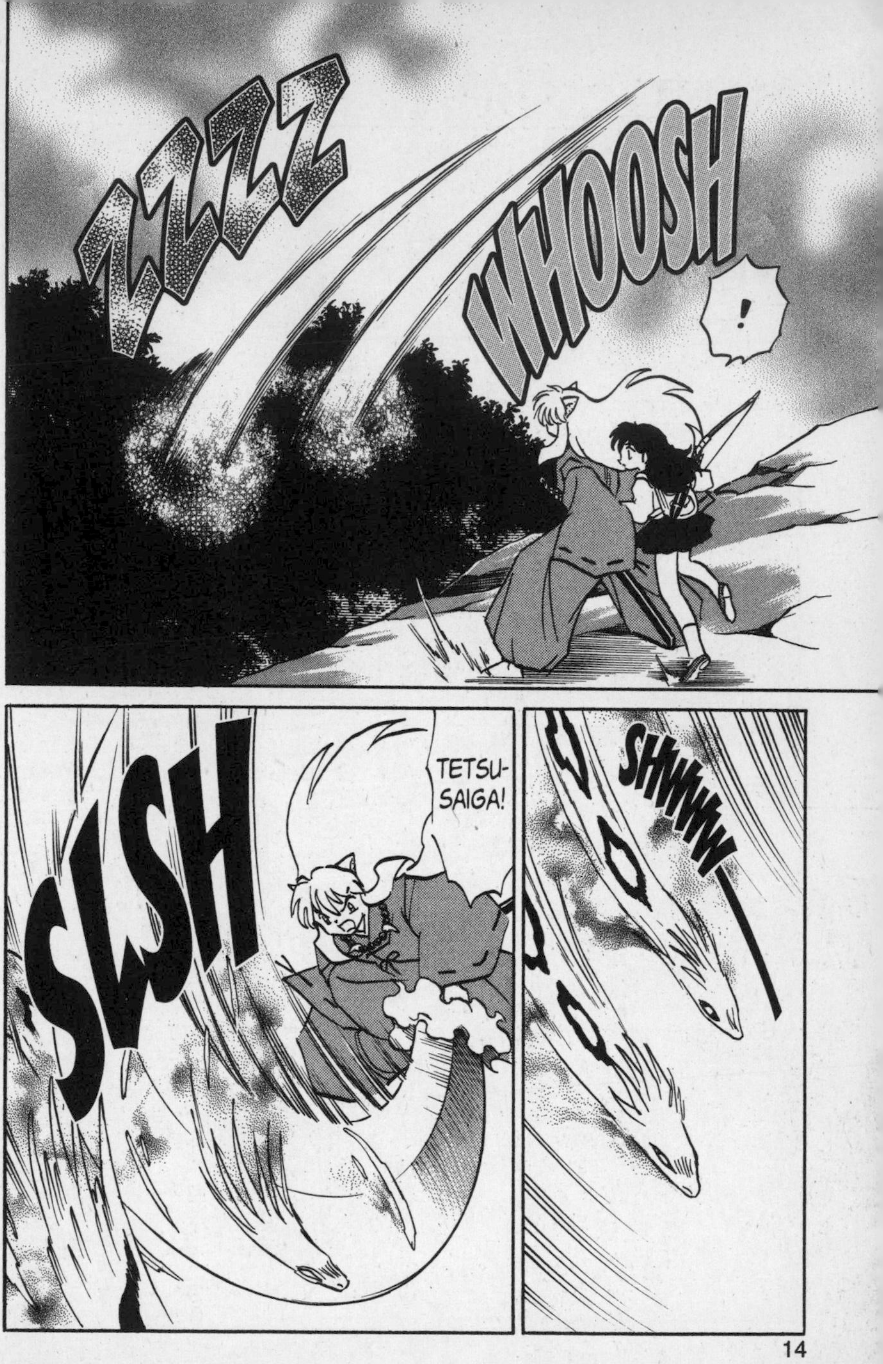
ZZZZZ
WHOOSH
!
SHWWWW
SLSH
TETSU-SAIGA!

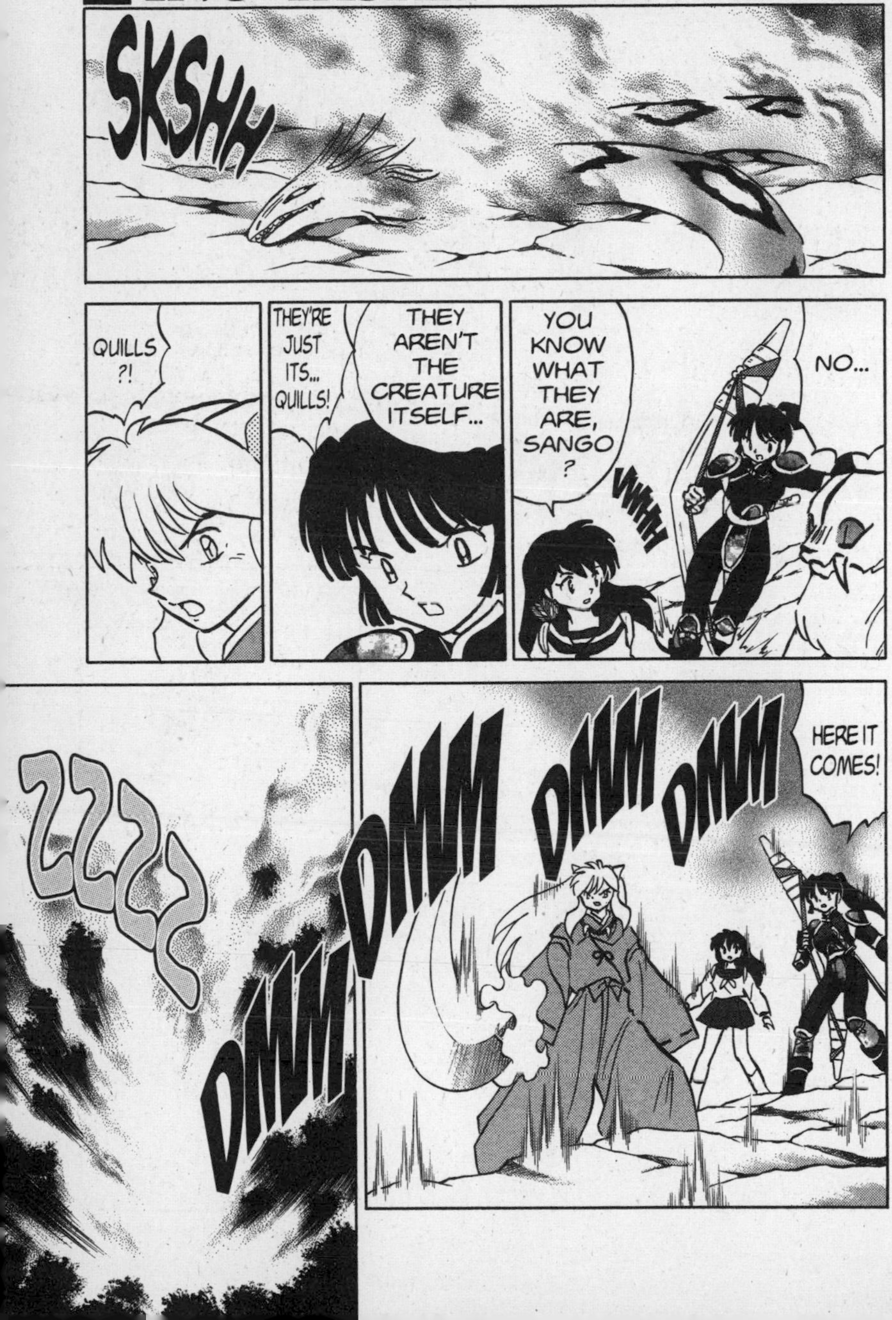
SKSHH
YOU KNOW WHAT THEY ARE, SANGO?
NO...
VWHH
THEY AREN'T THE CREATURE ITSELF...
THEY'RE JUST ITS... QUILLS!
QUILLS?!
HERE IT COMES!
DMM DMM DMM DMM DMM
ZZZZ

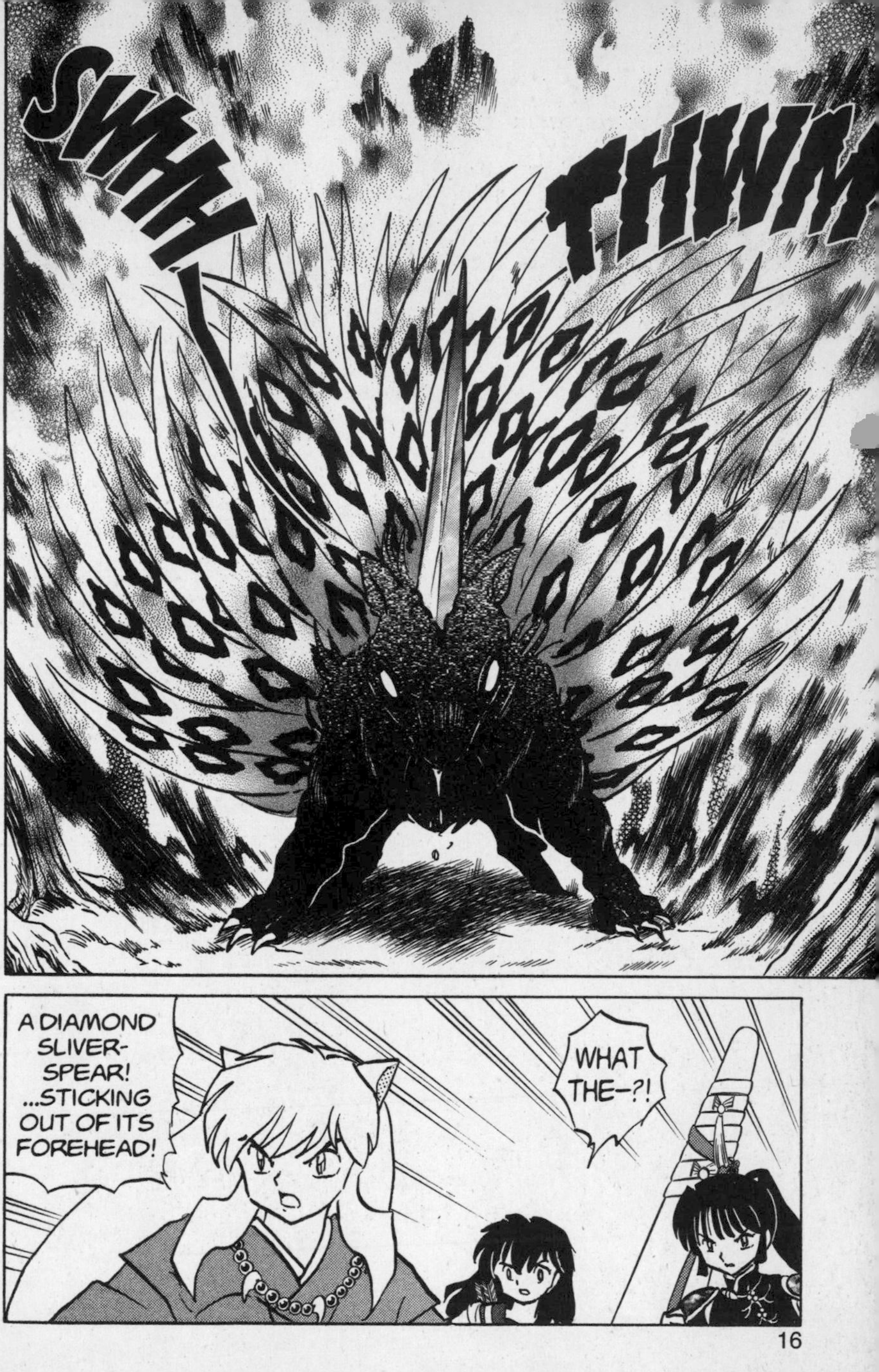
THWM
SWH
WHAT THE–?!
A DIAMOND SLIVER-SPEAR! ...STICKING OUT OF ITS FOREHEAD!

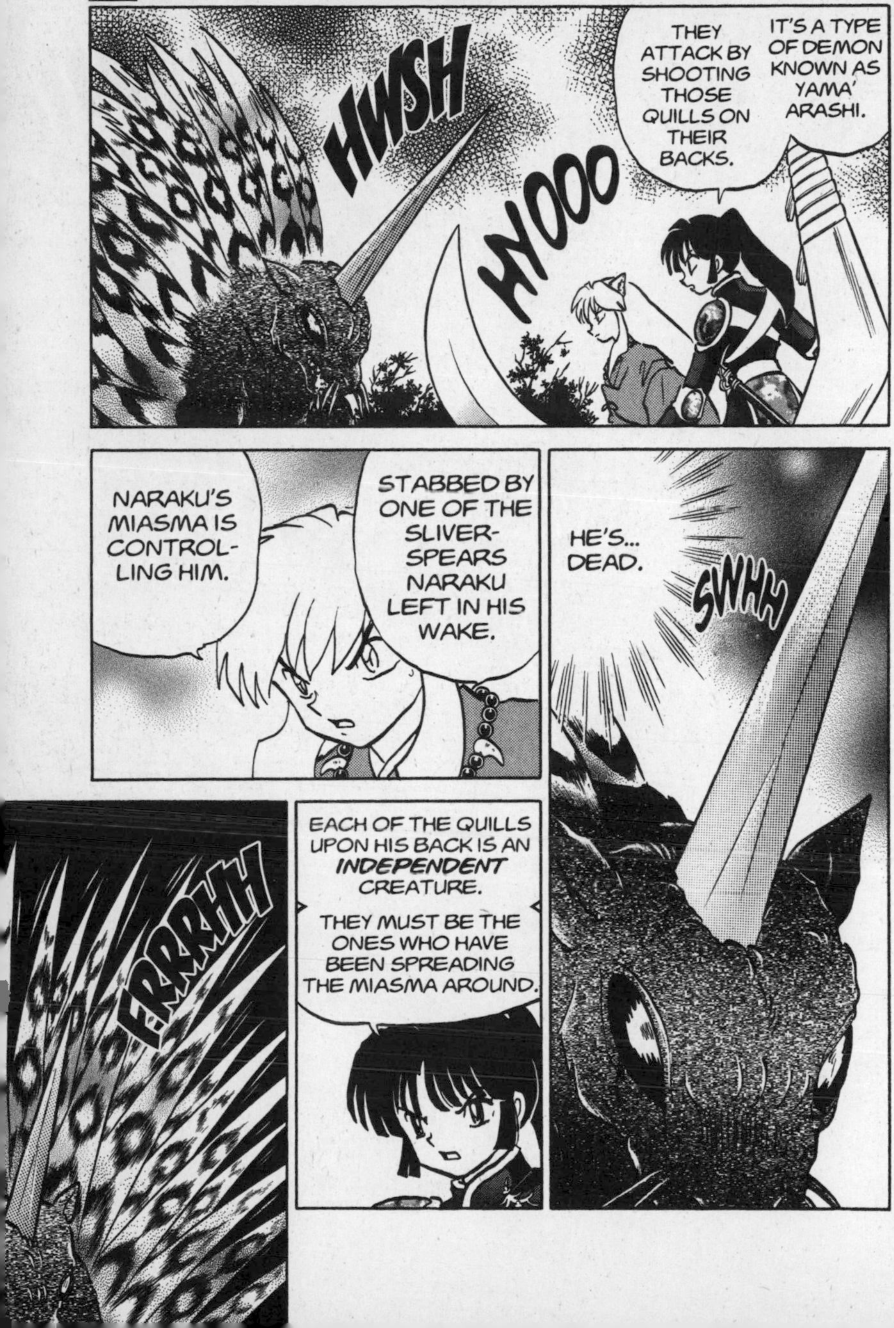
IT'S A TYPE OF DEMON KNOWN AS YAMA' ARASHI.
THEY ATTACK BY SHOOTING THOSE QUILLS ON THEIR BACKS.
HYOOO
HWSH
HE'S... DEAD.
SWHH
STABBED BY ONE OF THE SLIVER-SPEARS NARAKU LEFT IN HIS WAKE.
NARAKU'S MIASMA IS CONTROL-LING HIM.
EACH OF THE QUILLS UPON HIS BACK IS AN *INDEPENDENT* CREATURE.
THEY MUST BE THE ONES WHO HAVE BEEN SPREADING THE MIASMA AROUND.
FRRRHH

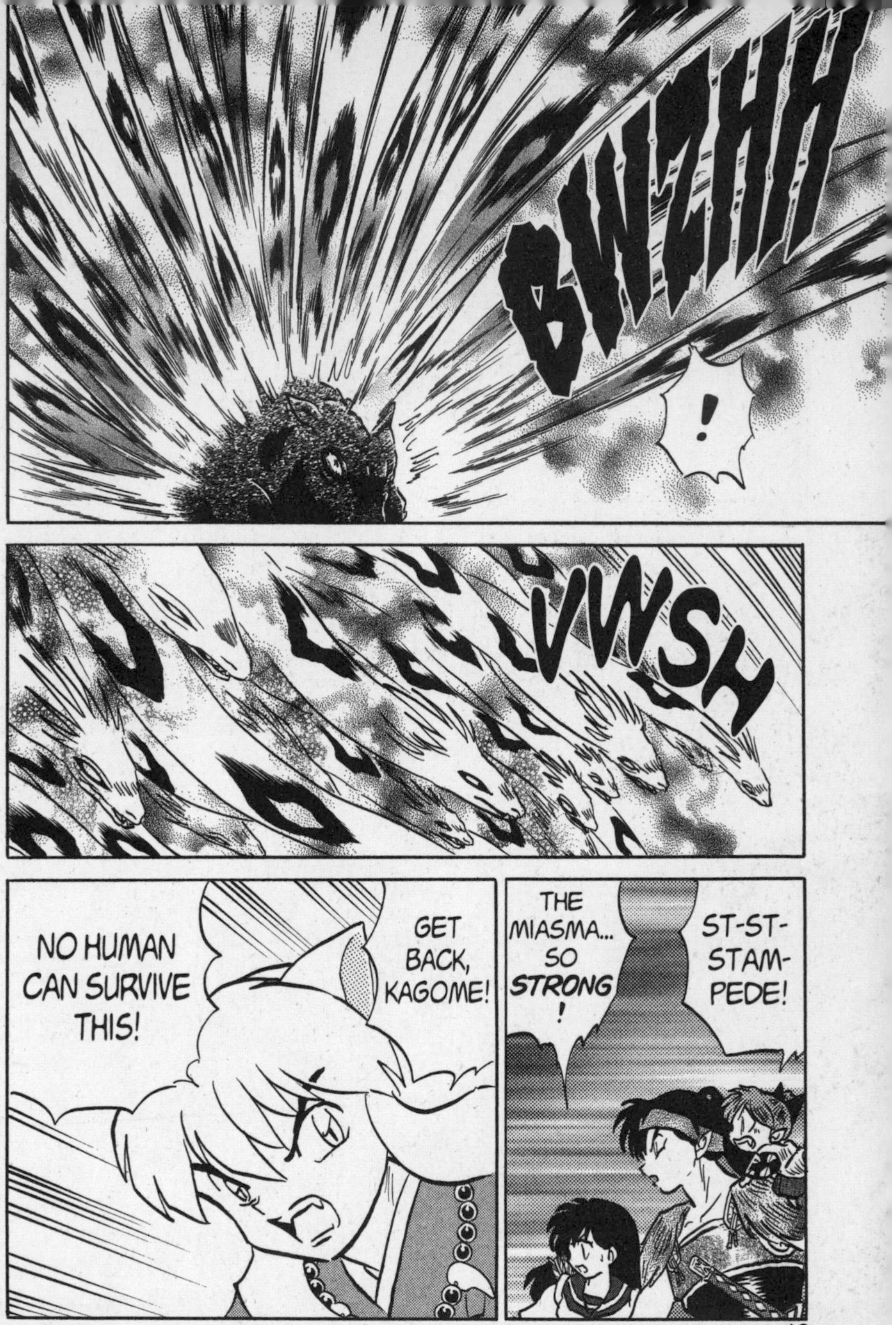
BWZHH
!
VWSH
ST-ST-STAMPEDE!
THE MIASMA... SO STRONG!
GET BACK, KAGOME!
NO HUMAN CAN SURVIVE THIS!

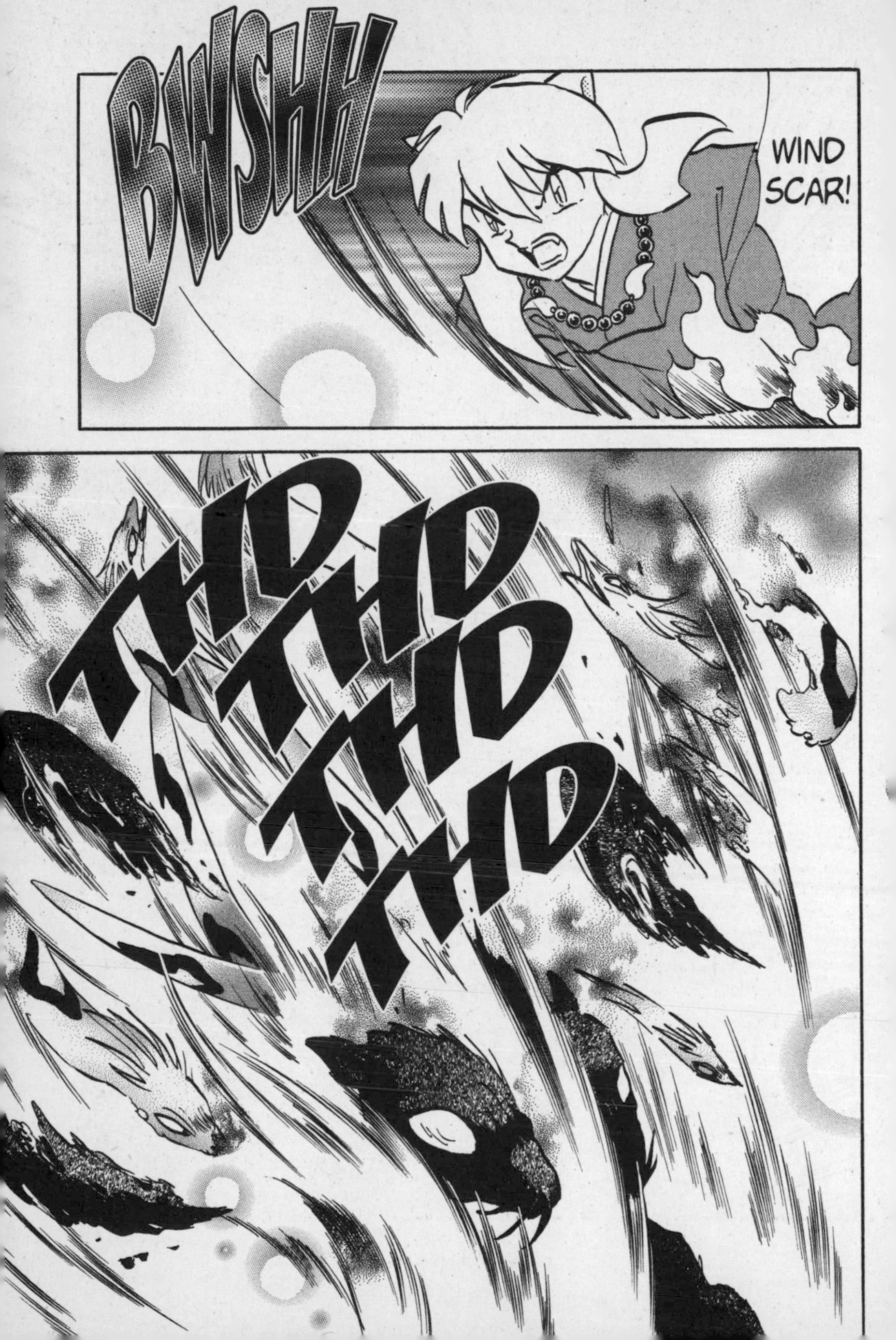
BWSHH
WIND SCAR!
THD THD THD THD

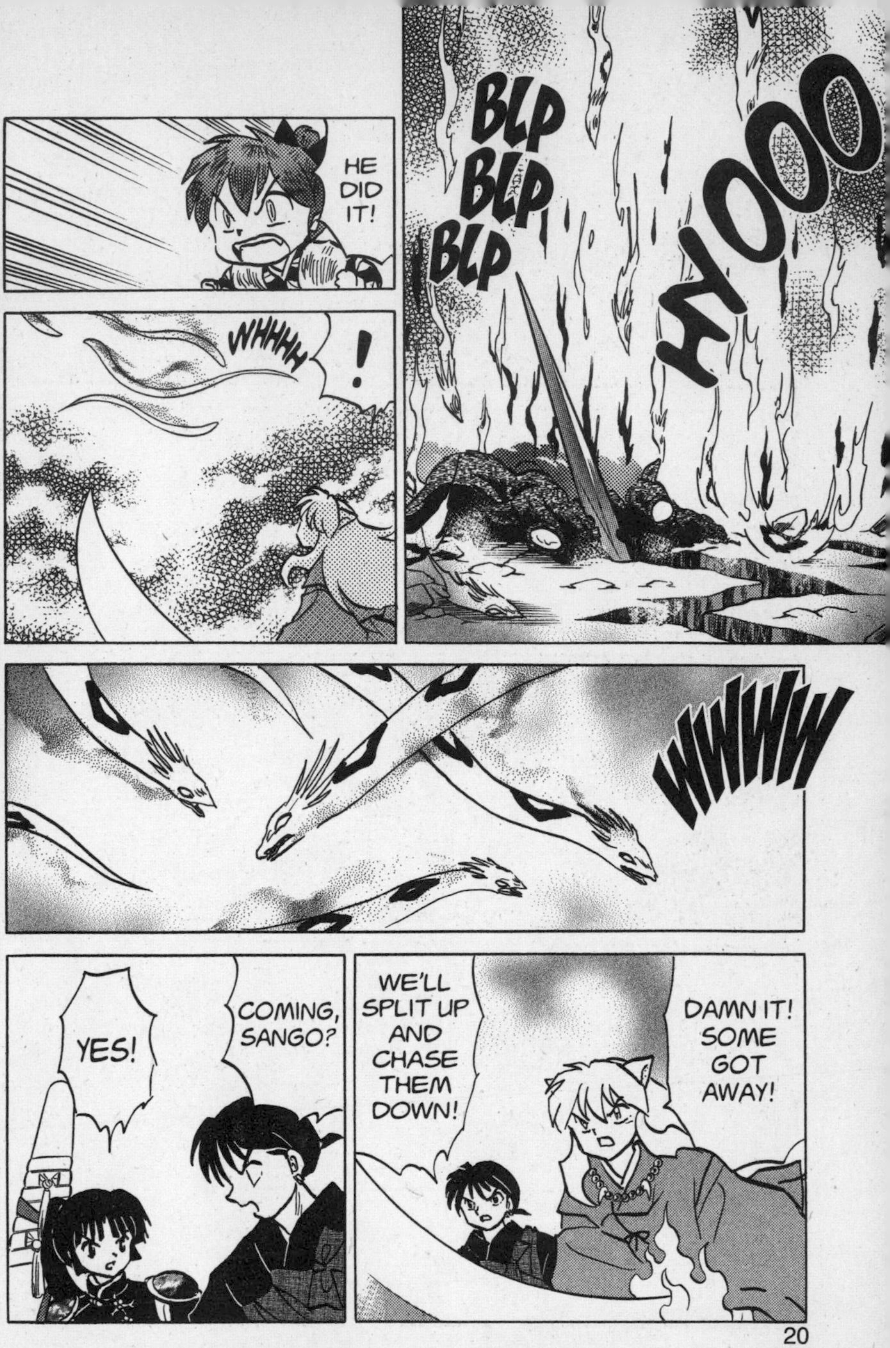
HYOOO
BLP BLP BLP
HE DID IT!
WHHHH
!
WWWWW
DAMN IT! SOME GOT AWAY!
WE'LL SPLIT UP AND CHASE THEM DOWN!
COMING, SANGO?
YES!

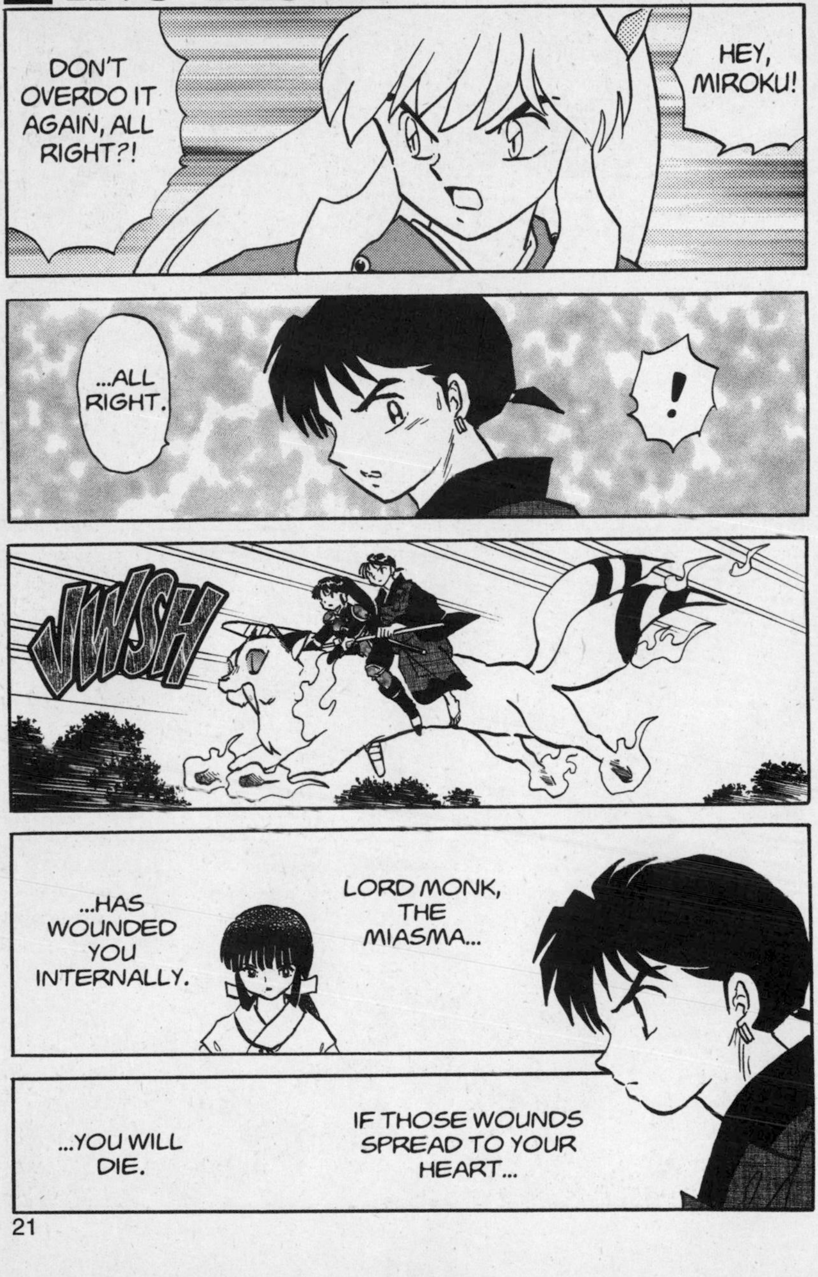
HEY, MIROKU!
DON'T OVERDO IT AGAIN, ALL RIGHT?!
!
...ALL RIGHT.
JWSH
LORD MONK, THE MIASMA...
...HAS WOUNDED YOU INTERNALLY.
IF THOSE WOUNDS SPREAD TO YOUR HEART...
...YOU WILL DIE.

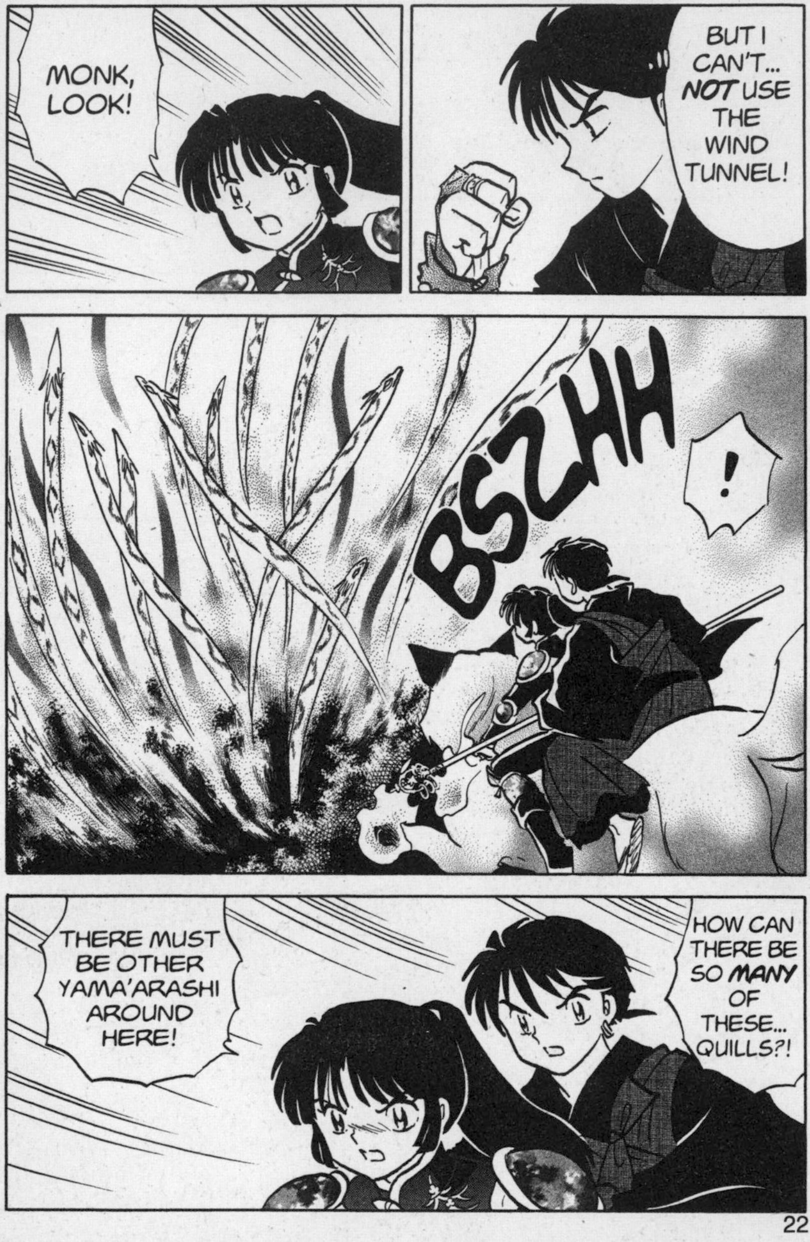
BUT I CAN'T... *NOT* USE THE WIND TUNNEL!
MONK, LOOK!
BSZHH
!
HOW CAN THERE BE SO *MANY* OF THESE... QUILLS?!
THERE MUST BE OTHER YAMA'ARASHI AROUND HERE!

SCROLL 2

THE HERD

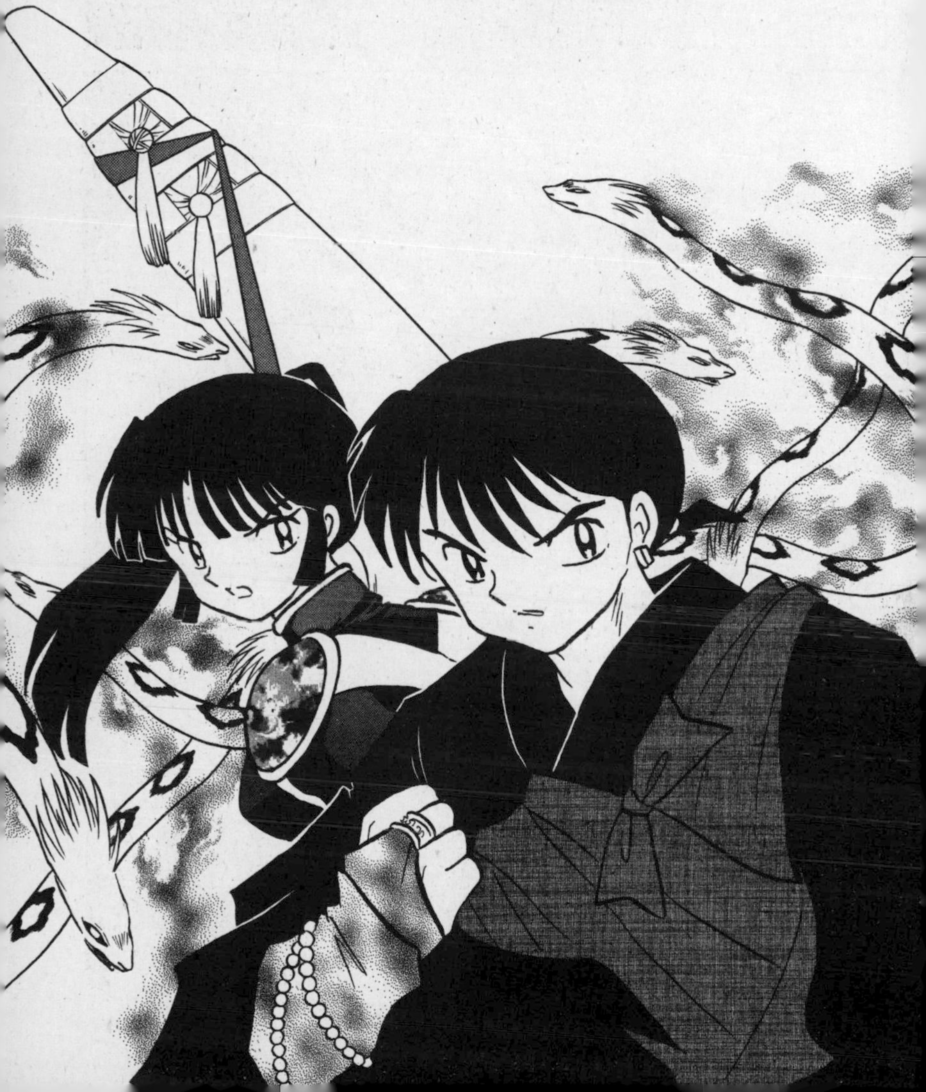

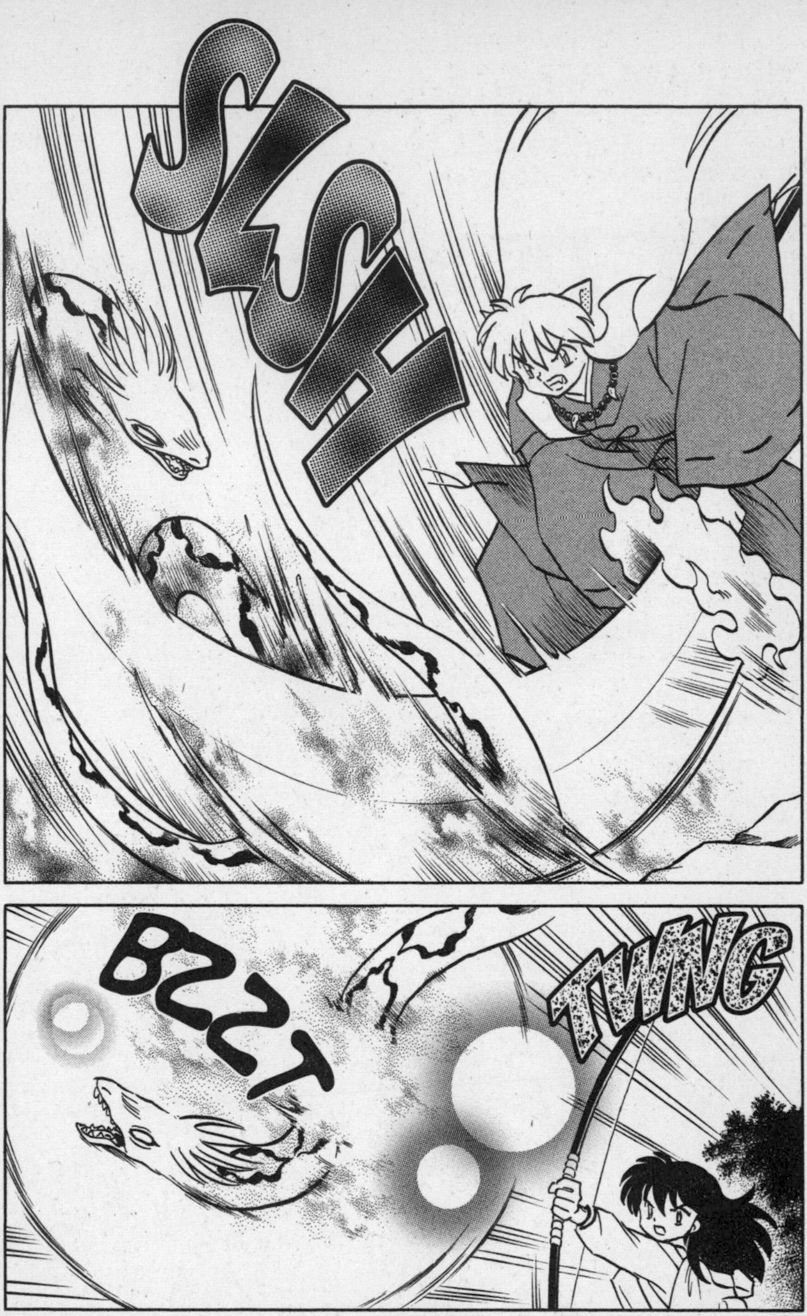
SLSH
TWNG
BZZT

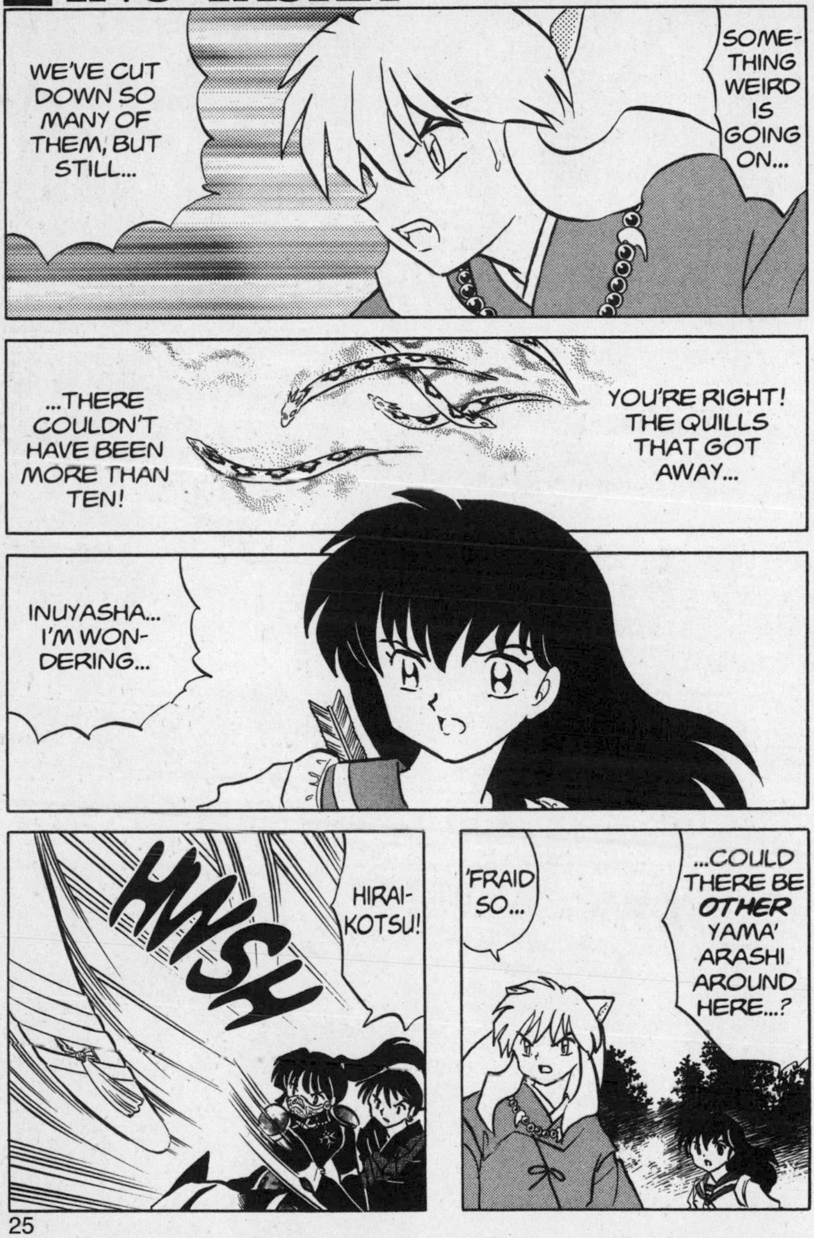
SOME-THING WEIRD IS GOING ON...
WE'VE CUT DOWN SO MANY OF THEM, BUT STILL...
YOU'RE RIGHT! THE QUILLS THAT GOT AWAY...
...THERE COULDN'T HAVE BEEN MORE THAN TEN!
INUYASHA... I'M WON-DERING...
...COULD THERE BE OTHER YAMA' ARASHI AROUND HERE...?
'FRAID SO...
HIRAI-KOTSU!
HWSH

KRK SNP
BZZT
BLP BLP BLP
VWSH
HAH!
WHPP
BZZT
VWHH HH
!

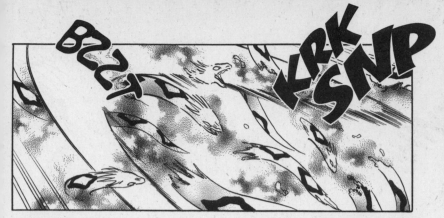

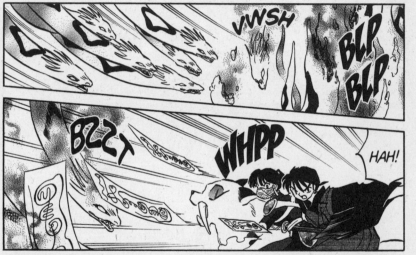

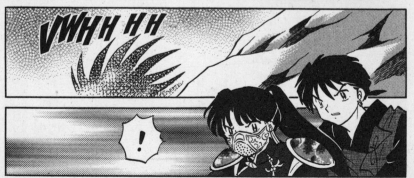

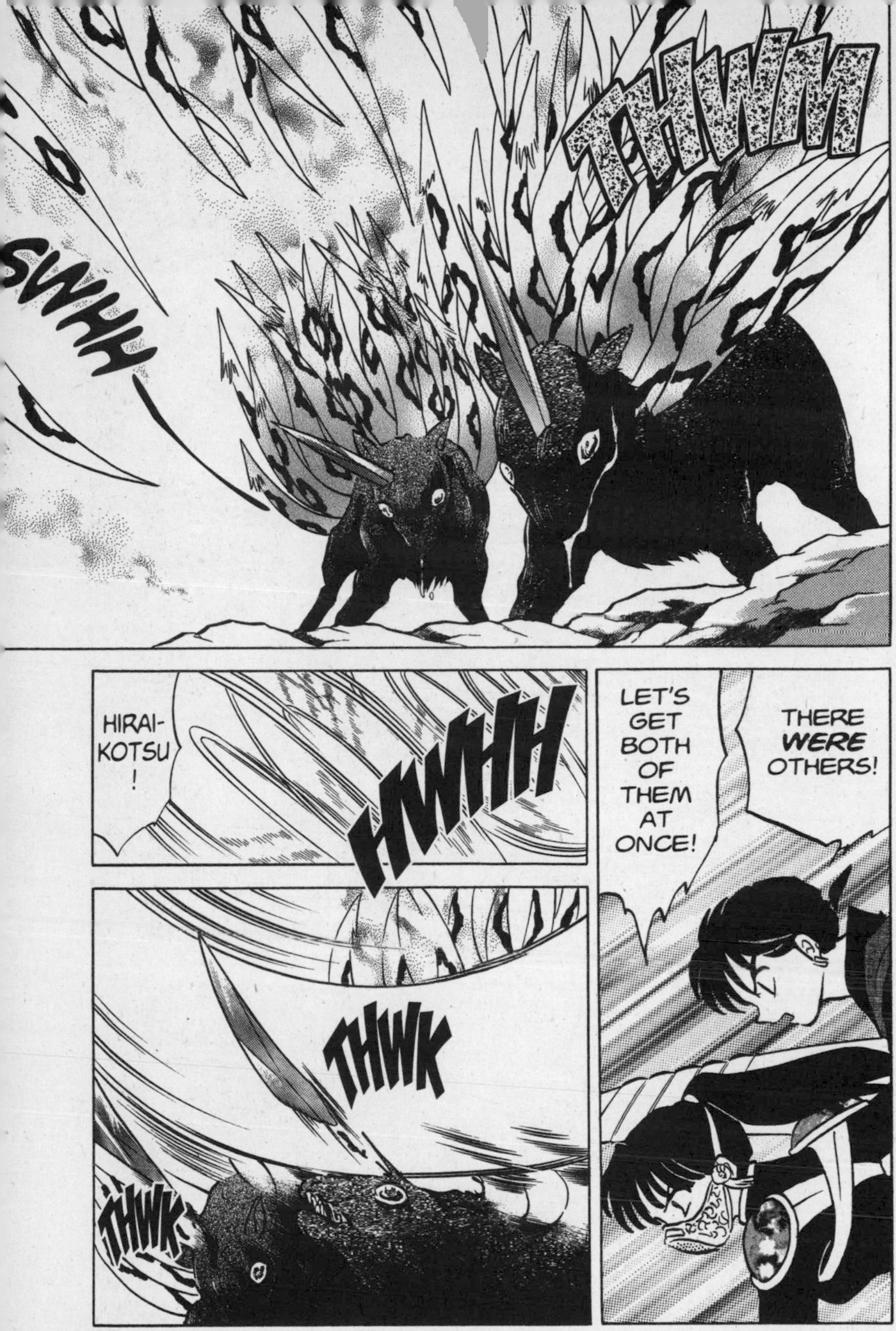
THWM
SWHH
THERE *WERE* OTHERS!
LET'S GET BOTH OF THEM AT ONCE!
HIRAI-KOTSU!
HWHH
THWK
THWK

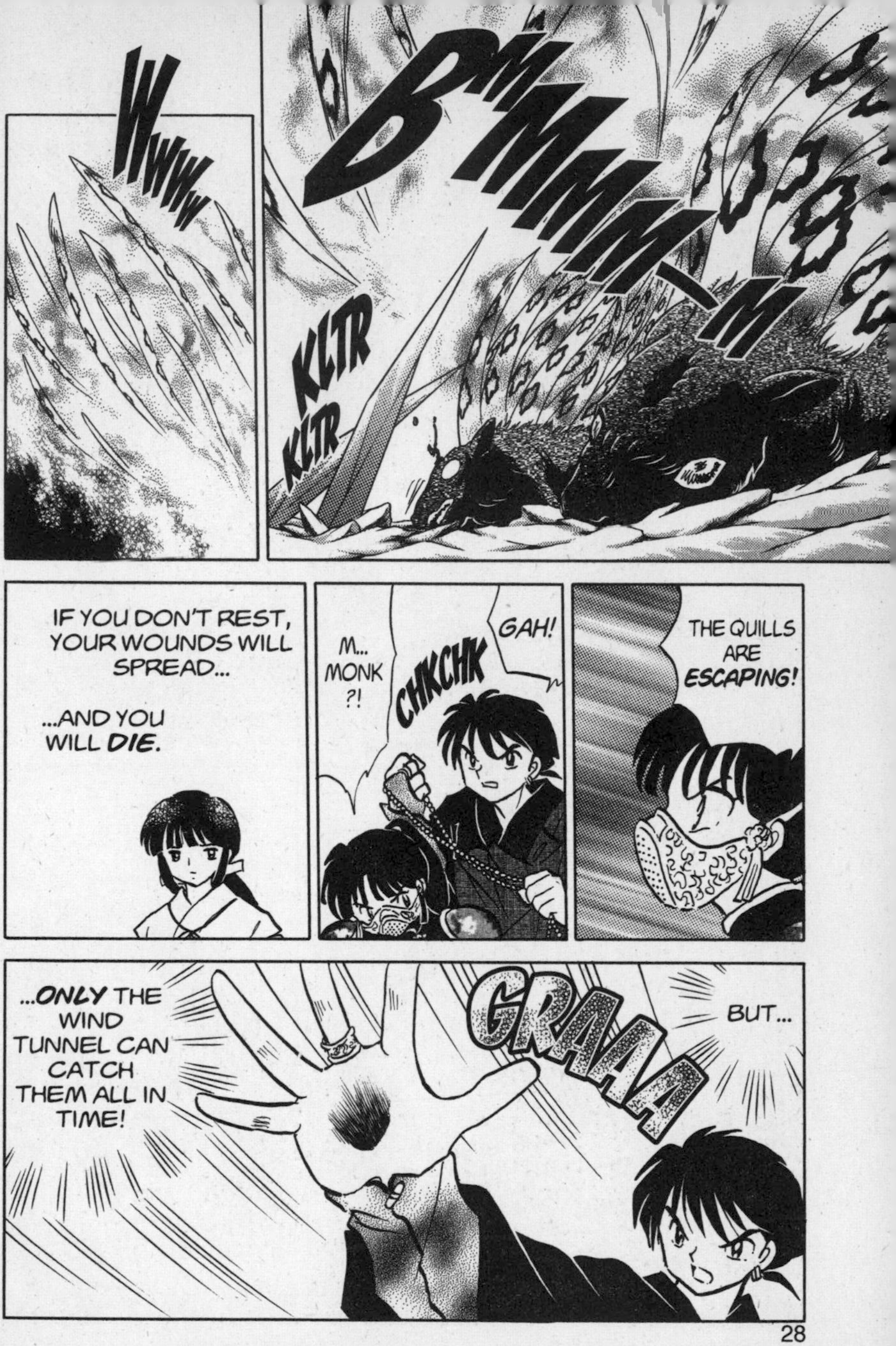
BAMMMM-M
KLTR KLTR
WWWWW
THE QUILLS ARE ESCAPING!
GAH!
M... MONK ?!
CHKCHK
IF YOU DON'T REST, YOUR WOUNDS WILL SPREAD...
...AND YOU WILL DIE.
BUT...
GRAAA
...ONLY THE WIND TUNNEL CAN CATCH THEM ALL IN TIME!

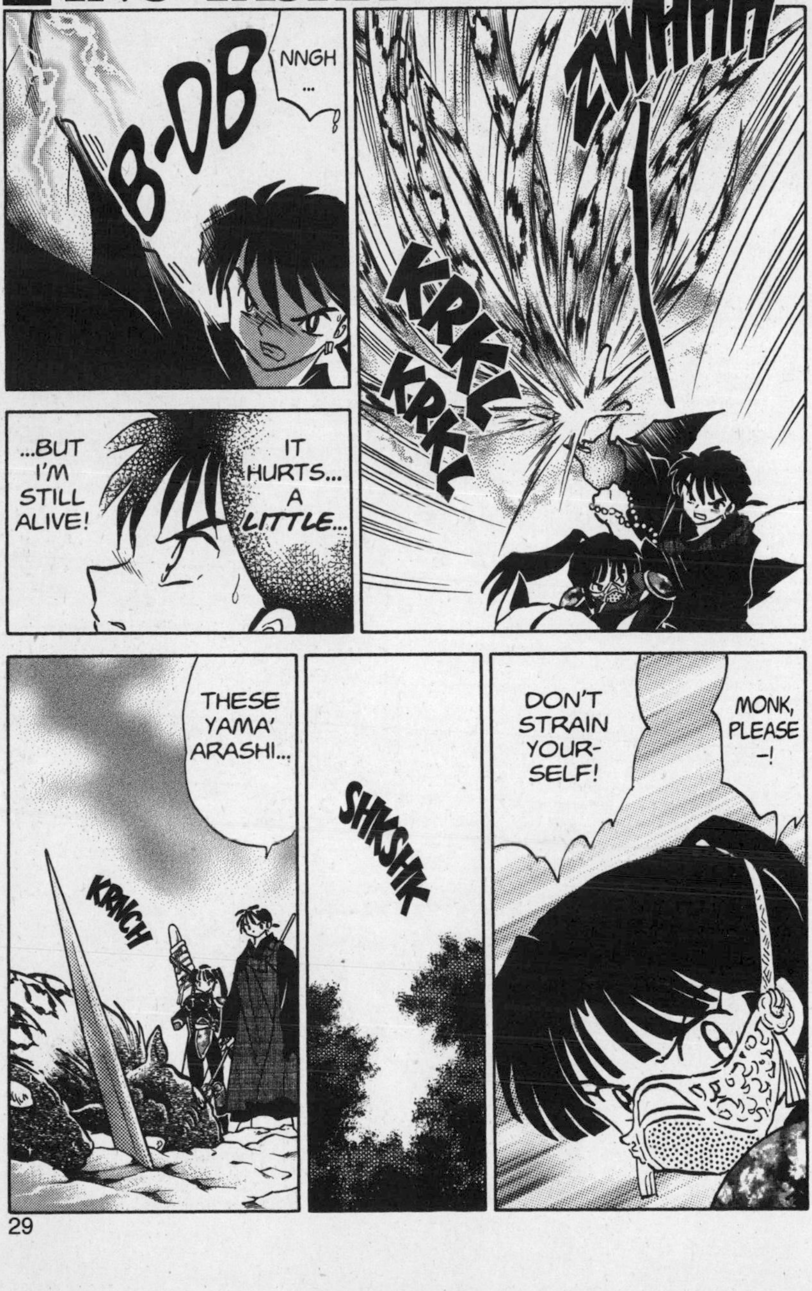
ZWHHHH
KRKKL
KRKKL
B-DB
NNGH ...
IT HURTS... A LITTLE...
...BUT I'M STILL ALIVE!
MONK, PLEASE —!
DON'T STRAIN YOURSELF!
SHKSHK
THESE YAMA' ARASHI...
KRNCH

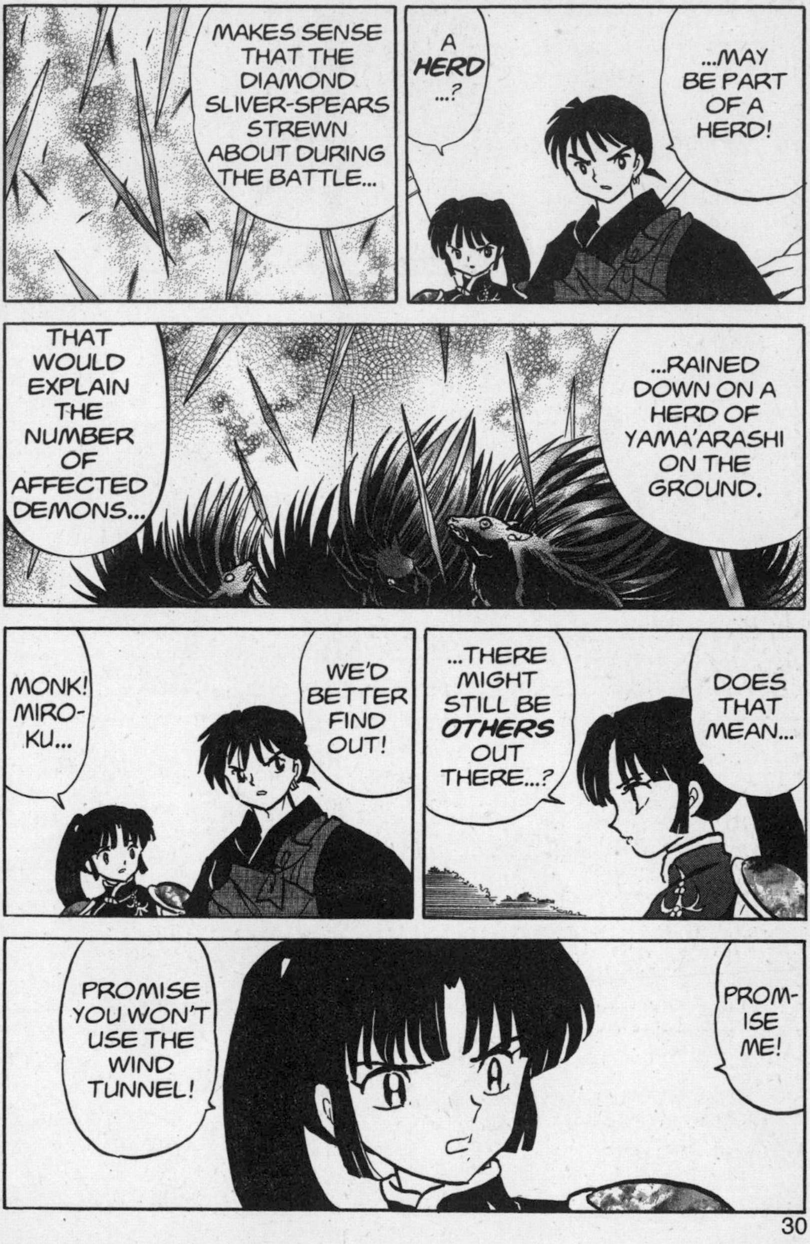
...MAY BE PART OF A HERD!
A HERD...?
MAKES SENSE THAT THE DIAMOND SLIVER-SPEARS STREWN ABOUT DURING THE BATTLE...
...RAINED DOWN ON A HERD OF YAMA'ARASHI ON THE GROUND.
THAT WOULD EXPLAIN THE NUMBER OF AFFECTED DEMONS...
DOES THAT MEAN...
...THERE MIGHT STILL BE OTHERS OUT THERE...?
WE'D BETTER FIND OUT!
MONK! MIRO-KU...
PROM-ISE ME!
PROMISE YOU WON'T USE THE WIND TUNNEL!

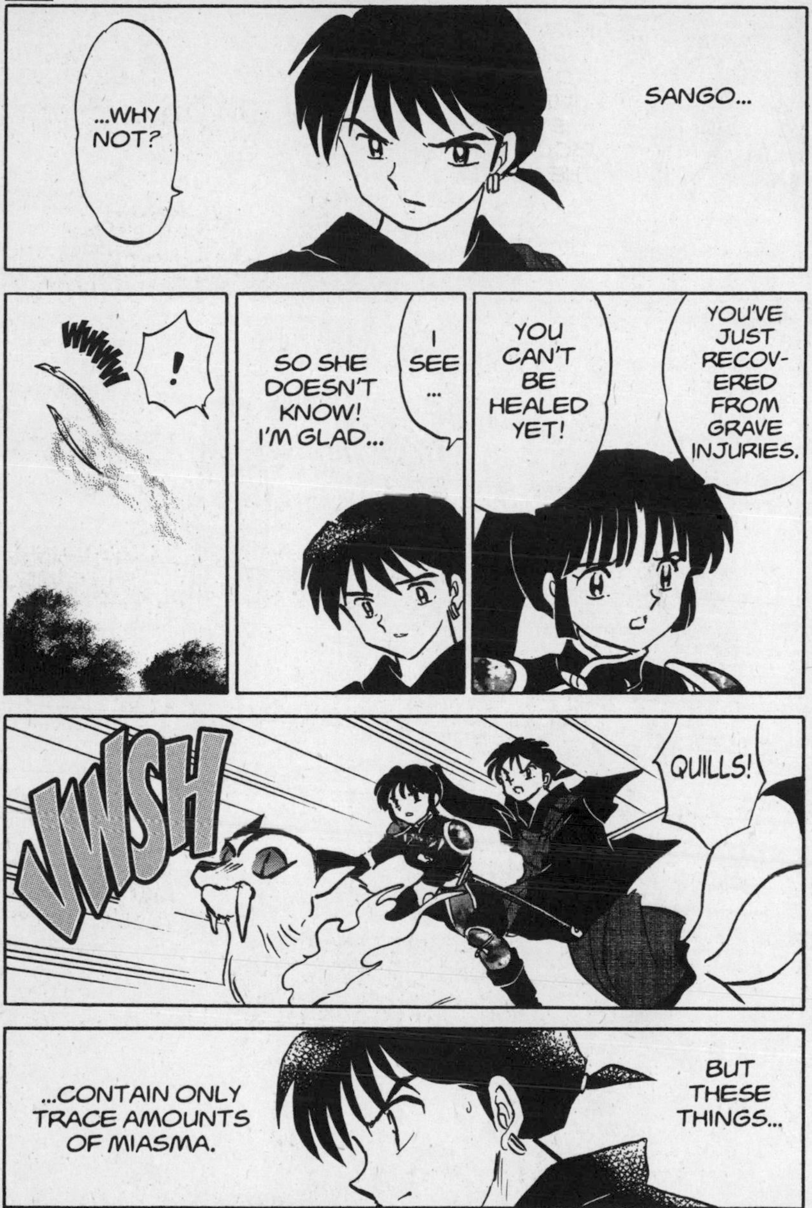
SANGO...
...WHY NOT?
YOU'VE JUST RECOV-ERED FROM GRAVE INJURIES.
YOU CAN'T BE HEALED YET!
I SEE ...
SO SHE DOESN'T KNOW! I'M GLAD...
!
WWWW
QUILLS!
VWSH
BUT THESE THINGS...
...CONTAIN ONLY TRACE AMOUNTS OF MIASMA.

NOT SO
MUCH THAT
MY
TUNNEL...

...CAN'T
HANDLE
THEM!

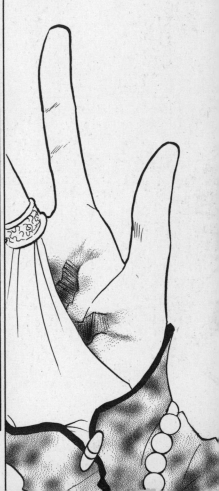

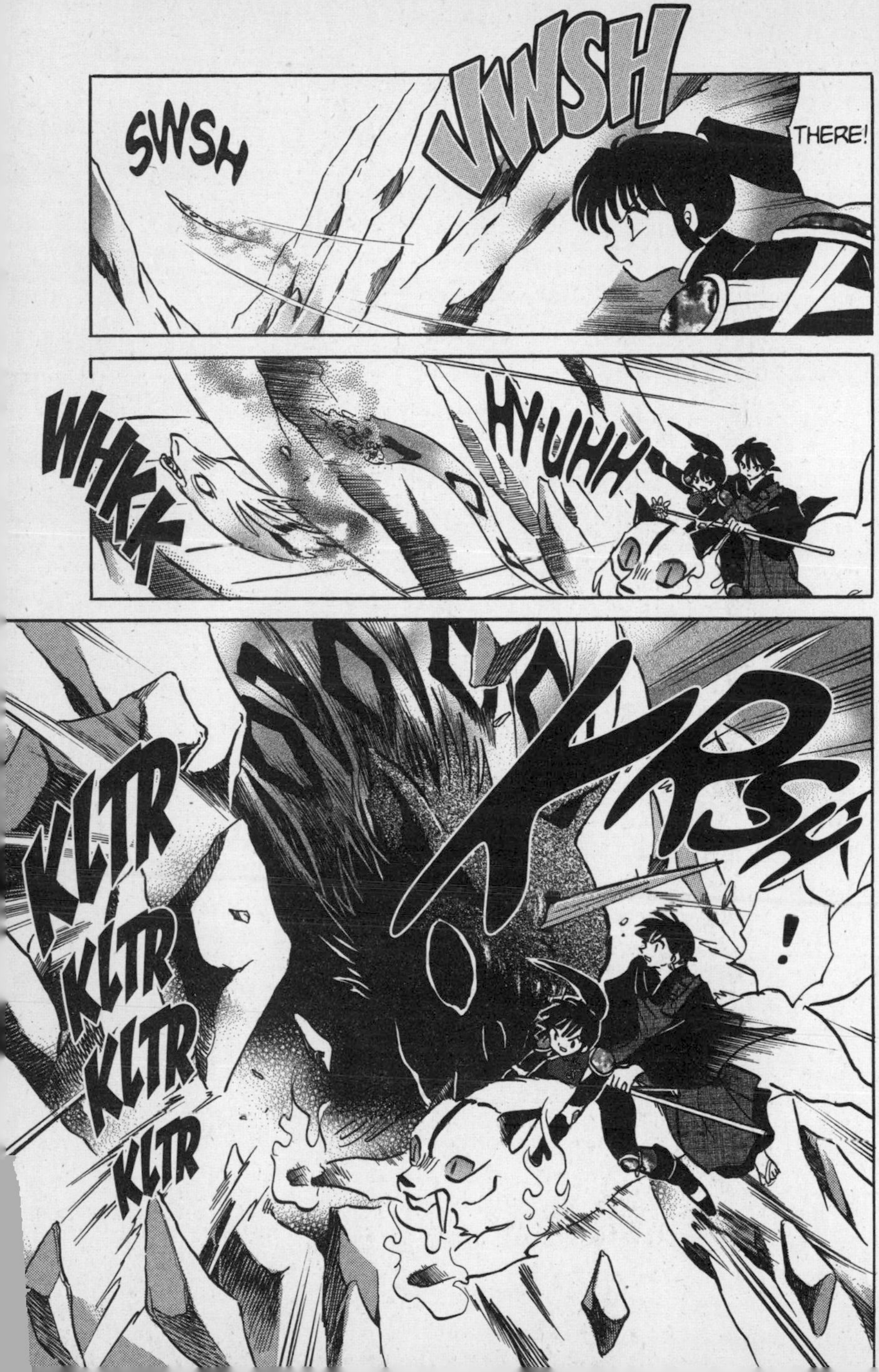
THERE!
VWSH
SWSH
HYUHH
WHKK
!
KRSH
KLTR
KLTR
KLTR
KLTR
KLTR

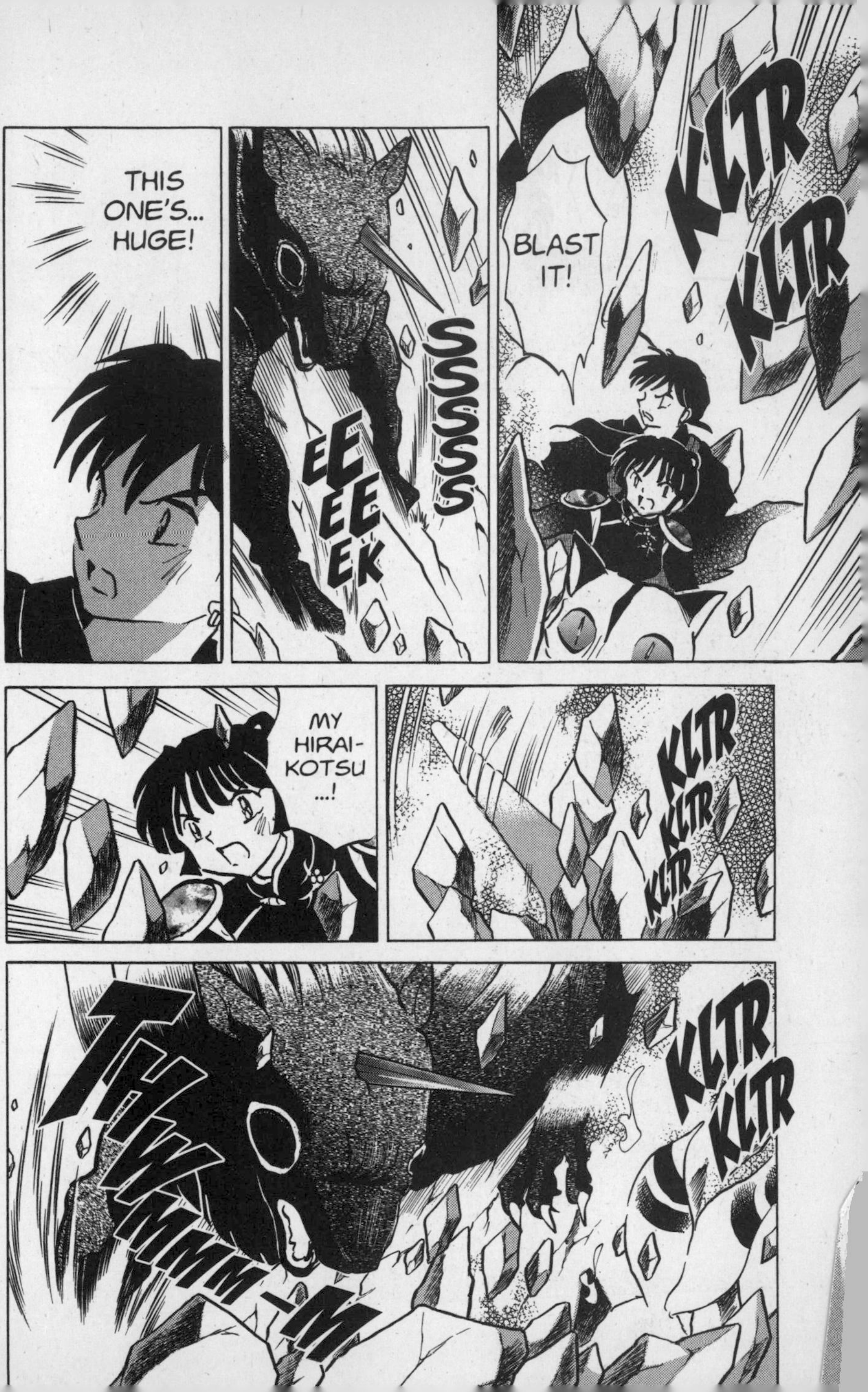

BLAST IT!
KLTR KLTR
SSSSSS
EEEEEK
THIS ONE'S... HUGE!
KLTR KLTR KLTR
MY HIRAI-KOTSU ...!
KLTR KLTR
THWMMM-M

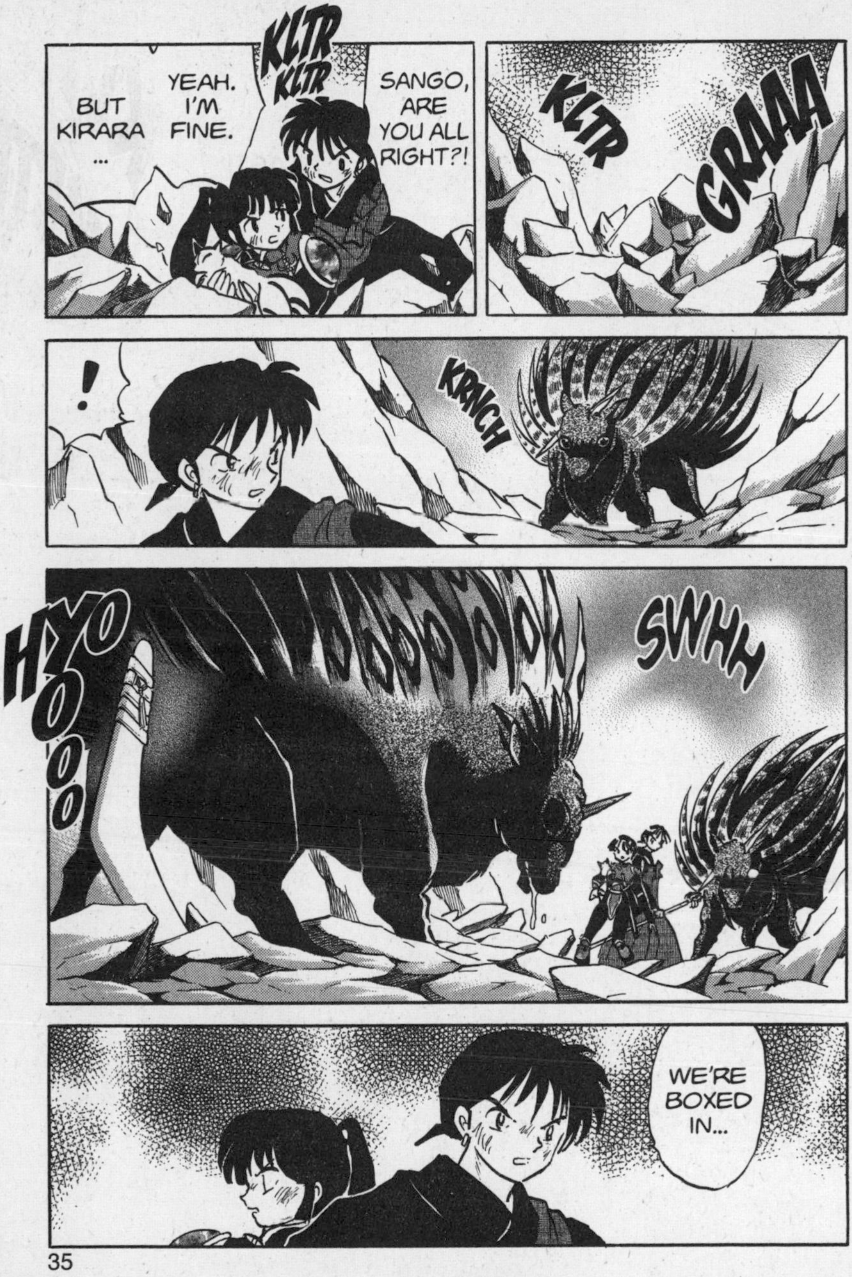
KLTR
GRAAA
SANGO, ARE YOU ALL RIGHT?!
KLTR KLTR
YEAH. I'M FINE.
BUT KIRARA ...
KRNCH
!
SWHH
HYOOOOO
WE'RE BOXED IN...

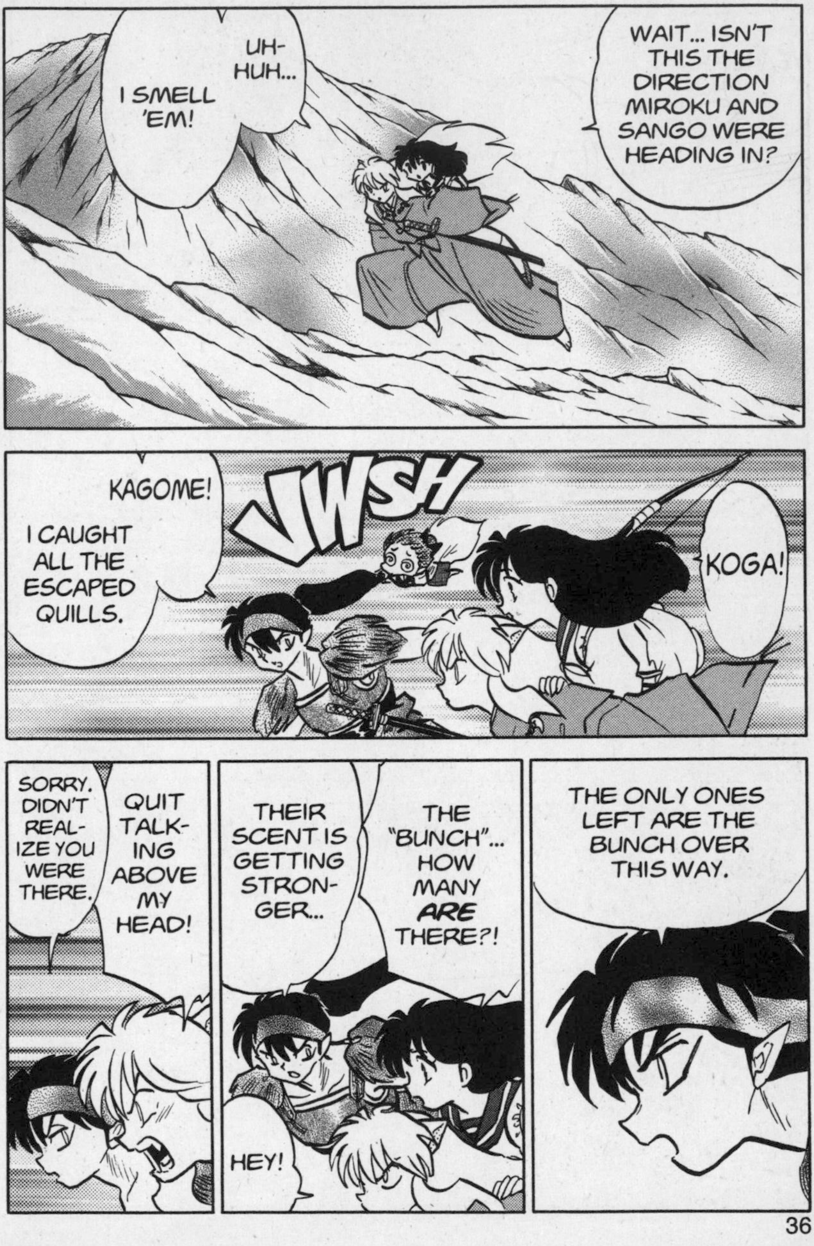
WAIT... ISN'T THIS THE DIRECTION MIROKU AND SANGO WERE HEADING IN?
UH-HUH... I SMELL 'EM!
KOGA!
VWSH
KAGOME! I CAUGHT ALL THE ESCAPED QUILLS.
THE ONLY ONES LEFT ARE THE BUNCH OVER THIS WAY.
THE "BUNCH"... HOW MANY *ARE* THERE?!
THEIR SCENT IS GETTING STRON-GER...
HEY!
QUIT TALK-ING ABOVE MY HEAD!
SORRY. DIDN'T REAL-IZE YOU WERE THERE.

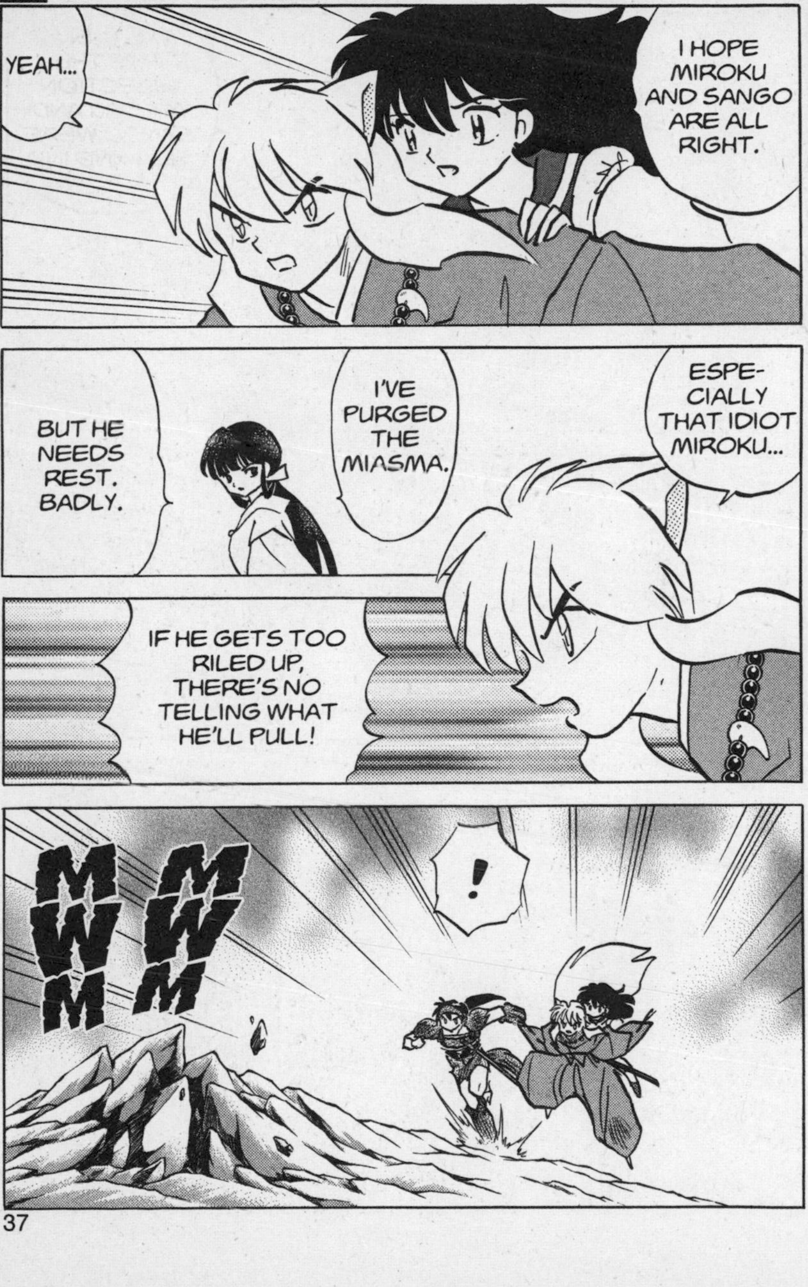
I HOPE MIROKU AND SANGO ARE ALL RIGHT.
YEAH...
ESPE-CIALLY THAT IDIOT MIROKU...
I'VE PURGED THE MIASMA.
BUT HE NEEDS REST. BADLY.
IF HE GETS TOO RILED UP, THERE'S NO TELLING WHAT HE'LL PULL!
!
MWWM
MWWM

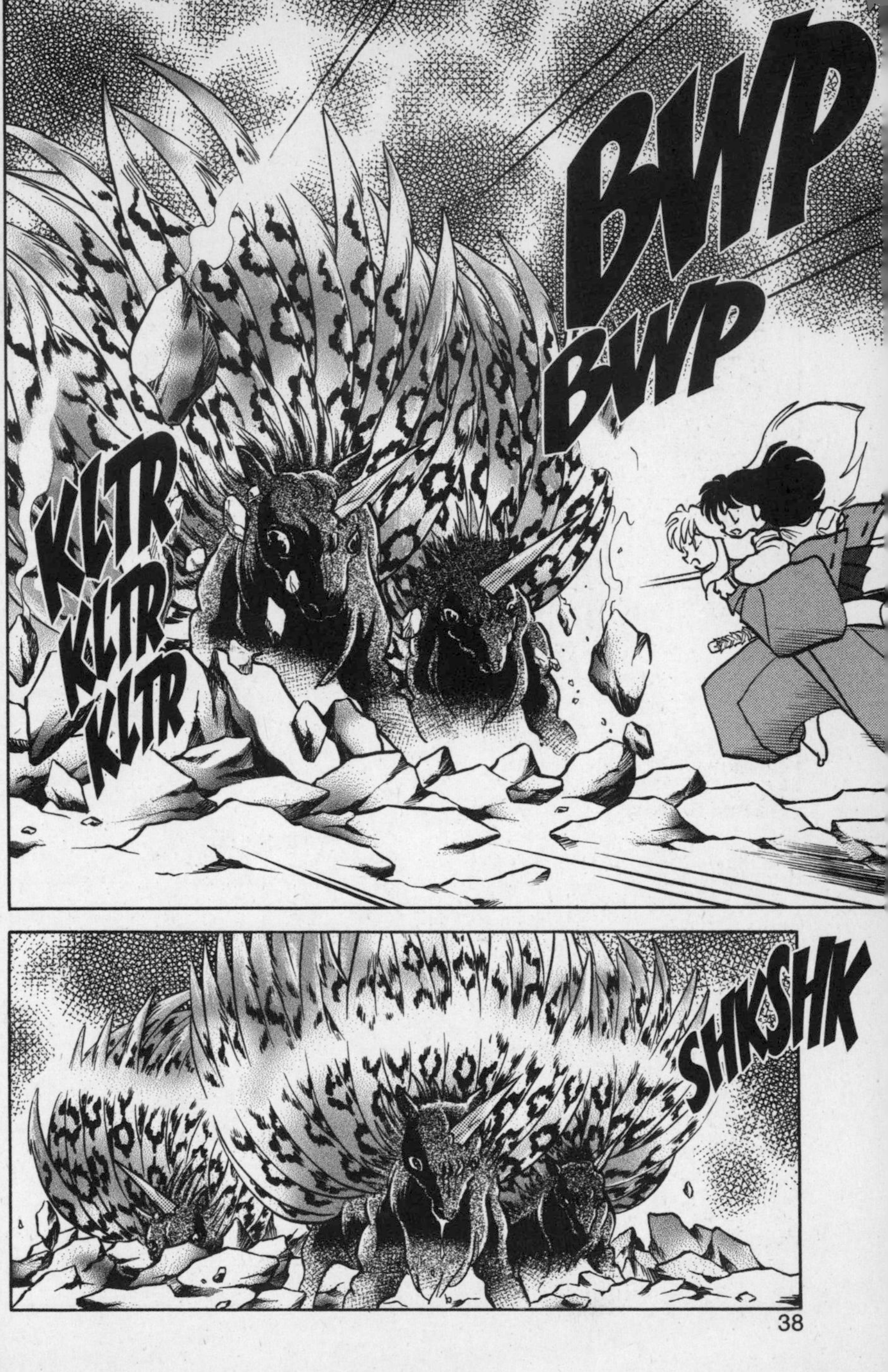
BWP
BWP
KLTR
KLTR
KLTR
SHKSHK

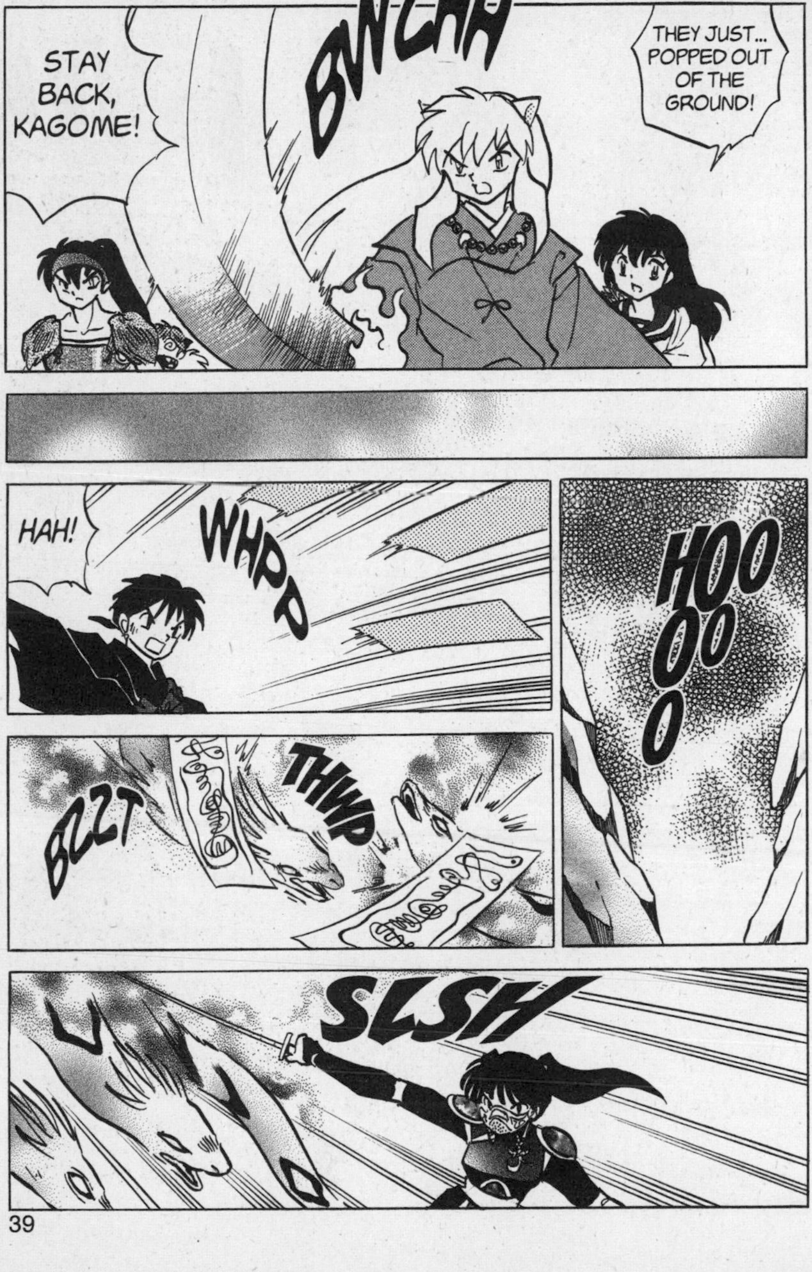
THEY JUST... POPPED OUT OF THE GROUND!
BWZHH
STAY BACK, KAGOME!
HOOOOOO
WHPP
HAH!
THWP
BZZT
SLSH

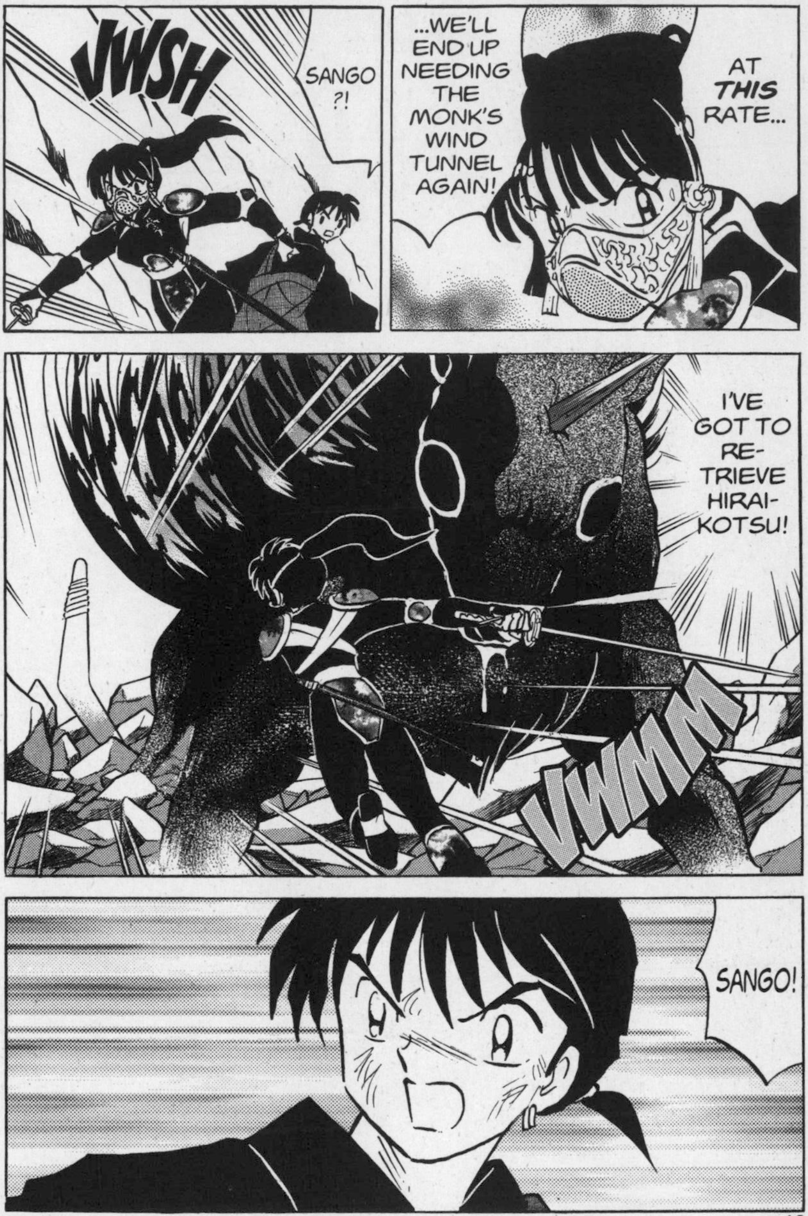
AT **THIS** RATE...
...WE'LL END UP NEEDING THE MONK'S WIND TUNNEL AGAIN!
JWSH
SANGO ?!
I'VE GOT TO RE-TRIEVE HIRAI-KOTSU!
VWMM
SANGO!

SCROLL 3

THE VALLEY OF MIASMA

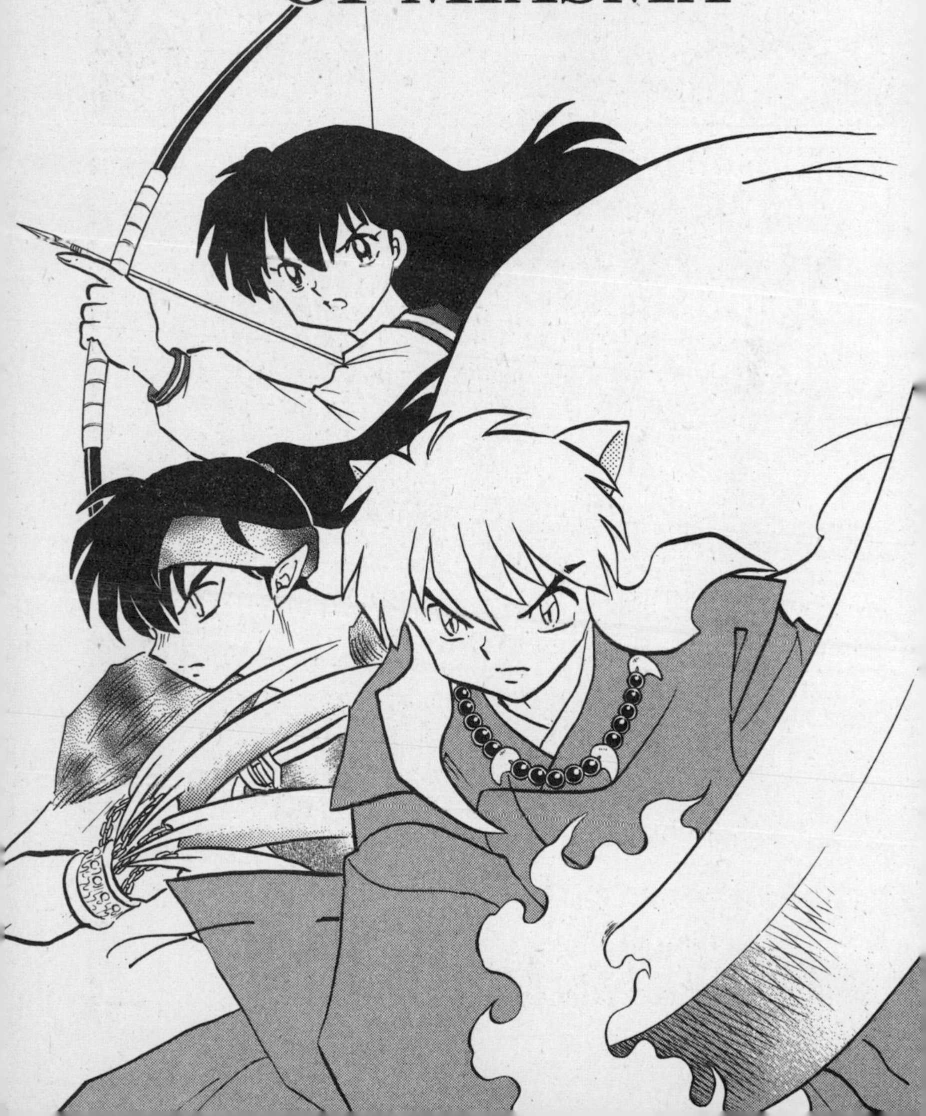

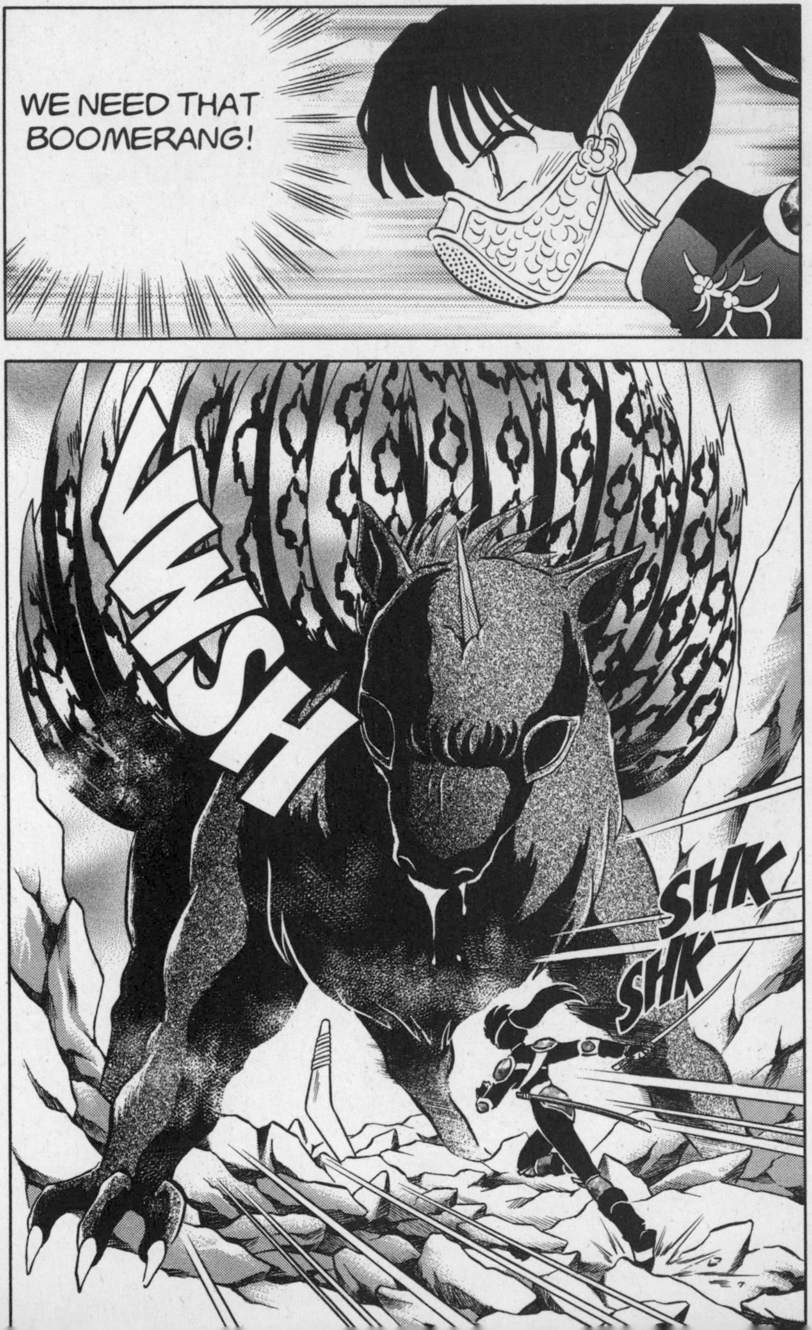
WE NEED THAT BOOMERANG!
VWSH
SHK
SHK

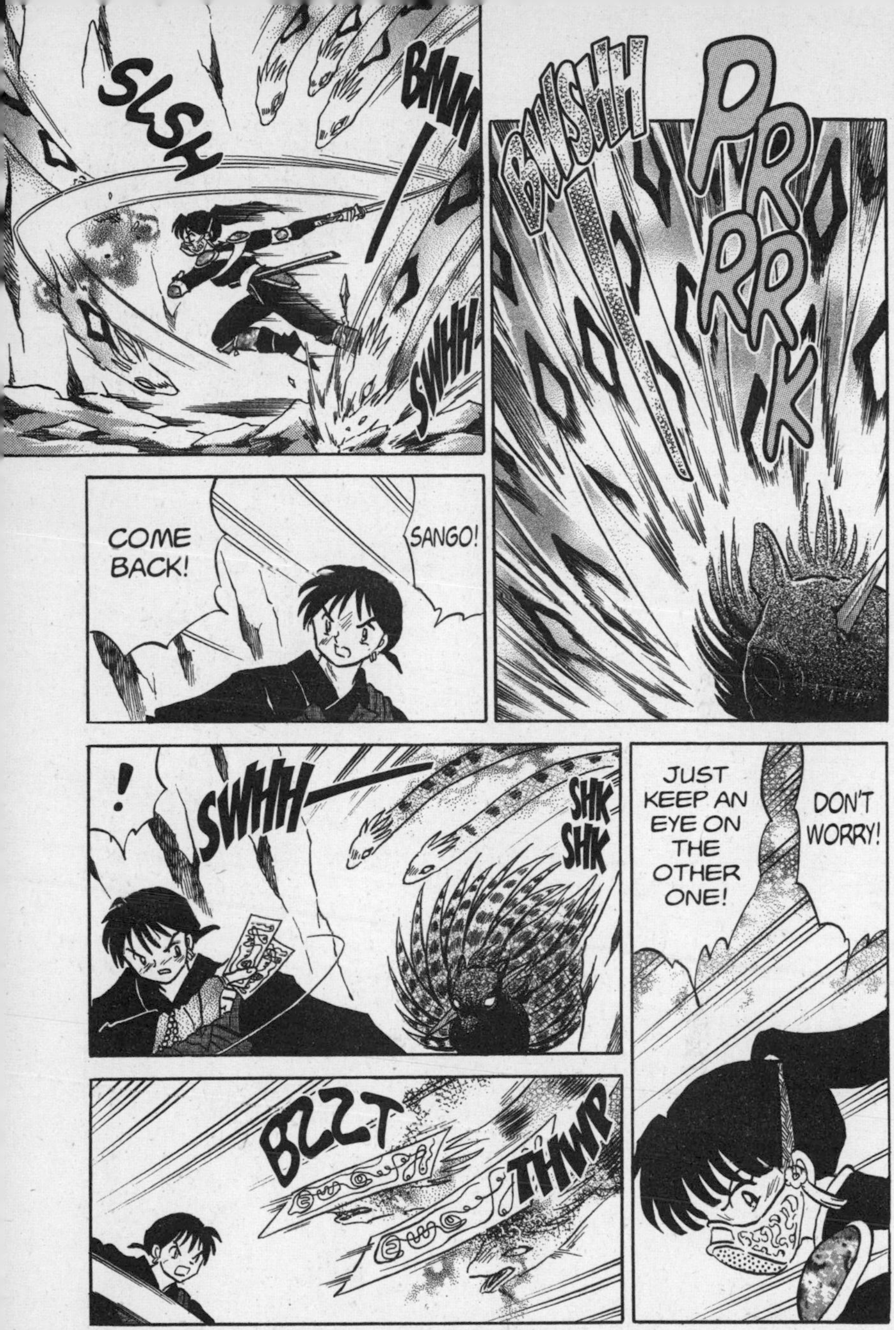
BWSHH
PRRRK
SLSH
BAMM
SWHH
SANGO!
COME BACK!
DON'T WORRY!
JUST KEEP AN EYE ON THE OTHER ONE!
!
SWHH
SHK SHK
BZZT
THWP

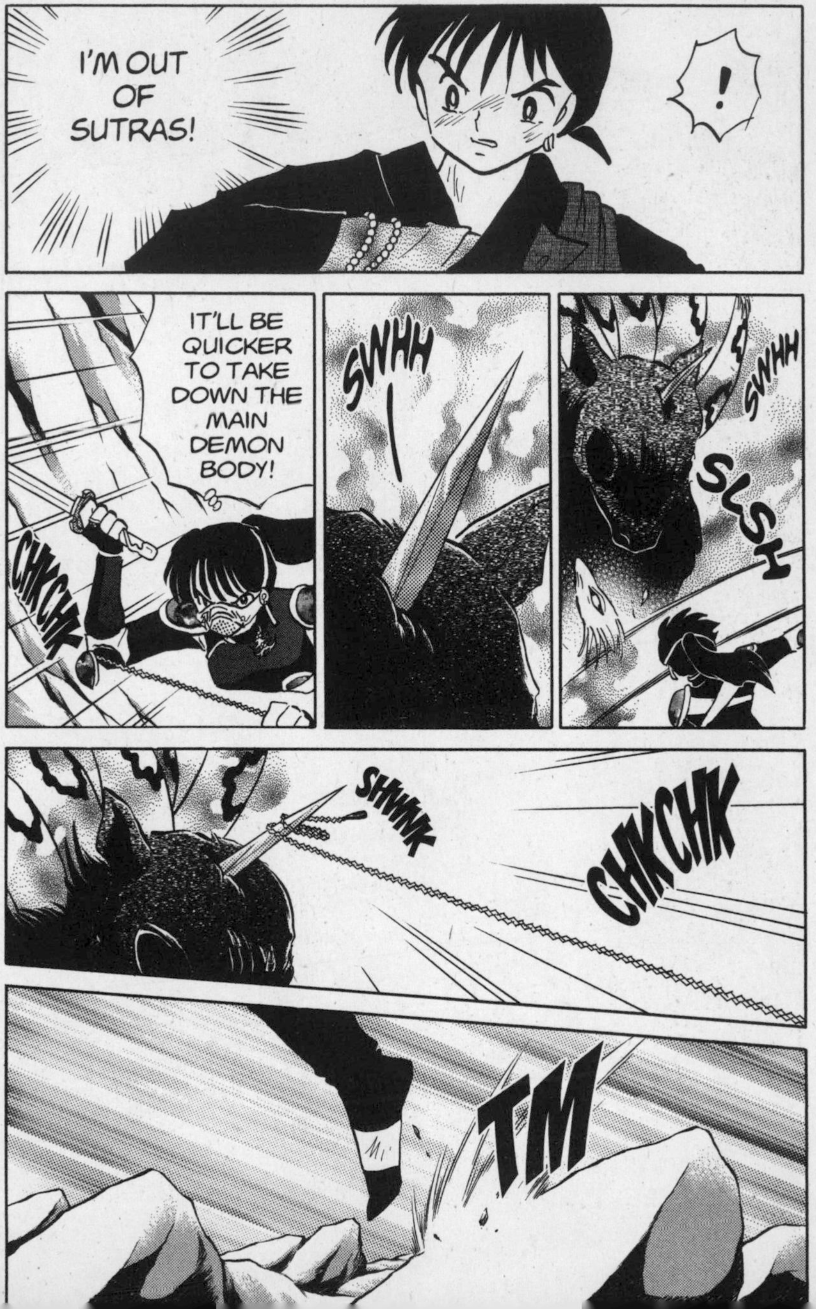
!
I'M OUT OF SUTRAS!
SWHH
SLSH
SWHH
IT'LL BE QUICKER TO TAKE DOWN THE MAIN DEMON BODY!
CHKCHK
CHKCHK
SHWNK
TM

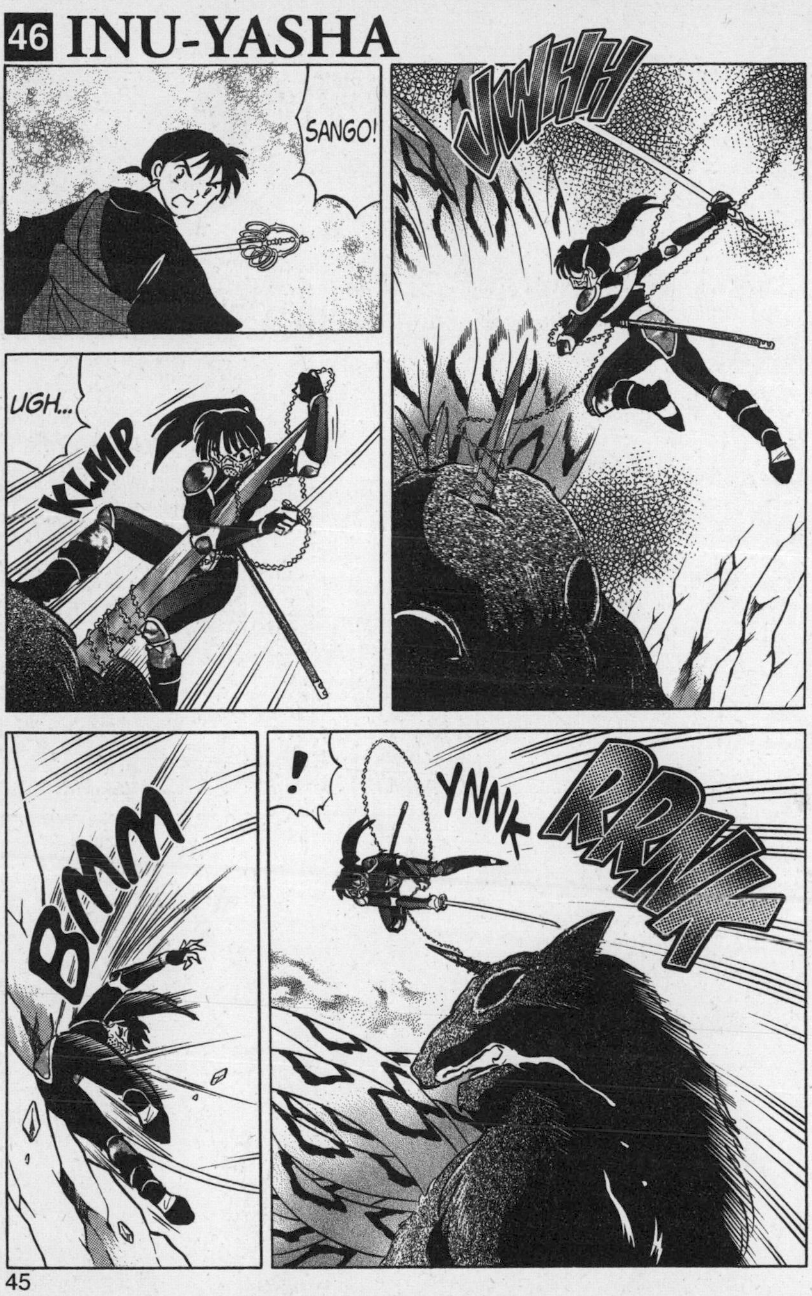
JWHH
SANGO!
UGH...
KLMP
!
YNNK
RRNK
BMM

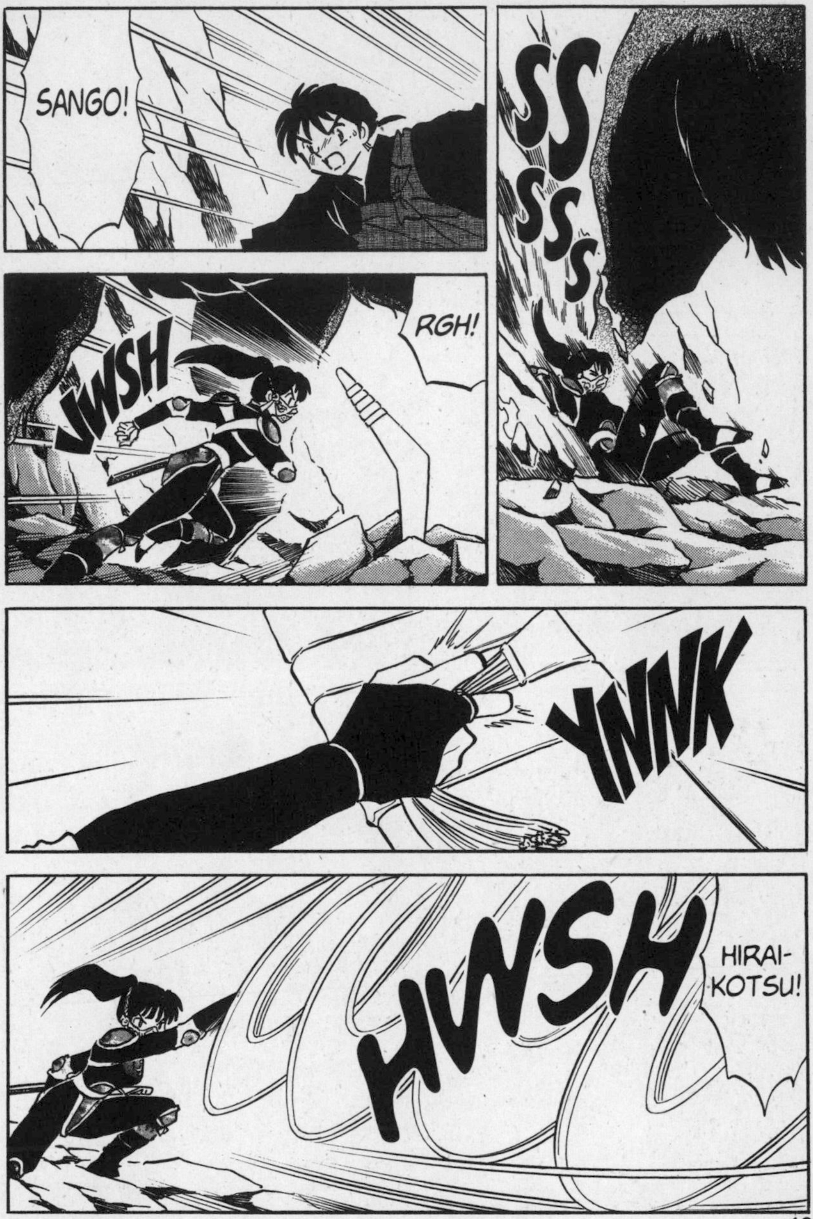
SSSSS
SANGO!
RGH!
VWSH
YNNK
HIRAI-KOTSU!
HWSH

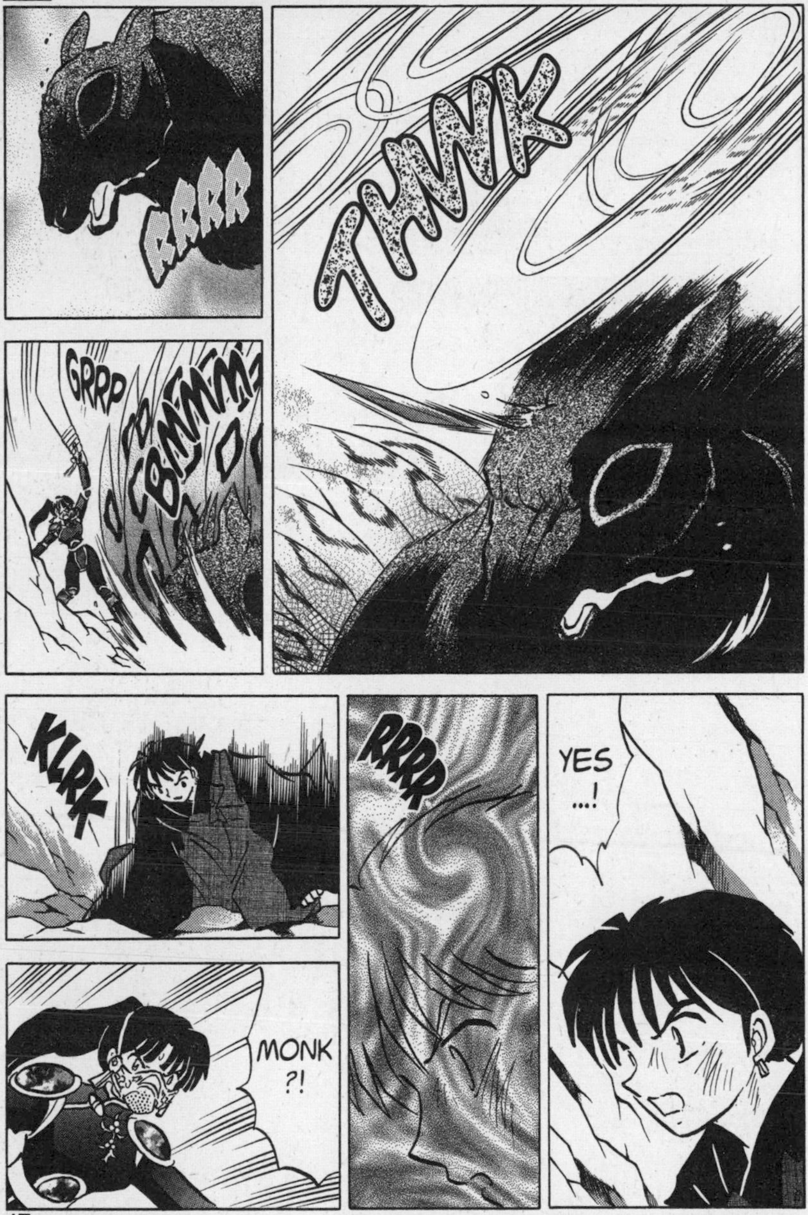
THWK
RRRR
GRRP
YES ...!
RRRR
KLRK
MONK ?!

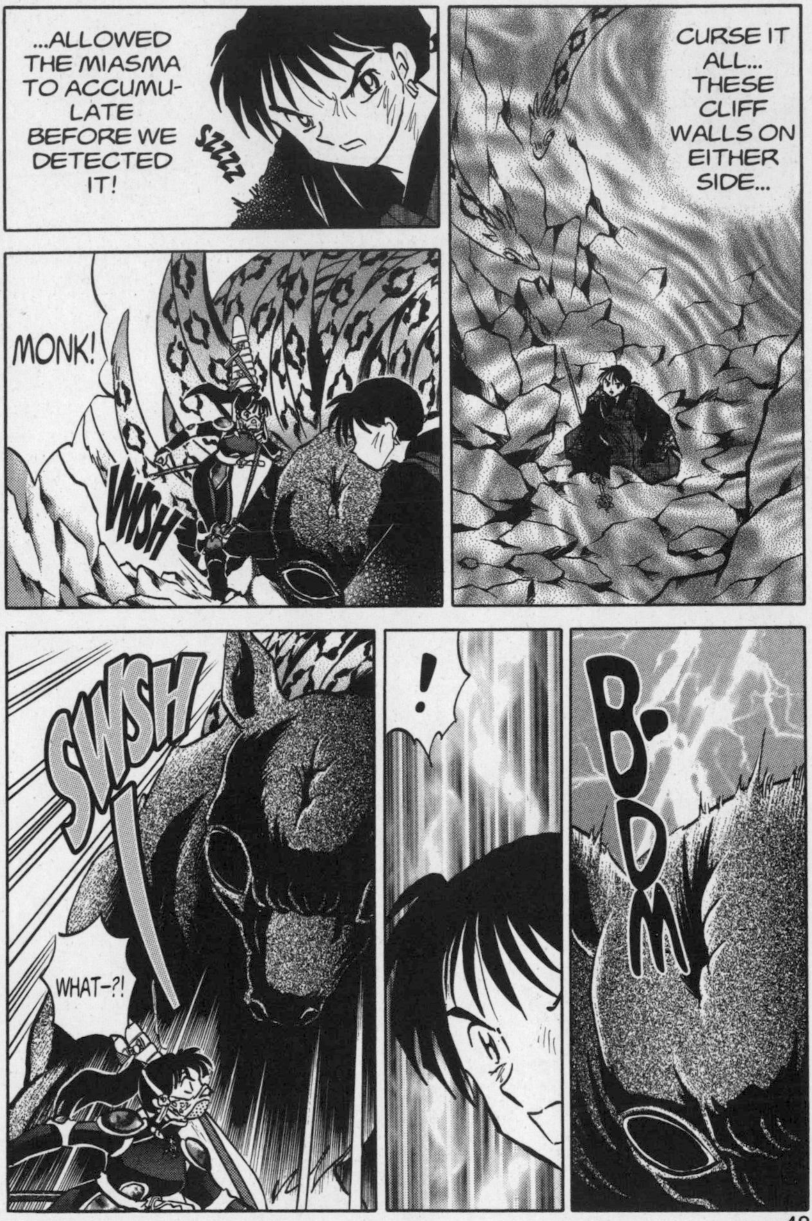
CURSE IT ALL... THESE CLIFF WALLS ON EITHER SIDE...
...ALLOWED THE MIASMA TO ACCUMU-LATE BEFORE WE DETECTED IT!
SZZZZ
MONK!
VWSH
B-DOM
!
SWSH
WHAT-?!

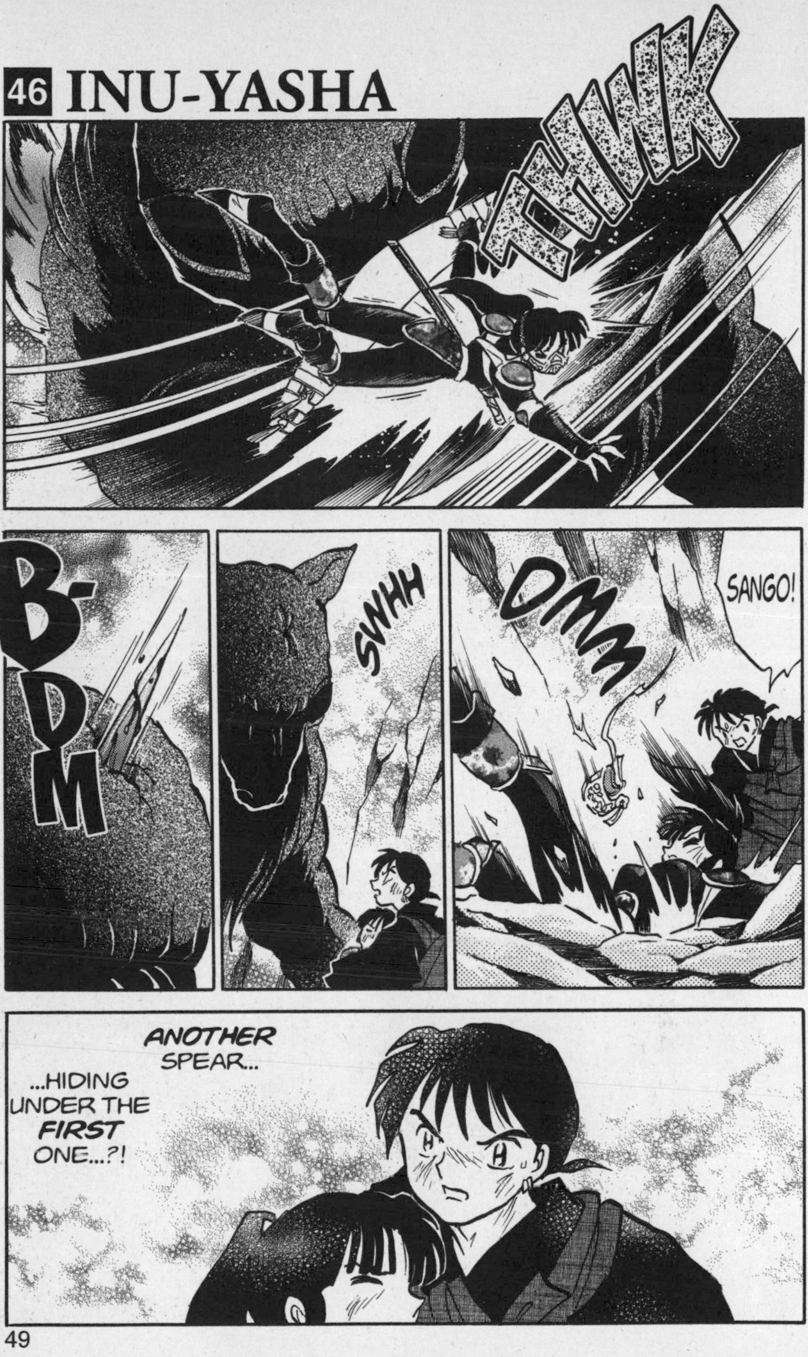
THWK
SANGO!
DMM
SWHH
B-DM
ANOTHER SPEAR...
...HIDING UNDER THE FIRST ONE...?!

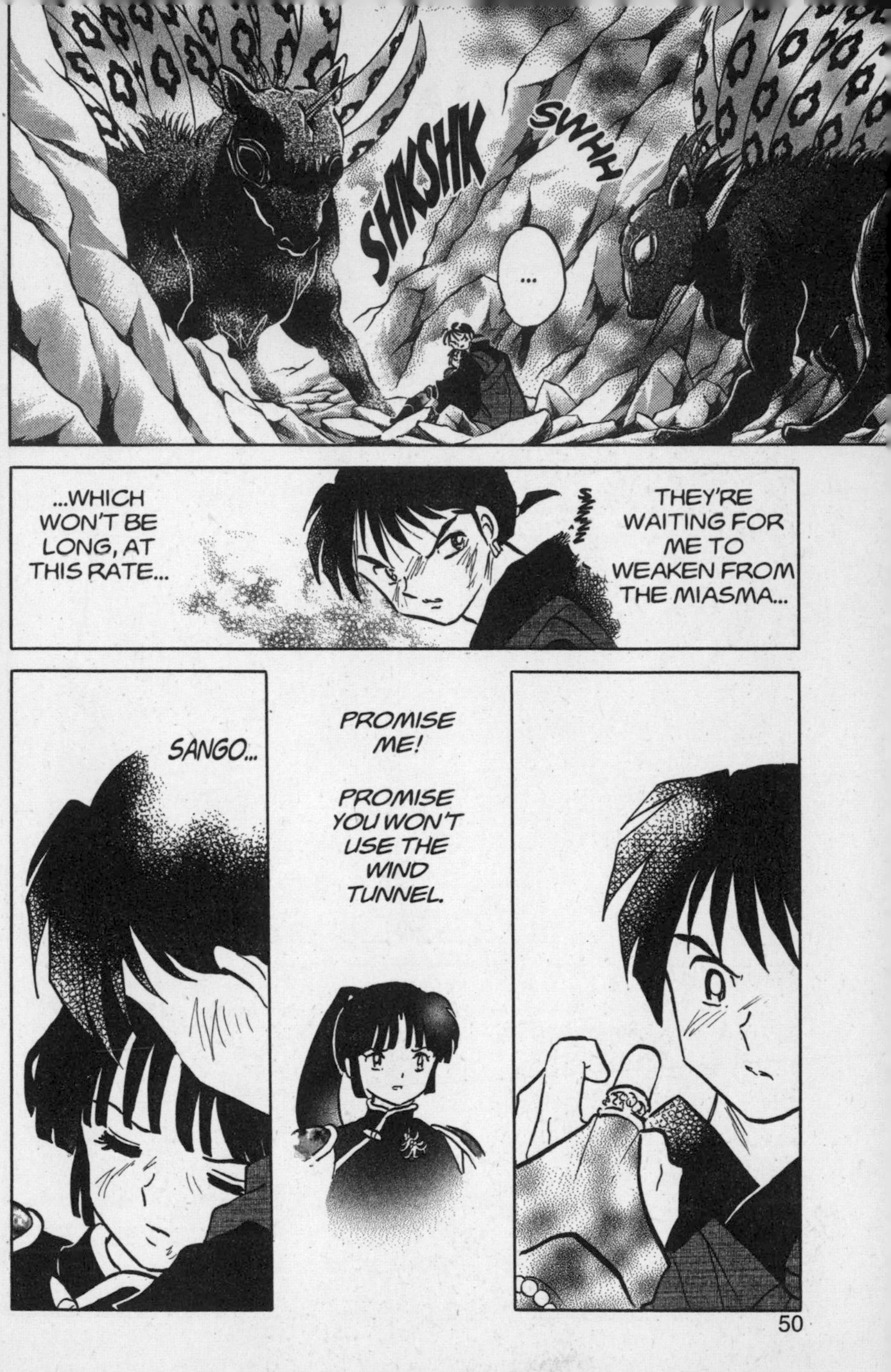
SWHH
SHKSHK
...
THEY'RE WAITING FOR ME TO WEAKEN FROM THE MIASMA...
...WHICH WON'T BE LONG, AT THIS RATE...
PROMISE ME!
PROMISE YOU WON'T USE THE WIND TUNNEL.
SANGO...

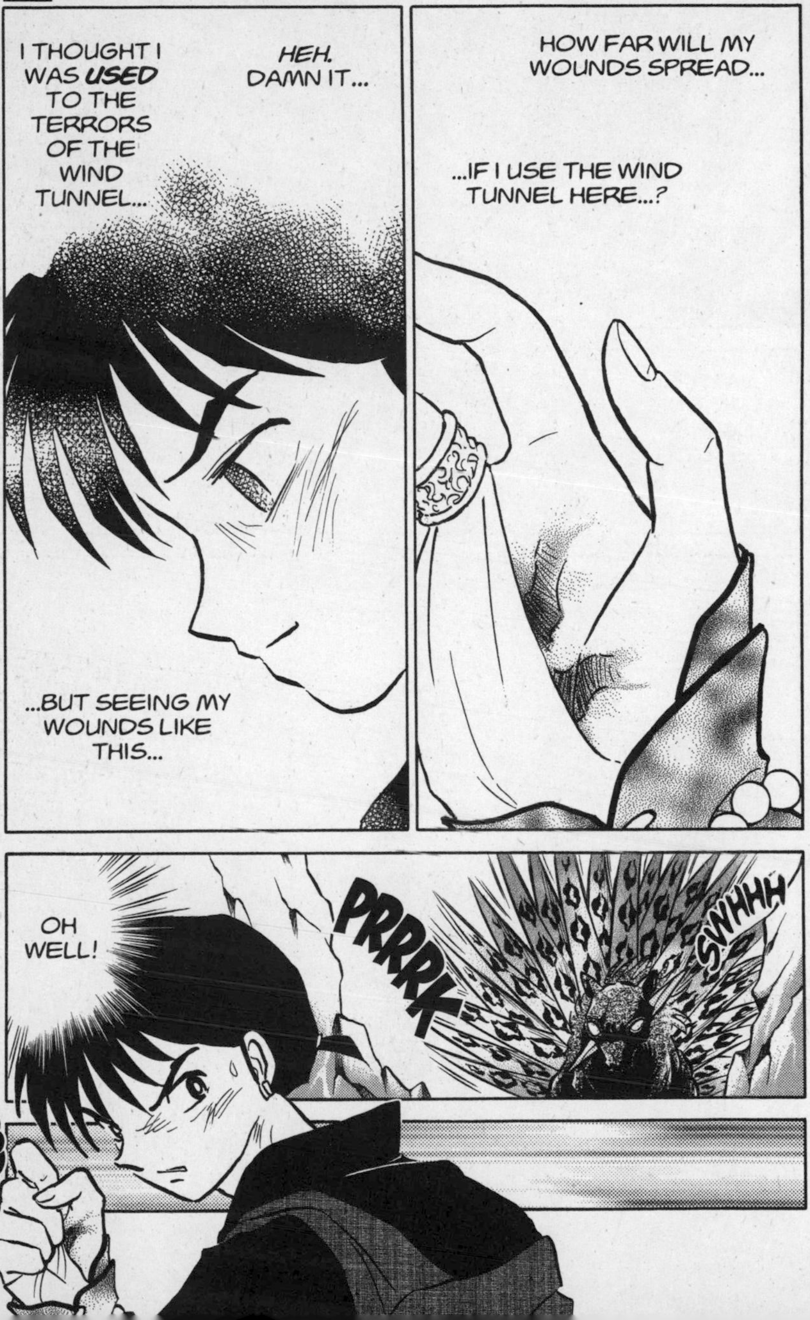
HOW FAR WILL MY WOUNDS SPREAD...
...IF I USE THE WIND TUNNEL HERE...?
HEH. DAMN IT...
I THOUGHT I WAS **USED** TO THE TERRORS OF THE WIND TUNNEL...
...BUT SEEING MY WOUNDS LIKE THIS...
SWHHH
PRRRK
OH WELL!
KRRRR

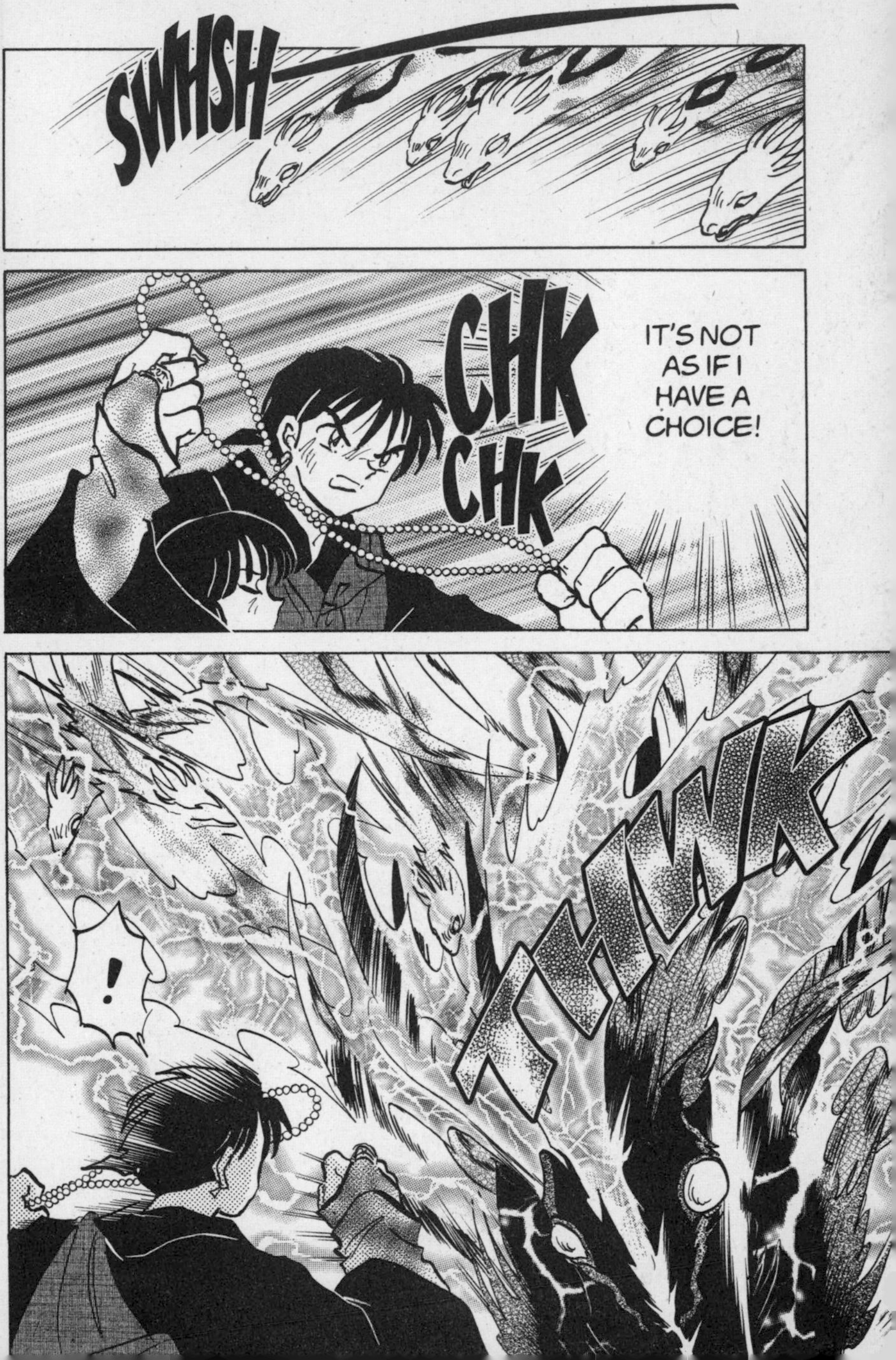
SWISH
IT'S NOT AS IF I HAVE A CHOICE!
CHK CHK
THWAK
!

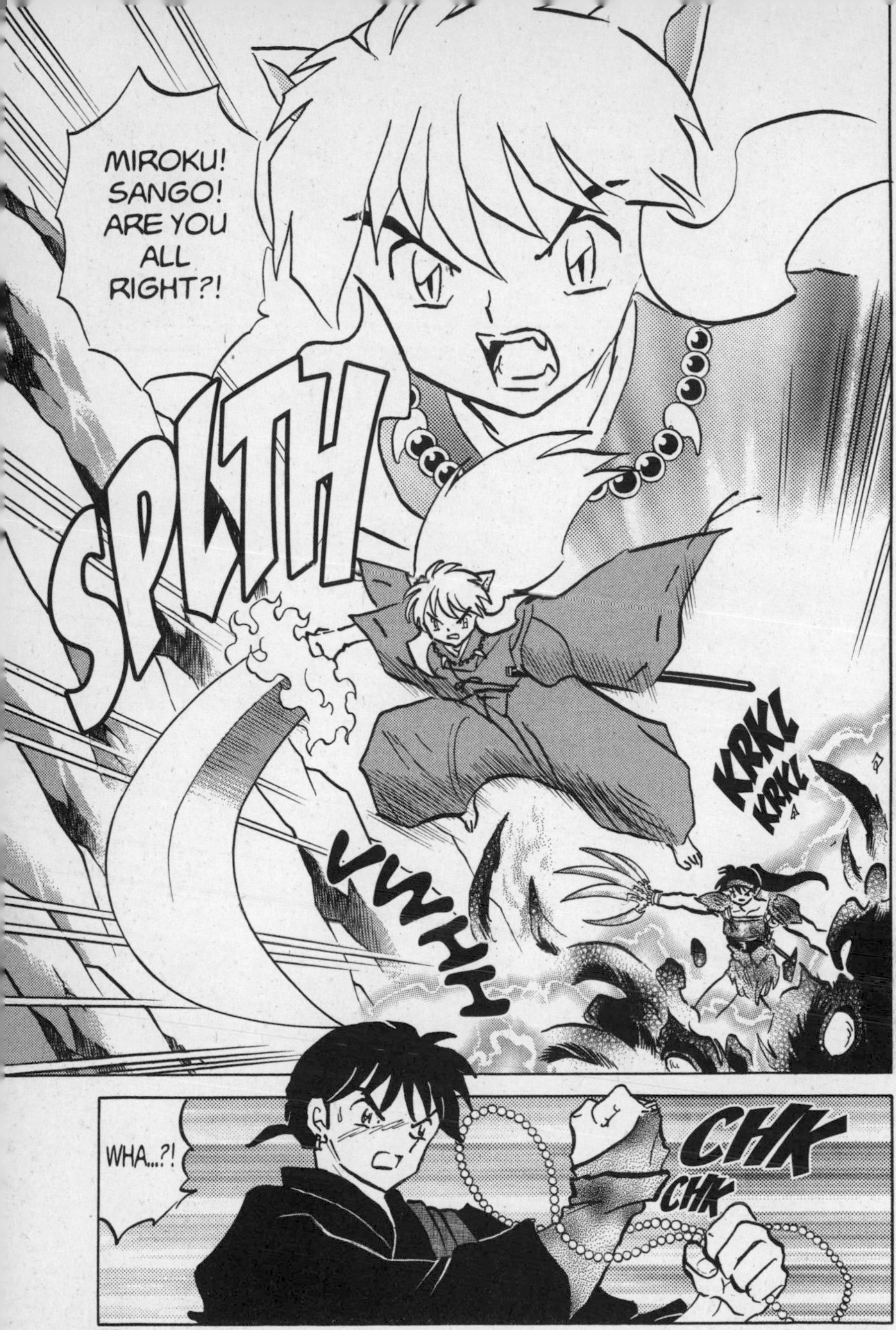
MIROKU! SANGO! ARE YOU ALL RIGHT?!
SPLTH
KRKI KRKI
VWHI
CHK CHK
WHA...?!

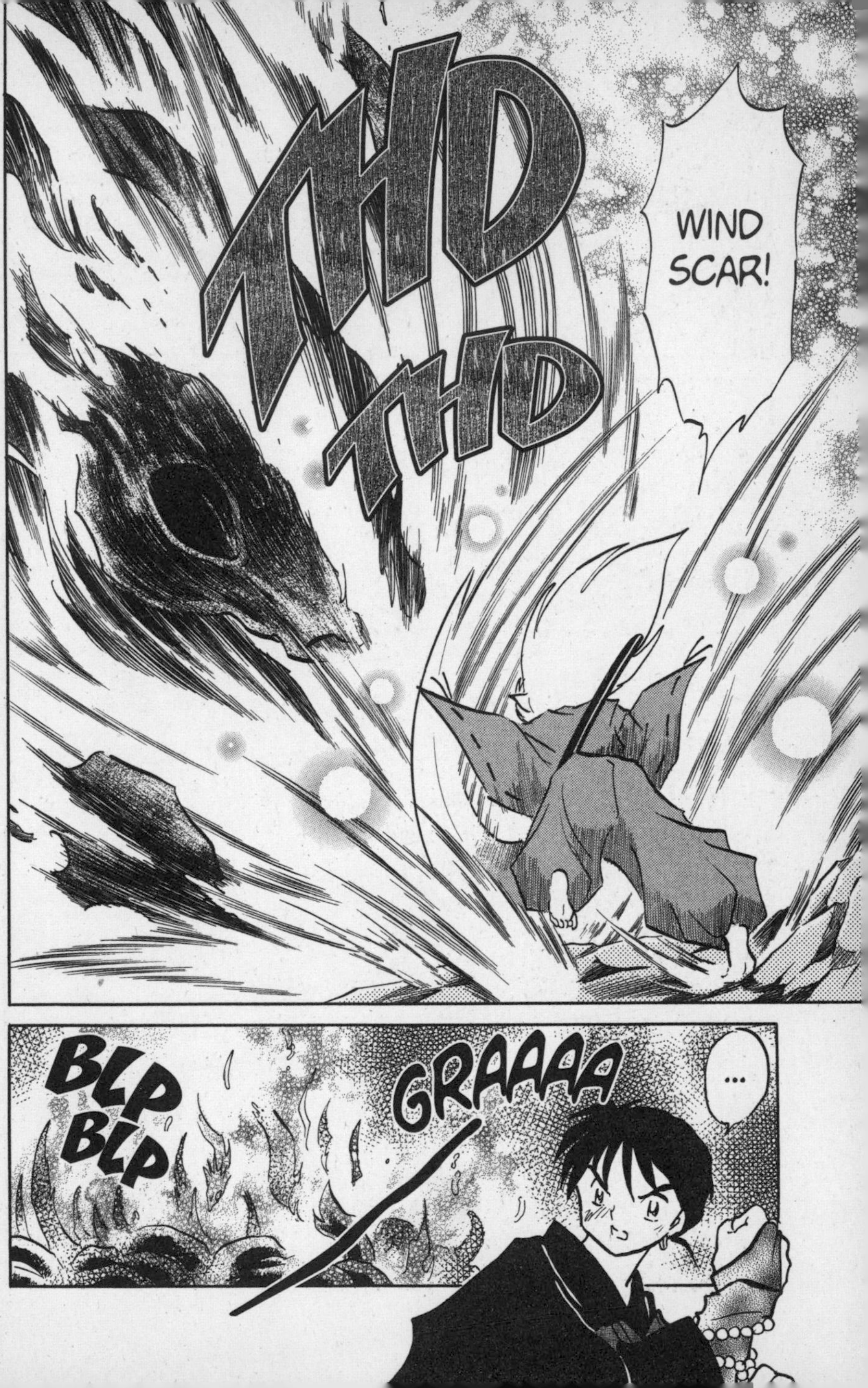
WIND SCAR!
THD THD
...
GRAAAA
BLP BLP

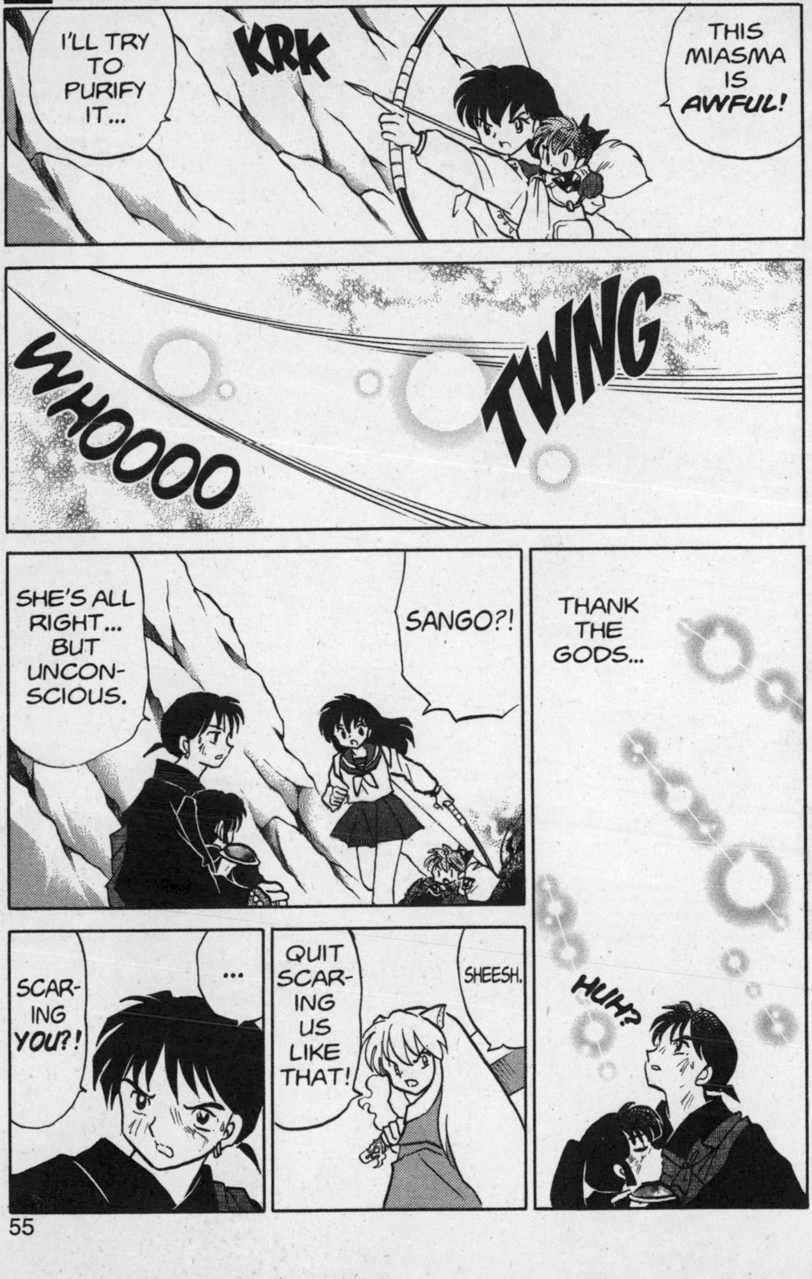
THIS MIASMA IS AWFUL!
KRK
I'LL TRY TO PURIFY IT...
TWNG
WHOOOO
THANK THE GODS...
HUH?
SANGO?!
SHE'S ALL RIGHT... BUT UNCONSCIOUS.
SHEESH.
QUIT SCARING US LIKE THAT!
...
SCARING YOU?!

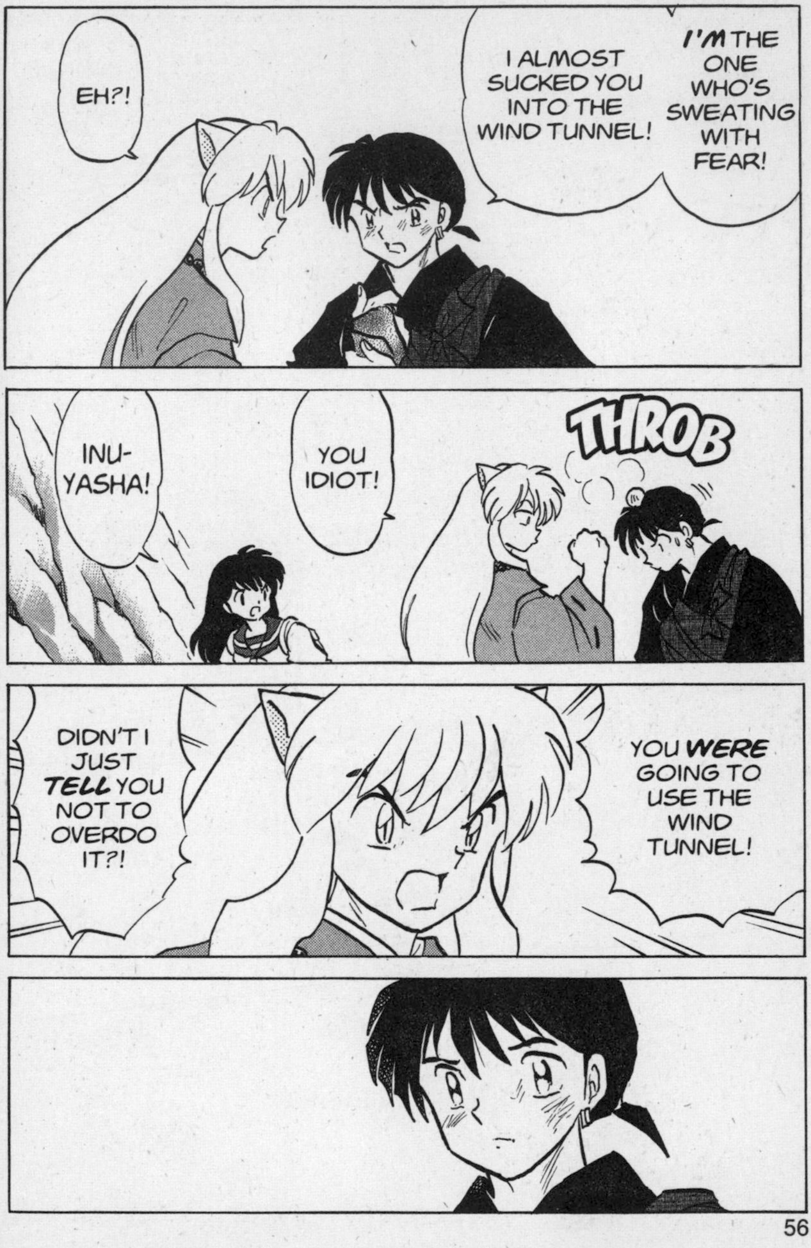
I'M THE ONE WHO'S SWEATING WITH FEAR!
I ALMOST SUCKED YOU INTO THE WIND TUNNEL!
EH?!
THROB
YOU IDIOT!
INU-YASHA!
YOU WERE GOING TO USE THE WIND TUNNEL!
DIDN'T I JUST TELL YOU NOT TO OVERDO IT?!

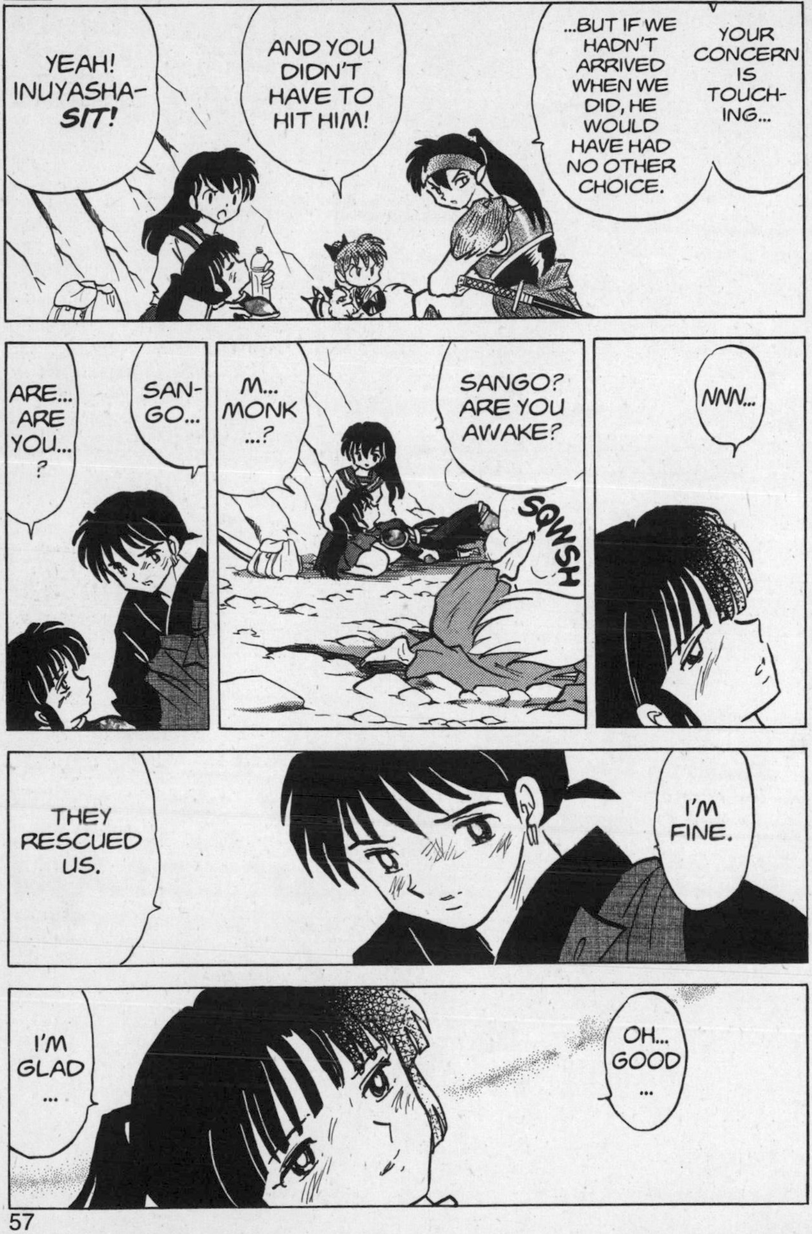
YOUR CONCERN IS TOUCHING...
...BUT IF WE HADN'T ARRIVED WHEN WE DID, HE WOULD HAVE HAD NO OTHER CHOICE.
AND YOU DIDN'T HAVE TO HIT HIM!
YEAH! INUYASHA- *SIT!*
NNN...
SANGO? ARE YOU AWAKE?
SQWSH
M... MONK ...?
SAN-GO...
ARE... ARE YOU... ?
I'M FINE.
THEY RESCUED US.
OH... GOOD ...
I'M GLAD ...

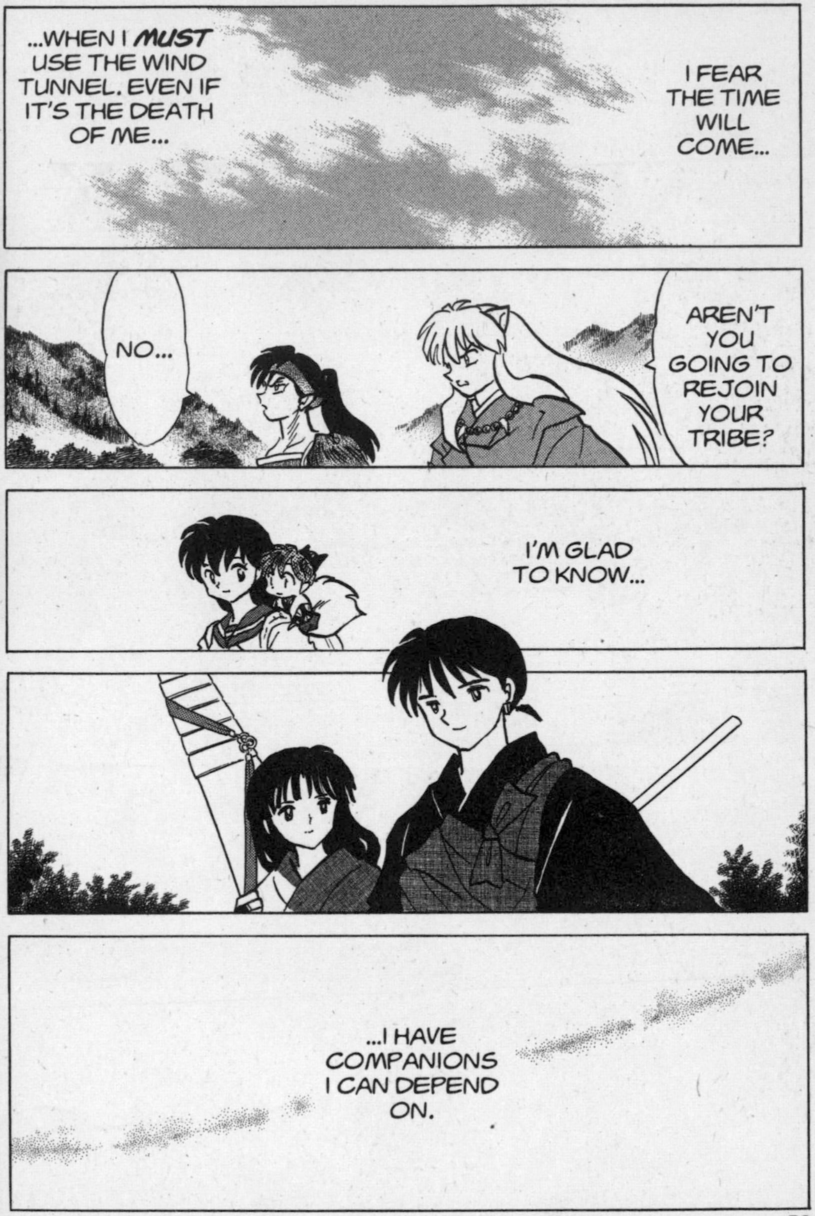
I FEAR THE TIME WILL COME...
...WHEN I MUST USE THE WIND TUNNEL. EVEN IF IT'S THE DEATH OF ME...
AREN'T YOU GOING TO REJOIN YOUR TRIBE?
NO...
I'M GLAD TO KNOW...
...I HAVE COMPANIONS I CAN DEPEND ON.

SCROLL 4

SPIDER SILK

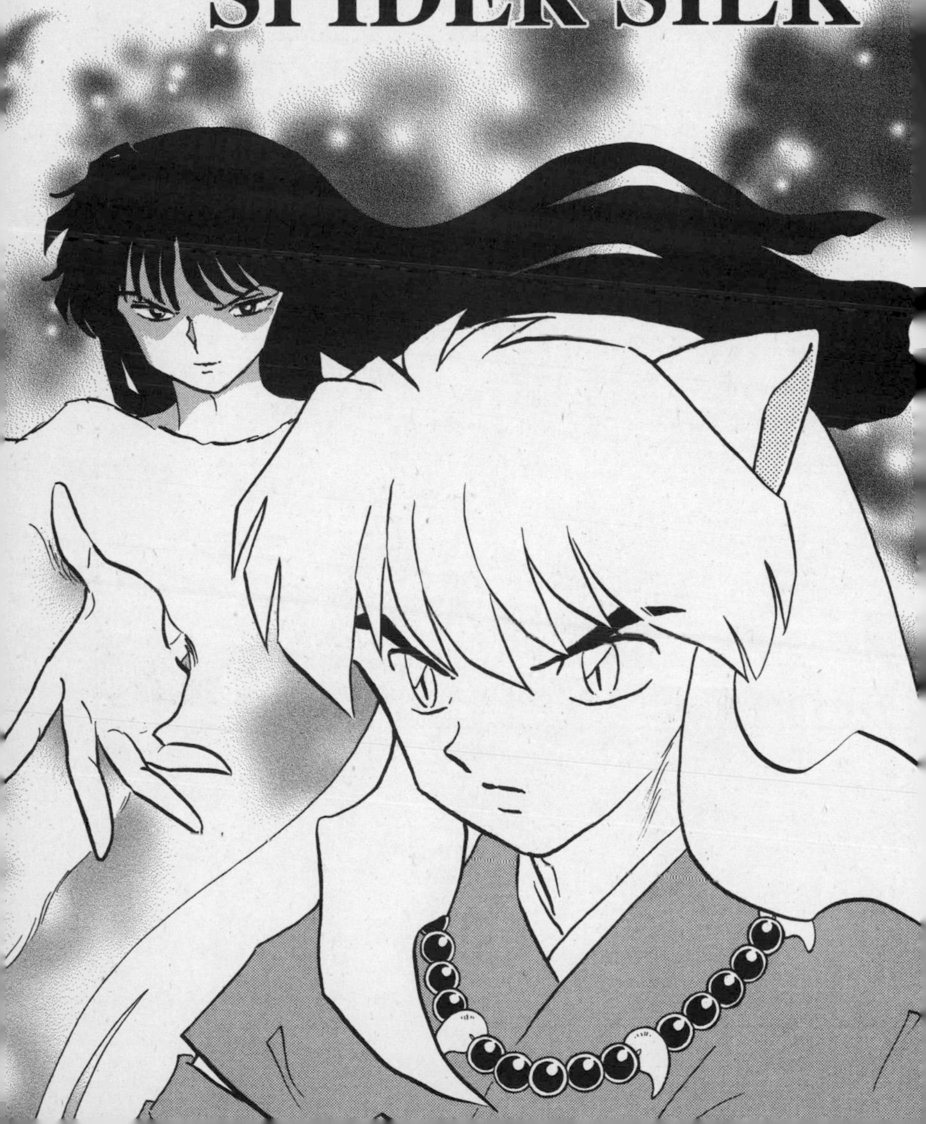

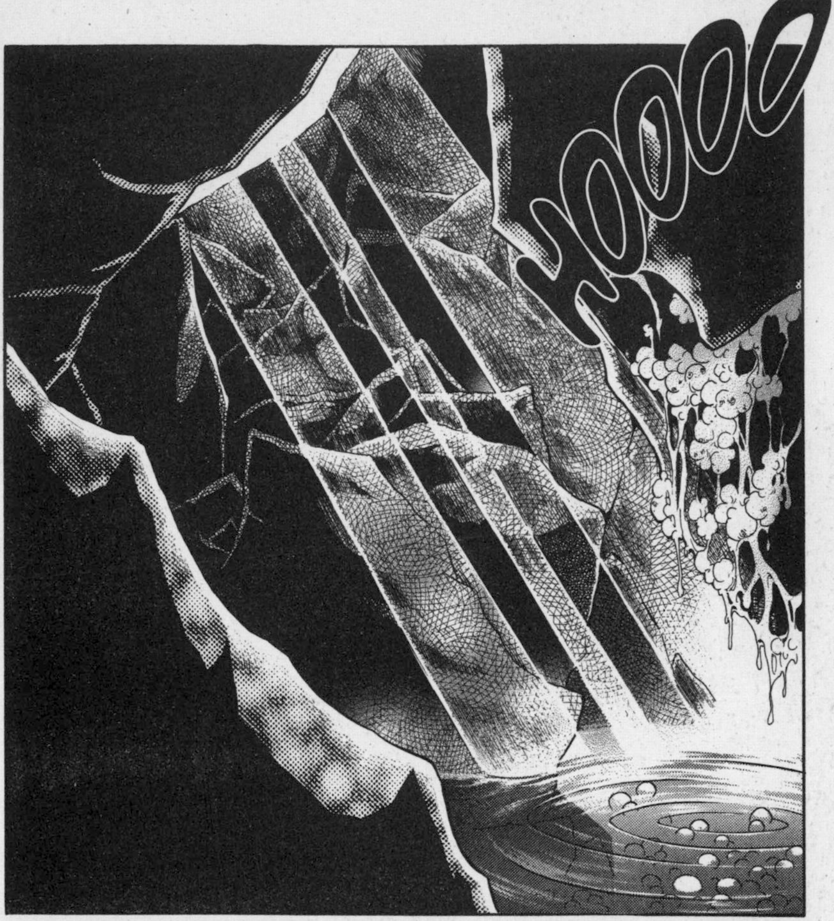

YOOOOO

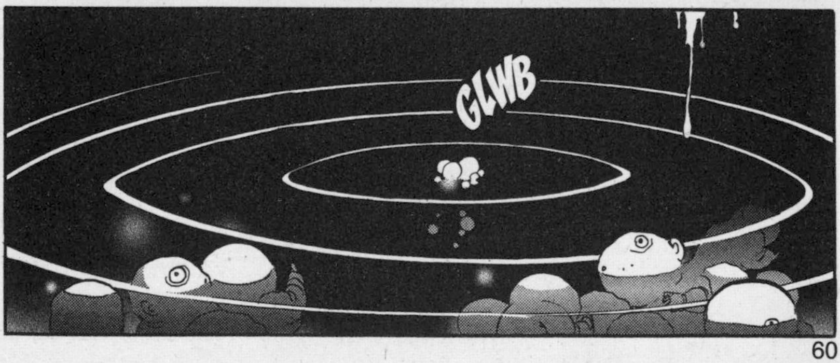

GLWB

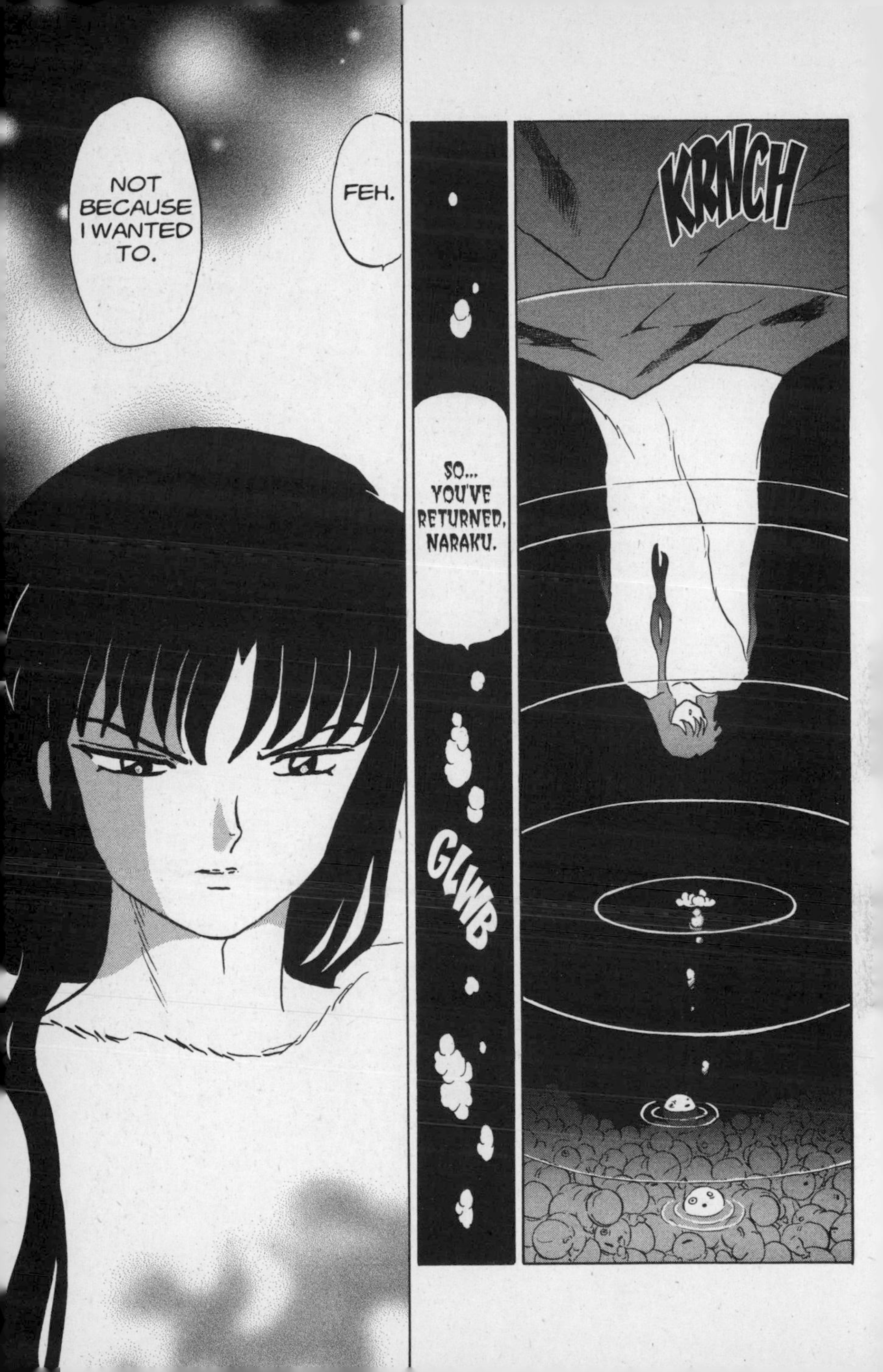
KRNCH
SO... YOU'VE RETURNED, NARAKU.
GLWB
FEH.
NOT BECAUSE I WANTED TO.

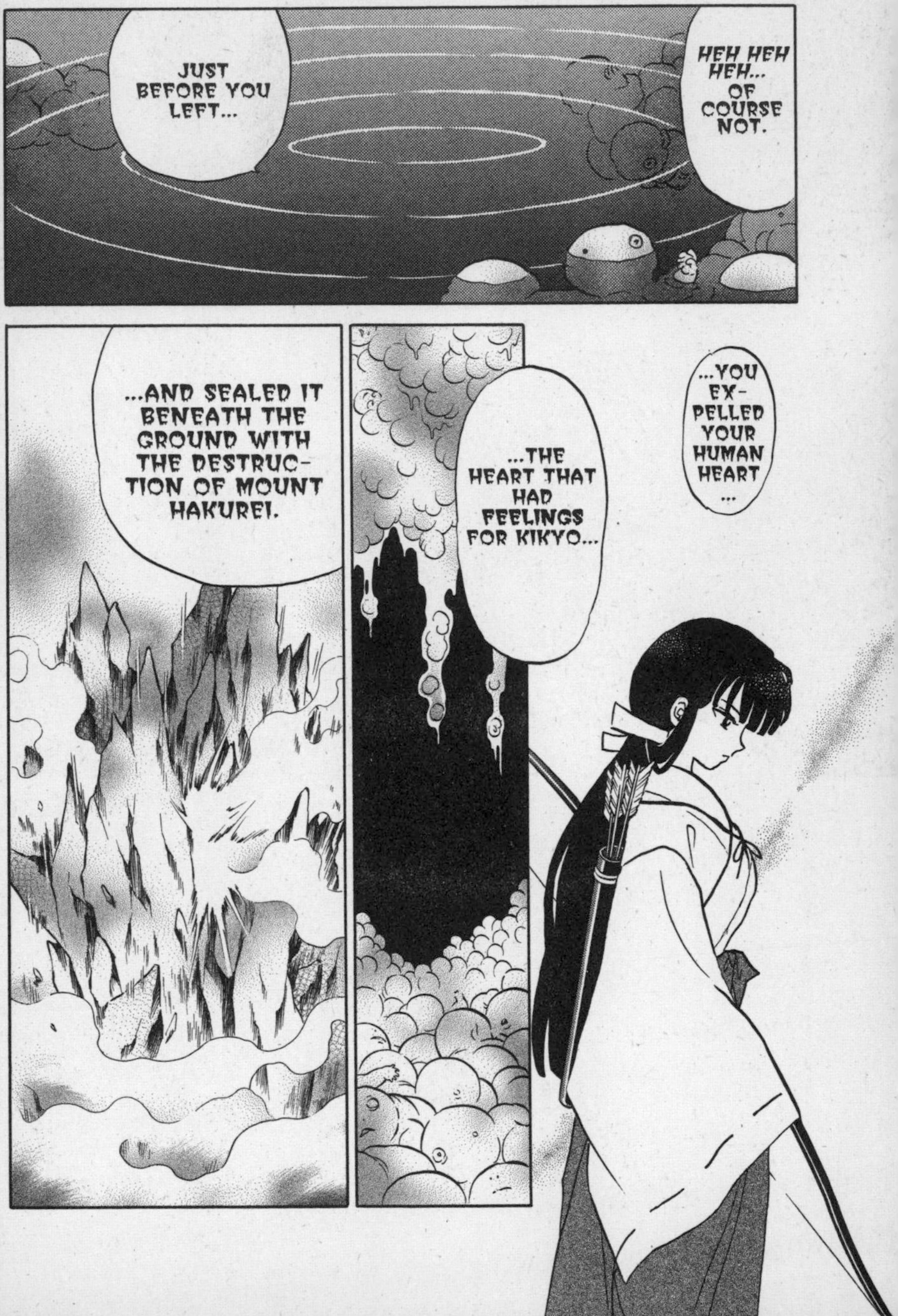
HEH HEH HEH... OF COURSE NOT.
JUST BEFORE YOU LEFT...
...YOU EXPELLED YOUR HUMAN HEART...
...THE HEART THAT HAD FEELINGS FOR KIKYO...
...AND SEALED IT BENEATH THE GROUND WITH THE DESTRUCTION OF MOUNT HAKUREI.

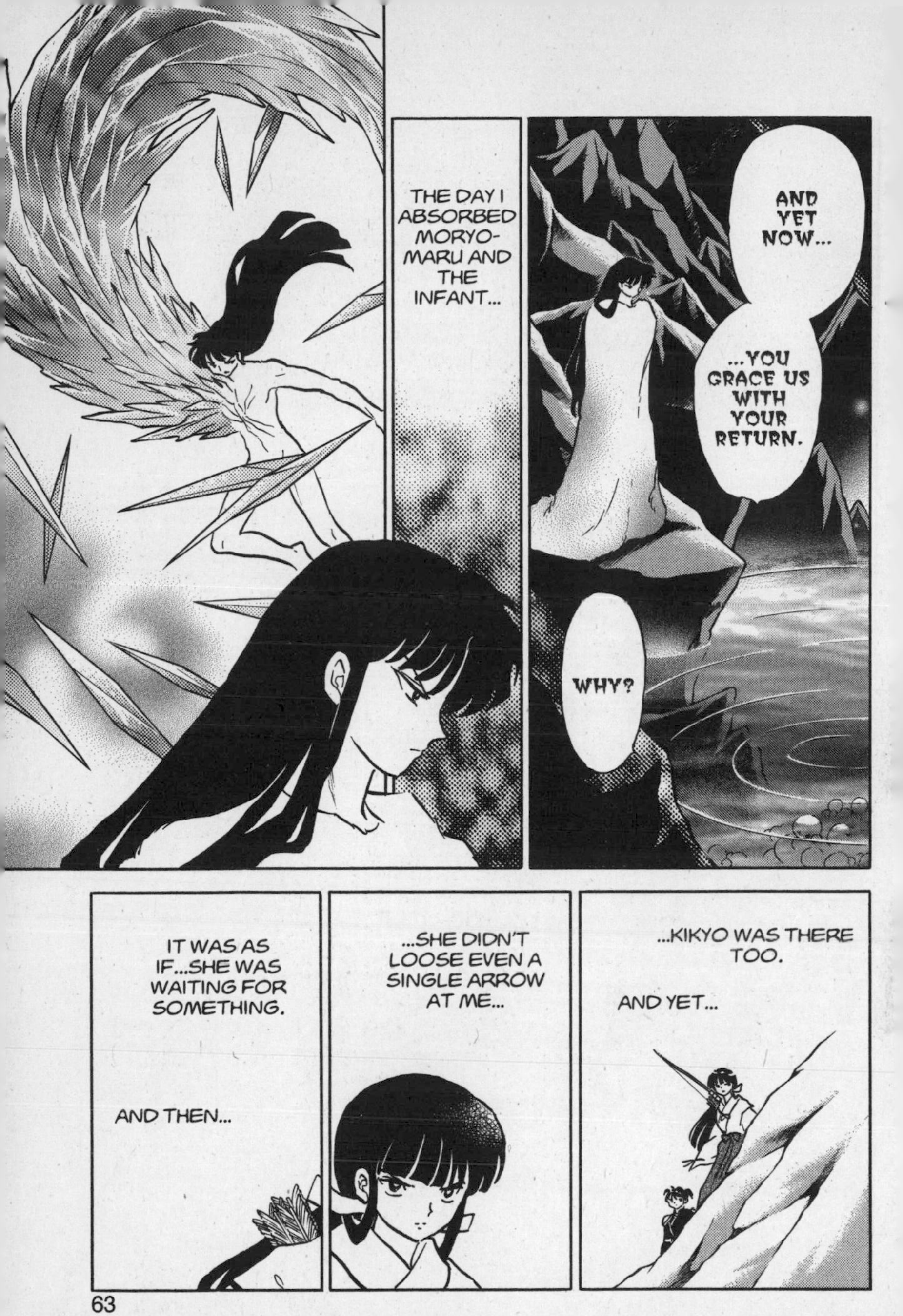
AND YET NOW...
...YOU GRACE US WITH YOUR RETURN.
WHY?
THE DAY I ABSORBED MORYO-MARU AND THE INFANT...
...KIKYO WAS THERE TOO.
AND YET...
...SHE DIDN'T LOOSE EVEN A SINGLE ARROW AT ME...
IT WAS AS IF...SHE WAS WAITING FOR SOMETHING.
AND THEN...

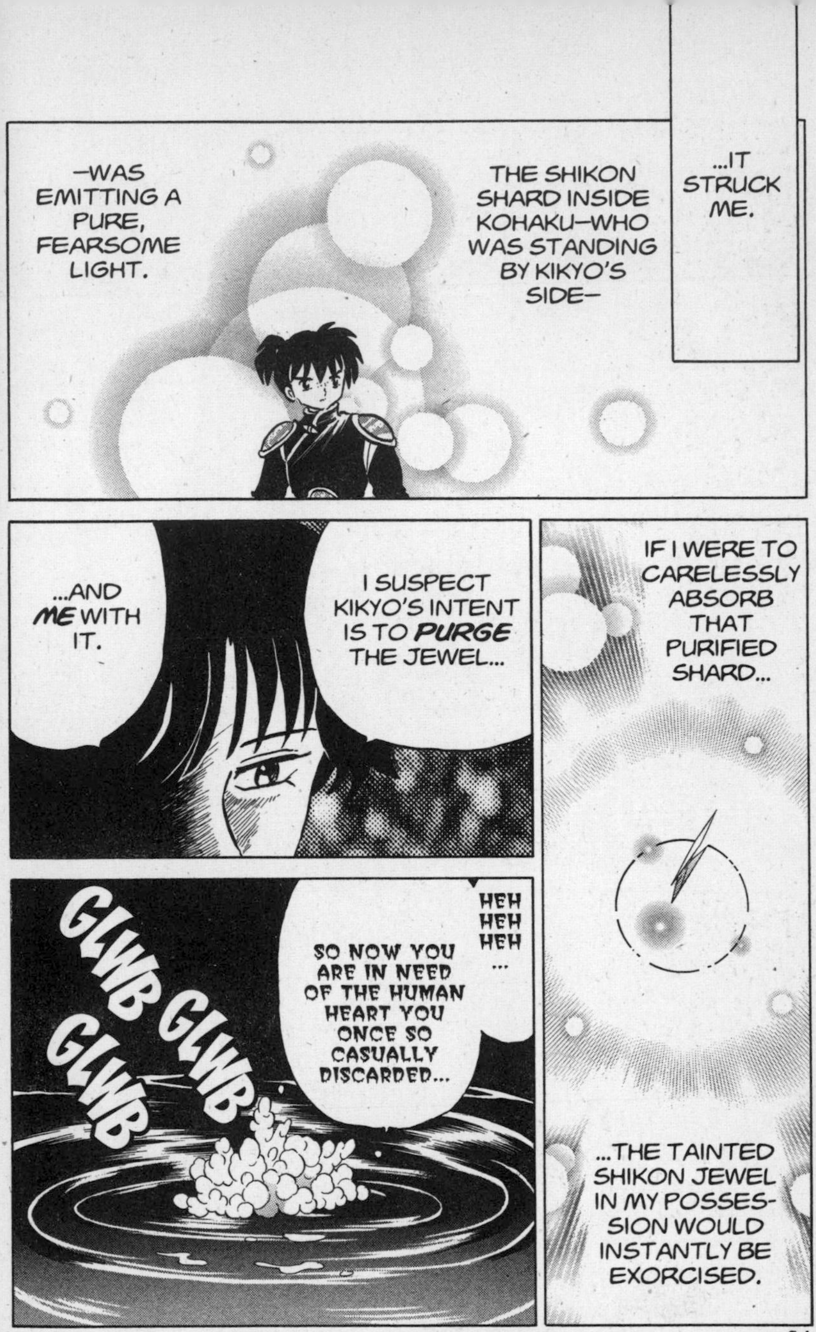
...IT STRUCK ME.
THE SHIKON SHARD INSIDE KOHAKU—WHO WAS STANDING BY KIKYO'S SIDE—
—WAS EMITTING A PURE, FEARSOME LIGHT.
IF I WERE TO CARELESSLY ABSORB THAT PURIFIED SHARD...
...THE TAINTED SHIKON JEWEL IN MY POSSES-SION WOULD INSTANTLY BE EXORCISED.
I SUSPECT KIKYO'S INTENT IS TO *PURGE* THE JEWEL...
...AND *ME* WITH IT.
HEH HEH HEH ...
SO NOW YOU ARE IN NEED OF THE HUMAN HEART YOU ONCE SO CASUALLY DISCARDED...
GLWB GLWB GLWB

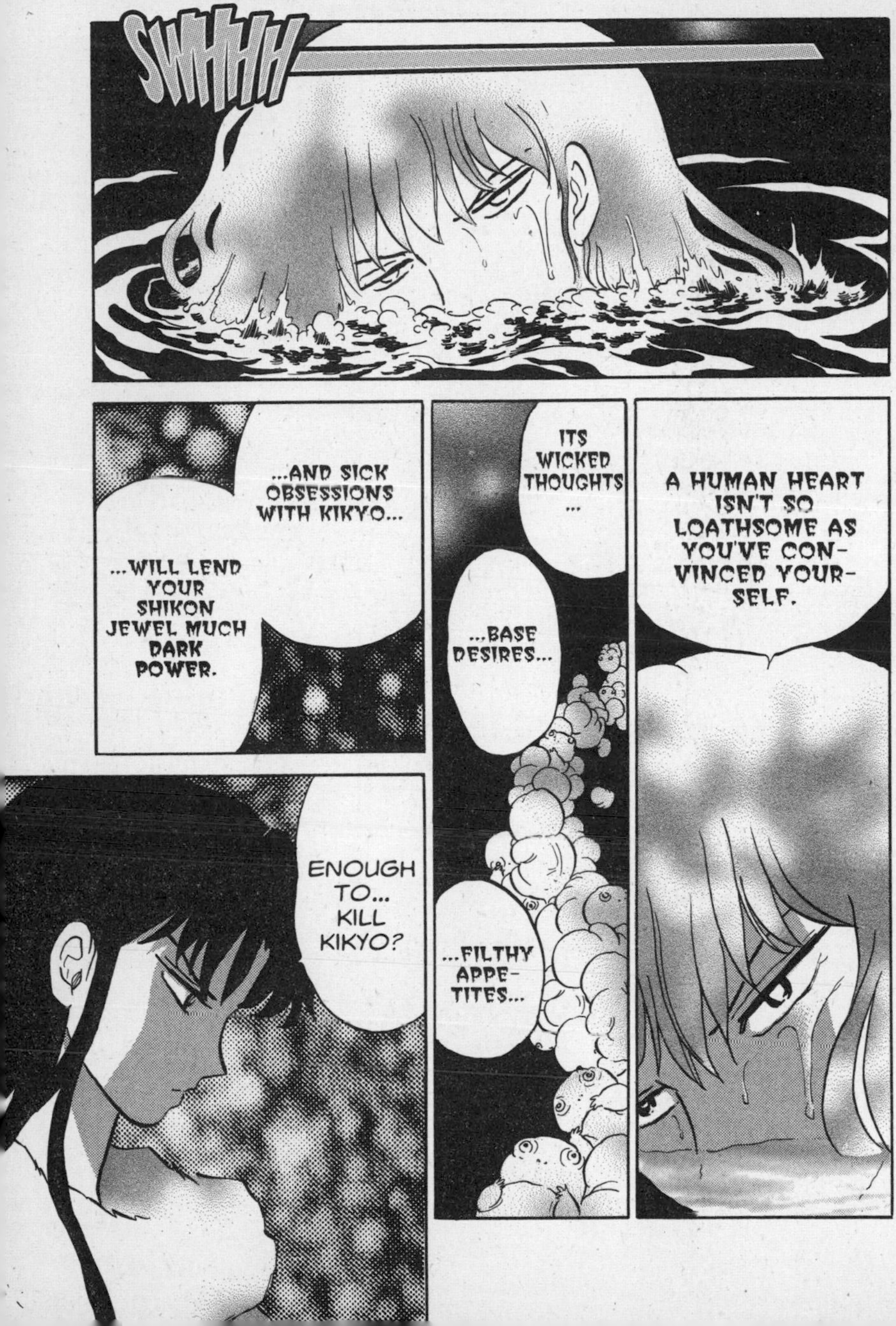
SWHHHH
A HUMAN HEART ISN'T SO LOATHSOME AS YOU'VE CONVINCED YOURSELF.
ITS WICKED THOUGHTS...
...BASE DESIRES...
...FILTHY APPETITES...
...AND SICK OBSESSIONS WITH KIKYO...
...WILL LEND YOUR SHIKON JEWEL MUCH DARK POWER.
ENOUGH TO... KILL KIKYO?

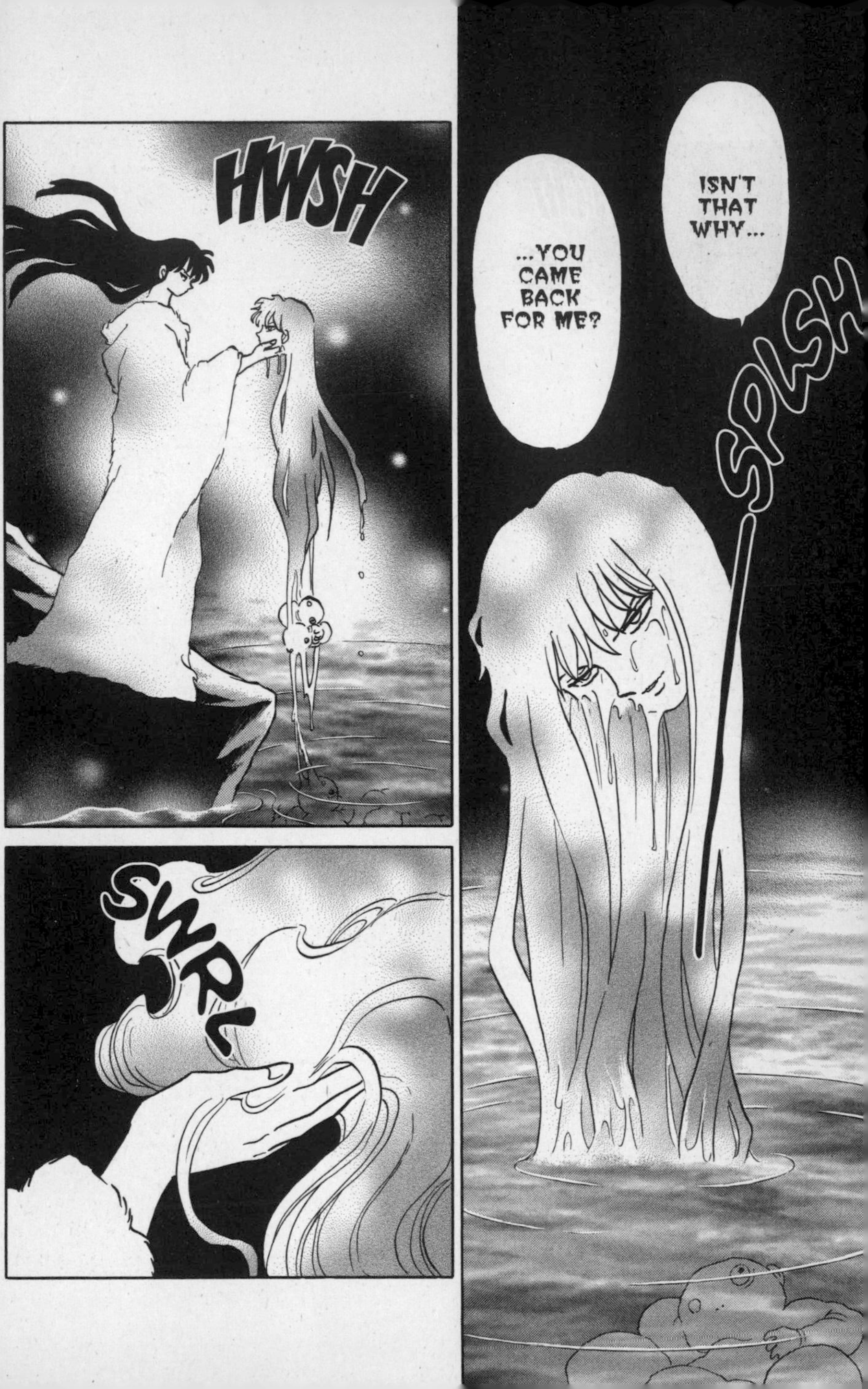
ISN'T THAT WHY...
...YOU CAME BACK FOR ME?
SPLSH
HWSH
SWRL

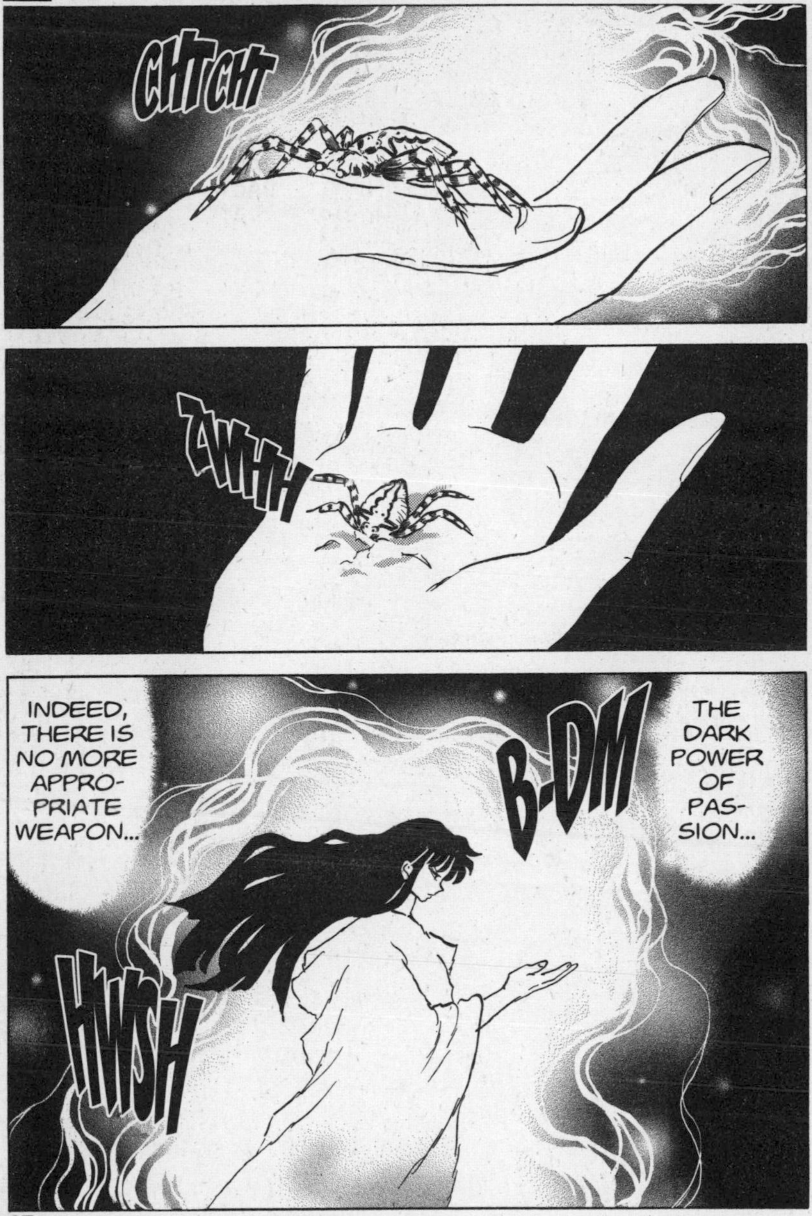
CHT CHT
ZWHH
THE DARK POWER OF PAS-SION...
B-DM
INDEED, THERE IS NO MORE APPRO-PRIATE WEAPON...
HWSH

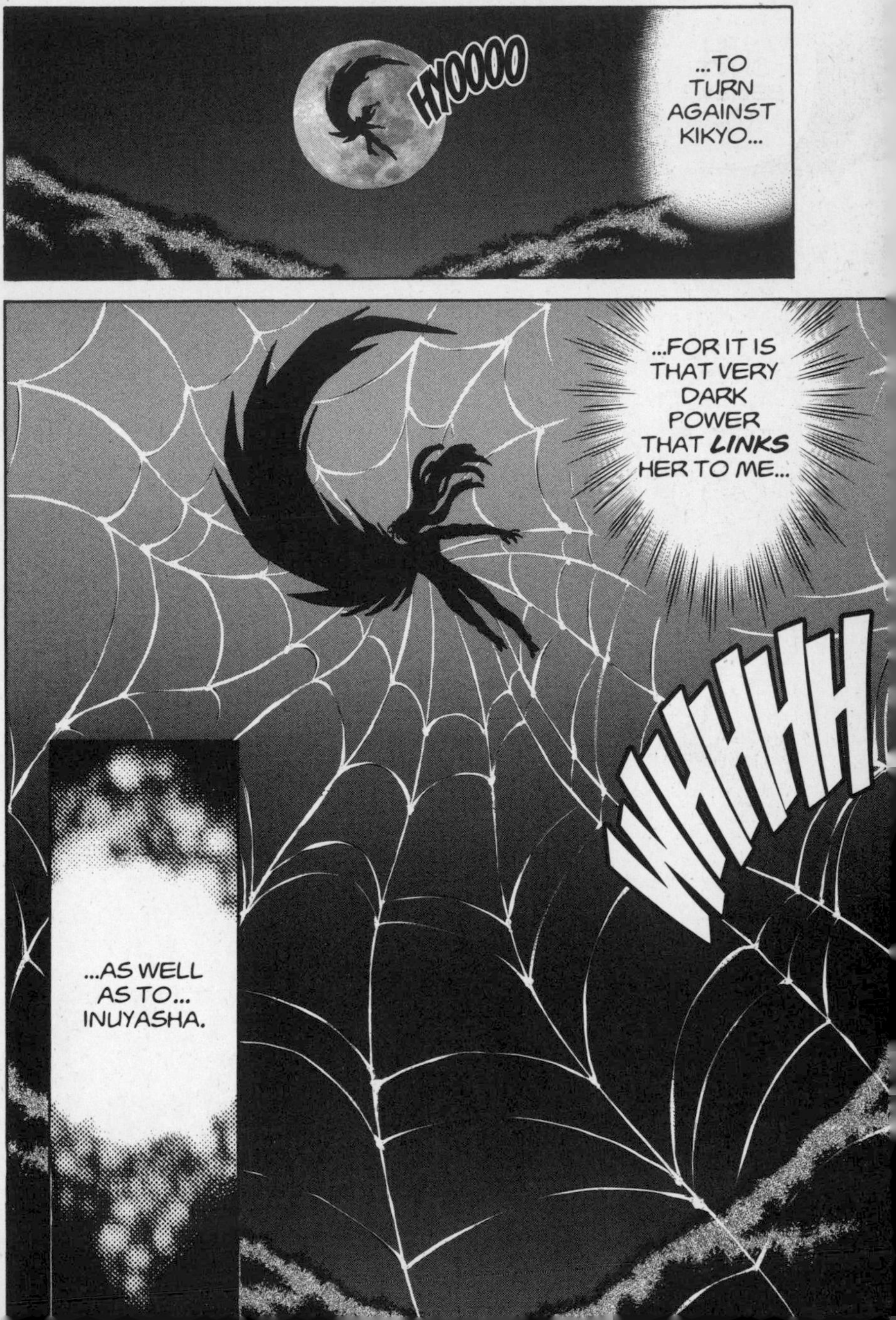
...TO TURN AGAINST KIKYO...
HYOOOO
...FOR IT IS THAT VERY DARK POWER THAT ***LINKS*** HER TO ME...
WHHHH
...AS WELL AS TO... INUYASHA.

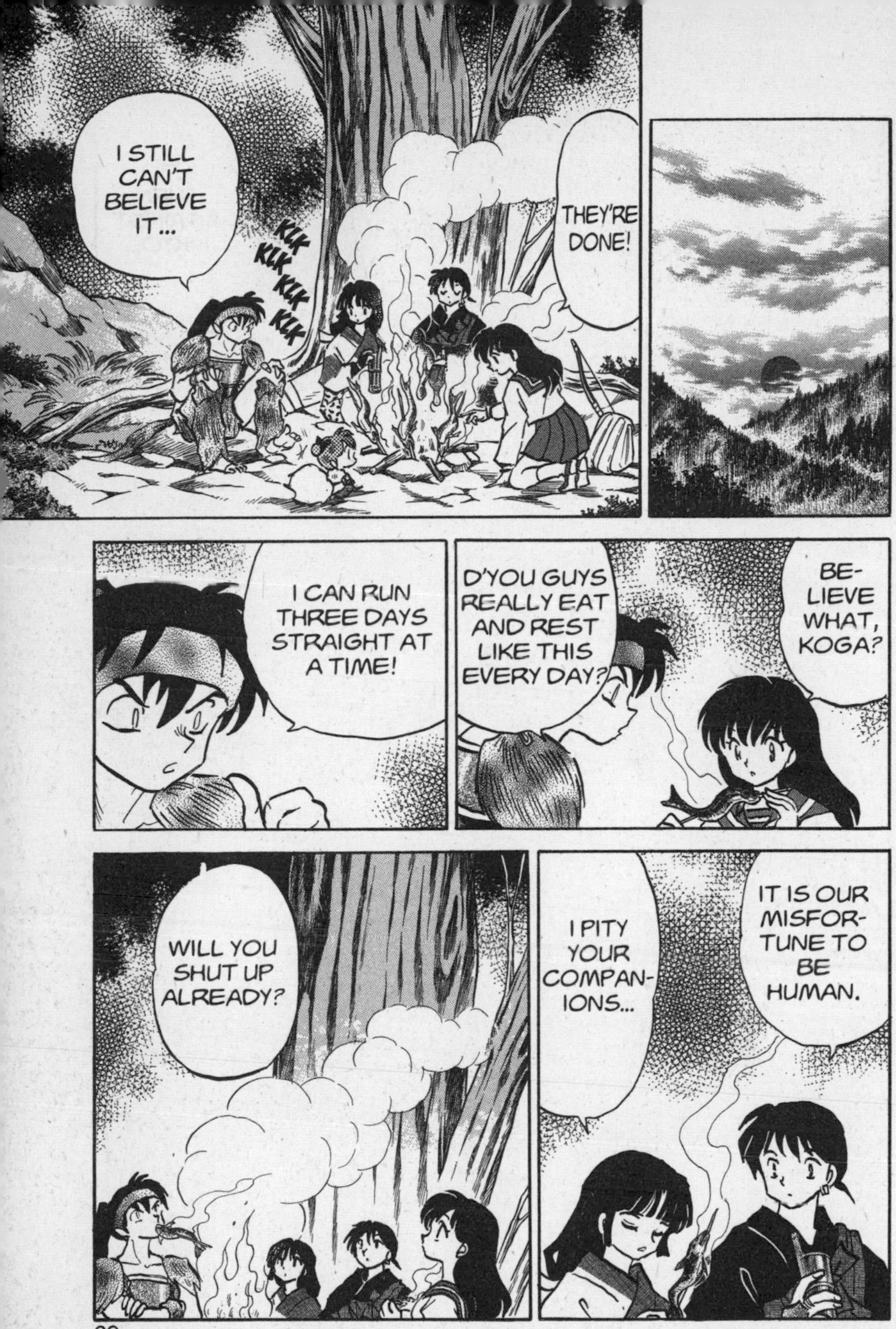
THEY'RE DONE!
I STILL CAN'T BELIEVE IT...
KLK KLK KLK KLK
BE-LIEVE WHAT, KOGA?
D'YOU GUYS REALLY EAT AND REST LIKE THIS EVERY DAY?
I CAN RUN THREE DAYS STRAIGHT AT A TIME!
IT IS OUR MISFOR-TUNE TO BE HUMAN.
I PITY YOUR COMPAN-IONS...
WILL YOU SHUT UP ALREADY?

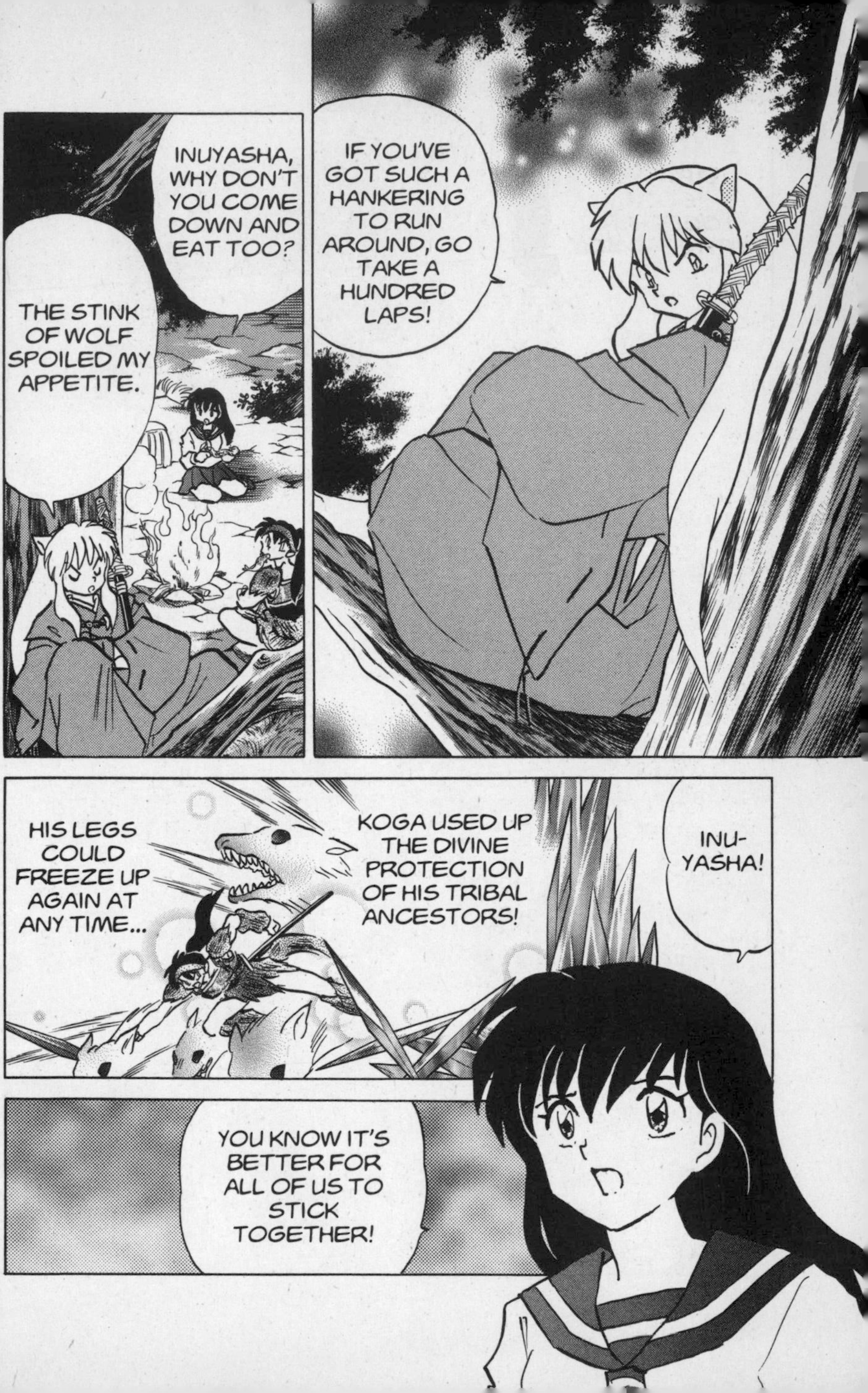
IF YOU'VE GOT SUCH A HANKERING TO RUN AROUND, GO TAKE A HUNDRED LAPS!
INUYASHA, WHY DON'T YOU COME DOWN AND EAT TOO?
THE STINK OF WOLF SPOILED MY APPETITE.
INU-YASHA!
KOGA USED UP THE DIVINE PROTECTION OF HIS TRIBAL ANCESTORS!
HIS LEGS COULD FREEZE UP AGAIN AT ANY TIME...
YOU KNOW IT'S BETTER FOR ALL OF US TO STICK TOGETHER!

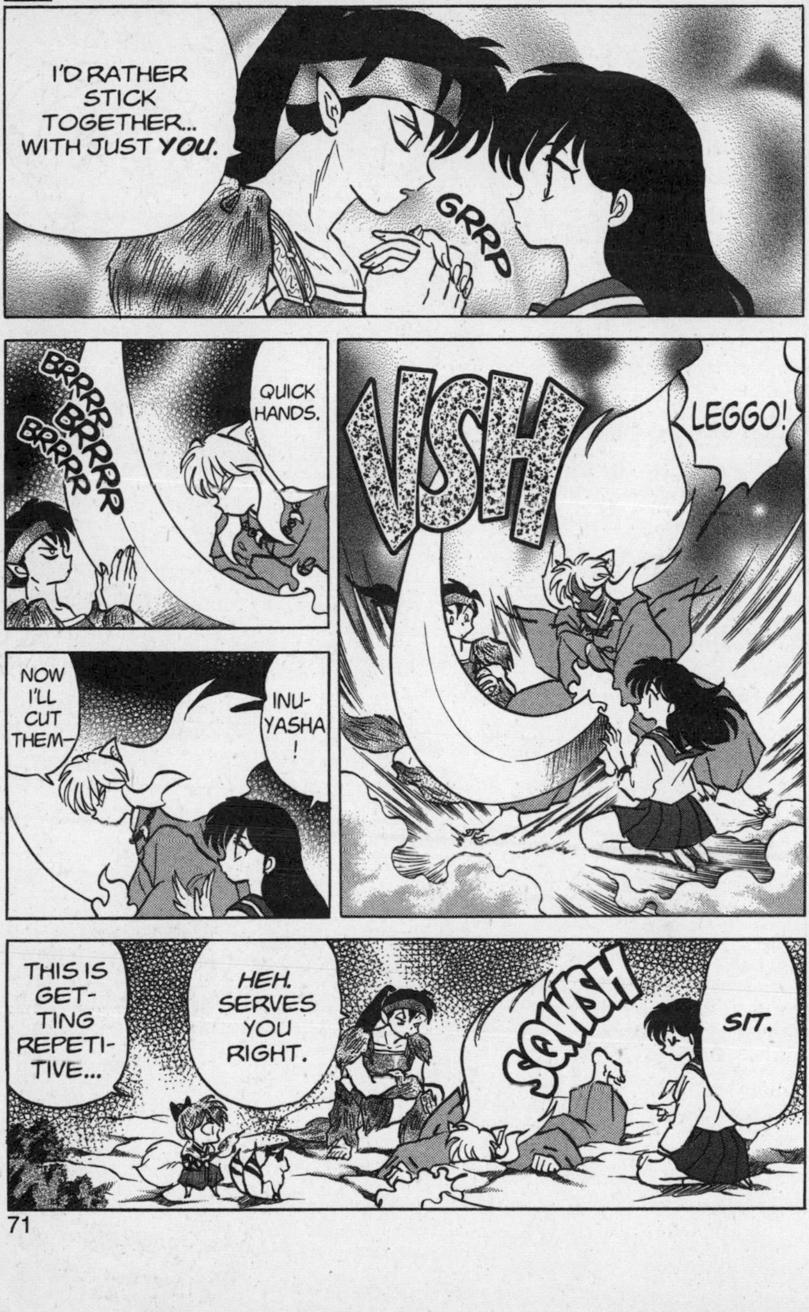
I'D RATHER STICK TOGETHER... WITH JUST YOU.
GRRP
LEGGO!
VSH
QUICK HANDS.
BRRRR BRRRRR BRRRRR
INU-YASHA!
NOW I'LL CUT THEM—
SIT.
SQWSH
HEH. SERVES YOU RIGHT.
THIS IS GETTING REPETITIVE...

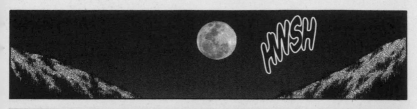

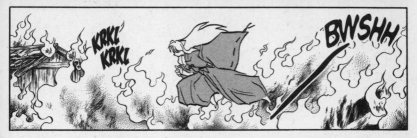

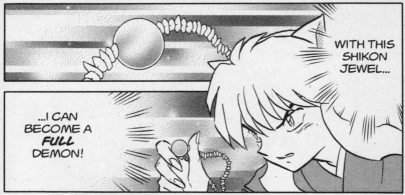

HWSH
SLWN
BWSHH
KRKL KRKL
WITH THIS SHIKON JEWEL...
...I CAN BECOME A FULL DEMON!
INUYASHA!
JWSH

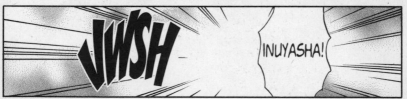

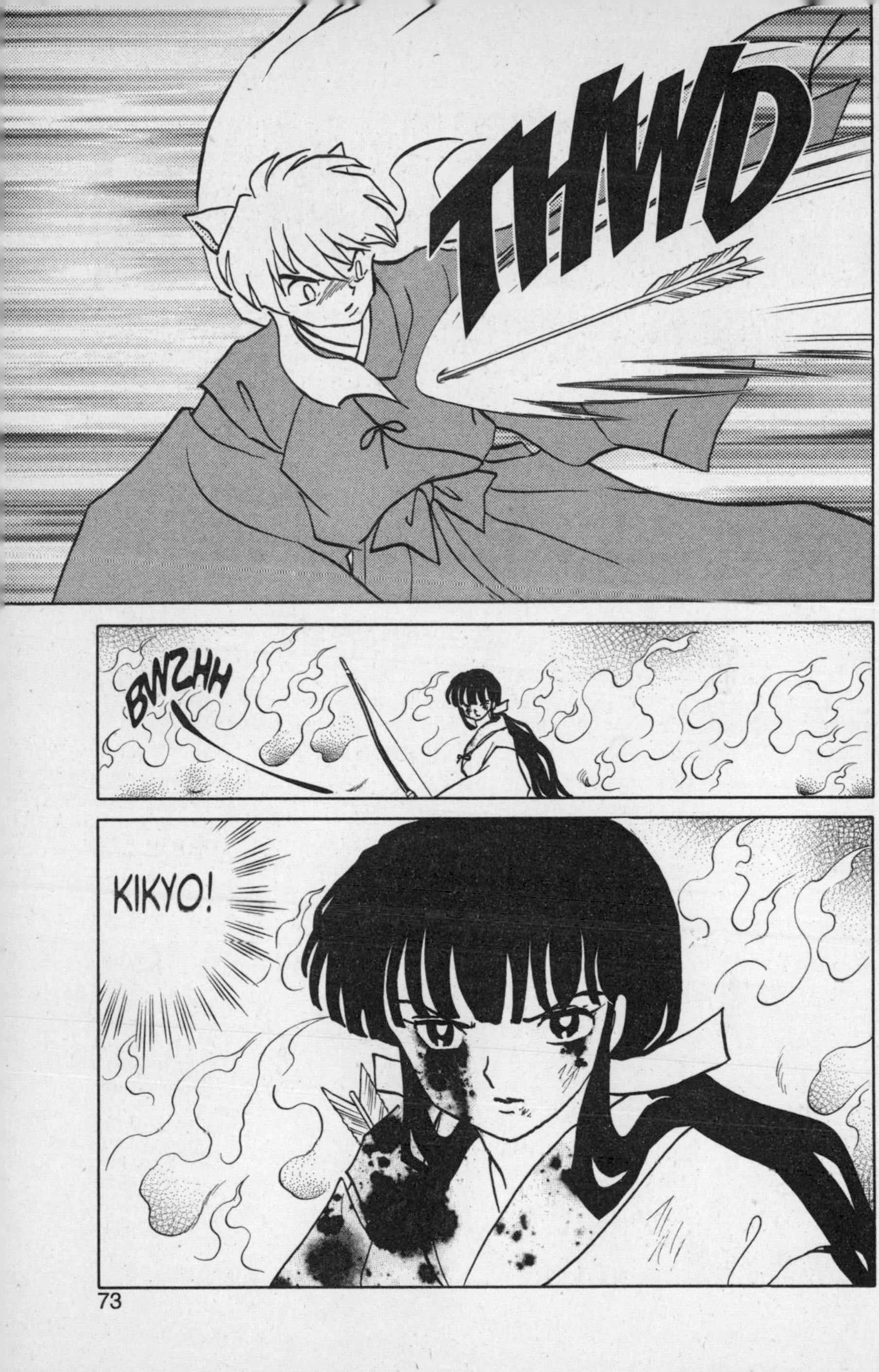
THWD
BWZHH
KIKYO!

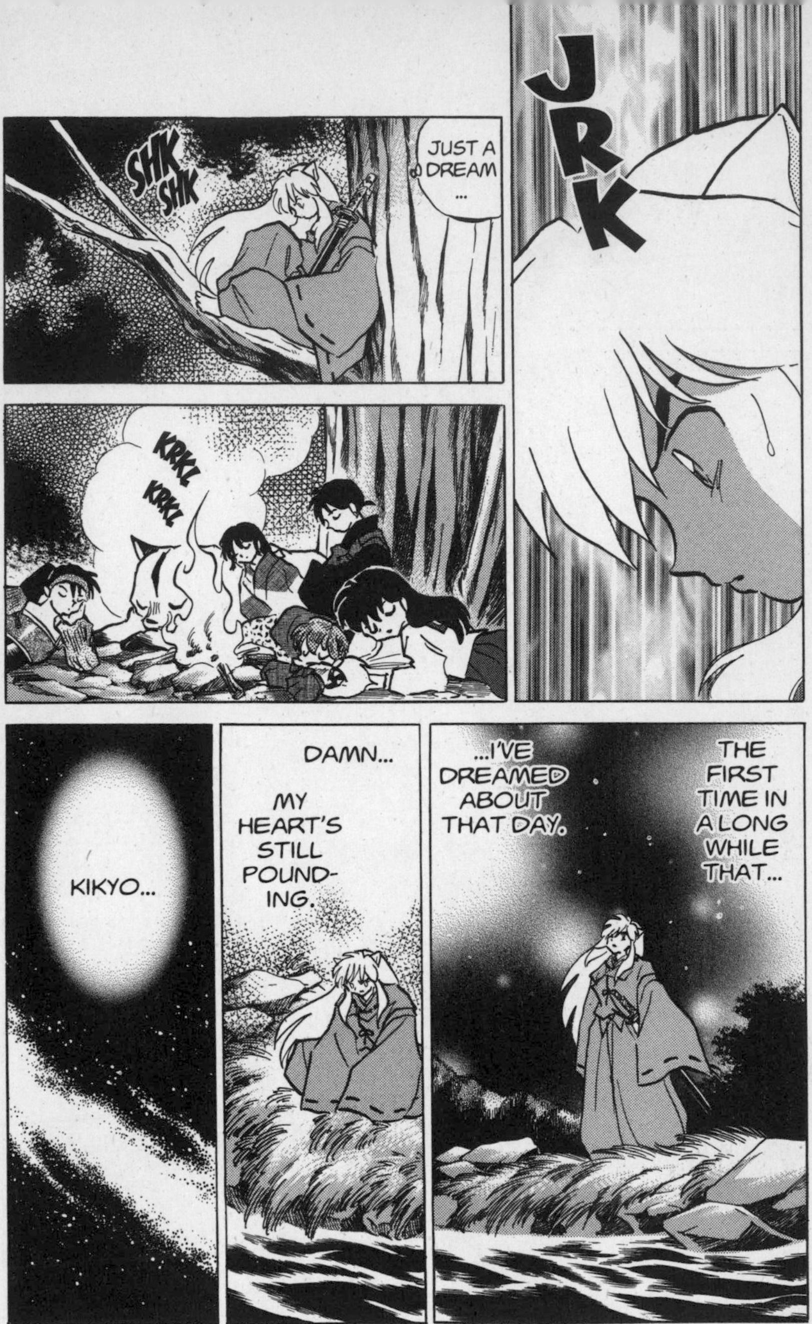
JRK
JUST A DREAM ...
SHK SHK
KRKL KRKL
THE FIRST TIME IN A LONG WHILE THAT...
...I'VE DREAMED ABOUT THAT DAY.
DAMN...
MY HEART'S STILL POUNDING.
KIKYO...

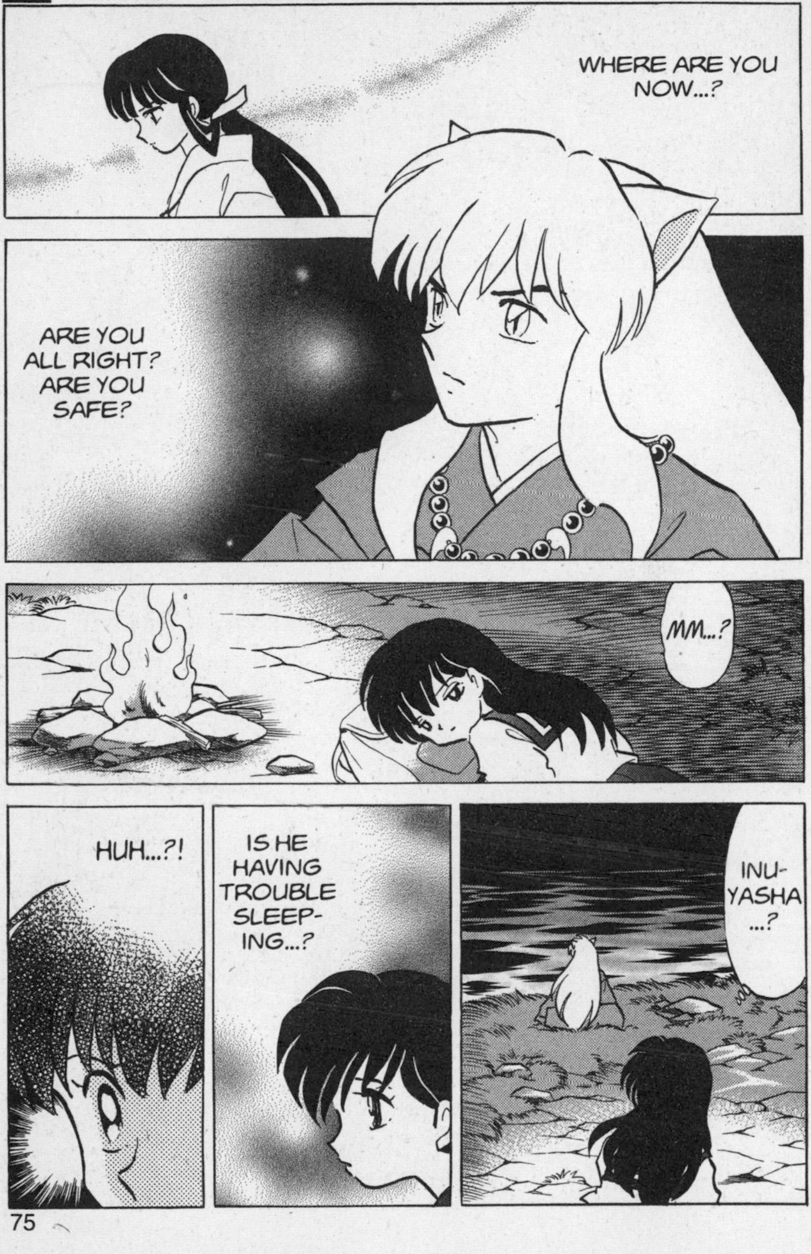
WHERE ARE YOU NOW...?
ARE YOU ALL RIGHT? ARE YOU SAFE?
MM...?
INU-YASHA ...?
IS HE HAVING TROUBLE SLEEP-ING...?
HUH...?!

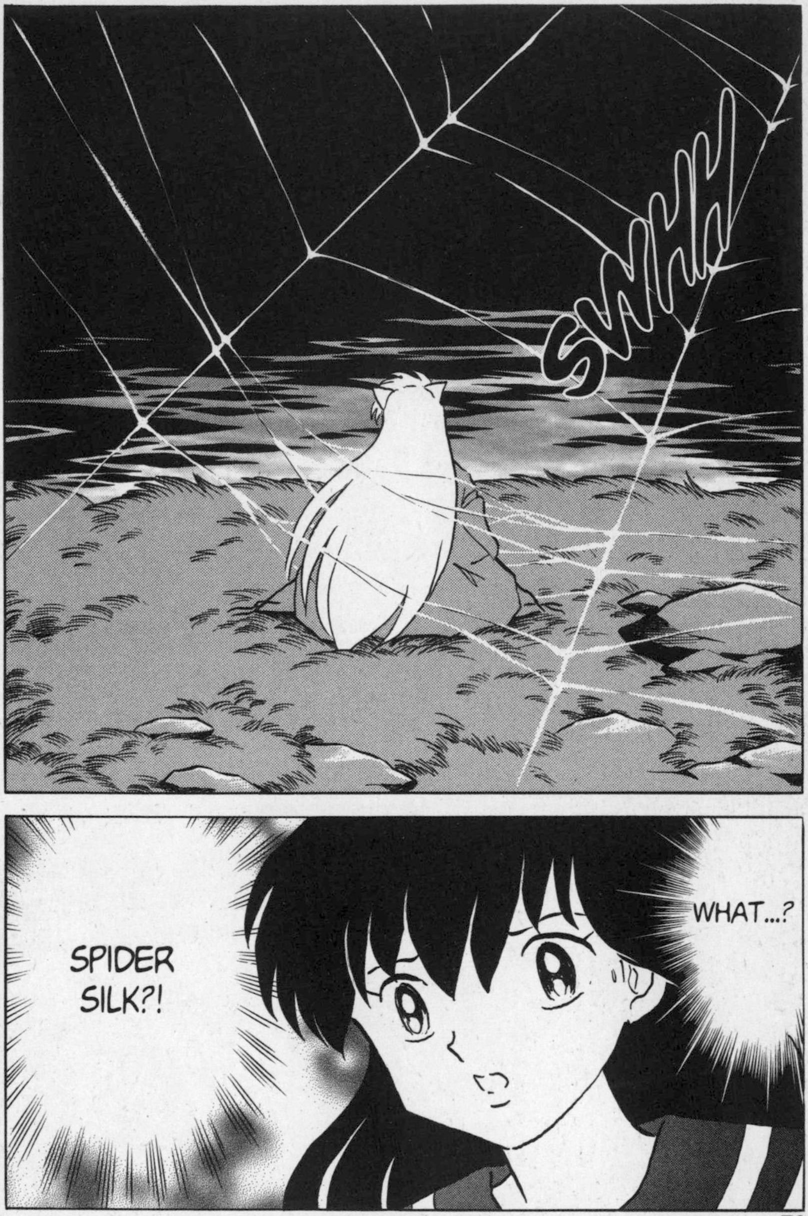
SWHH
WHAT...?
SPIDER SILK?!

SCROLL 5
THE CLINGING STRANDS

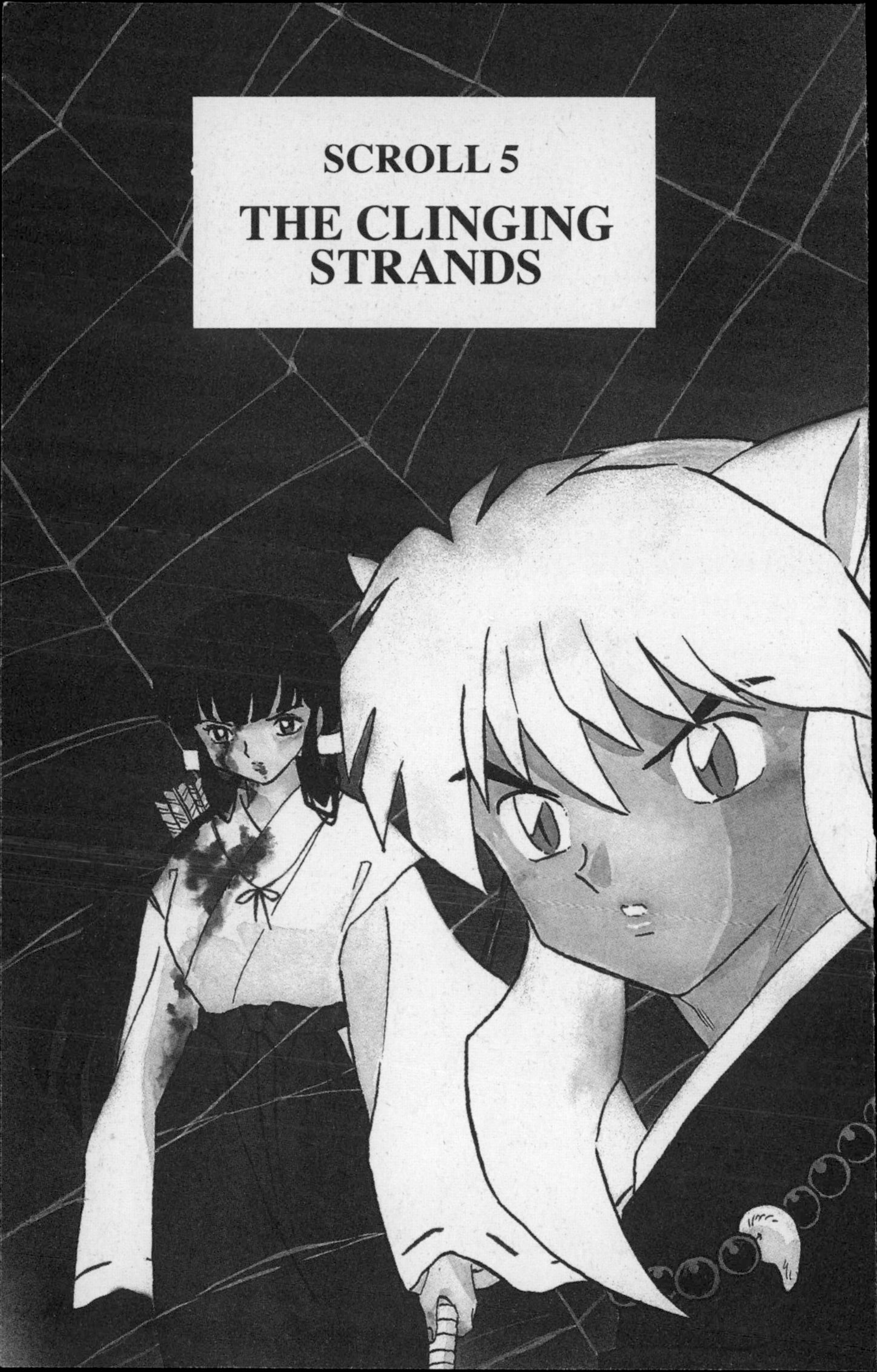

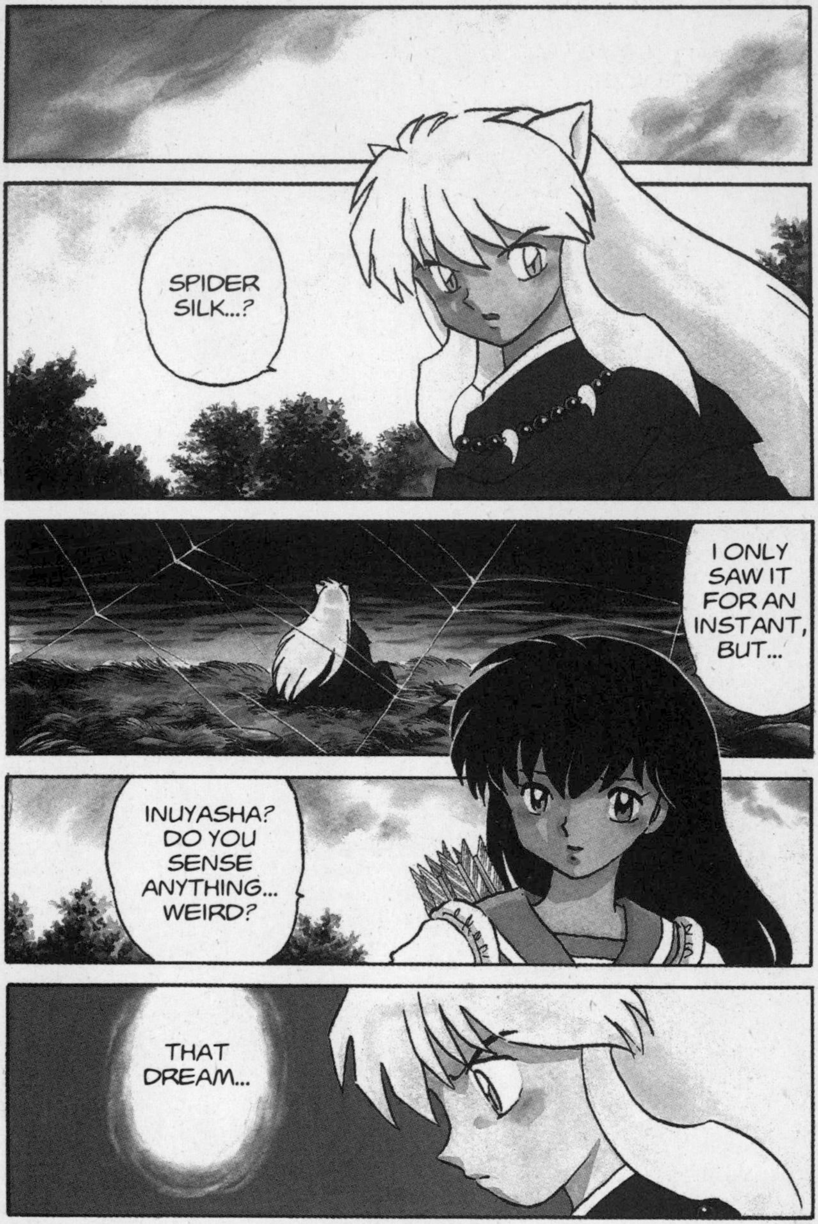
SPIDER SILK...?
I ONLY SAW IT FOR AN INSTANT, BUT...
INUYASHA? DO YOU SENSE ANYTHING... WEIRD?
THAT DREAM...

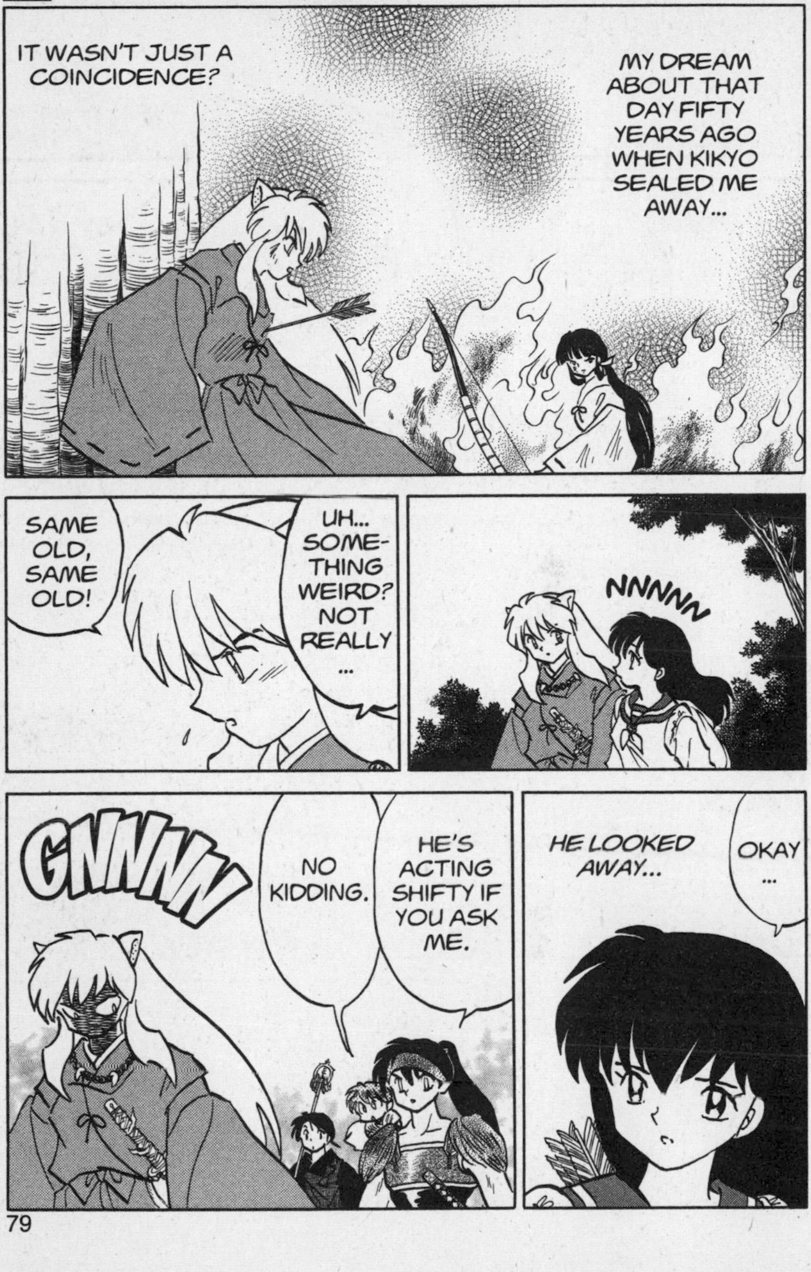
MY DREAM ABOUT THAT DAY FIFTY YEARS AGO WHEN KIKYO SEALED ME AWAY...
IT WASN'T JUST A COINCIDENCE?
NNNNN
UH... SOME-THING WEIRD? NOT REALLY ...
SAME OLD, SAME OLD!
OKAY ...
HE LOOKED AWAY...
HE'S ACTING SHIFTY IF YOU ASK ME.
NO KIDDING.
GNNNNN

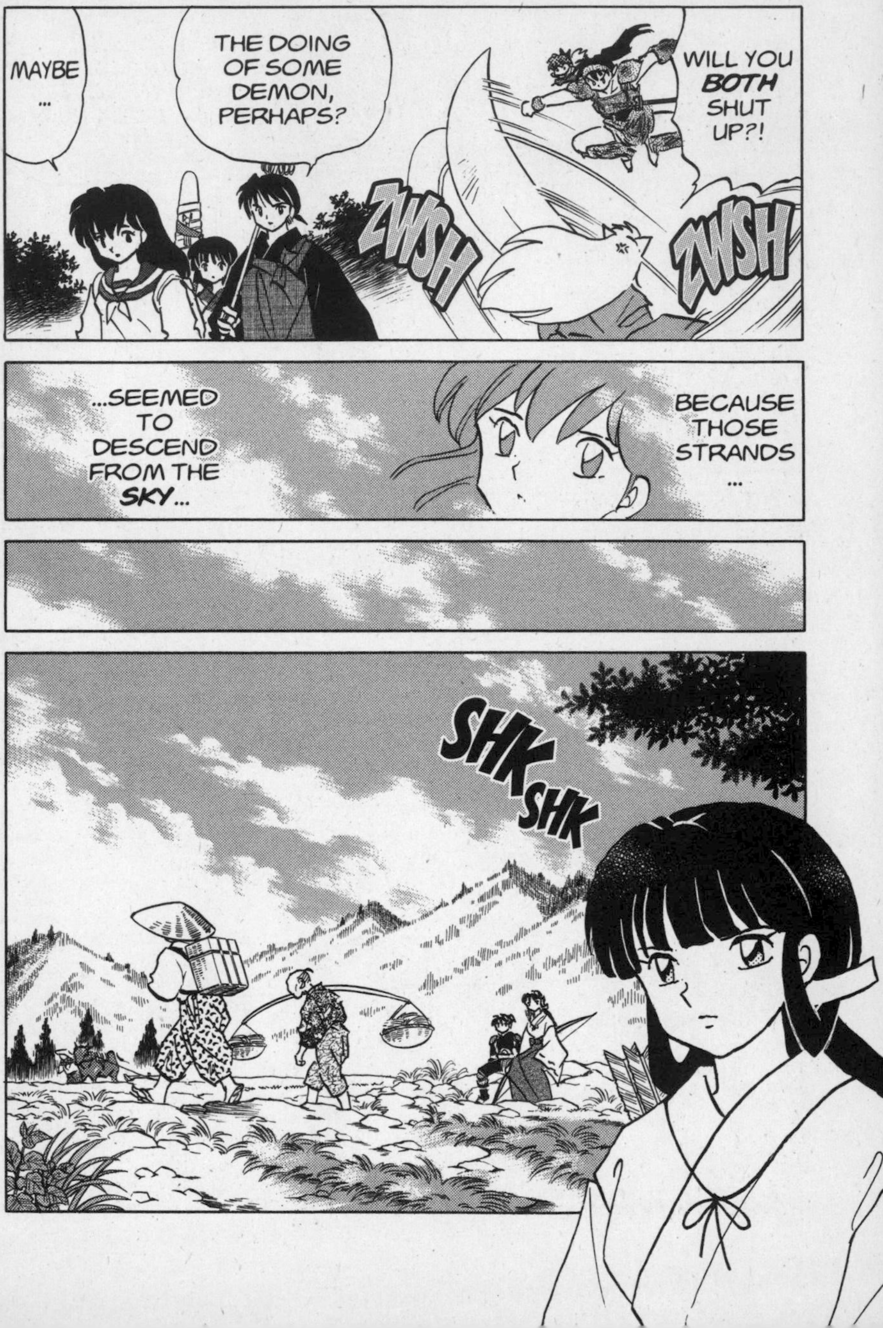
WILL YOU BOTH SHUT UP?!
ZWSH
ZWSH
THE DOING OF SOME DEMON, PERHAPS?
MAYBE ...
BECAUSE THOSE STRANDS ...
...SEEMED TO DESCEND FROM THE SKY...
SHK SHK

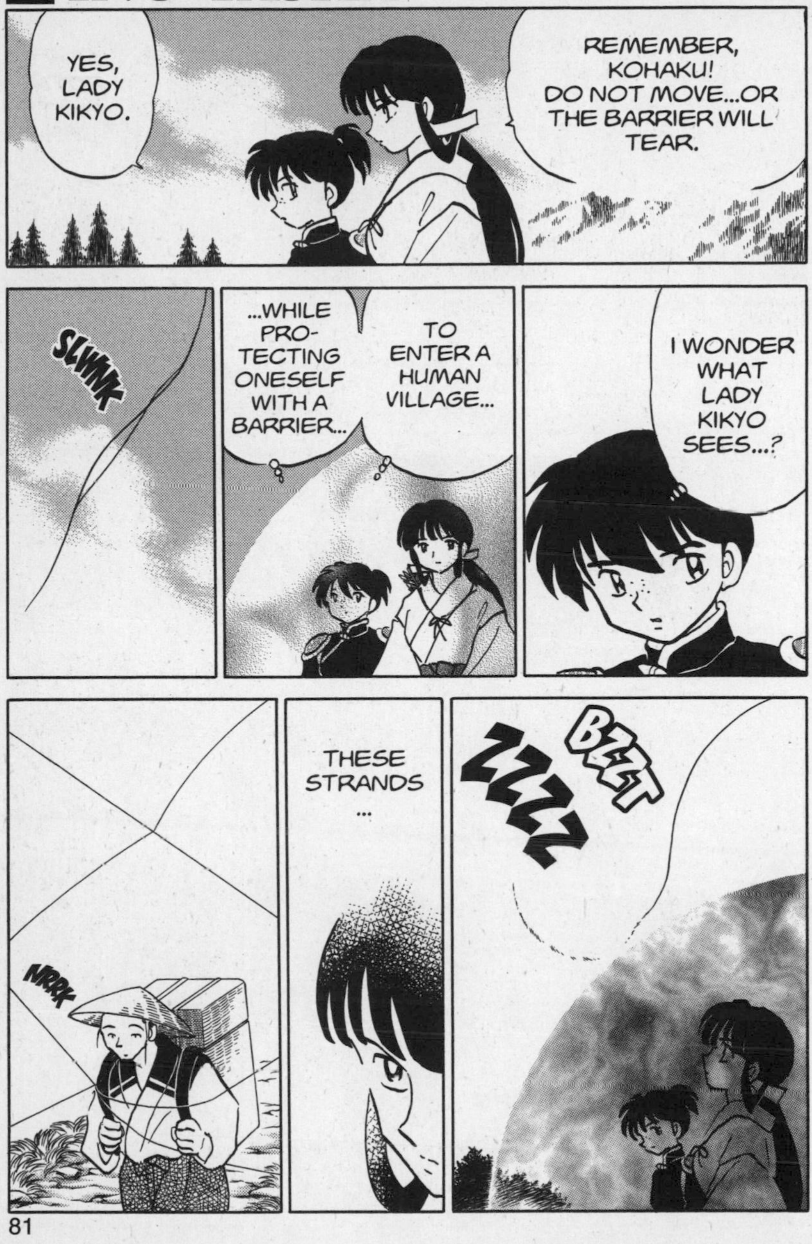
REMEMBER, KOHAKU! DO NOT MOVE...OR THE BARRIER WILL TEAR.
YES, LADY KIKYO.
I WONDER WHAT LADY KIKYO SEES...?
TO ENTER A HUMAN VILLAGE...
...WHILE PRO-TECTING ONESELF WITH A BARRIER...
SLWNK
BZZT
ZZZZ
THESE STRANDS ...
NRRK

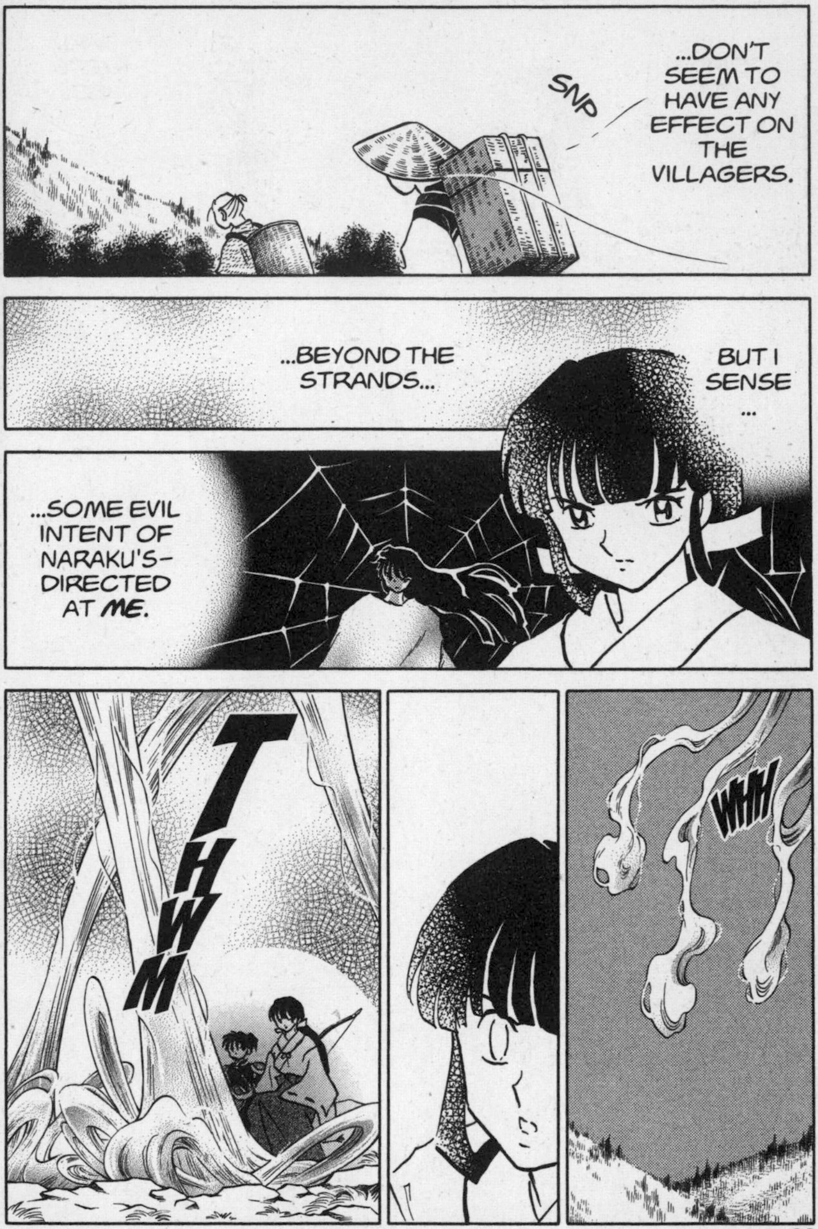
...DON'T SEEM TO HAVE ANY EFFECT ON THE VILLAGERS.
SNP
BUT I SENSE ...
...BEYOND THE STRANDS...
...SOME EVIL INTENT OF NARAKU'S- DIRECTED AT *ME*.
WHH
THWM

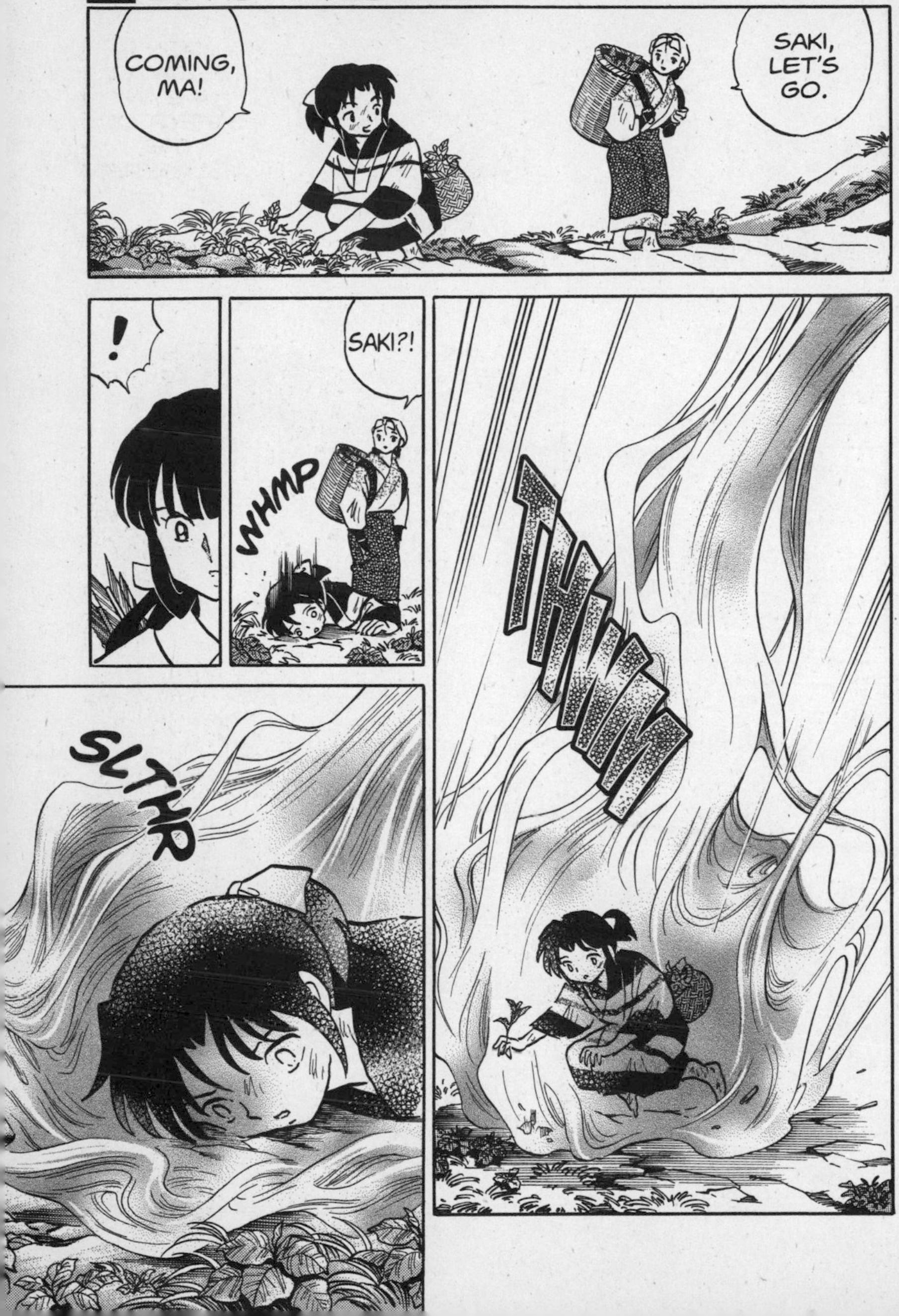
SAKI, LET'S GO.
COMING, MA!
THWM
SAKI?!
WHMP
!
SLTHR

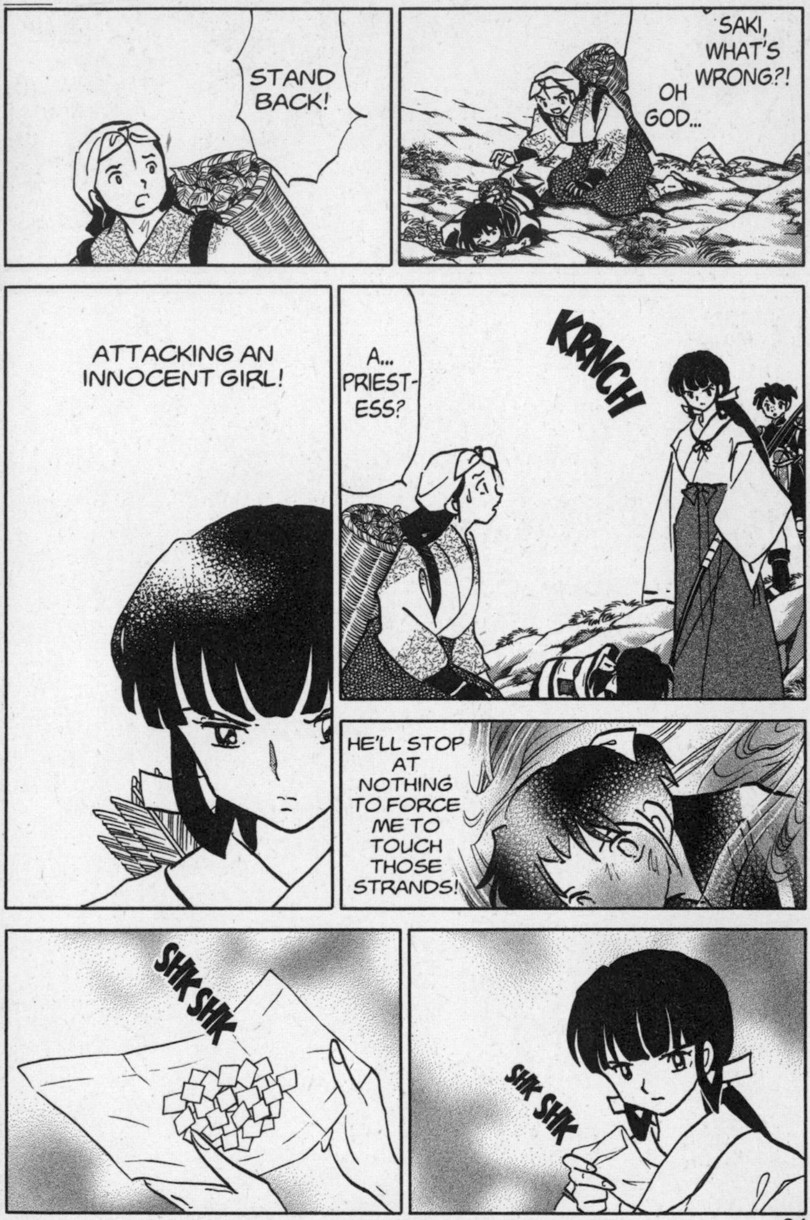
SAKI, WHAT'S WRONG?!
OH GOD...
STAND BACK!
KRNCH
A... PRIEST-ESS?
HE'LL STOP AT NOTHING TO FORCE ME TO TOUCH THOSE STRANDS!
ATTACKING AN INNOCENT GIRL!
SHK SHK
SHK SHK

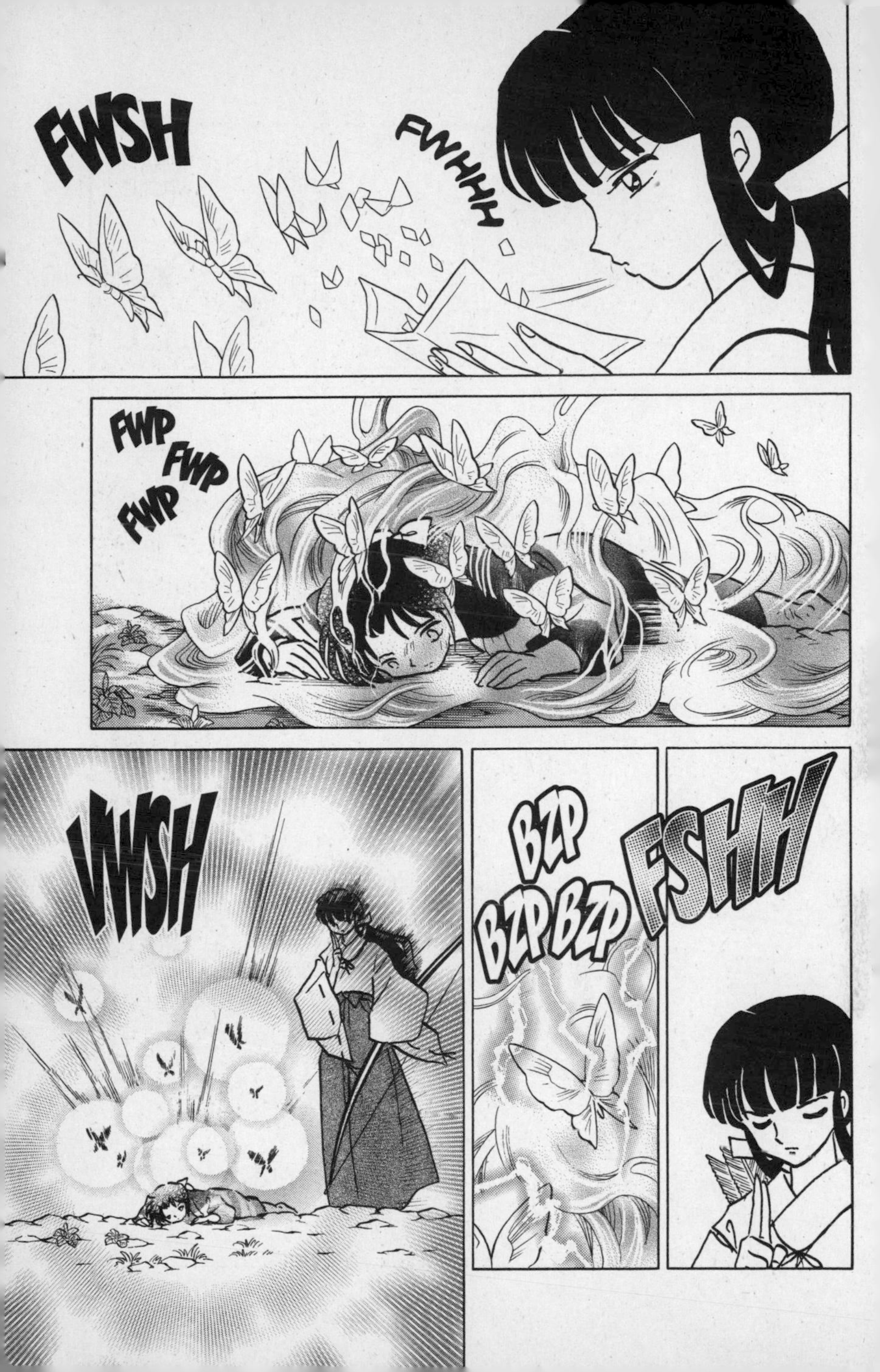
FWHHH
FWSH
FWP FWP FWP
FSHH
BZP BZP BZP
VWSH

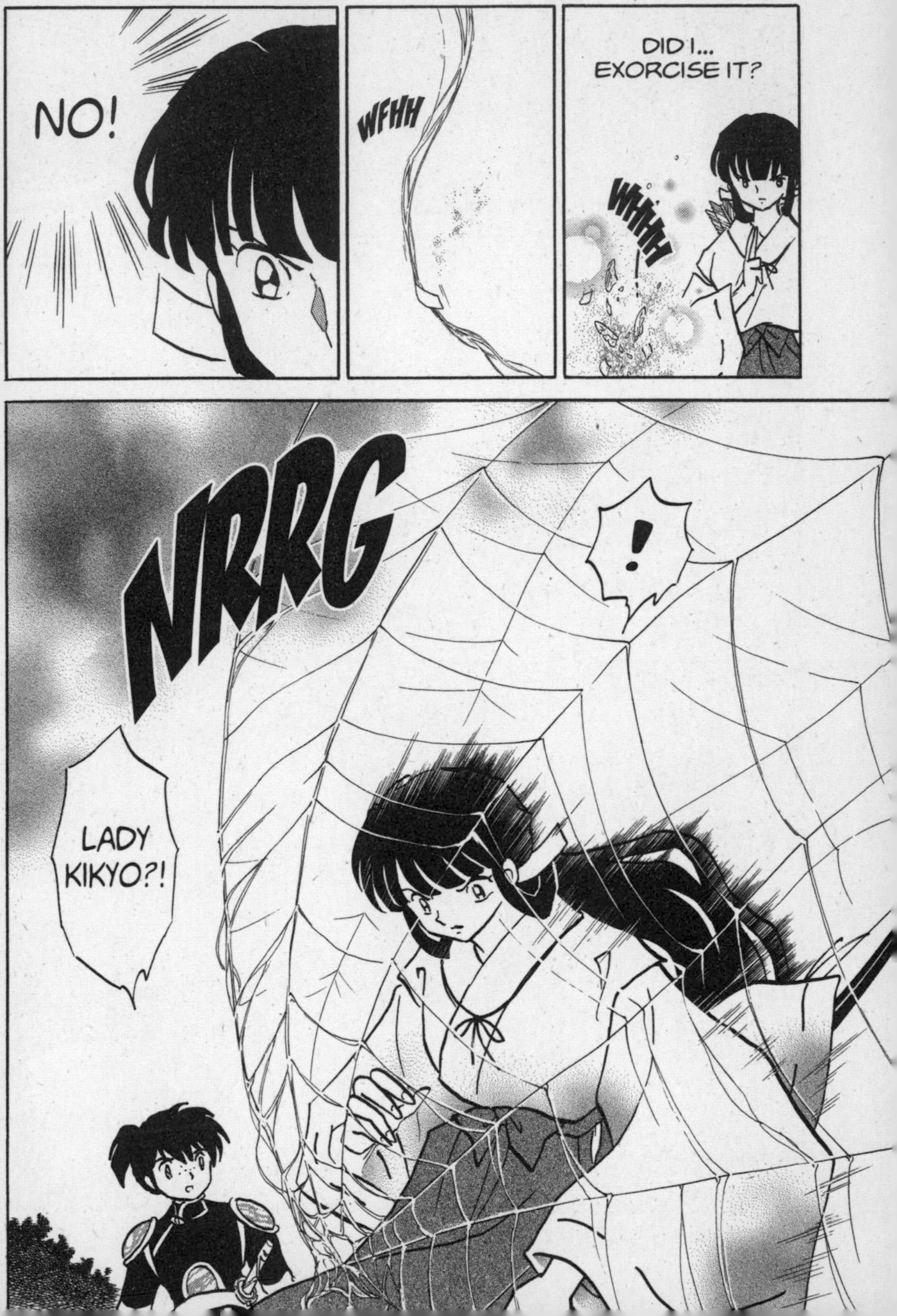
DID I...
EXORCISE IT?
WHHH
WFHH
NO!
NRRG
!
LADY KIKYO?!

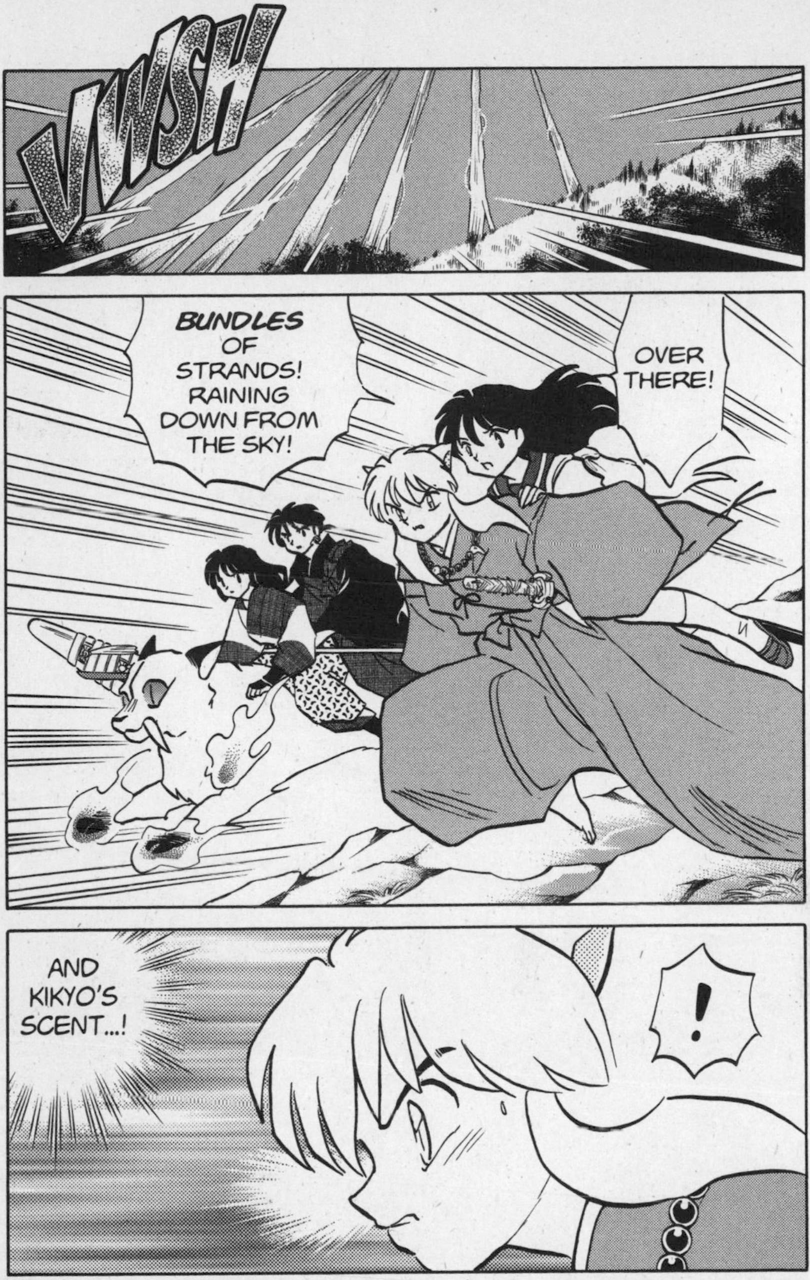
VWSH
OVER THERE!
BUNDLES OF STRANDS! RAINING DOWN FROM THE SKY!
!
AND KIKYO'S SCENT...!

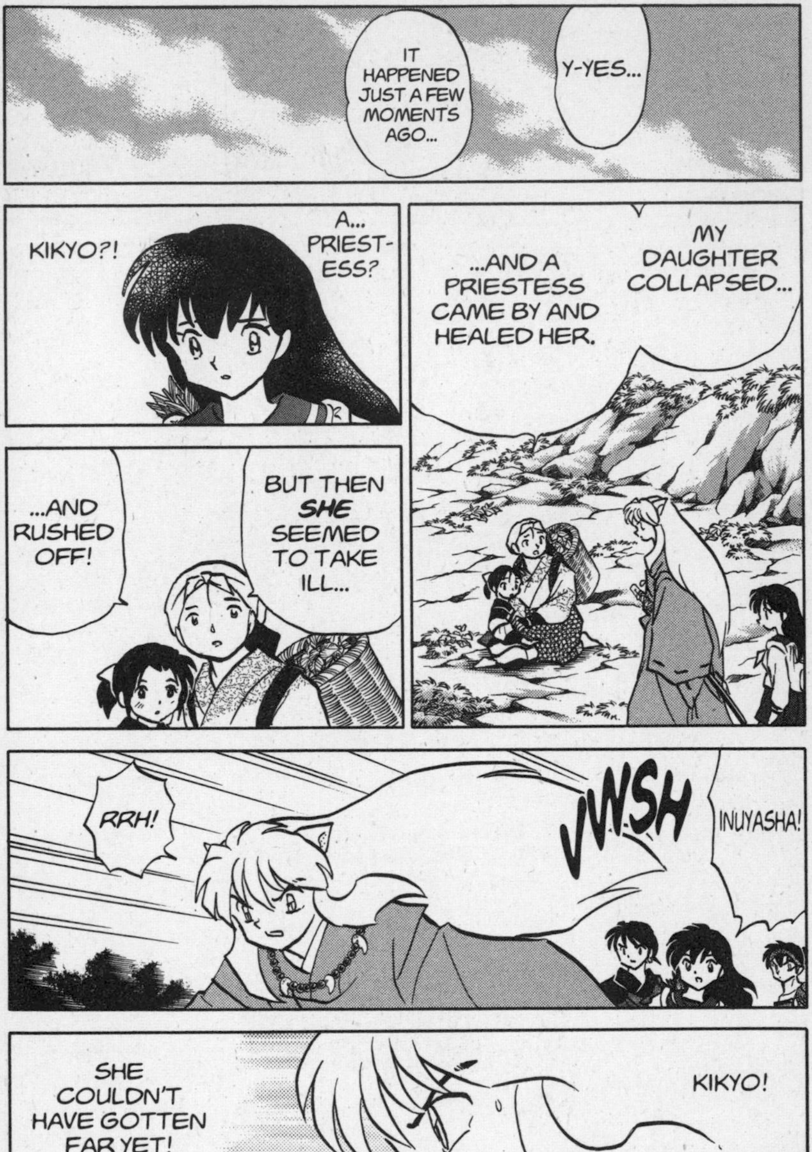
Y-YES...
IT HAPPENED JUST A FEW MOMENTS AGO...
MY DAUGHTER COLLAPSED...
...AND A PRIESTESS CAME BY AND HEALED HER.
A... PRIEST-ESS?
KIKYO?!
BUT THEN SHE SEEMED TO TAKE ILL...
...AND RUSHED OFF!
INUYASHA!
VWSH
RRH!
KIKYO!
SHE COULDN'T HAVE GOTTEN FAR YET!

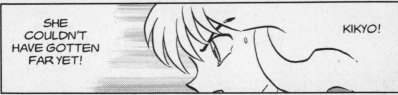

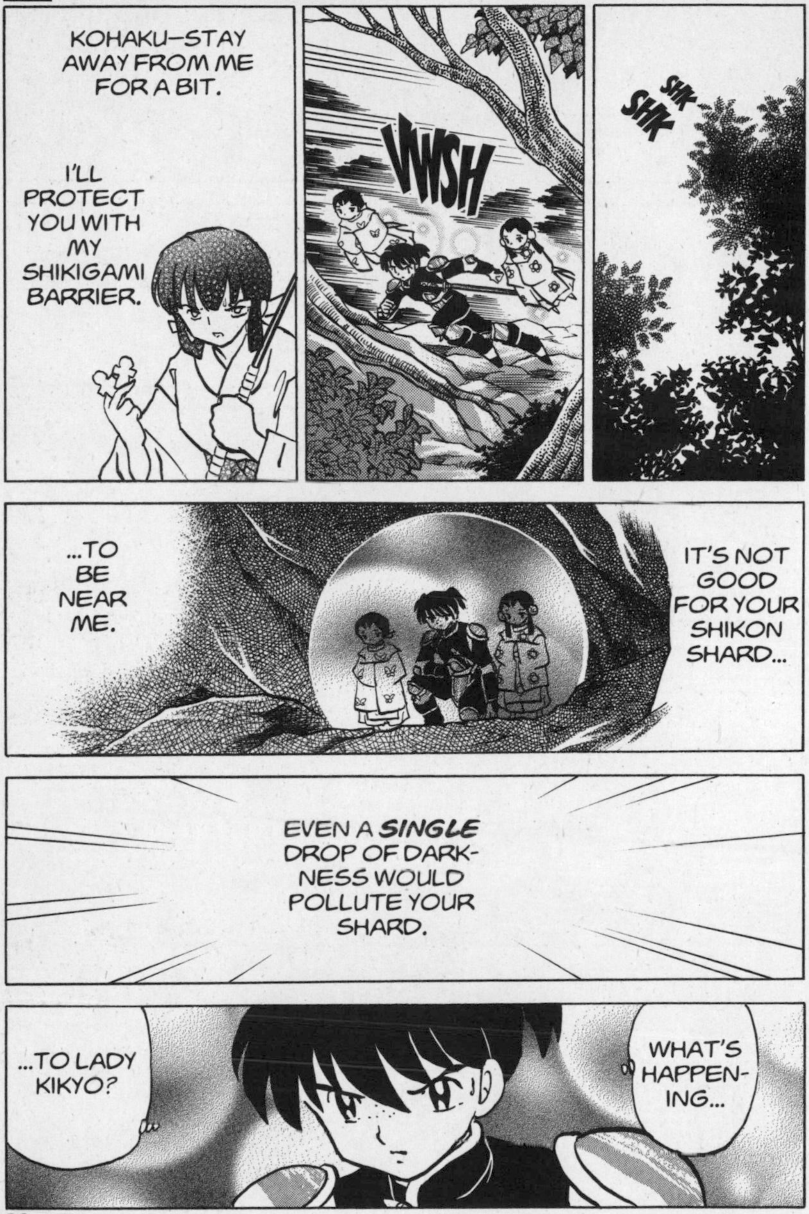
SHK SHK
VWSH
KOHAKU—STAY AWAY FROM ME FOR A BIT.
I'LL PROTECT YOU WITH MY SHIKIGAMI BARRIER.
IT'S NOT GOOD FOR YOUR SHIKON SHARD...
...TO BE NEAR ME.
EVEN A SINGLE DROP OF DARKNESS WOULD POLLUTE YOUR SHARD.
WHAT'S HAPPENING...
...TO LADY KIKYO?

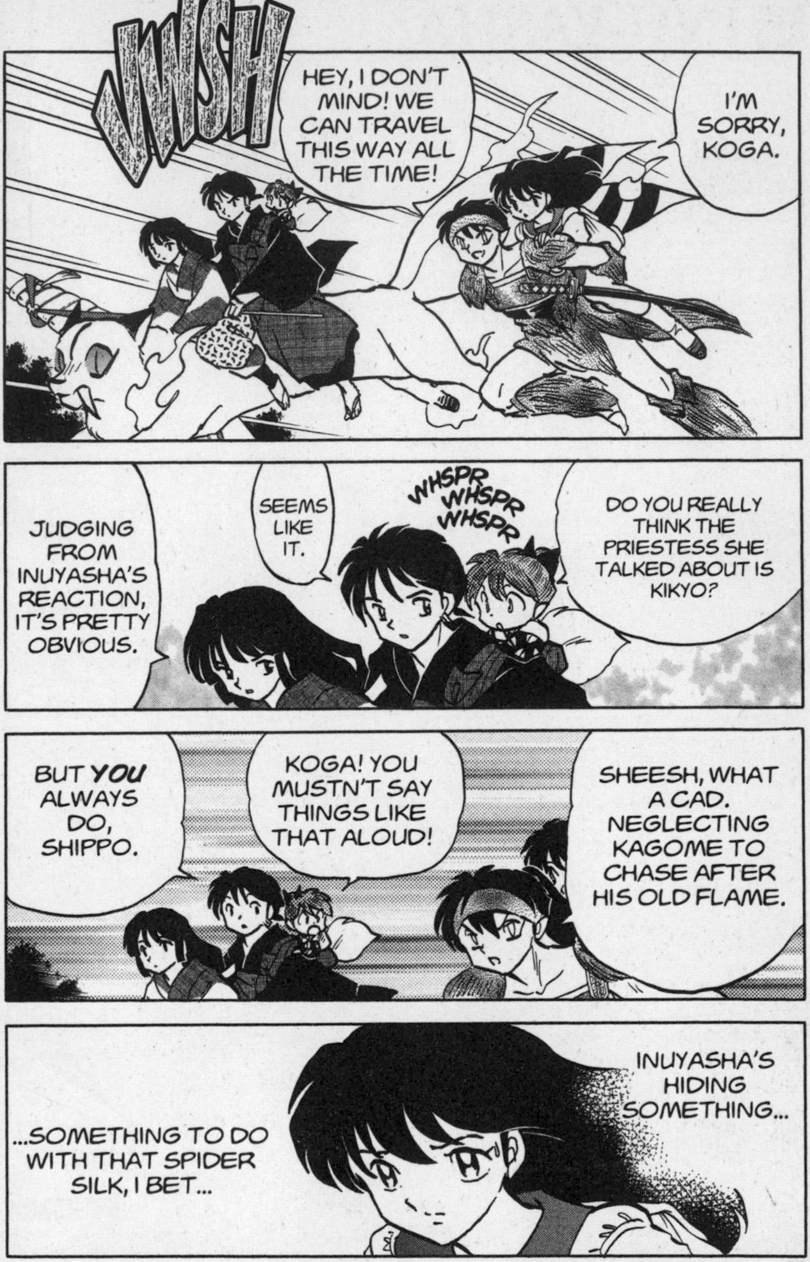
I'M SORRY, KOGA.
HEY, I DON'T MIND! WE CAN TRAVEL THIS WAY ALL THE TIME!
JWSH
DO YOU REALLY THINK THE PRIESTESS SHE TALKED ABOUT IS KIKYO?
WHSPR WHSPR WHSPR
SEEMS LIKE IT.
JUDGING FROM INUYASHA'S REACTION, IT'S PRETTY OBVIOUS.
SHEESH, WHAT A CAD. NEGLECTING KAGOME TO CHASE AFTER HIS OLD FLAME.
KOGA! YOU MUSTN'T SAY THINGS LIKE THAT ALOUD!
BUT ***YOU*** ALWAYS DO, SHIPPO.
INUYASHA'S HIDING SOMETHING...
...SOMETHING TO DO WITH THAT SPIDER SILK, I BET...

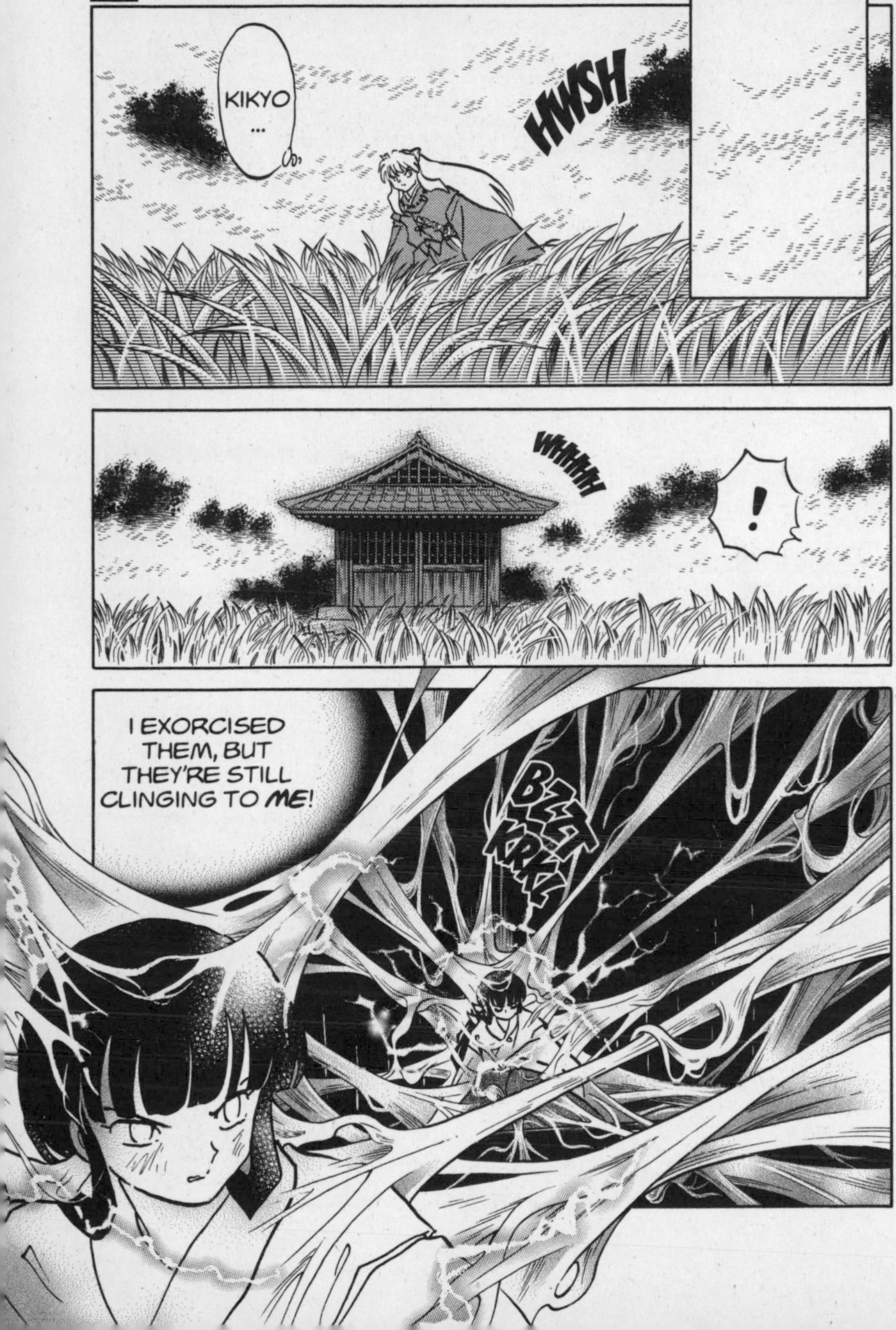
HWSH
KIKYO ...
WHHHHH
!
I EXORCISED THEM, BUT THEY'RE STILL CLINGING TO *ME*!
BZZT KRKL

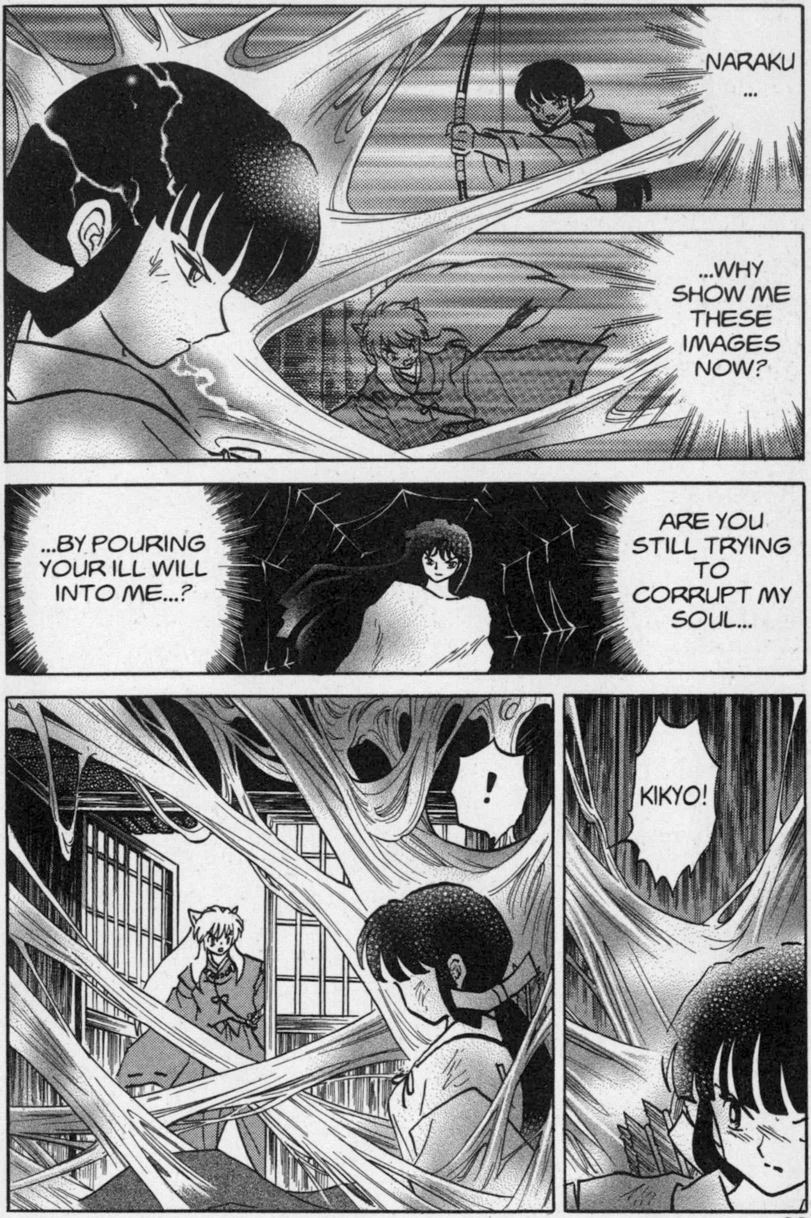
NARAKU ...
...WHY SHOW ME THESE IMAGES NOW?
ARE YOU STILL TRYING TO CORRUPT MY SOUL...
...BY POURING YOUR ILL WILL INTO ME...?
KIKYO!
!

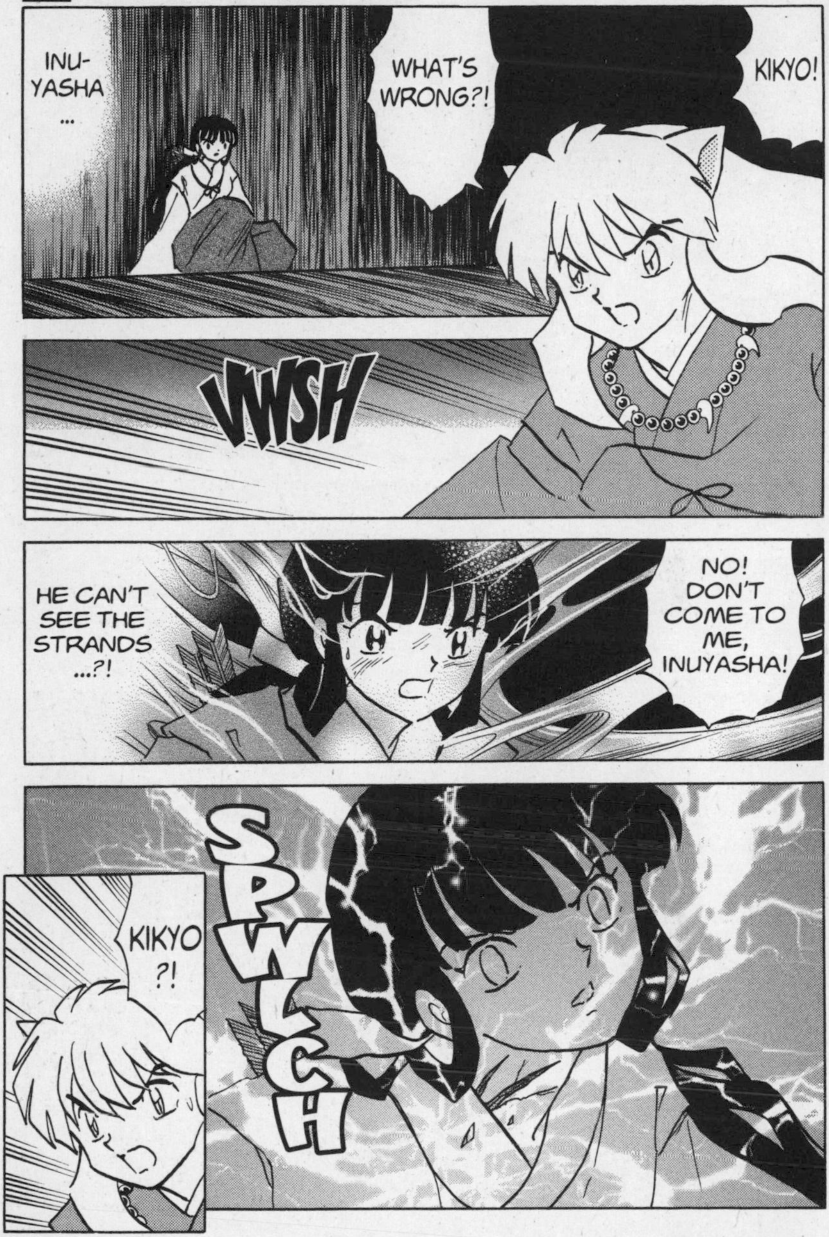
KIKYO!
WHAT'S WRONG?!
INU-YASHA ...
VWISH
NO! DON'T COME TO ME, INUYASHA!
HE CAN'T SEE THE STRANDS ...?!
SPWLCH
KIKYO ?!

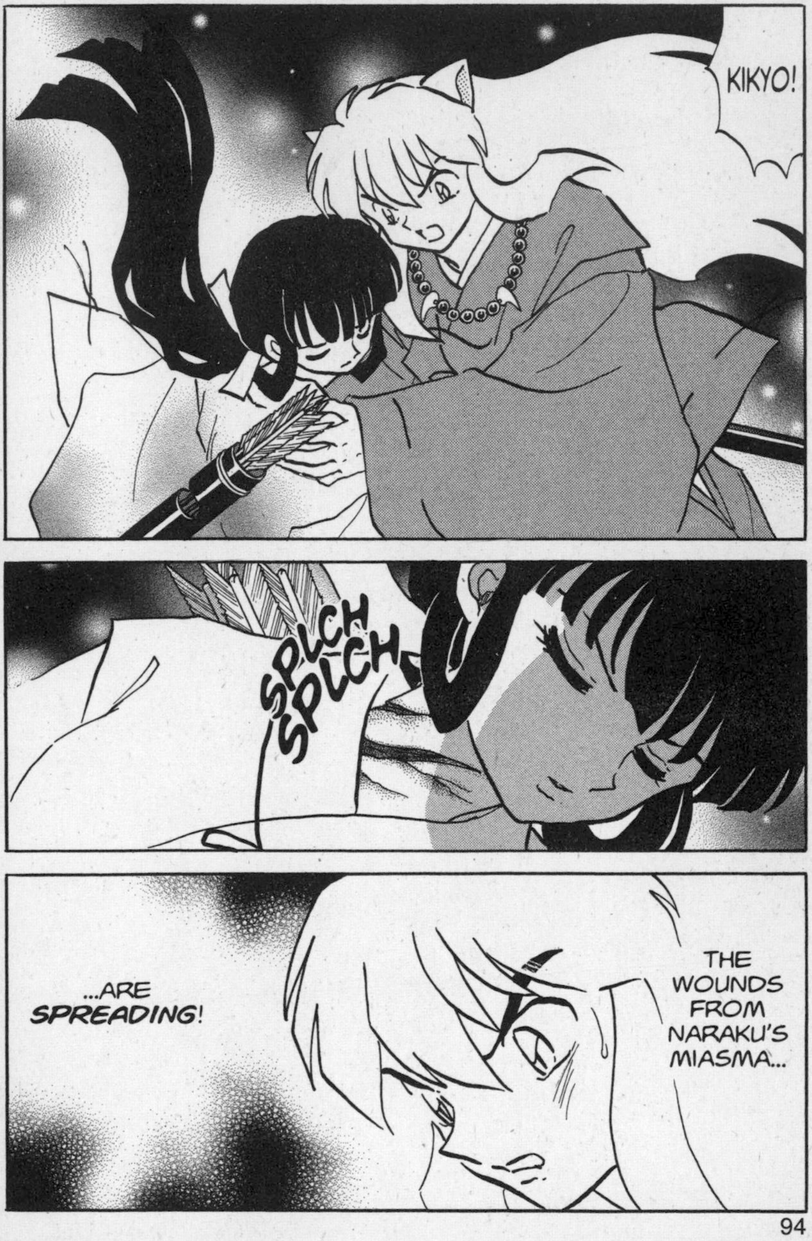
KIKYO!
SPLCH SPLCH
THE WOUNDS FROM NARAKU'S MIASMA...
...ARE SPREADING!

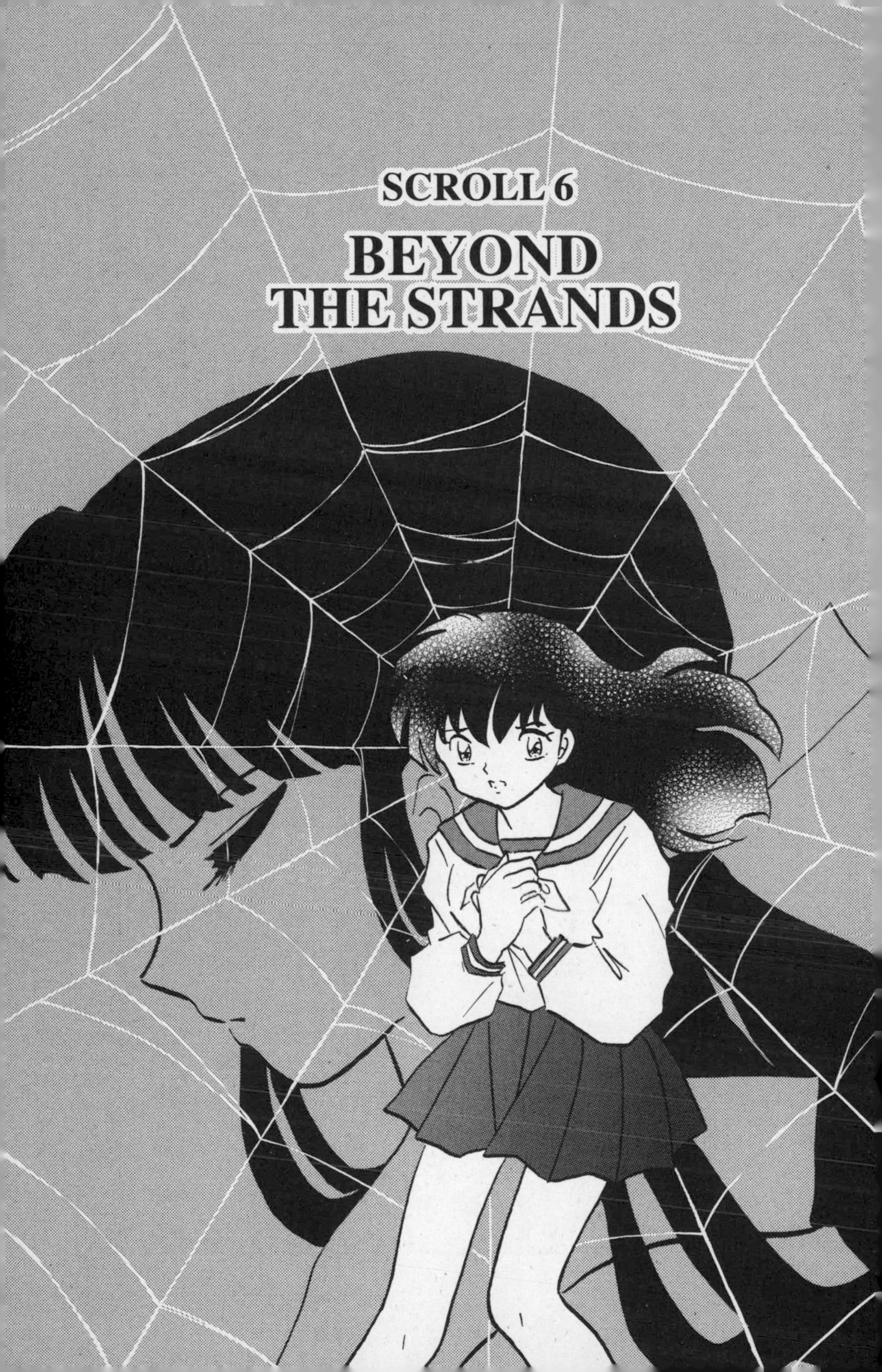
SCROLL 6
BEYOND THE STRANDS

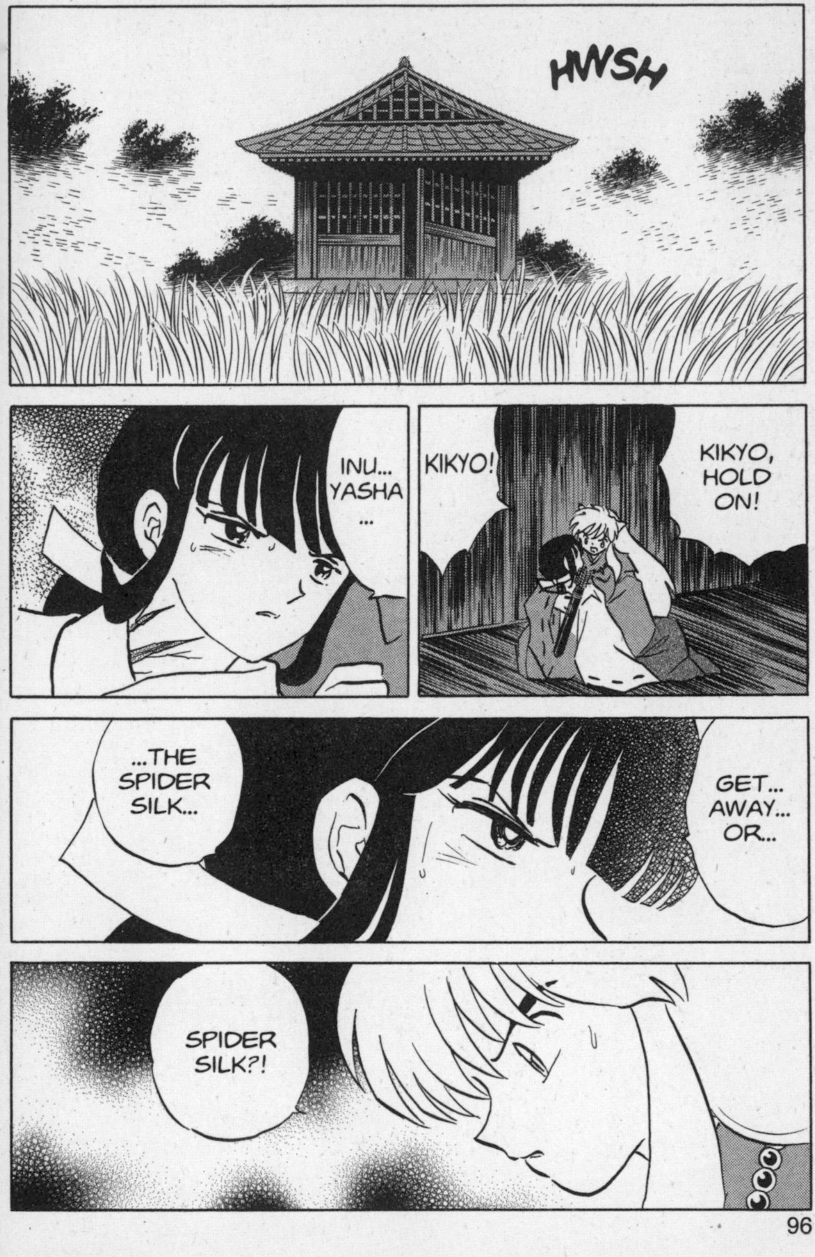
HWSH
KIKYO, HOLD ON!
KIKYO!
INU... YASHA ...
GET... AWAY... OR...
...THE SPIDER SILK...
SPIDER SILK?!

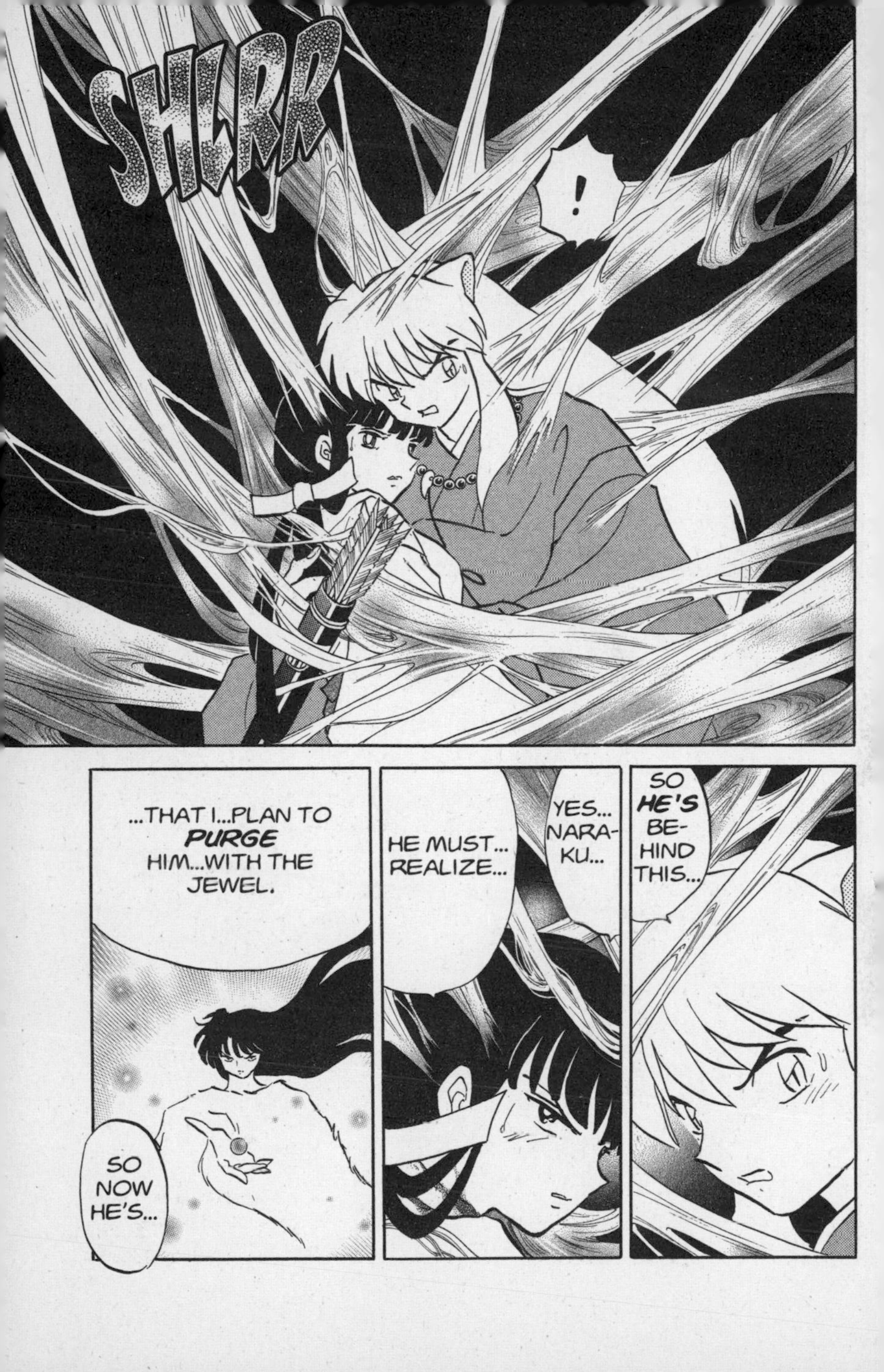
SHLRR
!
SO HE'S BE-HIND THIS...
YES... NARA-KU...
HE MUST... REALIZE...
...THAT I...PLAN TO PURGE HIM...WITH THE JEWEL.
SO NOW HE'S...

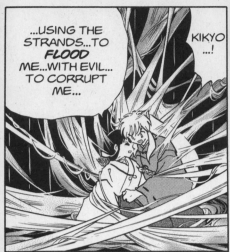

SPLCH
KIKYO ...!
...USING THE STRANDS...TO FLOOD ME...WITH EVIL... TO CORRUPT ME...
SAVE YOUR BREATH!
I'LL GET YOU OUT OF HERE!
ZWSH

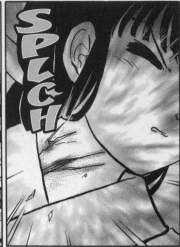

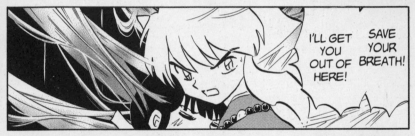

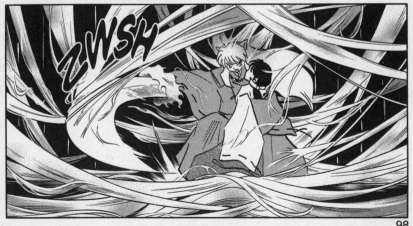

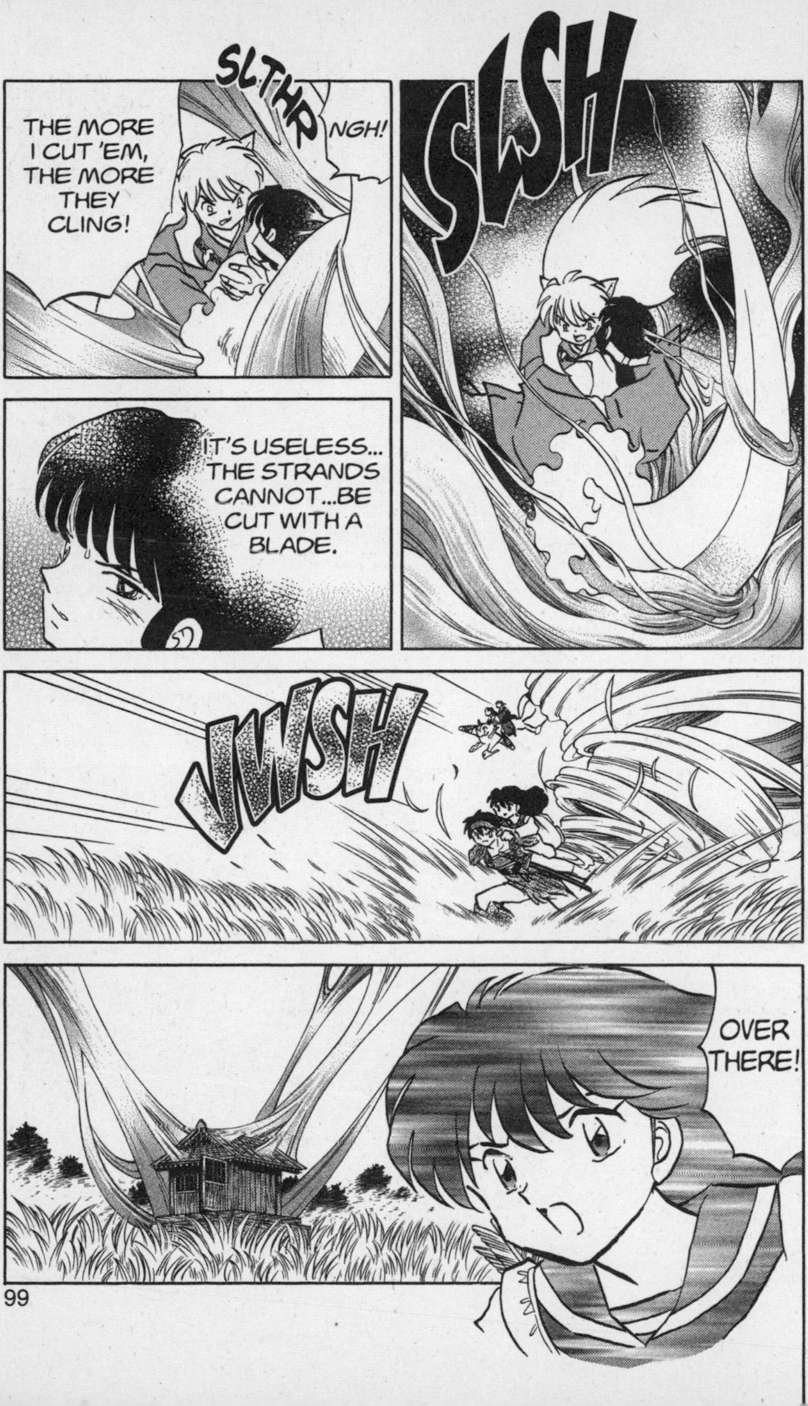
SLSH
SLTHR
NGH!
THE MORE I CUT 'EM, THE MORE THEY CLING!
IT'S USELESS... THE STRANDS CANNOT...BE CUT WITH A BLADE.
JWSH
OVER THERE!

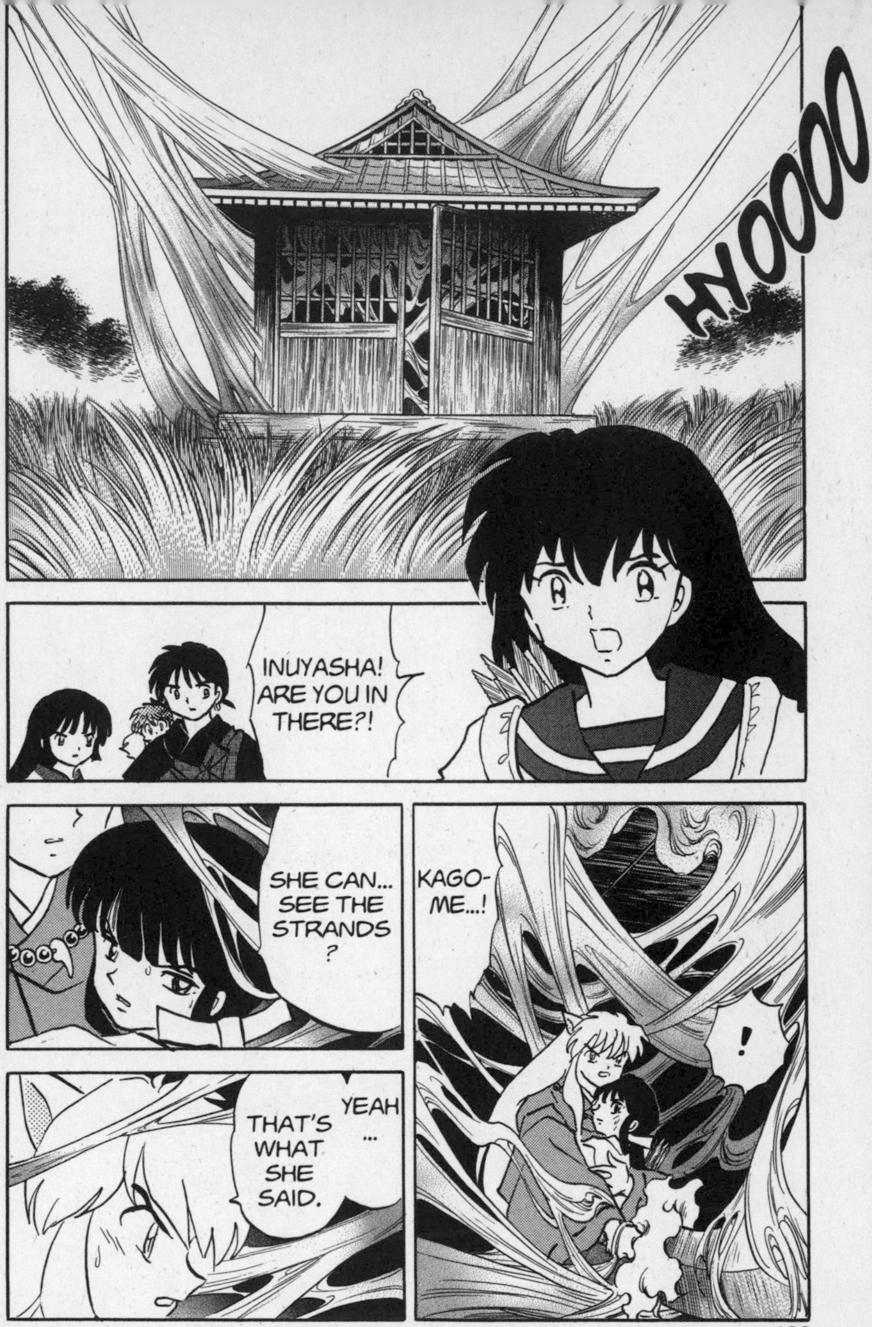
HYOOOO
INUYASHA! ARE YOU IN THERE?!
KAGO-ME...!
!
SHE CAN... SEE THE STRANDS?
YEAH...
THAT'S WHAT SHE SAID.

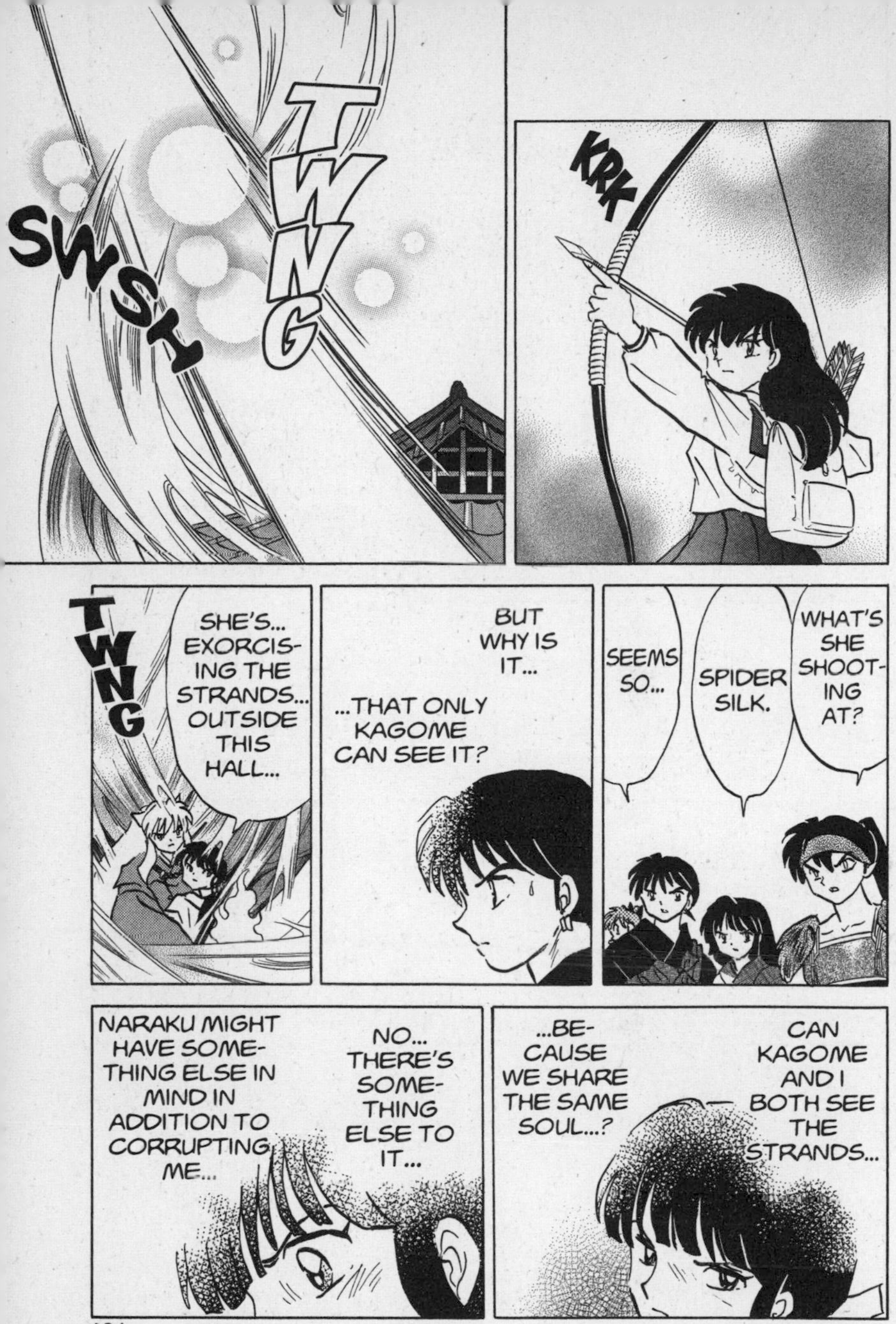
KRK
TWNG
SWSH
WHAT'S SHE SHOOTING AT?
SPIDER SILK.
SEEMS SO...
BUT WHY IS IT...
...THAT ONLY KAGOME CAN SEE IT?
TWNG
SHE'S... EXORCISING THE STRANDS... OUTSIDE THIS HALL...
CAN KAGOME AND I BOTH SEE THE STRANDS...
...BECAUSE WE SHARE THE SAME SOUL...?
NO... THERE'S SOMETHING ELSE TO IT...
NARAKU MIGHT HAVE SOMETHING ELSE IN MIND IN ADDITION TO CORRUPTING ME...

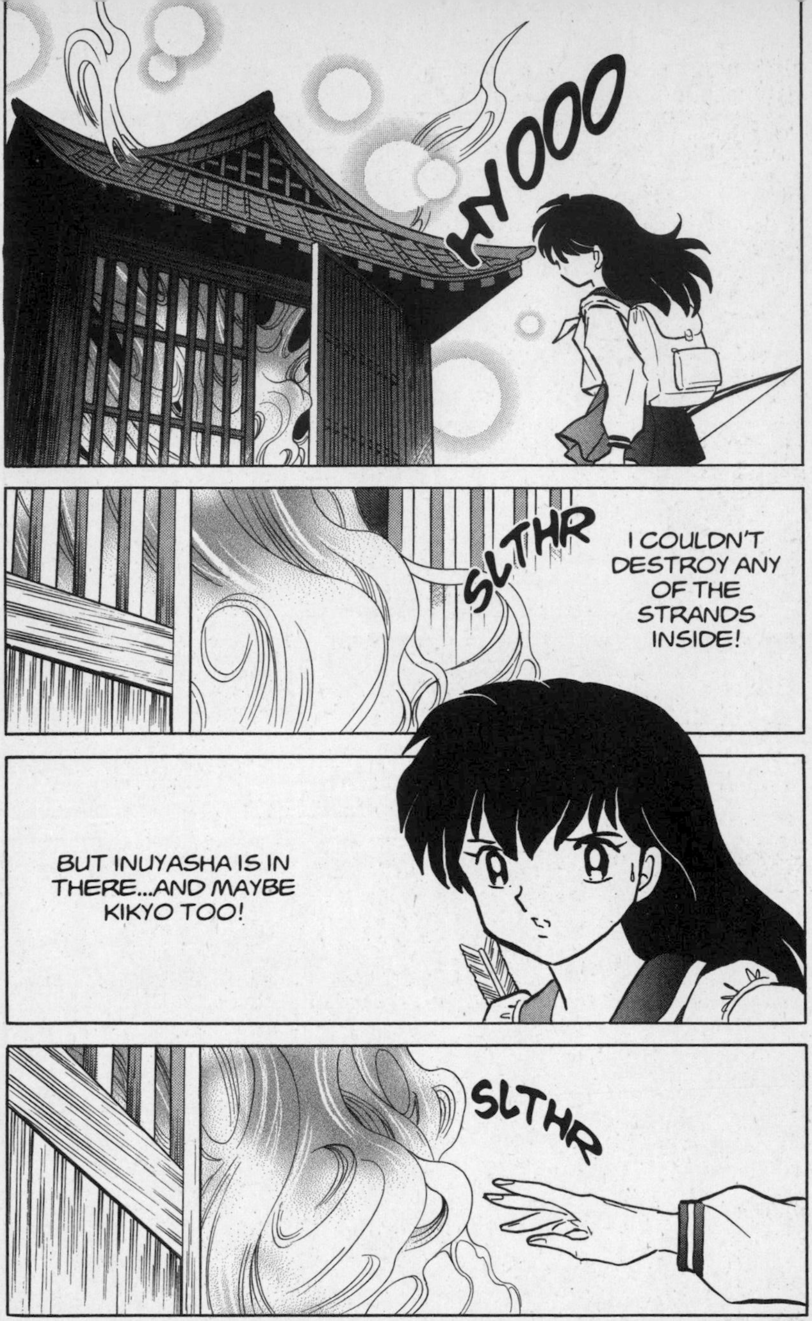
HYOOO
I COULDN'T DESTROY ANY OF THE STRANDS INSIDE!
SLTHR
BUT INUYASHA IS IN THERE...AND MAYBE KIKYO TOO!
SLTHR

KAGO-ME—!

SHNNNG

DON'T TOUCH THE STRANDS!!

KIKYO...!

HUH...?!

LADY KAGO-ME!

KAGO-ME!

YRNK

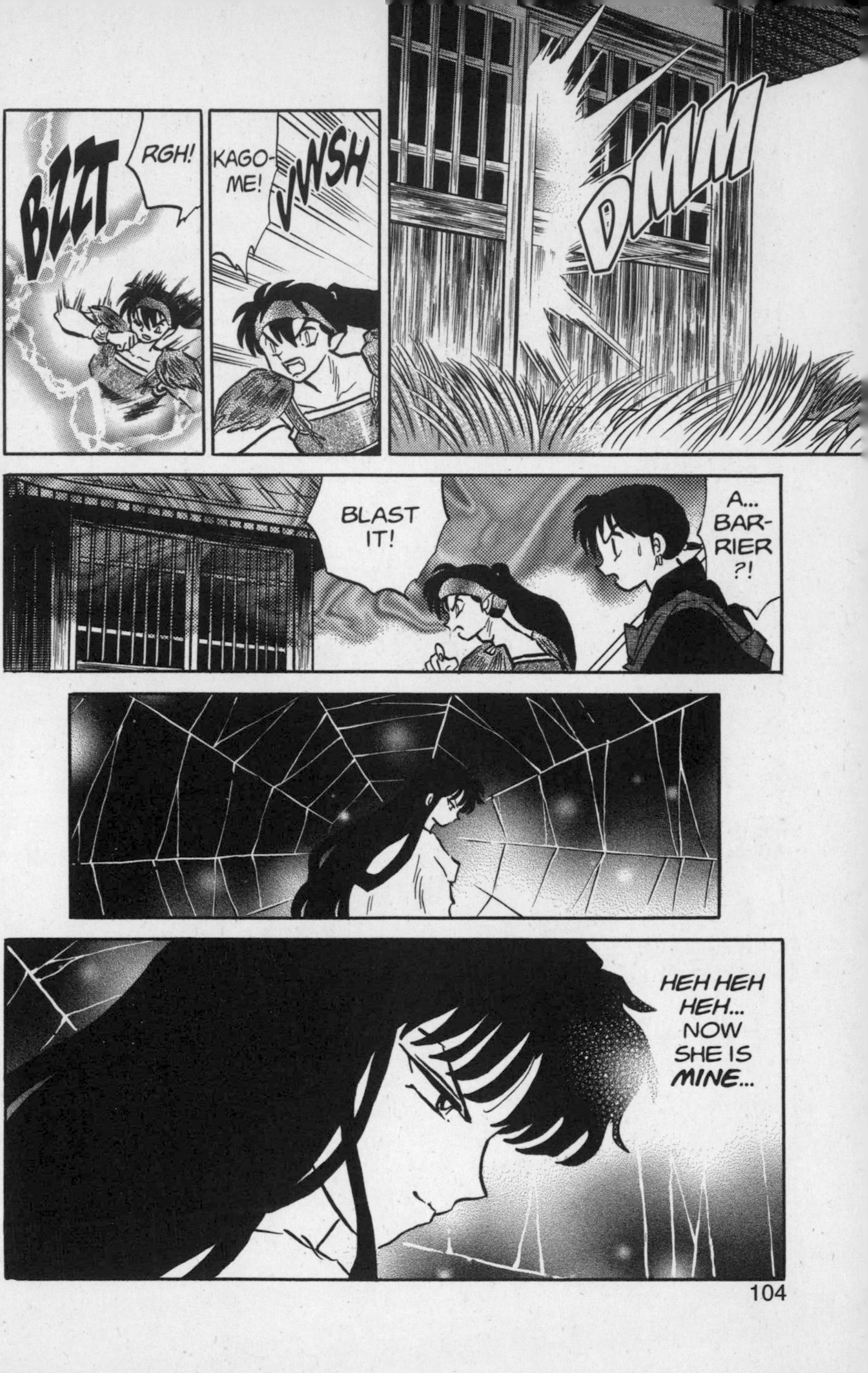
DMM
KAGO-ME!
VWSH
RGH!
BZZT
A... BARRIER?!
BLAST IT!
HEH HEH HEH... NOW SHE IS MINE...

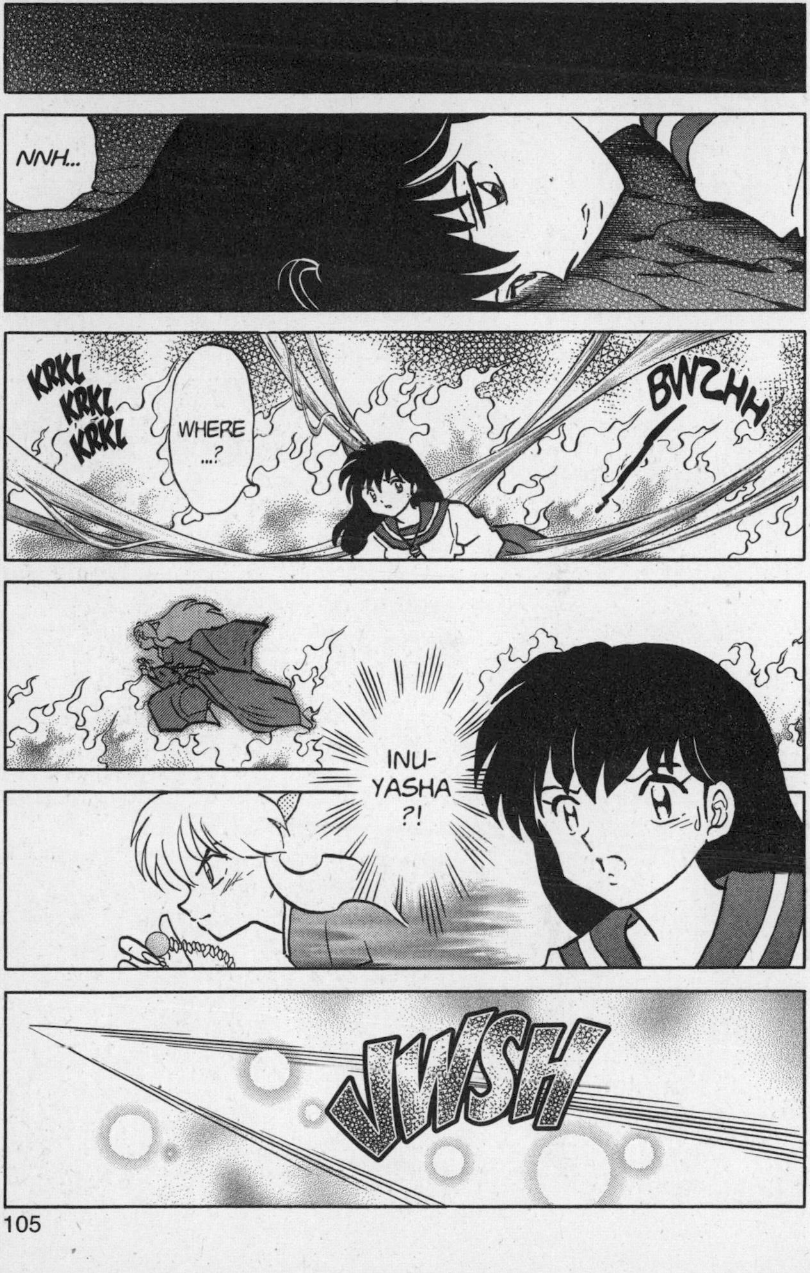
NNH...
BWSHH
WHERE ...?
KRKL KRKL KRKL
INU-YASHA ?!
JWSH

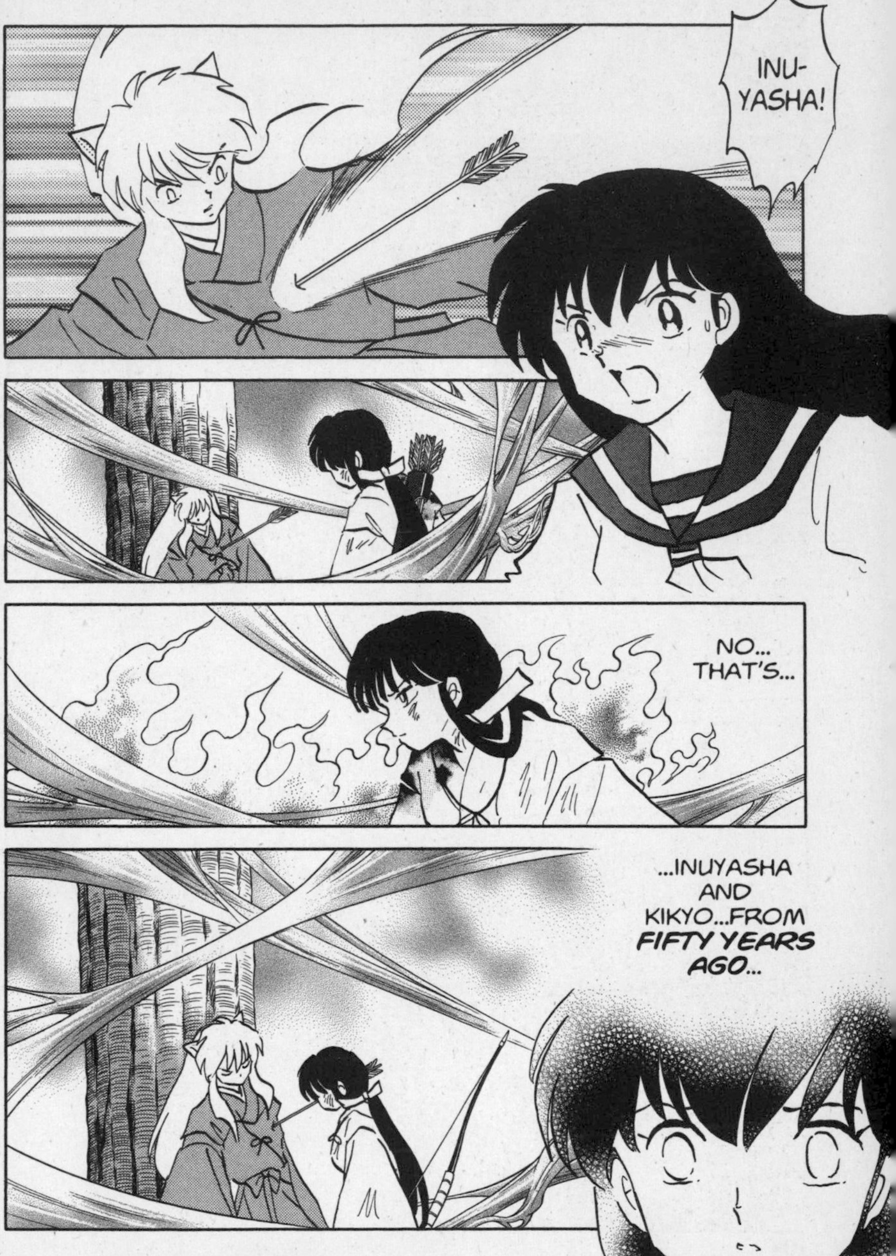
INU-
YASHA!
NO... THAT'S...
...INUYASHA AND KIKYO...FROM *FIFTY YEARS AGO...*

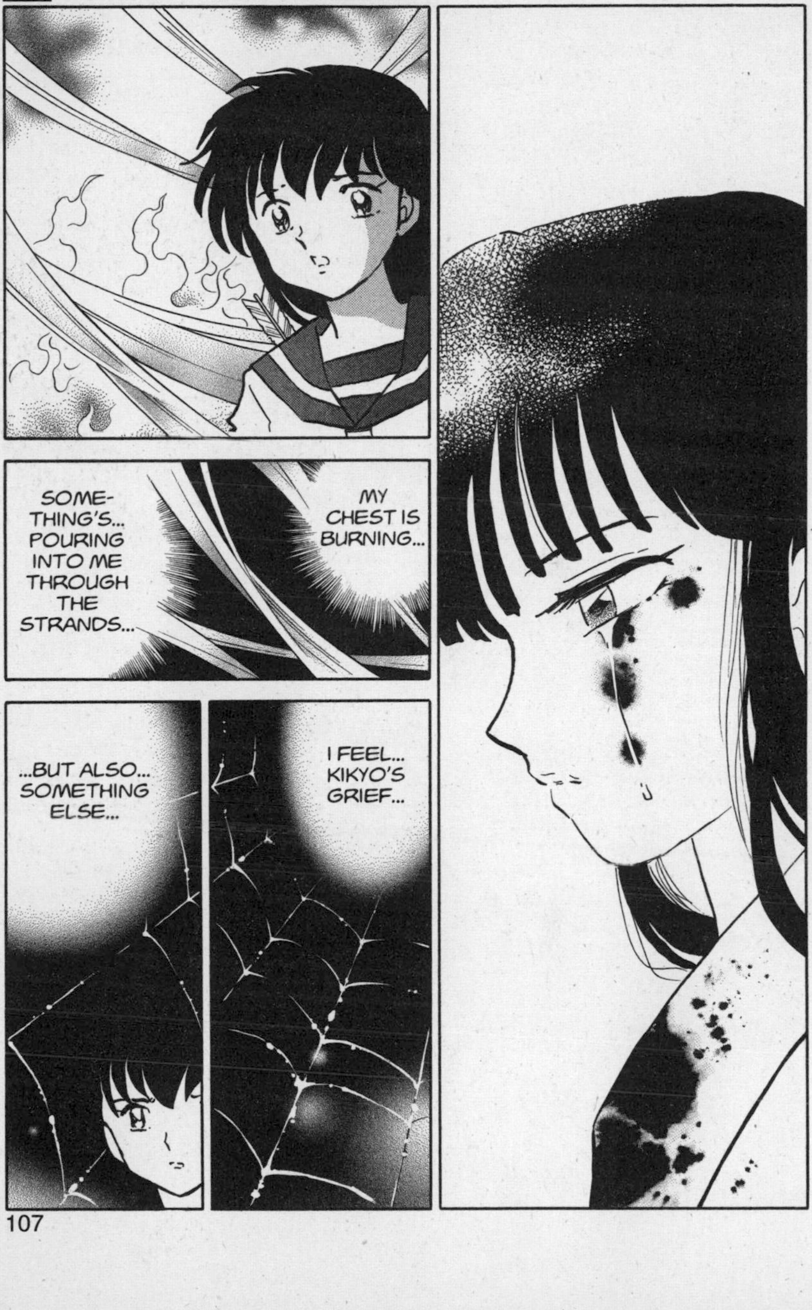
MY CHEST IS BURNING...
SOMETHING'S... POURING INTO ME THROUGH THE STRANDS...
I FEEL... KIKYO'S GRIEF...
...BUT ALSO... SOMETHING ELSE...

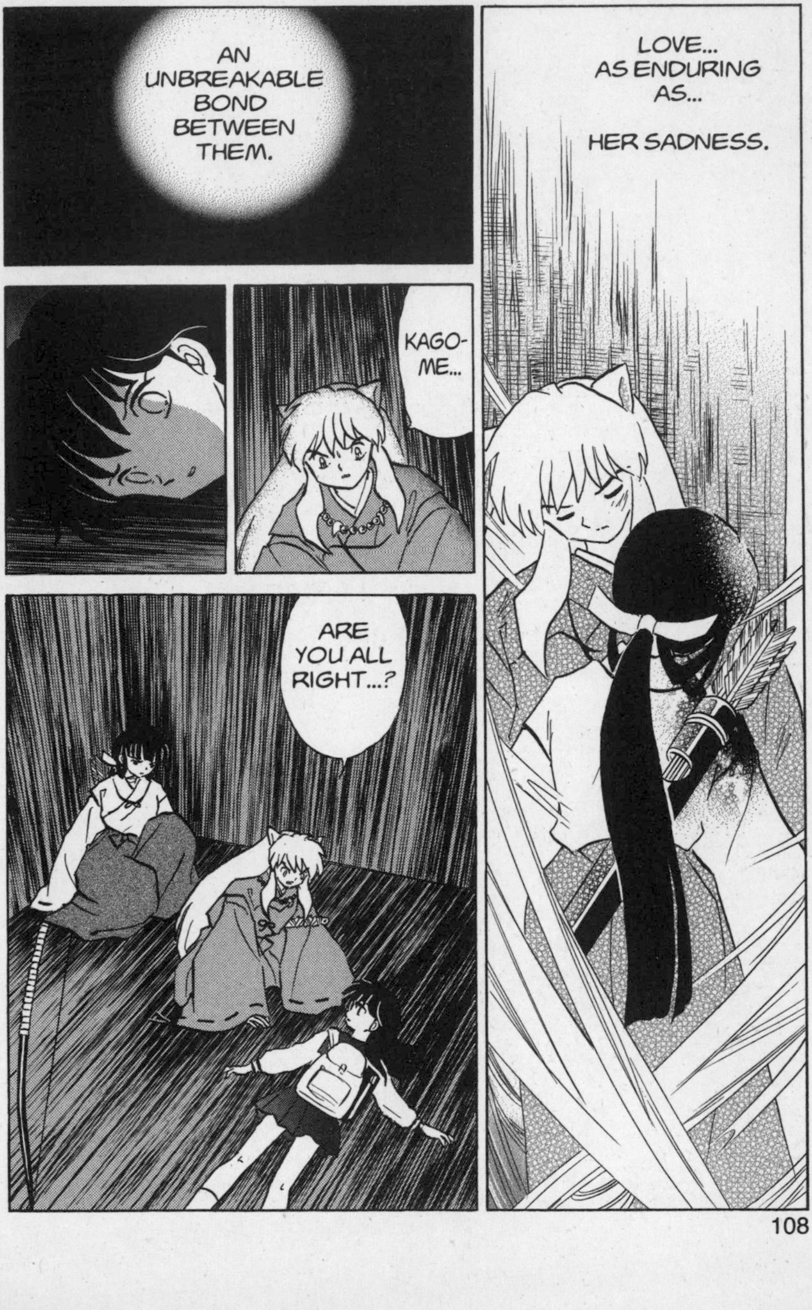
LOVE... AS ENDURING AS...
HER SADNESS.
AN UNBREAKABLE BOND BETWEEN THEM.
KAGO-ME...
ARE YOU ALL RIGHT...?

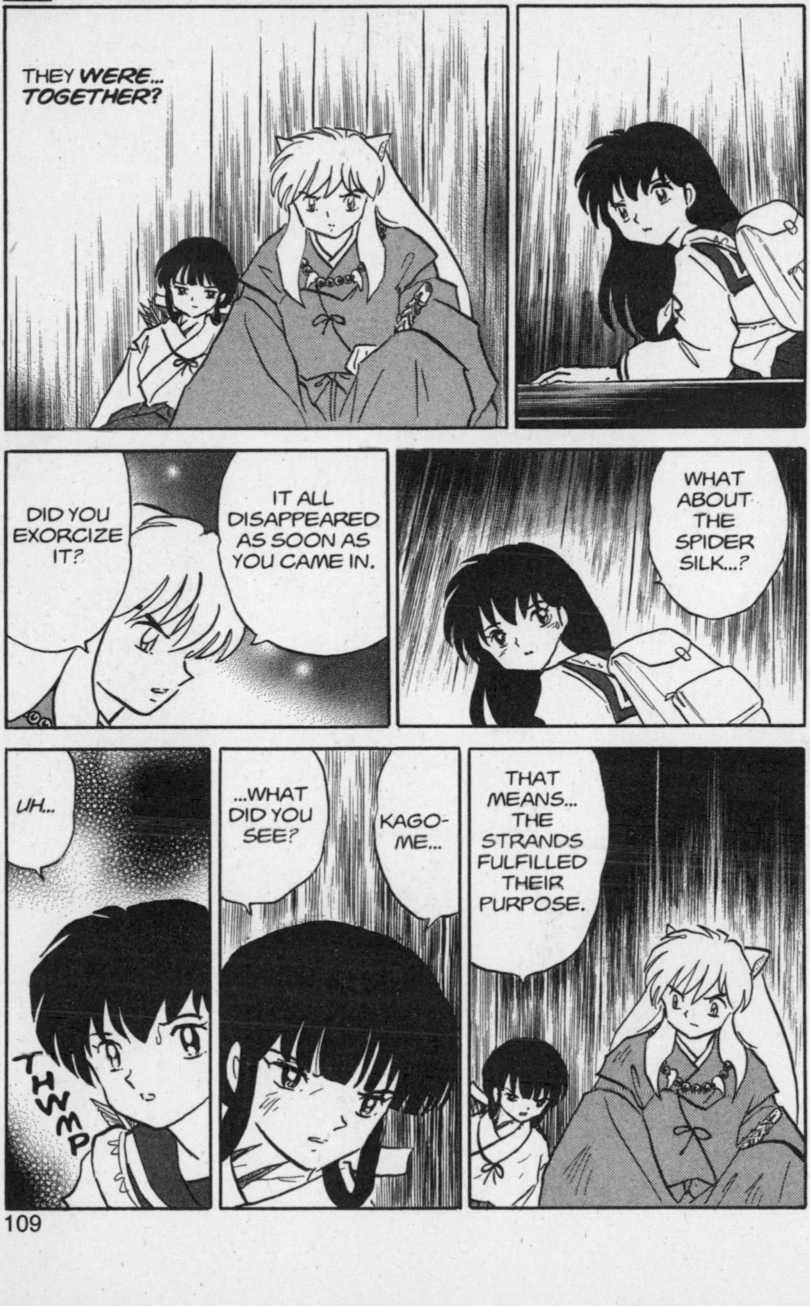
THEY WERE... TOGETHER?
WHAT ABOUT THE SPIDER SILK...?
IT ALL DISAPPEARED AS SOON AS YOU CAME IN.
DID YOU EXORCIZE IT?
THAT MEANS... THE STRANDS FULFILLED THEIR PURPOSE.
KAGO-ME...
...WHAT DID YOU SEE?
UH...
THWMP

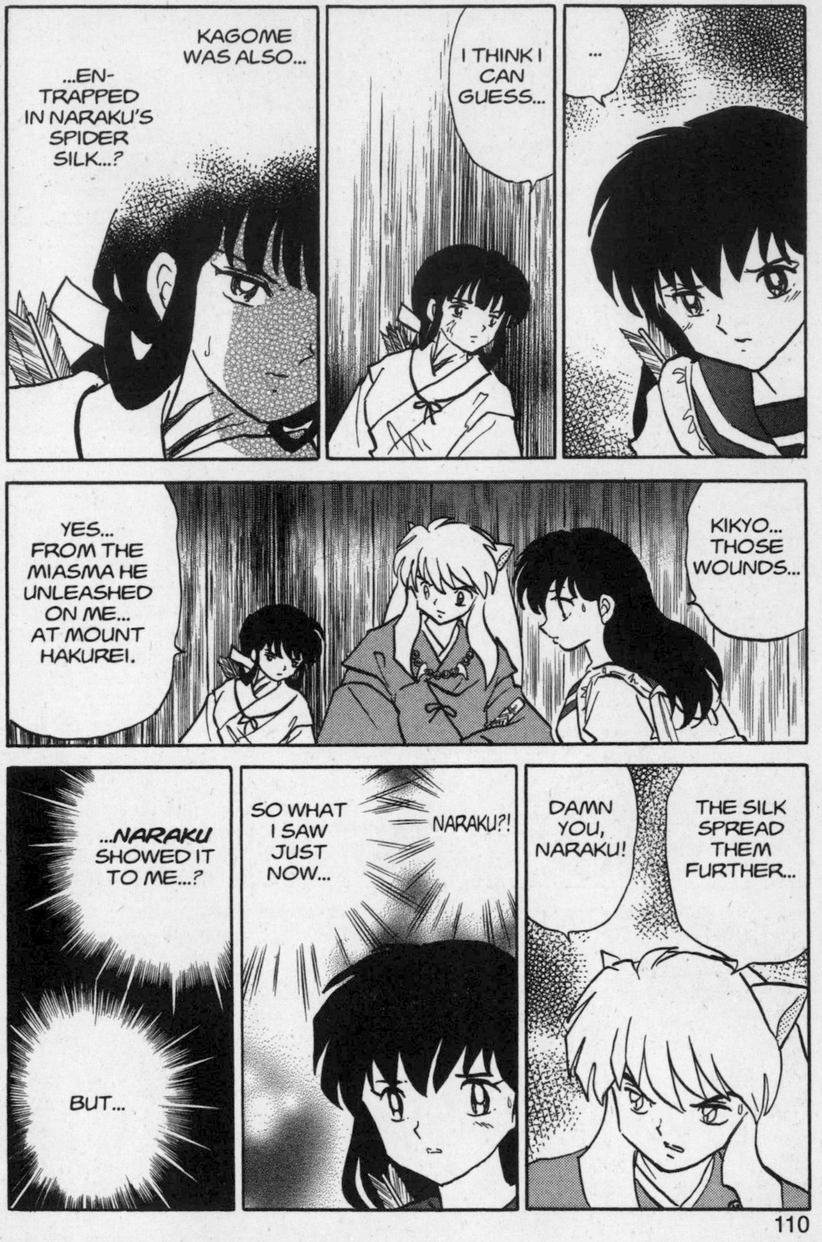
...
I THINK I CAN GUESS...
KAGOME WAS ALSO...
...EN-TRAPPED IN NARAKU'S SPIDER SILK...?
KIKYO... THOSE WOUNDS...
YES... FROM THE MIASMA HE UNLEASHED ON ME... AT MOUNT HAKUREI.
THE SILK SPREAD THEM FURTHER...
DAMN YOU, NARAKU!
NARAKU?!
SO WHAT I SAW JUST NOW...
...*NARAKU* SHOWED IT TO ME...?
BUT...

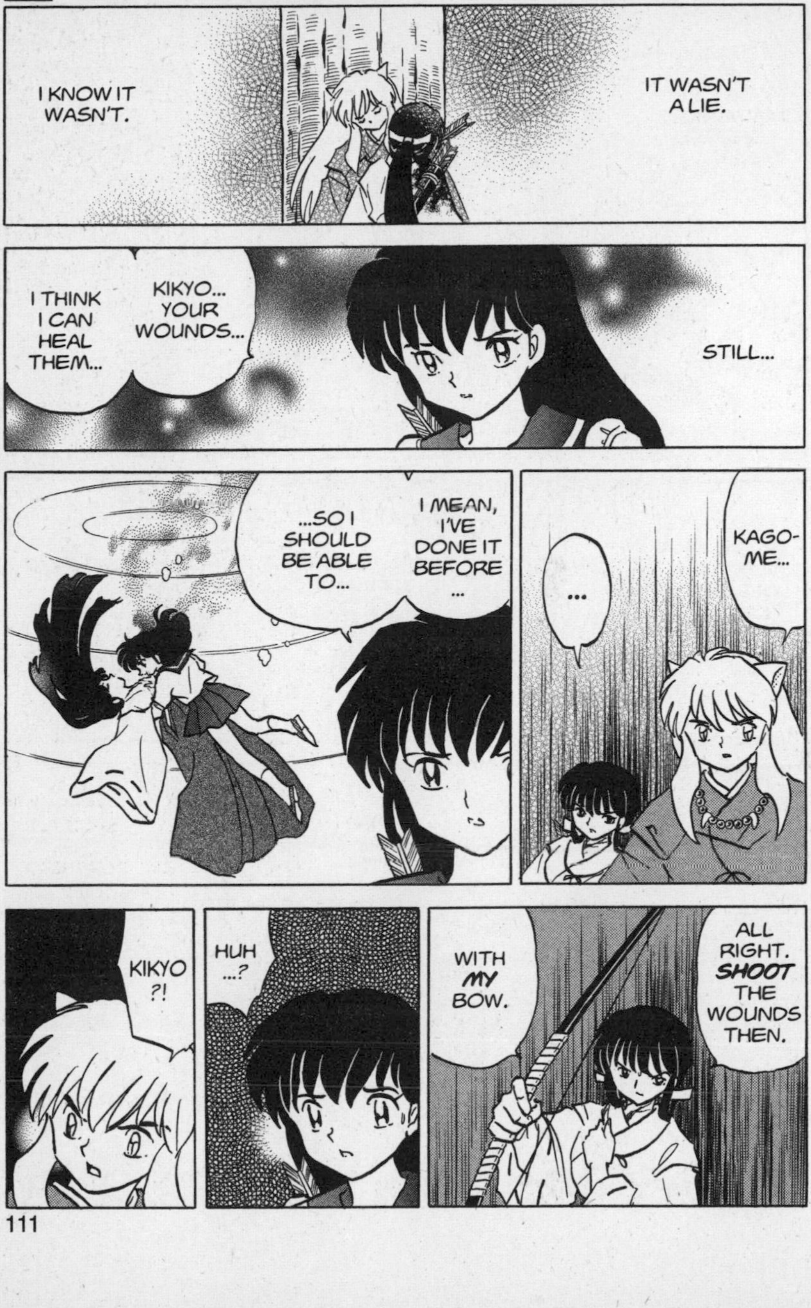
IT WASN'T A LIE.
I KNOW IT WASN'T.
STILL...
KIKYO... YOUR WOUNDS...
I THINK I CAN HEAL THEM...
KAGO-ME...
...
I MEAN, I'VE DONE IT BEFORE...
...SO I SHOULD BE ABLE TO...
ALL RIGHT. **SHOOT** THE WOUNDS THEN.
WITH ***MY*** BOW.
HUH...?
KIKYO?!

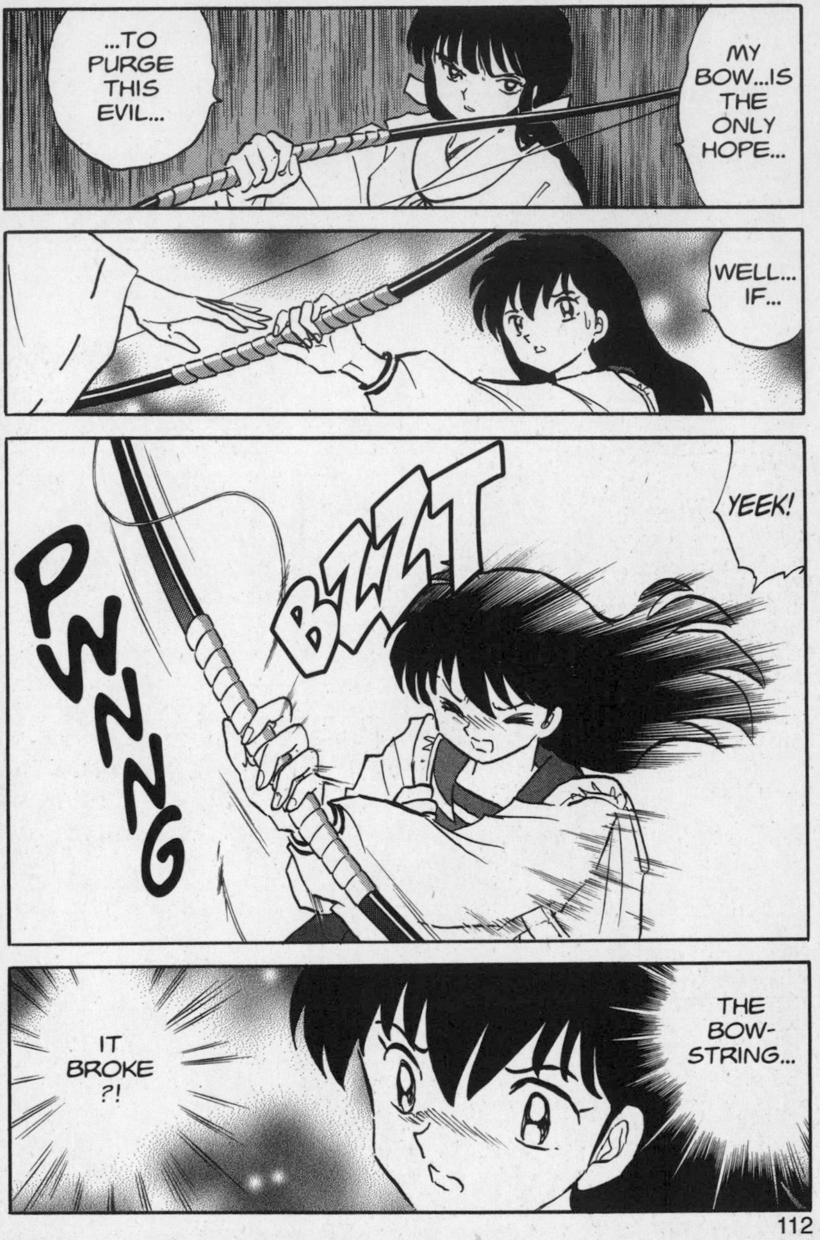
MY BOW...IS THE ONLY HOPE...
...TO PURGE THIS EVIL...
WELL... IF...
YEEK!
BZZT
PWNNG
THE BOW-STRING...
IT BROKE ?!

SCROLL 7

THE BROKEN BOWSTRING

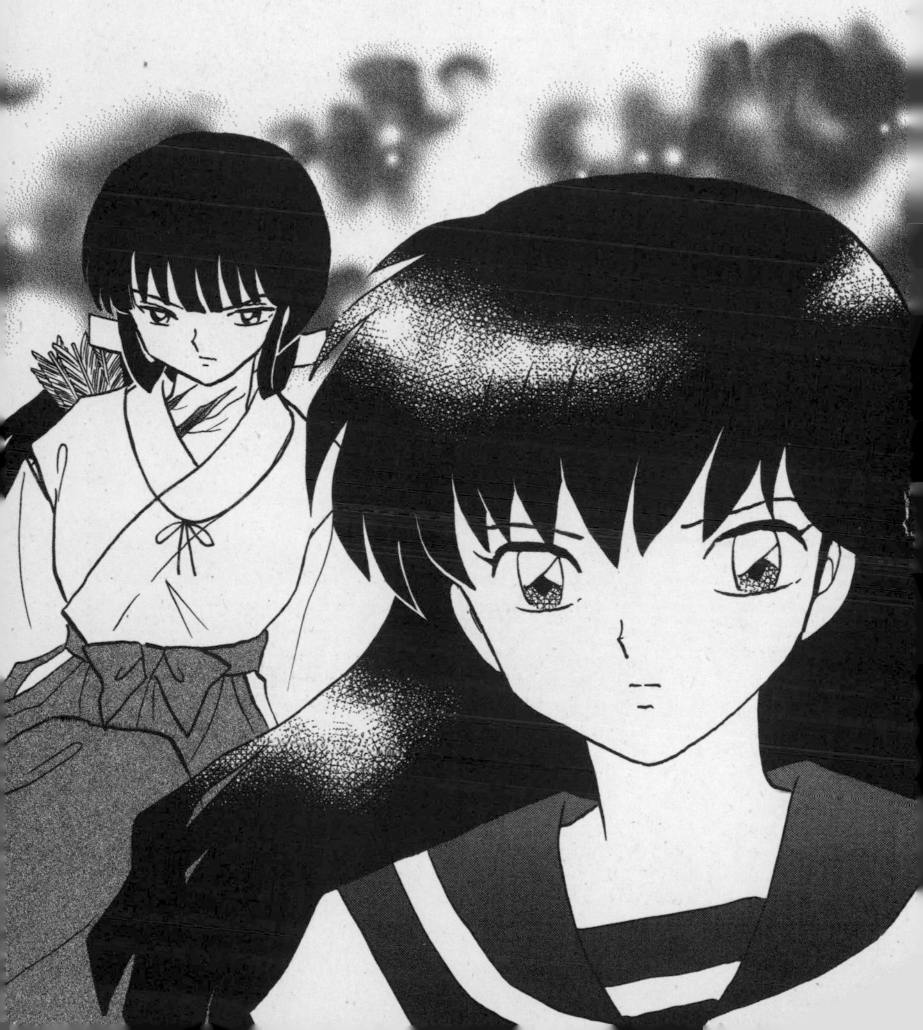

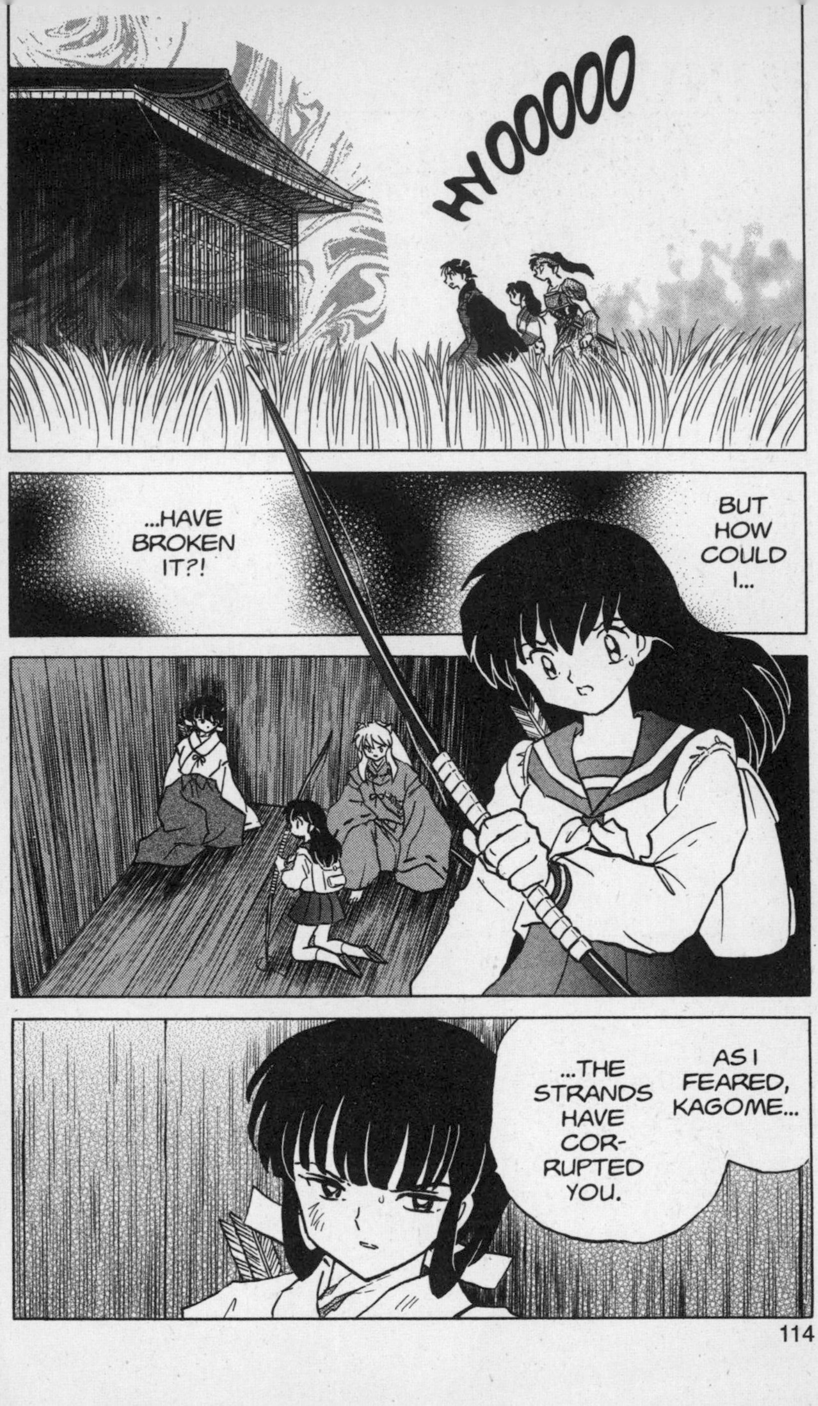
HYOOOOO
BUT HOW COULD I...
...HAVE BROKEN IT?!
AS I FEARED, KAGOME...
...THE STRANDS HAVE COR-RUPTED YOU.

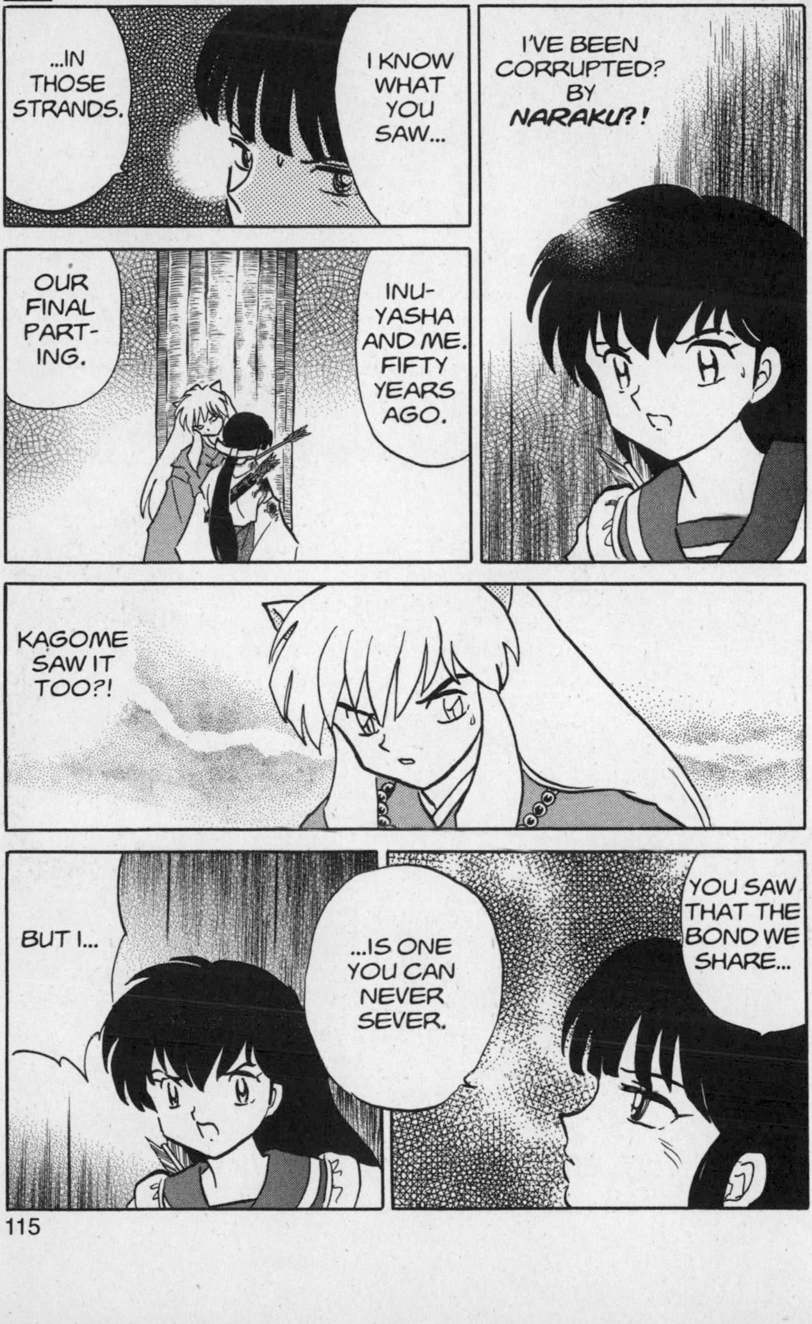
I'VE BEEN CORRUPTED? BY NARAKU?!
I KNOW WHAT YOU SAW...
...IN THOSE STRANDS.
INU-YASHA AND ME. FIFTY YEARS AGO.
OUR FINAL PARTING.
KAGOME SAW IT TOO?!
YOU SAW THAT THE BOND WE SHARE...
...IS ONE YOU CAN NEVER SEVER.
BUT I...

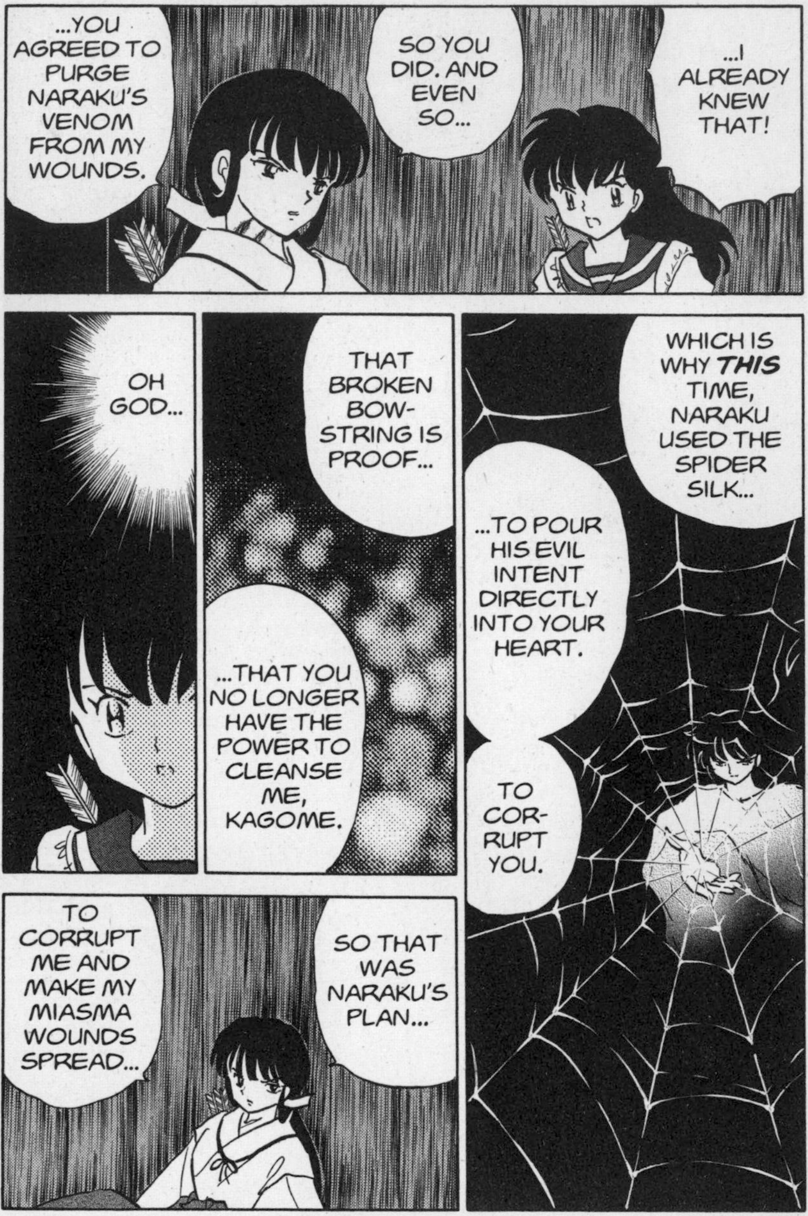
...I ALREADY KNEW THAT!
SO YOU DID. AND EVEN SO...
...YOU AGREED TO PURGE NARAKU'S VENOM FROM MY WOUNDS.
WHICH IS WHY *THIS* TIME, NARAKU USED THE SPIDER SILK...
...TO POUR HIS EVIL INTENT DIRECTLY INTO YOUR HEART.
TO COR-RUPT YOU.
THAT BROKEN BOW-STRING IS PROOF...
...THAT YOU NO LONGER HAVE THE POWER TO CLEANSE ME, KAGOME.
OH GOD...
SO THAT WAS NARAKU'S PLAN...
TO CORRUPT ME AND MAKE MY MIASMA WOUNDS SPREAD...

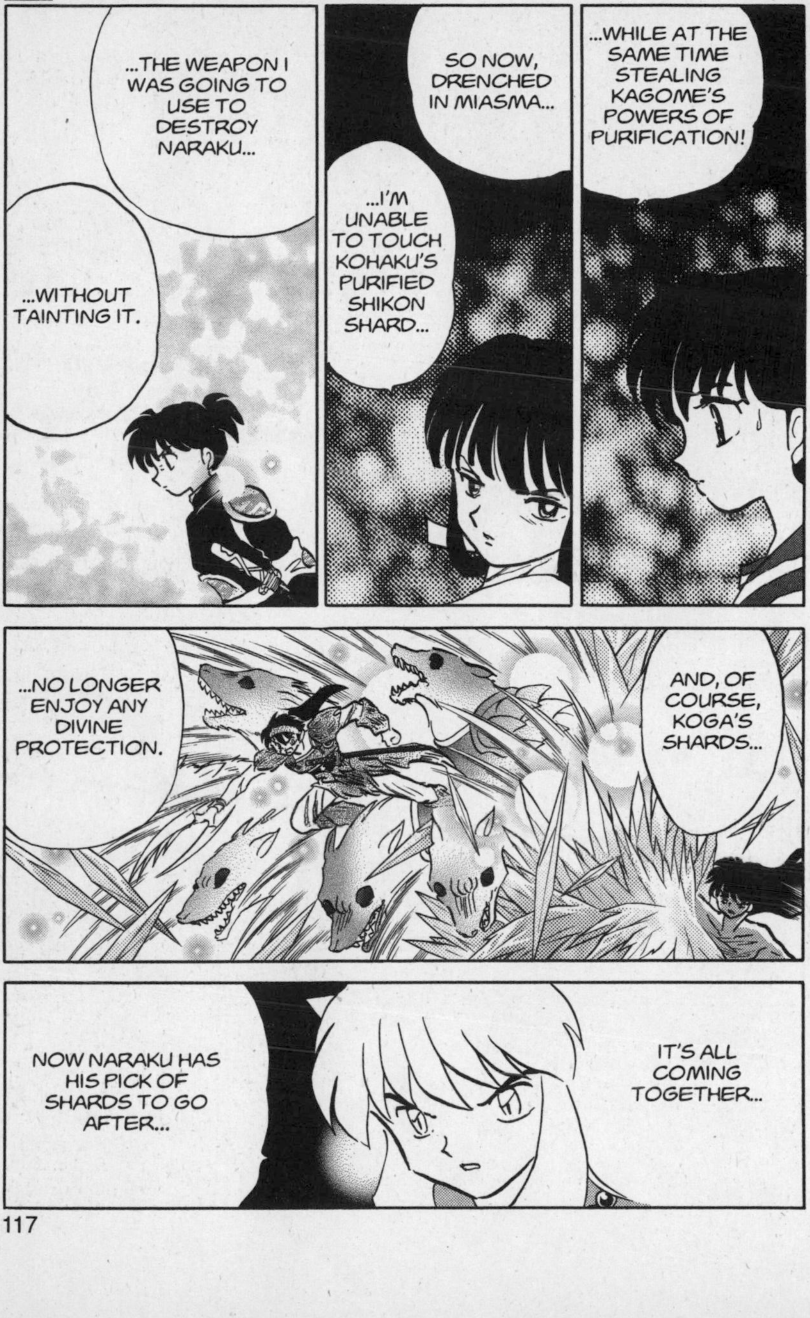
...WHILE AT THE SAME TIME STEALING KAGOME'S POWERS OF PURIFICATION!
SO NOW, DRENCHED IN MIASMA...
...I'M UNABLE TO TOUCH KOHAKU'S PURIFIED SHIKON SHARD...
...THE WEAPON I WAS GOING TO USE TO DESTROY NARAKU...
...WITHOUT TAINTING IT.
AND, OF COURSE, KOGA'S SHARDS...
...NO LONGER ENJOY ANY DIVINE PROTECTION.
IT'S ALL COMING TOGETHER...
NOW NARAKU HAS HIS PICK OF SHARDS TO GO AFTER...

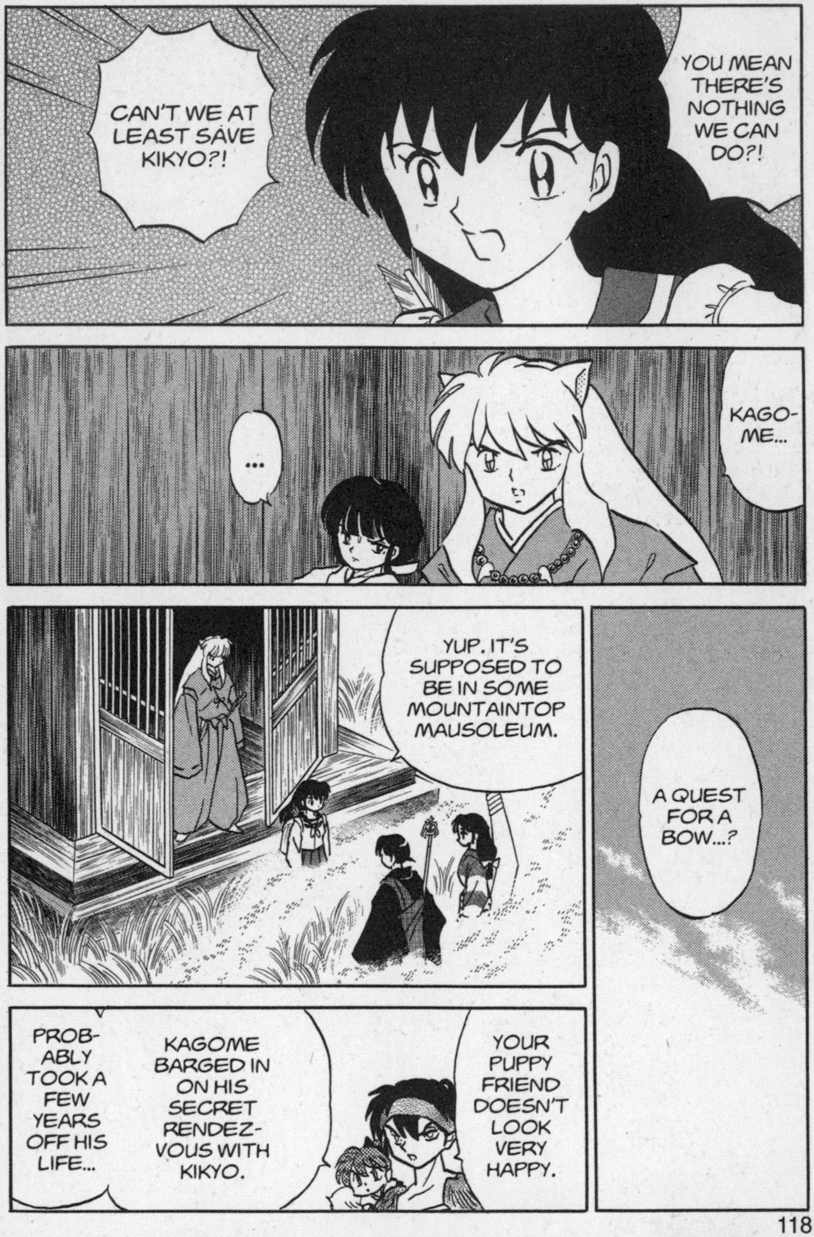
YOU MEAN THERE'S NOTHING WE CAN DO?!
CAN'T WE AT LEAST SAVE KIKYO?!
KAGO-ME...
...
A QUEST FOR A BOW...?
YUP. IT'S SUPPOSED TO BE IN SOME MOUNTAINTOP MAUSOLEUM.
YOUR PUPPY FRIEND DOESN'T LOOK VERY HAPPY.
KAGOME BARGED IN ON HIS SECRET RENDEZ-VOUS WITH KIKYO.
PROB-ABLY TOOK A FEW YEARS OFF HIS LIFE...

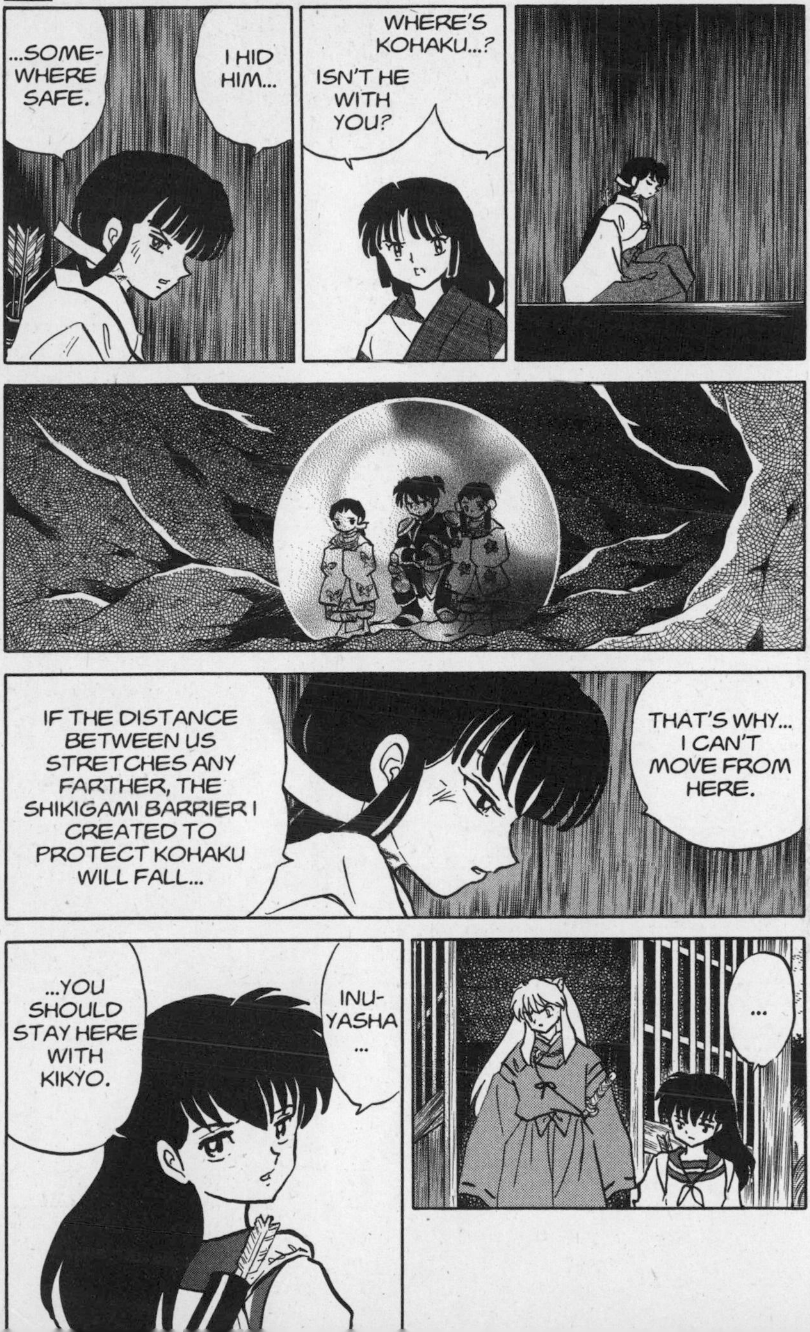
WHERE'S KOHAKU...? ISN'T HE WITH YOU?
I HID HIM...
...SOME-WHERE SAFE.
IF THE DISTANCE BETWEEN US STRETCHES ANY FARTHER, THE SHIKIGAMI BARRIER I CREATED TO PROTECT KOHAKU WILL FALL...
THAT'S WHY... I CAN'T MOVE FROM HERE.
...
INU-YASHA ...
...YOU SHOULD STAY HERE WITH KIKYO.

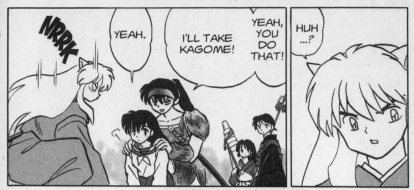

HUH ...?
YEAH, YOU DO THAT!
I'LL TAKE KAGOME!
YEAH.
NRRK
BE-SIDES ...
I DON'T REALLY WANT TO SEE YOUR FACE FOR A WHILE.
...
SORRY... I MUST REALLY BE CORRUPTED.
THWMP THWMP THWMP
SEEM THE SAME TO ME...

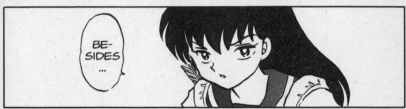

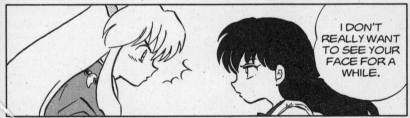

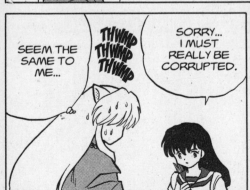

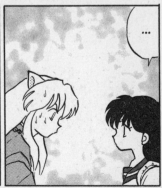

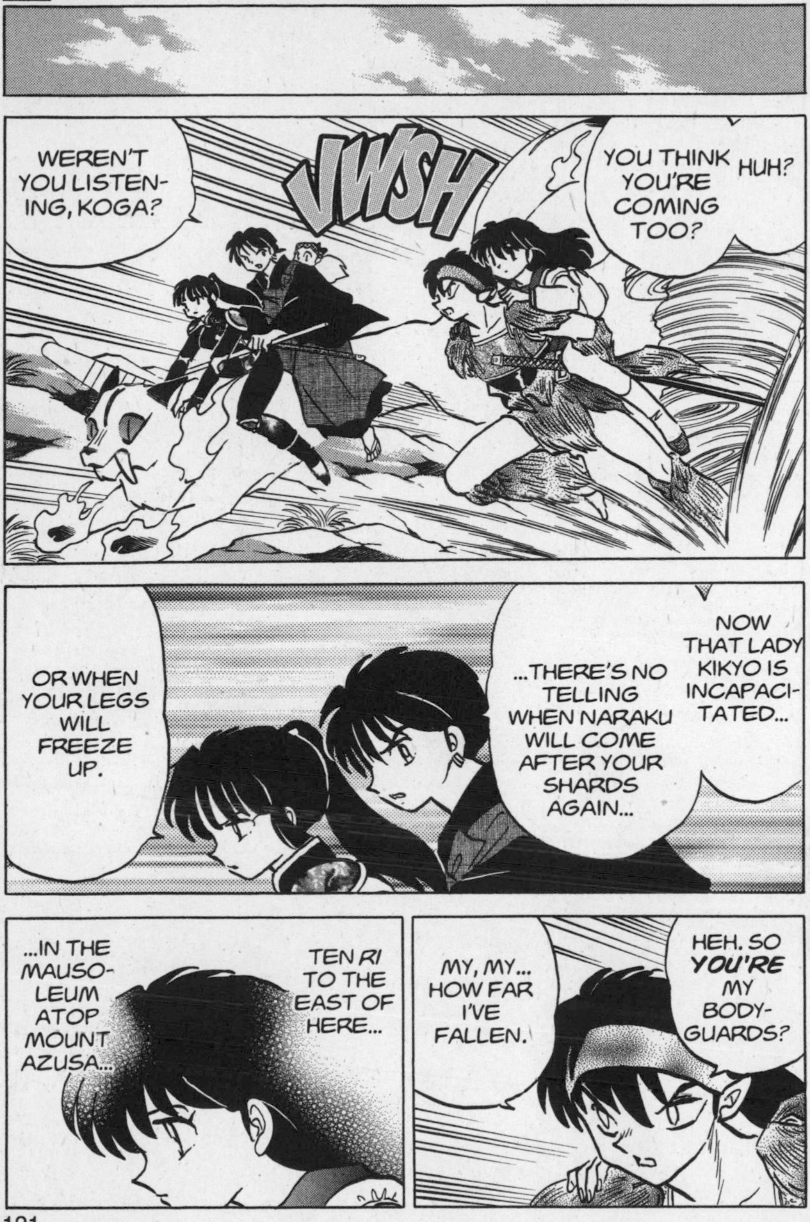
HUH?
YOU THINK YOU'RE COMING TOO?
VWSH
WEREN'T YOU LISTEN-ING, KOGA?
NOW THAT LADY KIKYO IS INCAPACI-TATED...
...THERE'S NO TELLING WHEN NARAKU WILL COME AFTER YOUR SHARDS AGAIN...
OR WHEN YOUR LEGS WILL FREEZE UP.
HEH. SO *YOU'RE* MY BODY-GUARDS?
MY, MY... HOW FAR I'VE FALLEN.
TEN *RI* TO THE EAST OF HERE...
...IN THE MAUSO-LEUM ATOP MOUNT AZUSA...

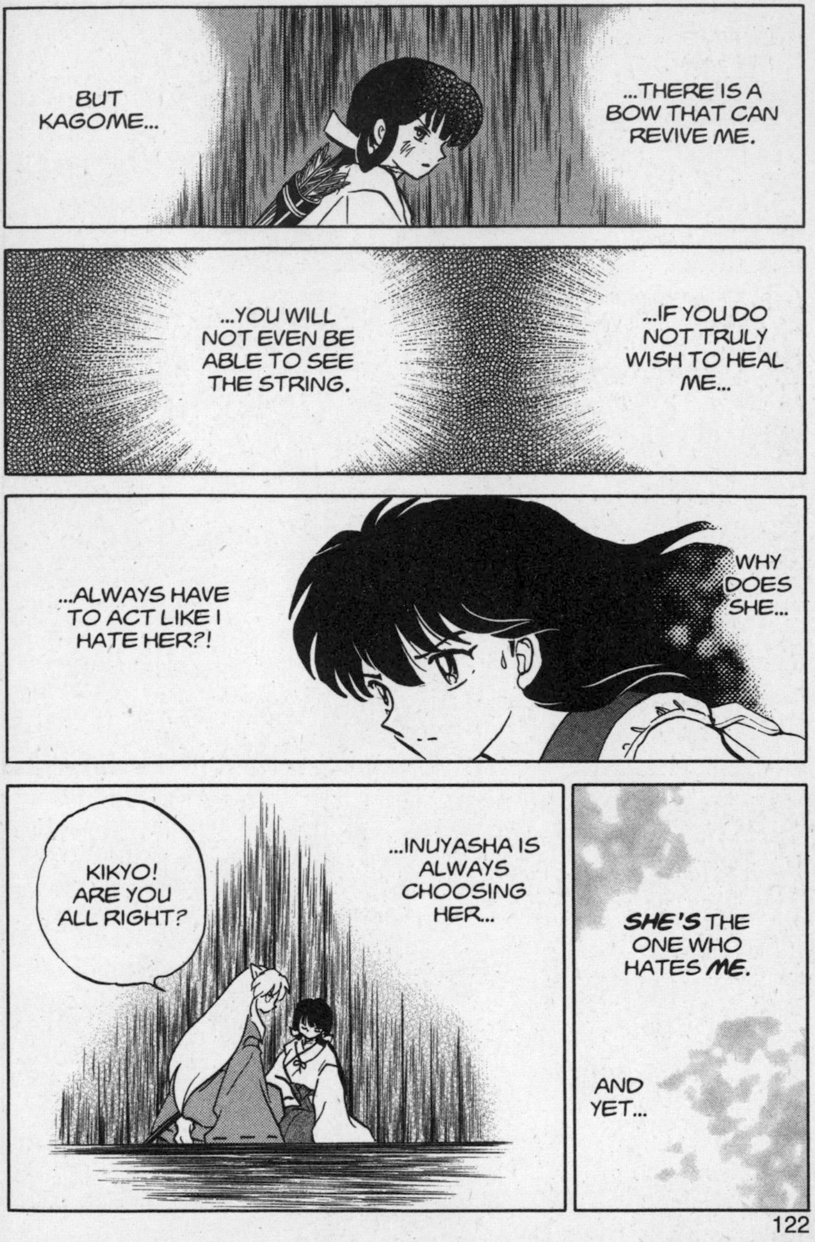
...THERE IS A BOW THAT CAN REVIVE ME.
BUT KAGOME...
...IF YOU DO NOT TRULY WISH TO HEAL ME...
...YOU WILL NOT EVEN BE ABLE TO SEE THE STRING.
WHY DOES SHE...
...ALWAYS HAVE TO ACT LIKE I HATE HER?!
SHE'S THE ONE WHO HATES ME.
AND YET...
...INUYASHA IS ALWAYS CHOOSING HER...
KIKYO! ARE YOU ALL RIGHT?

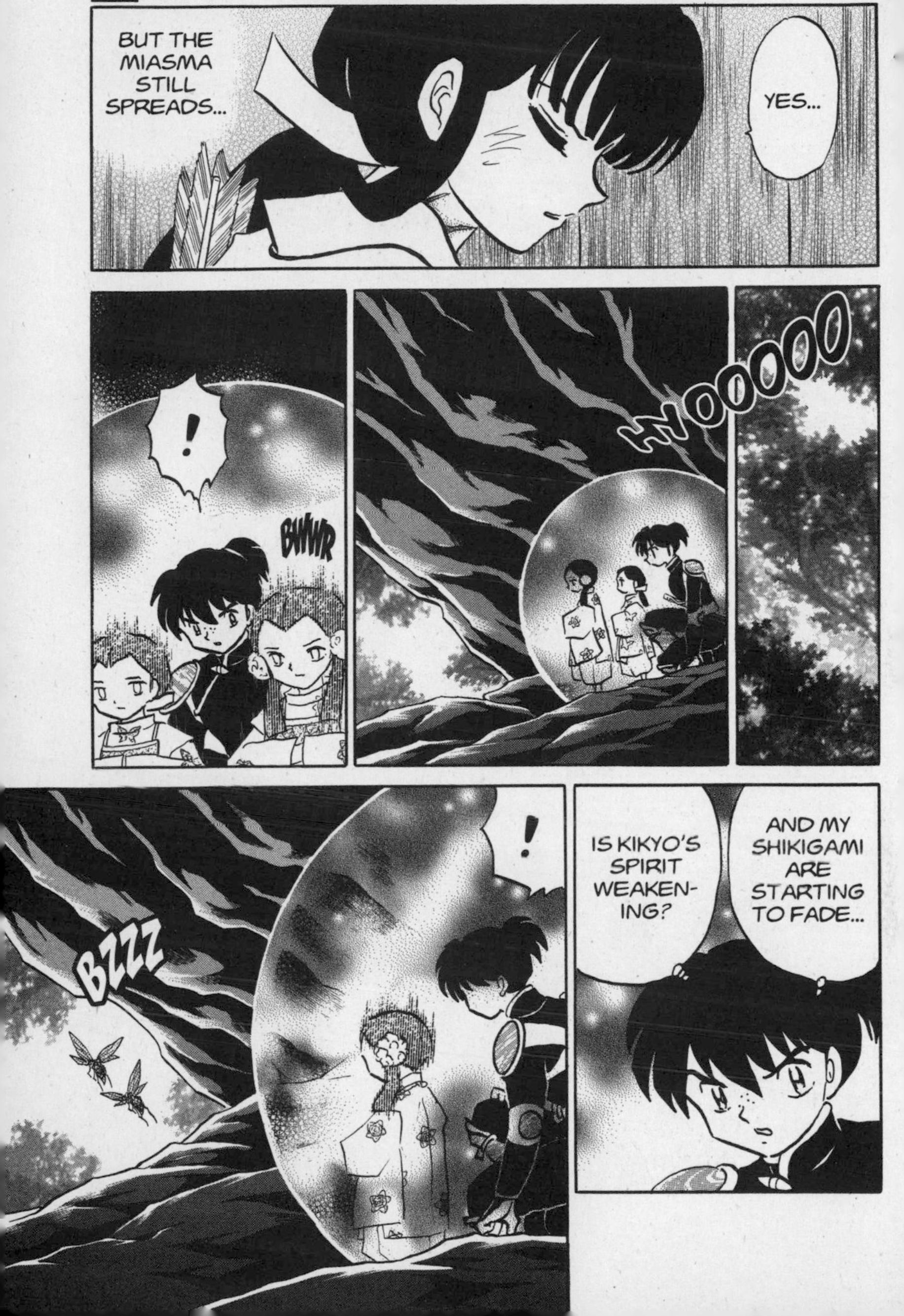
YES...
BUT THE MIASMA STILL SPREADS...
HYOOOOO
!
BWWR
AND MY SHIKIGAMI ARE STARTING TO FADE...
IS KIKYO'S SPIRIT WEAKEN-ING?
!
BZZZ

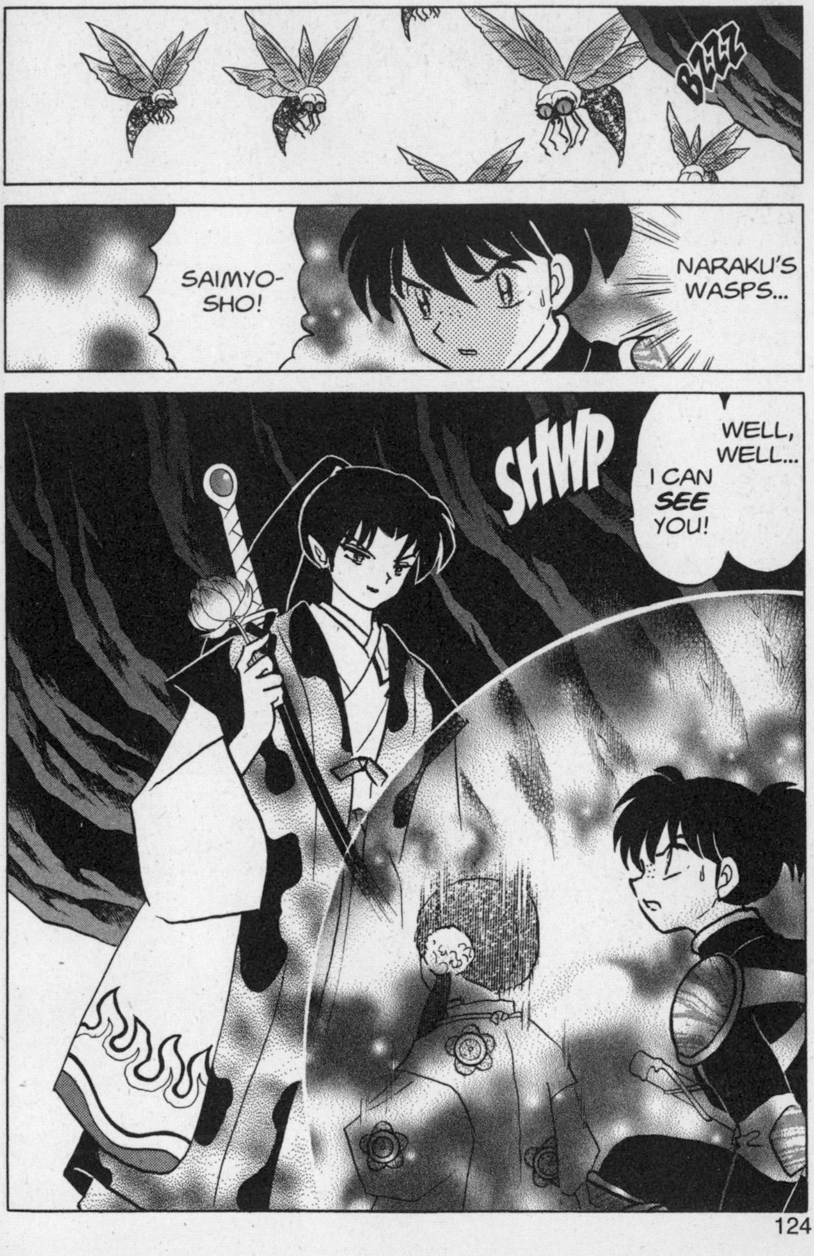
BZZZ
NARAKU'S WASPS...
SAIMYO-SHO!
SHWP
WELL, WELL... I CAN **SEE** YOU!

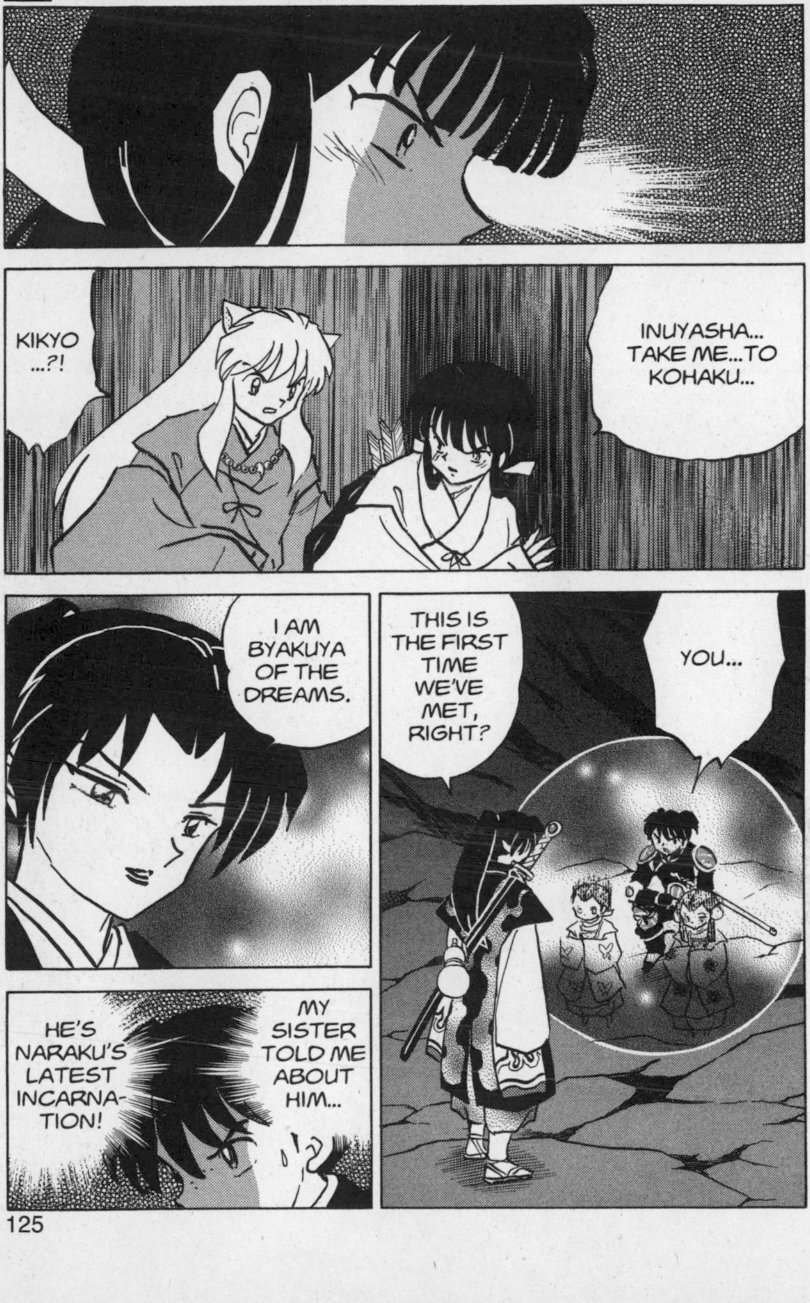
INUYASHA... TAKE ME...TO KOHAKU...
KIKYO ...?!
YOU...
THIS IS THE FIRST TIME WE'VE MET, RIGHT?
I AM BYAKUYA OF THE DREAMS.
MY SISTER TOLD ME ABOUT HIM...
HE'S NARAKU'S LATEST INCARNATION!

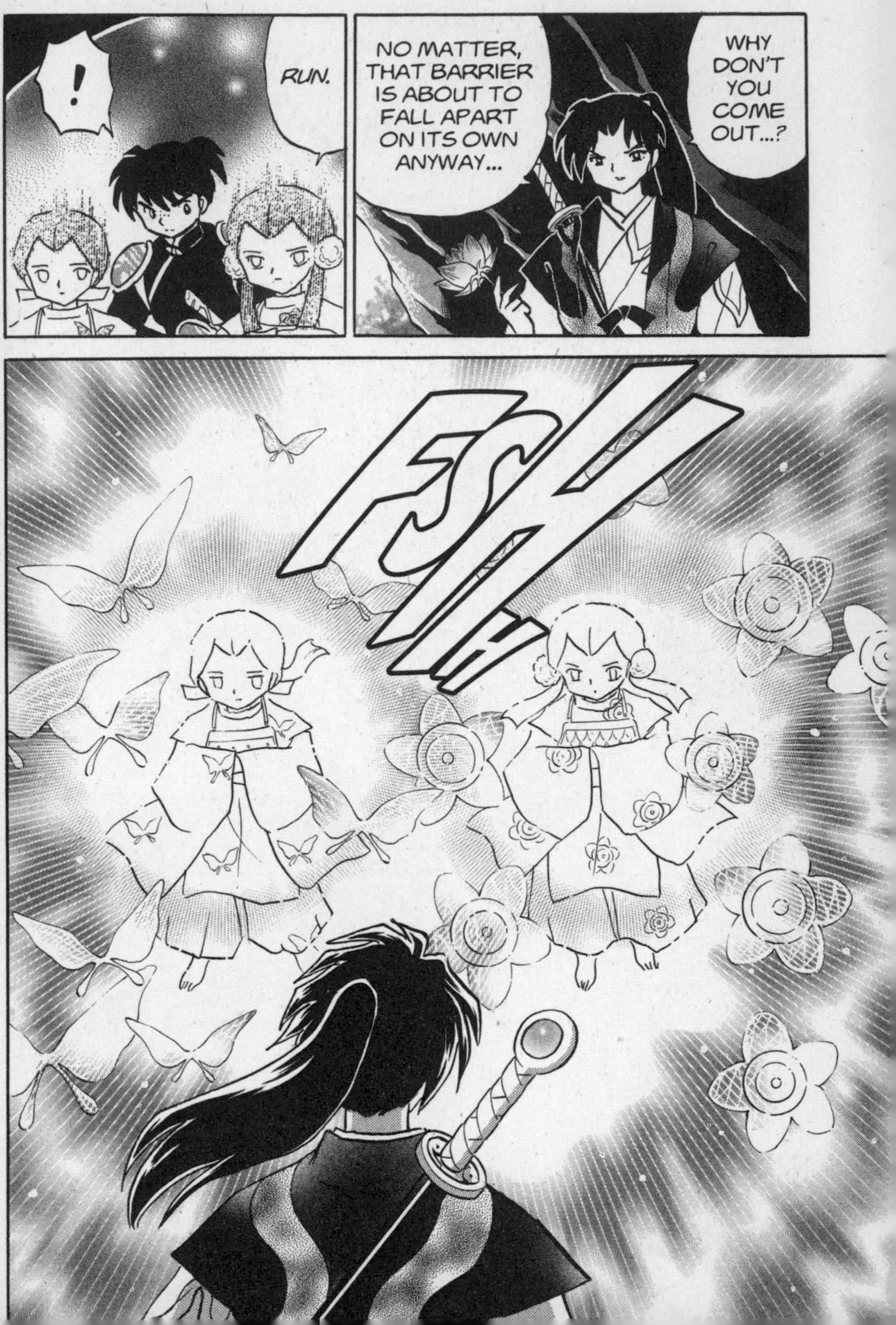
WHY DON'T YOU COME OUT...?
NO MATTER, THAT BARRIER IS ABOUT TO FALL APART ON ITS OWN ANYWAY...
RUN.
!
FSHH

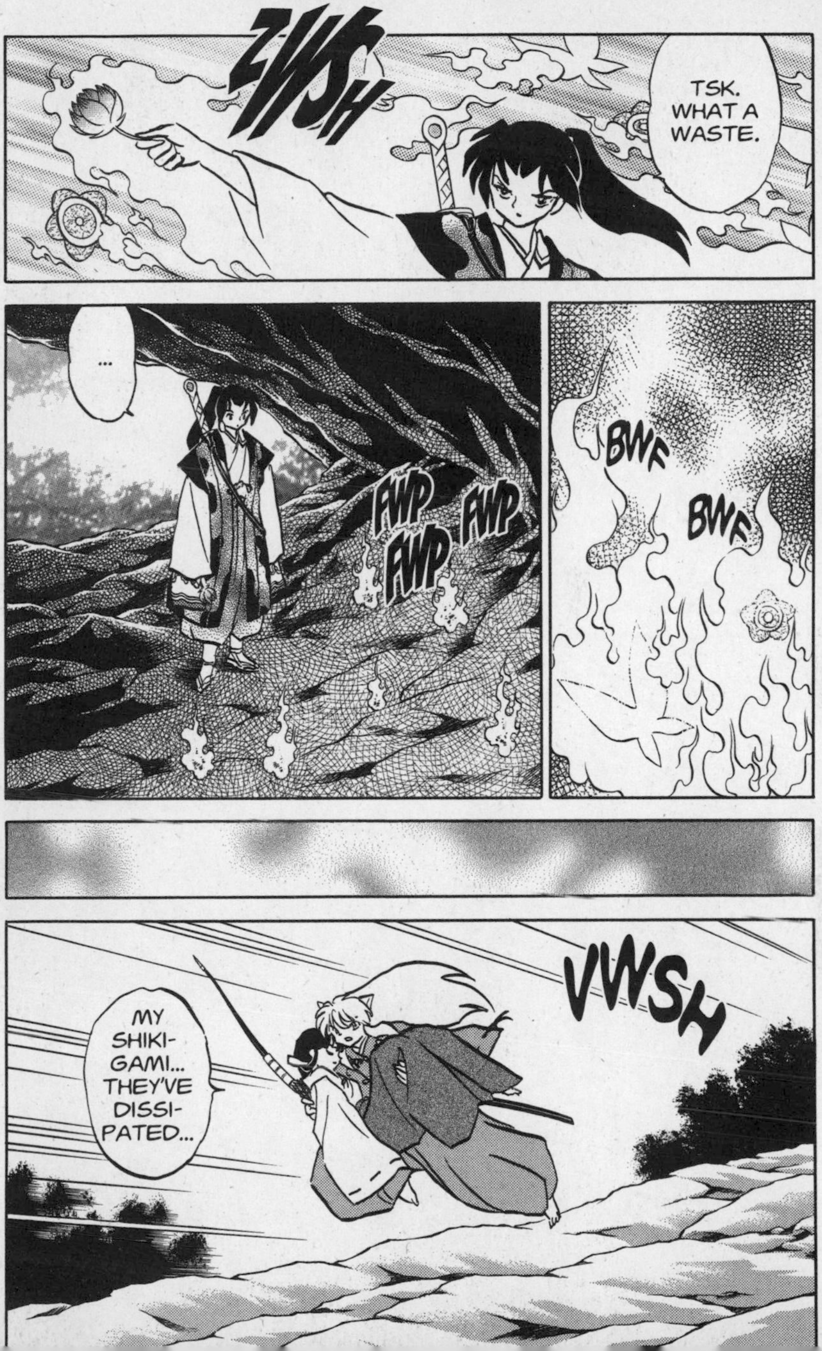
TSK. WHAT A WASTE.
ZWSH
BWF
BWF
...
FWP
FWP
FWP
VWSH
MY SHIKI-GAMI... THEY'VE DISSI-PATED...

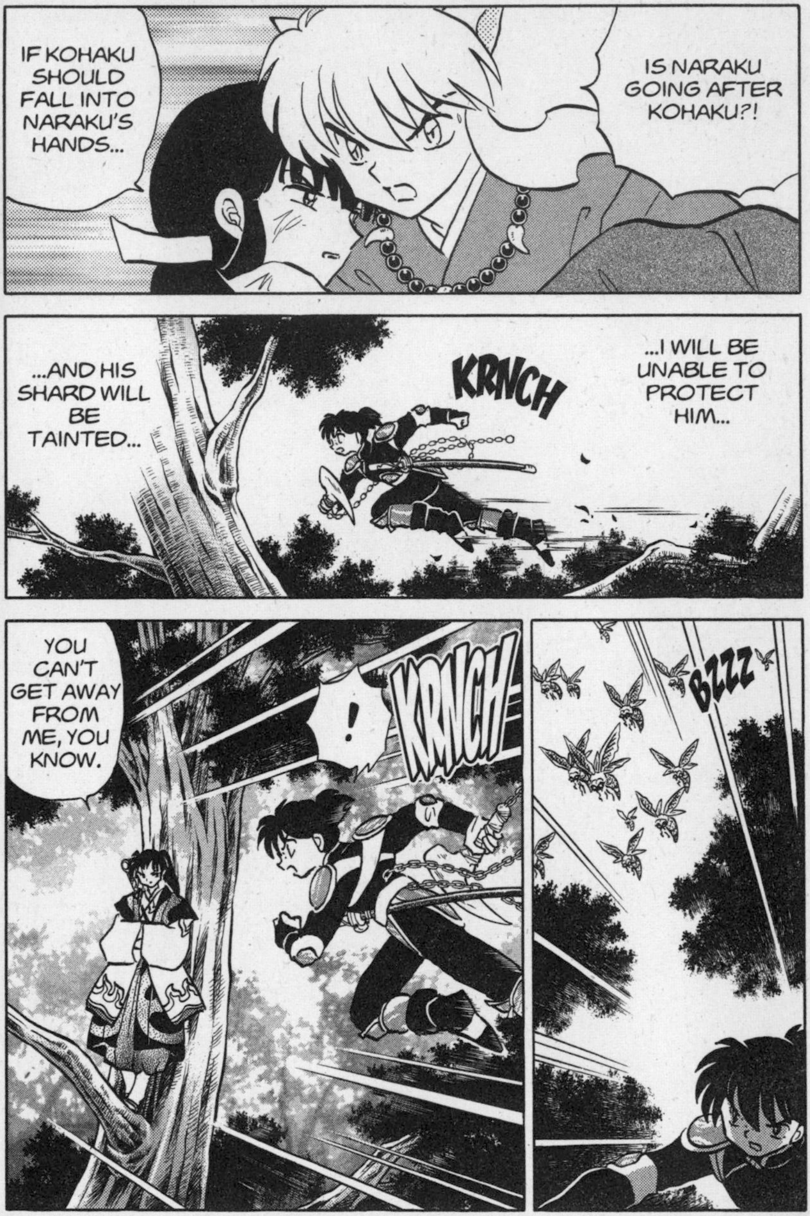
IS NARAKU GOING AFTER KOHAKU?!
IF KOHAKU SHOULD FALL INTO NARAKU'S HANDS...
...AND HIS SHARD WILL BE TAINTED...
KRNCH
...I WILL BE UNABLE TO PROTECT HIM...
BZZZ
KRNCH
!
YOU CAN'T GET AWAY FROM ME, YOU KNOW.

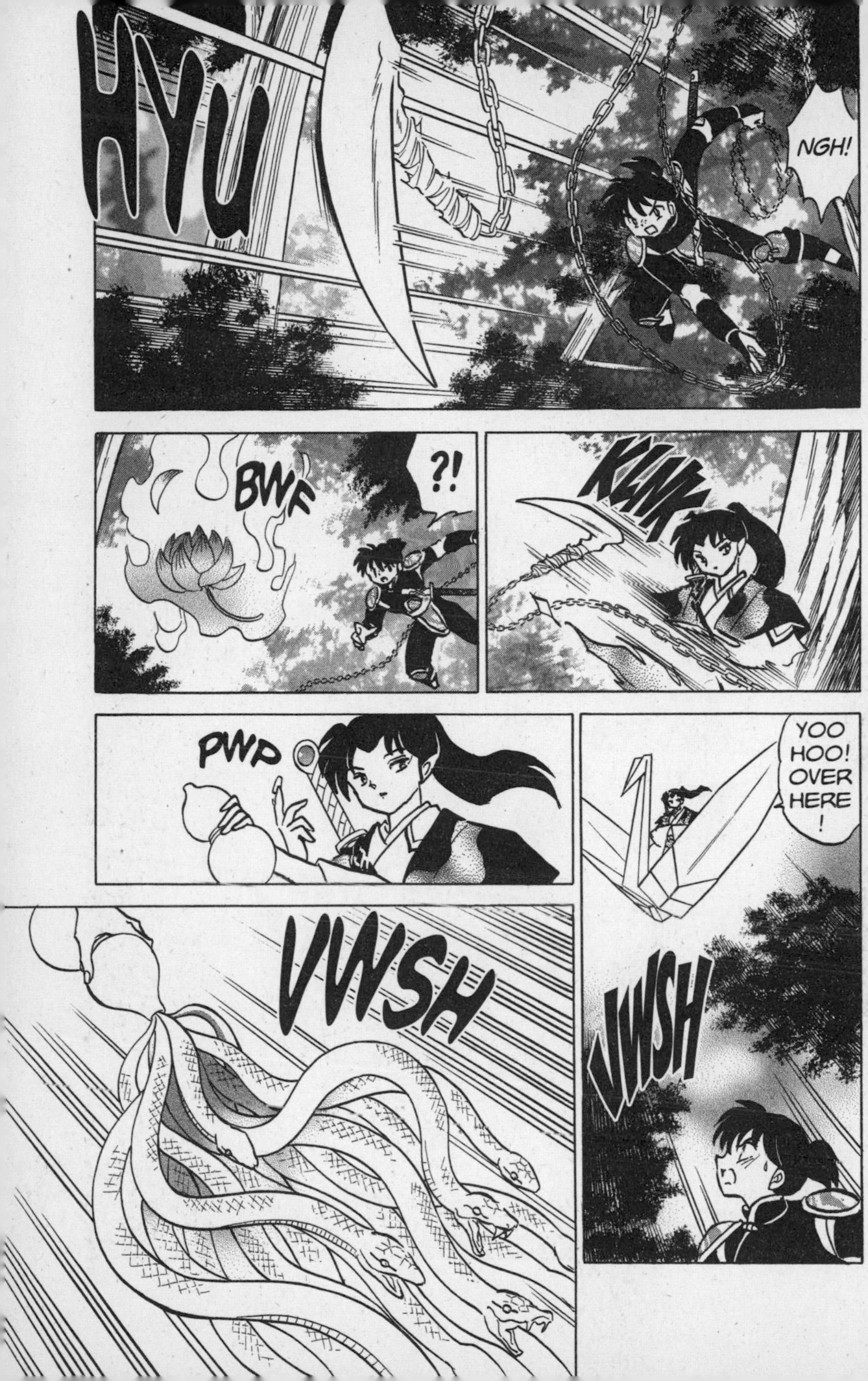
NGH!
HYU
KLINK
?!
BWF
YOO HOO! OVER HERE!
PWP
JWSH
VWSH

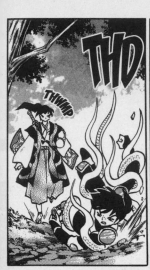

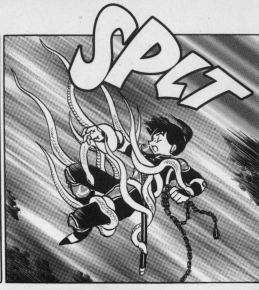

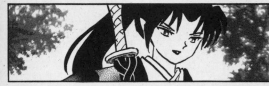

SPLIT
THD
THWMP
NOW, SHALL WE GET GOING?
BACK TO NARAKU, I MEAN.
NRRG
KOHAKU!

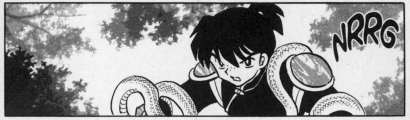

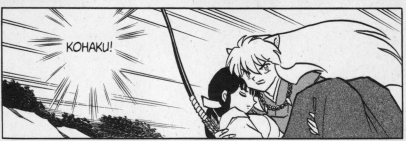

SCROLL 8
MOUNT AZUSA

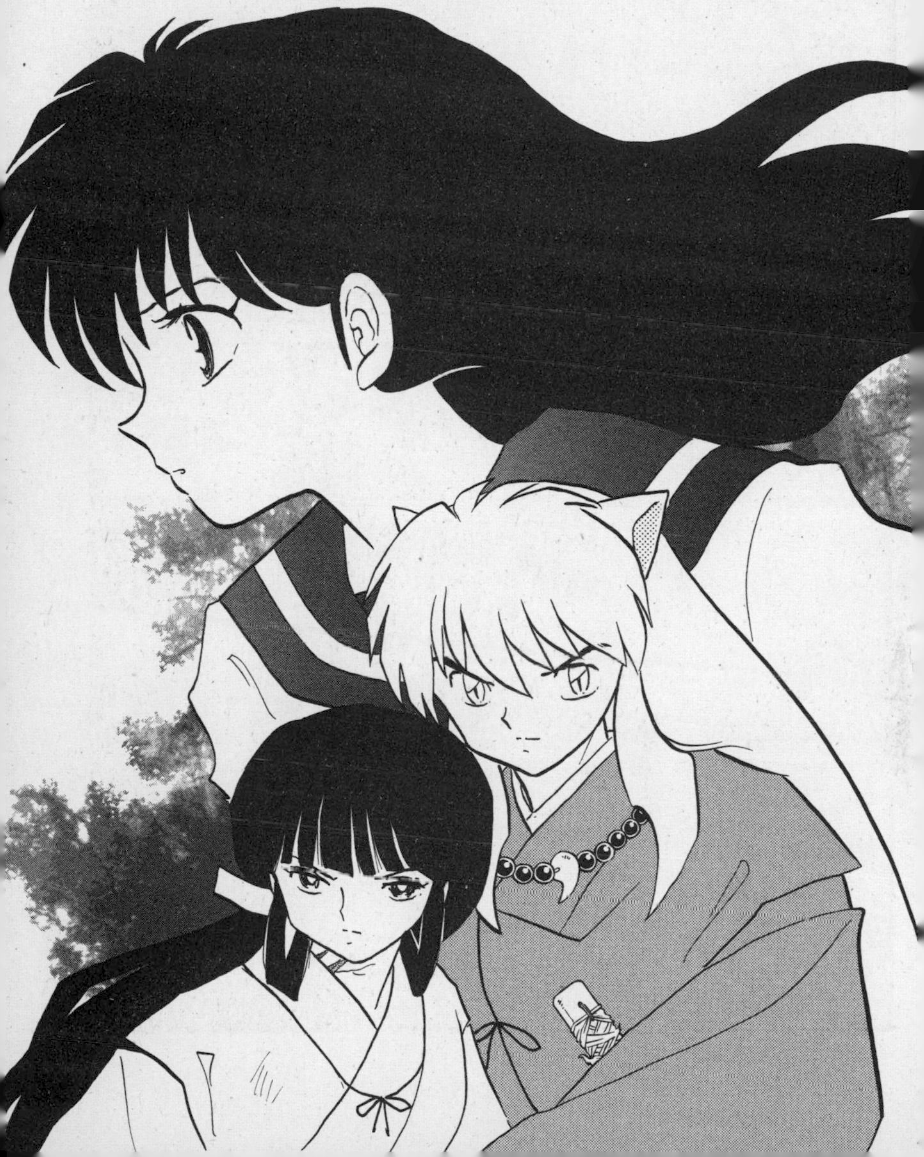

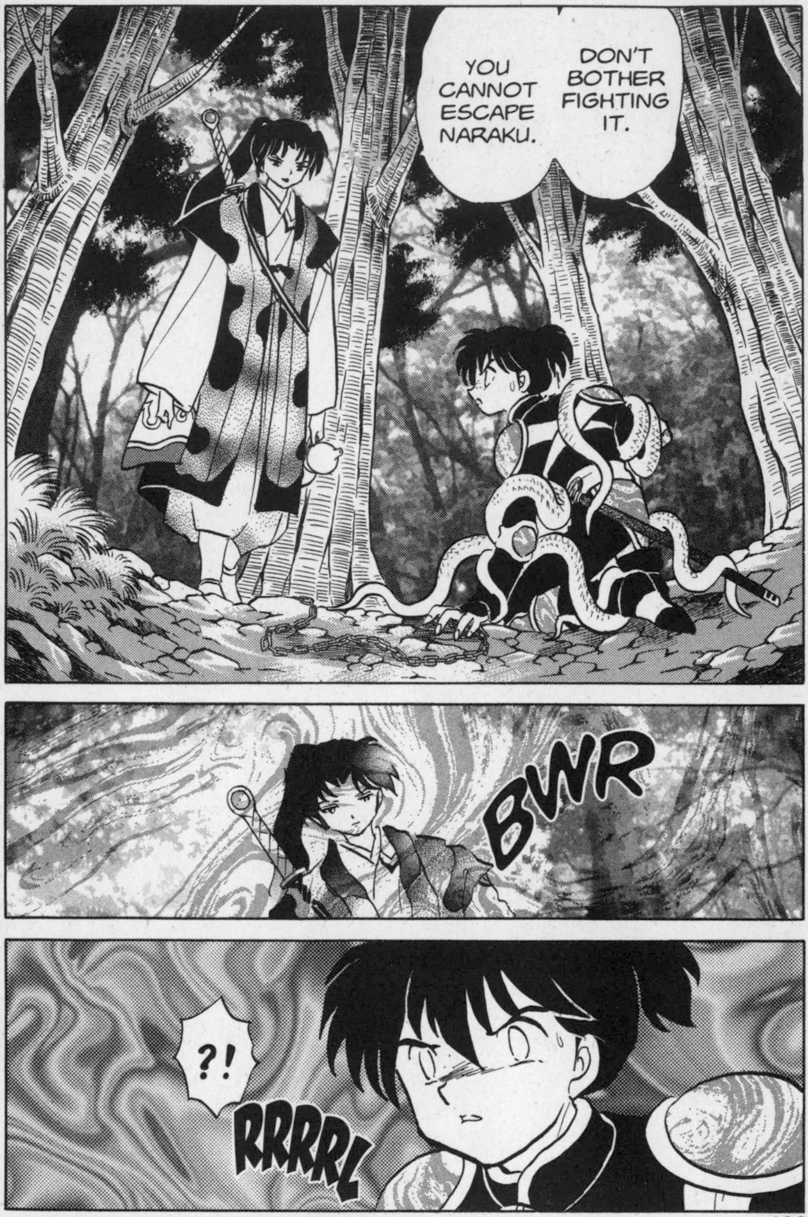
DON'T BOTHER FIGHTING IT.
YOU CANNOT ESCAPE NARAKU.
BWR
?!
RRRRL

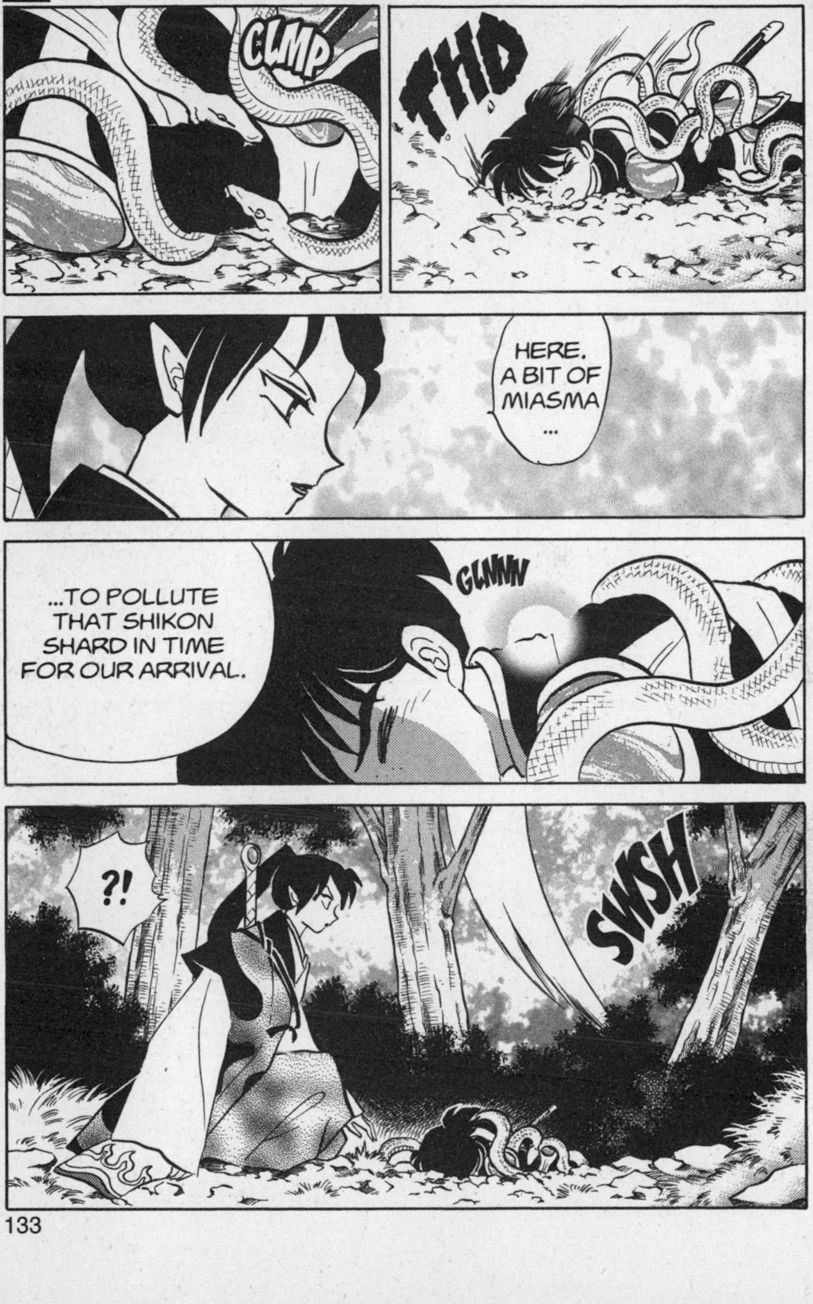
THD
CLMP
HERE. A BIT OF MIASMA ...
GLNNN
...TO POLLUTE THAT SHIKON SHARD IN TIME FOR OUR ARRIVAL.
SWSH
?!

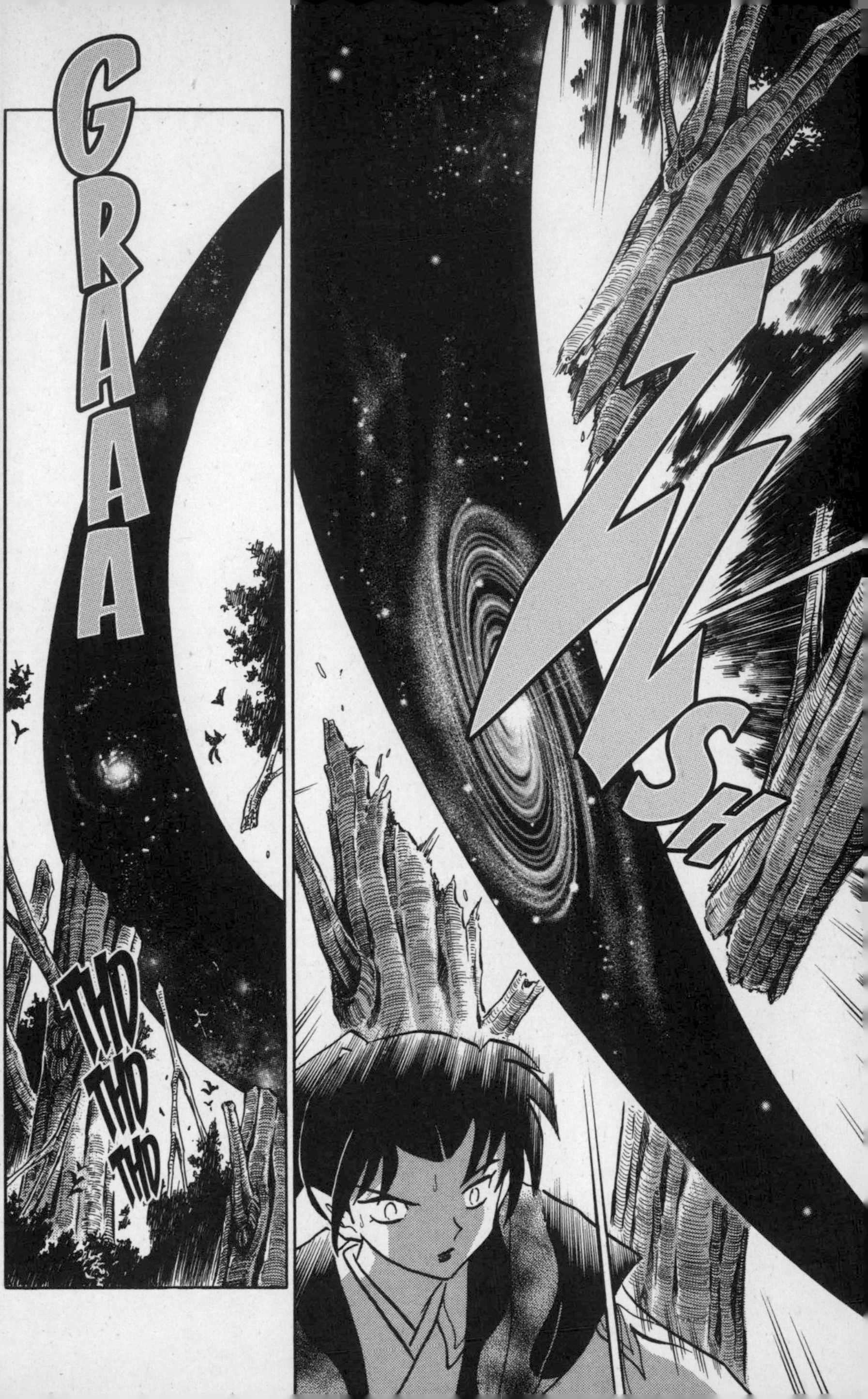
ZZSH
GRAAA
THD THD THD

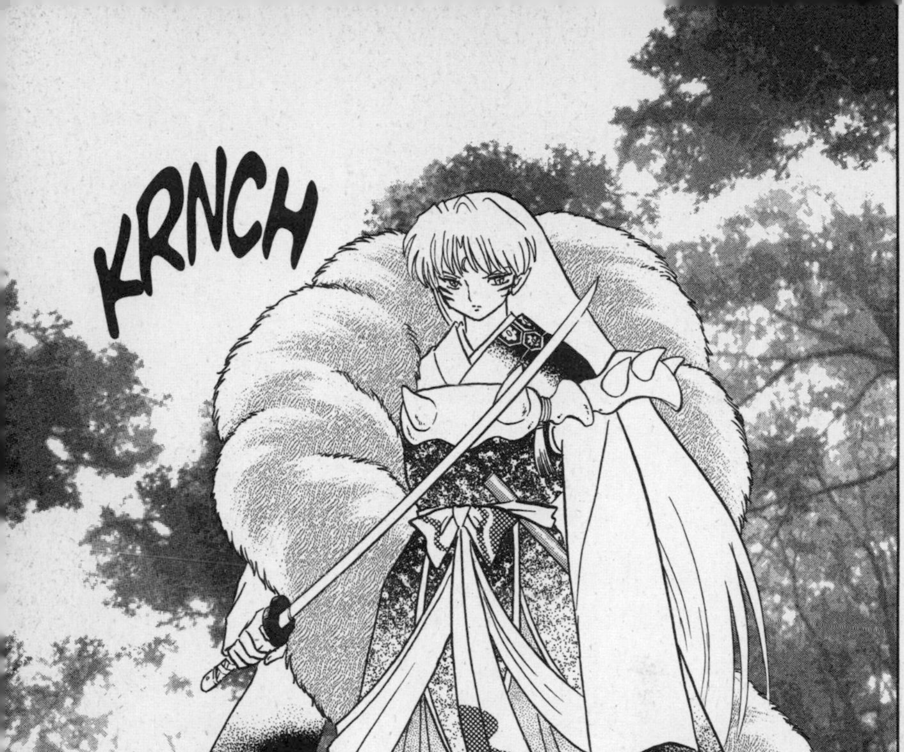
KRNCH

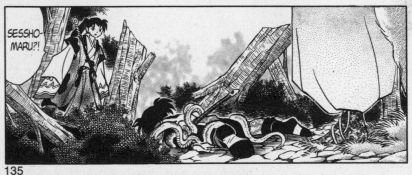

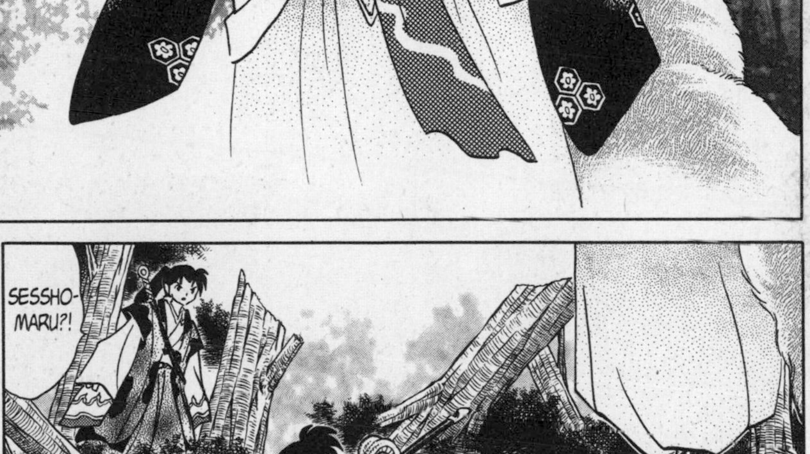
SESSHO-
MARU?!

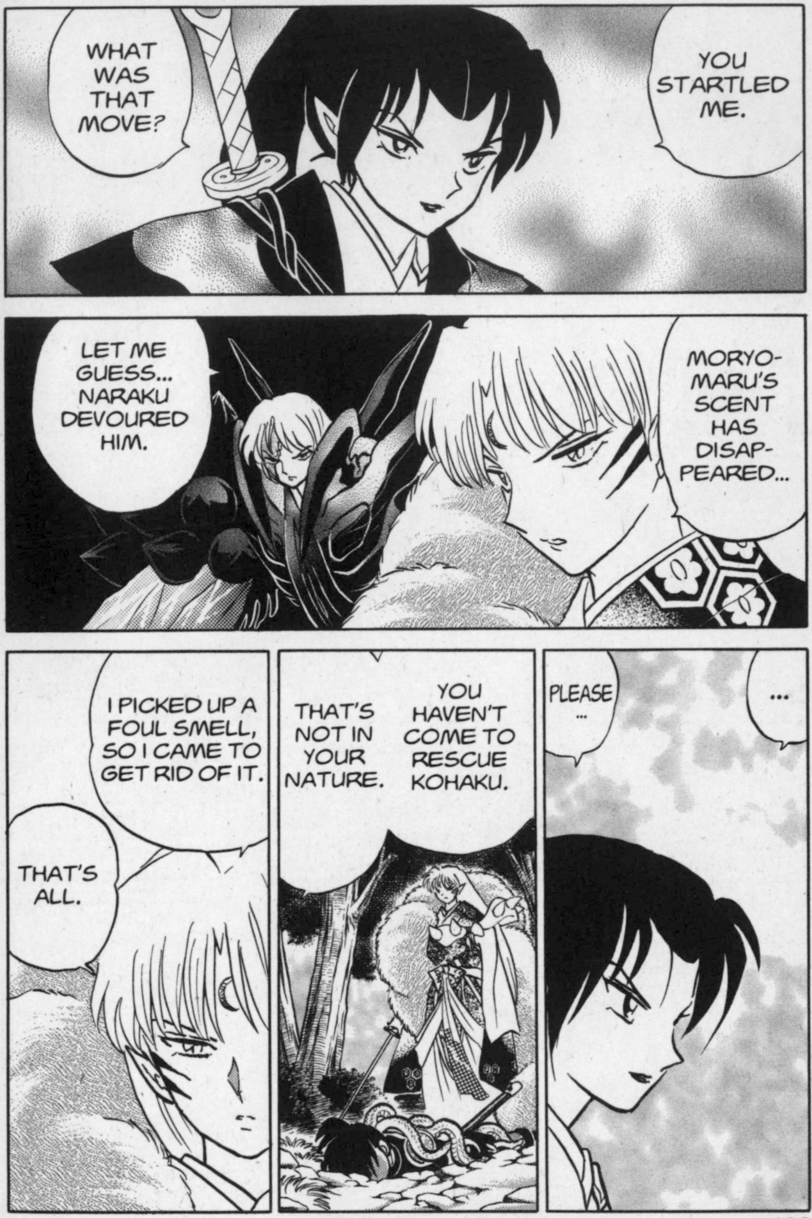
YOU STARTLED ME.
WHAT WAS THAT MOVE?
MORYO-MARU'S SCENT HAS DISAP-PEARED...
LET ME GUESS... NARAKU DEVOURED HIM.
...
PLEASE...
YOU HAVEN'T COME TO RESCUE KOHAKU.
THAT'S NOT IN YOUR NATURE.
I PICKED UP A FOUL SMELL, SO I CAME TO GET RID OF IT.
THAT'S ALL.

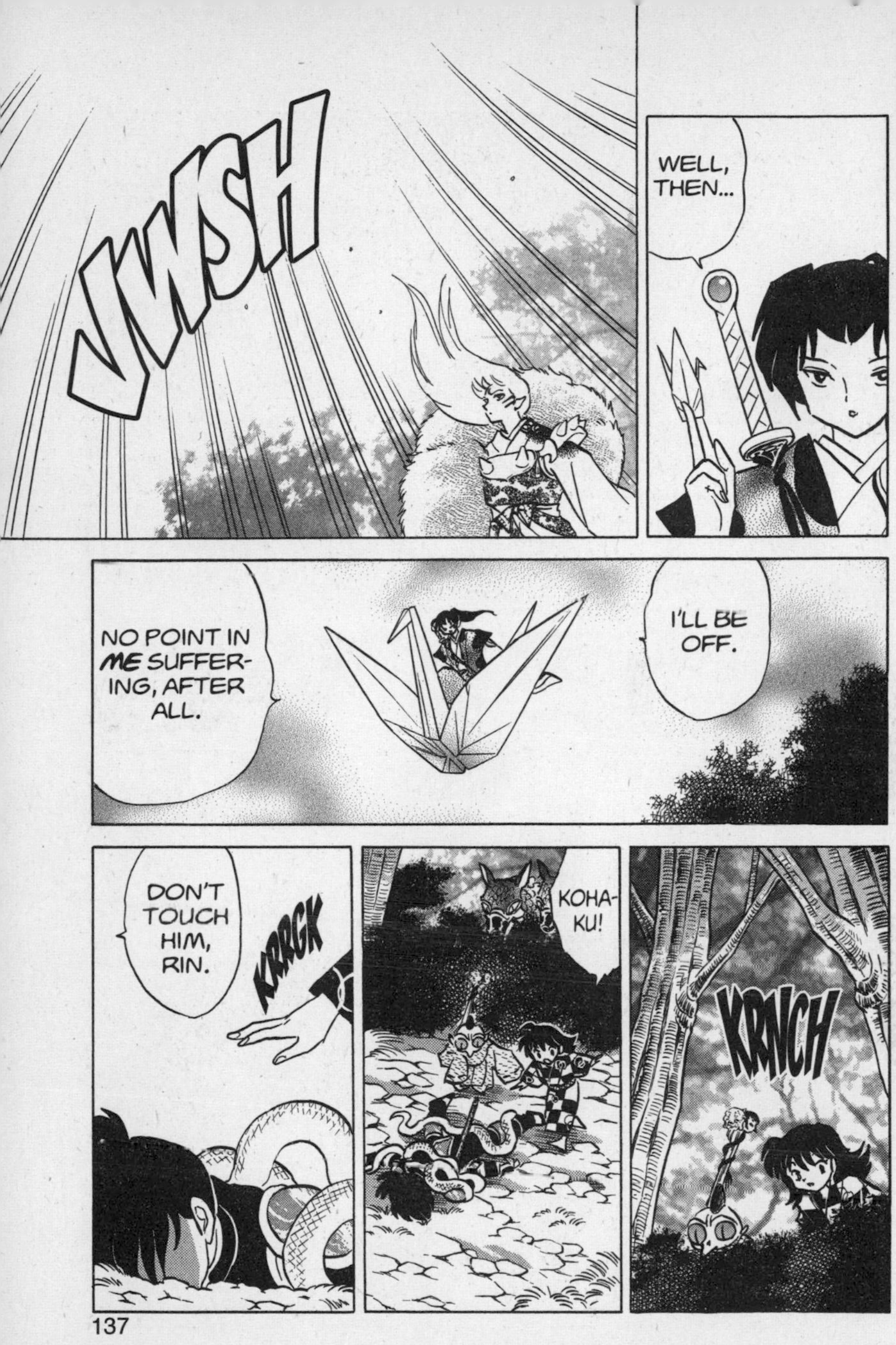
WELL, THEN...
VWSH
I'LL BE OFF.
NO POINT IN ME SUFFERING, AFTER ALL.
KRNCH
KOHA-KU!
DON'T TOUCH HIM, RIN.
KRRGK

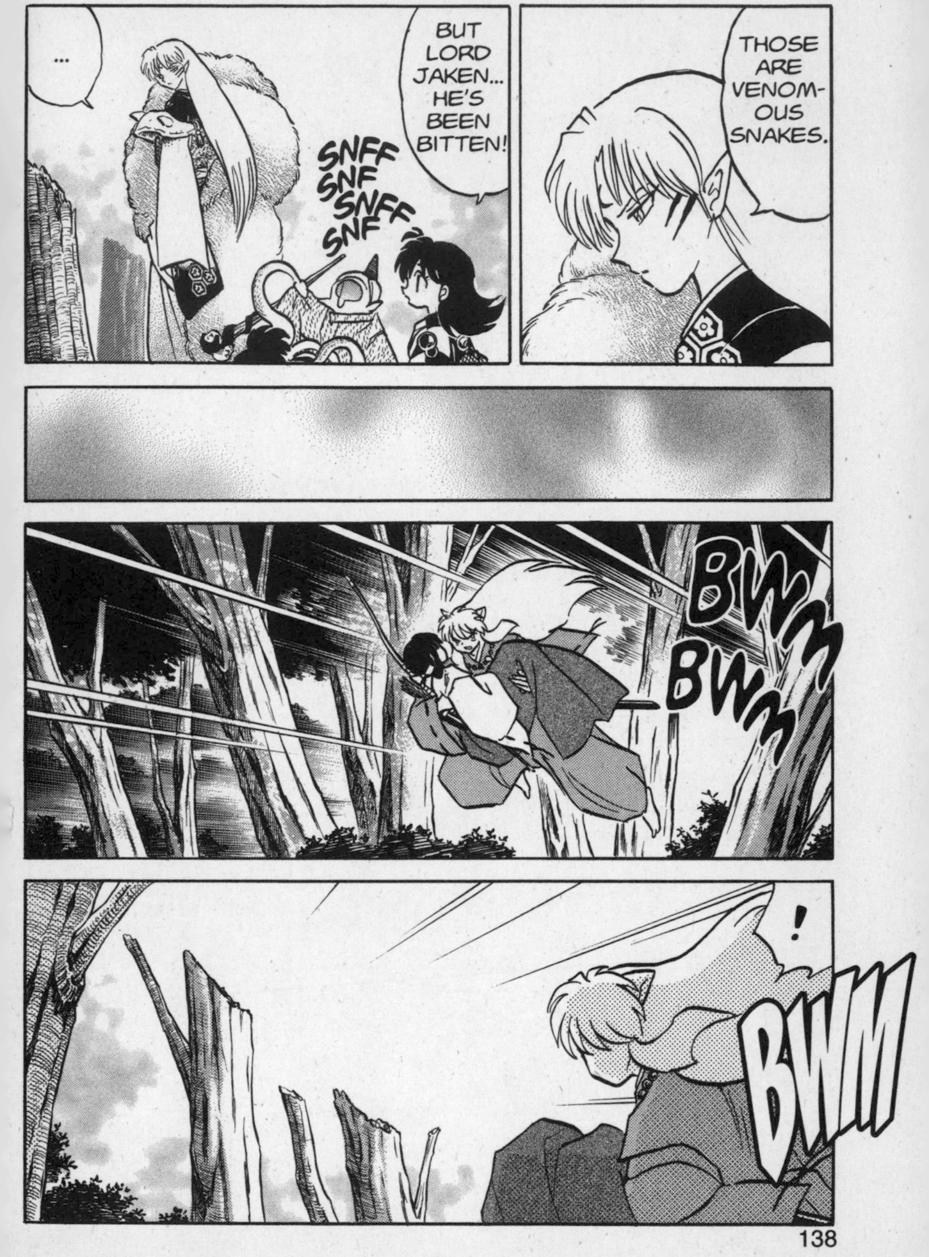

THOSE ARE VENOMOUS SNAKES.
BUT LORD JAKEN... HE'S BEEN BITTEN!
...
SNFF SNF SNFF SNF
BWM BWM
!
BWM

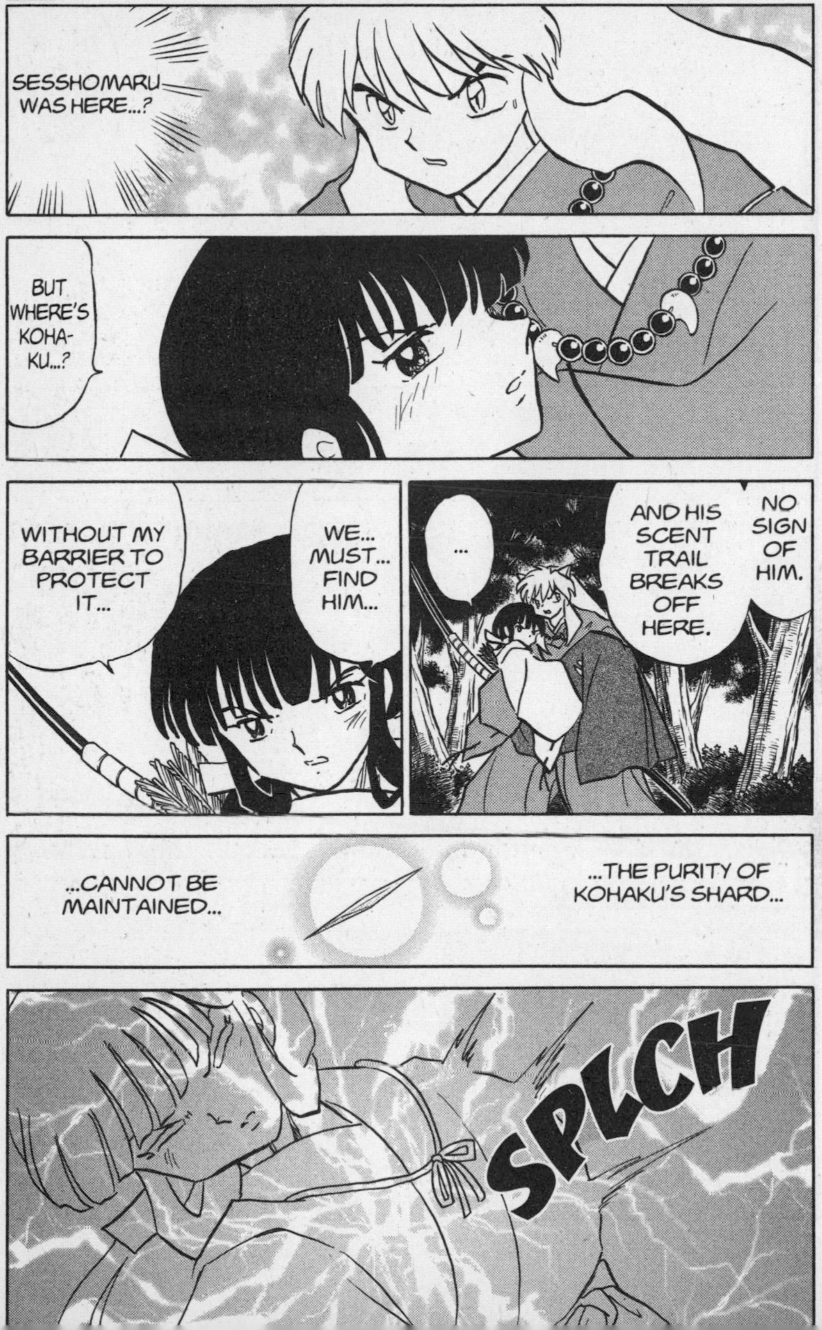
SESSHOMARU WAS HERE...?
BUT WHERE'S KOHAKU...?
NO SIGN OF HIM.
AND HIS SCENT TRAIL BREAKS OFF HERE.
...
WE... MUST... FIND HIM...
WITHOUT MY BARRIER TO PROTECT IT...
...THE PURITY OF KOHAKU'S SHARD...
...CANNOT BE MAINTAINED...
SPLCH

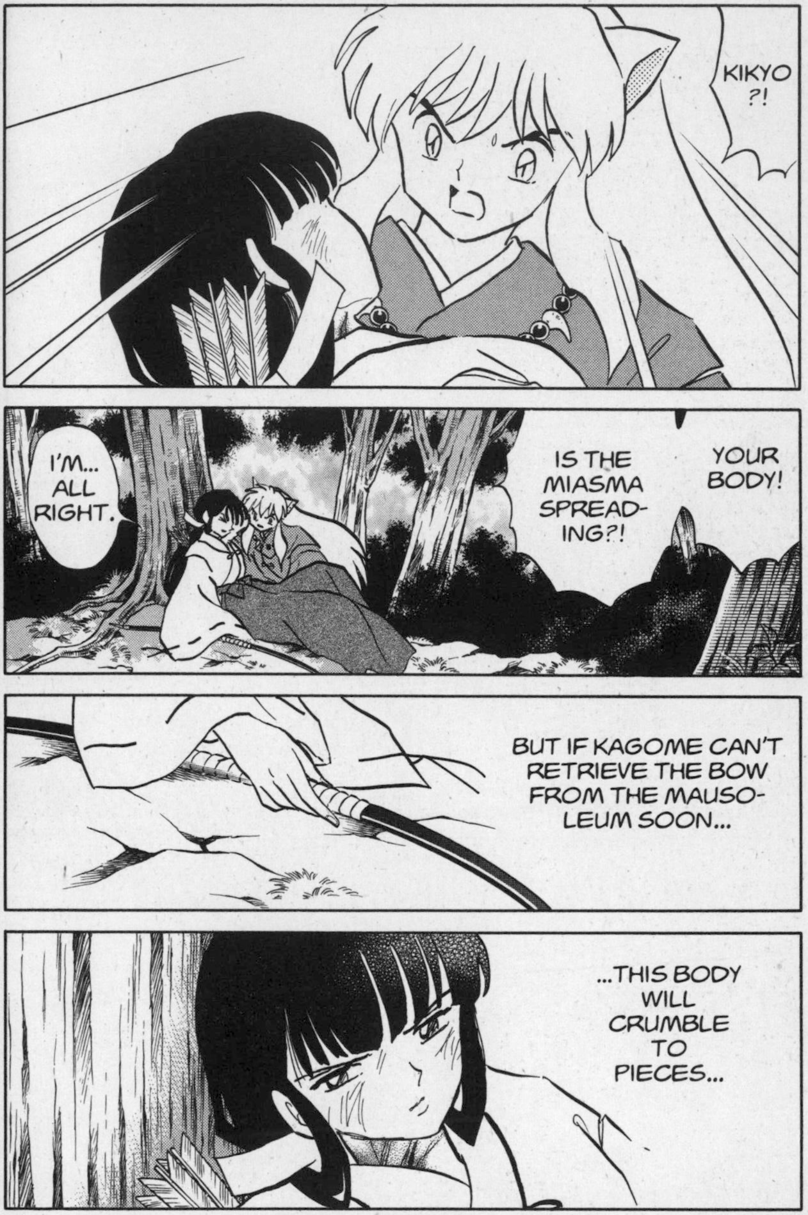
KIKYO ?!
YOUR BODY!
IS THE MIASMA SPREAD-ING?!
I'M... ALL RIGHT.
BUT IF KAGOME CAN'T RETRIEVE THE BOW FROM THE MAUSO-LEUM SOON...
...THIS BODY WILL CRUMBLE TO PIECES...

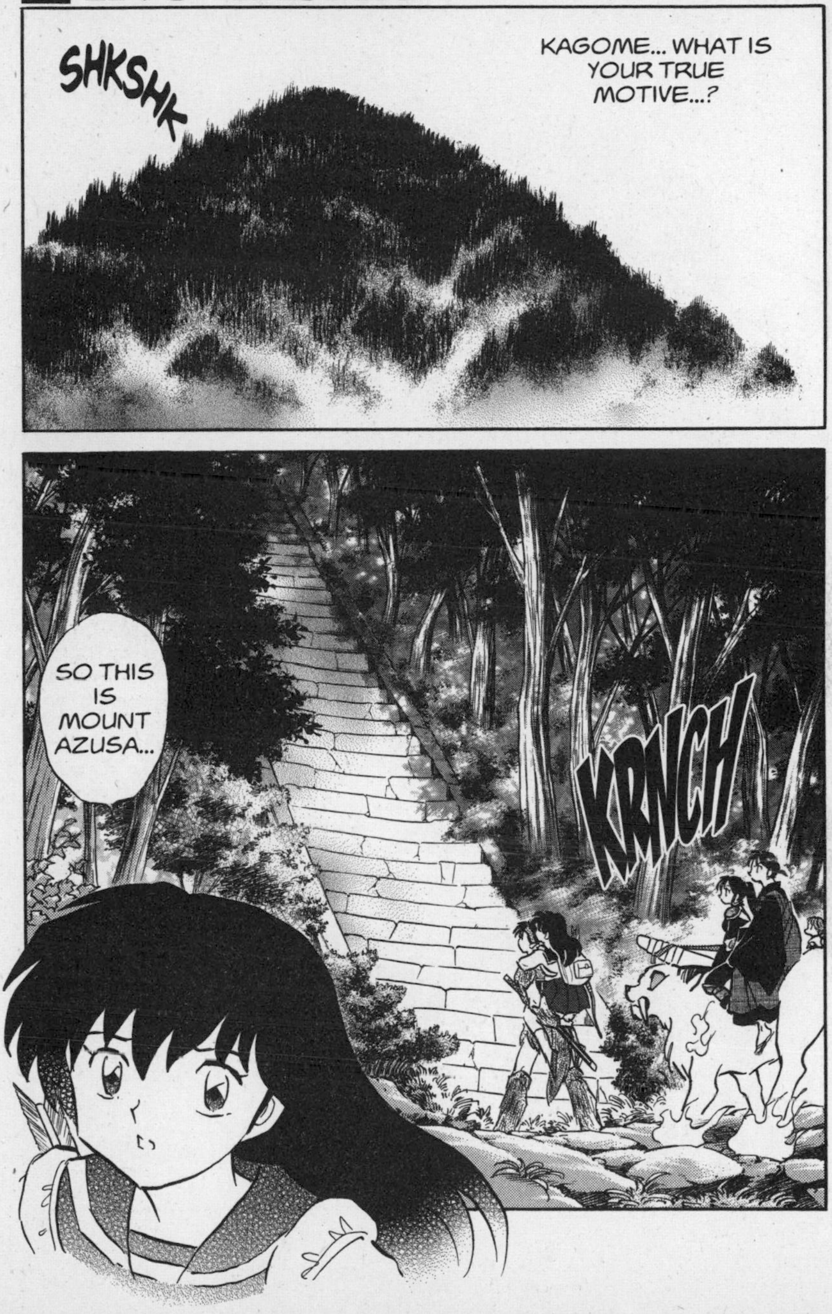
KAGOME... WHAT IS YOUR TRUE MOTIVE...?
SHKSHK
KRNCH
SO THIS IS MOUNT AZUSA...

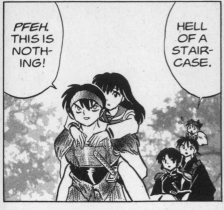

HWOOOO
HELL OF A STAIRCASE.
PFEH. THIS IS NOTHING!
LOOM
THAT'S GOT TO BE THE MAUSOLEUM.
ALL RIGHT THEN!
LET'S GO!
TMP

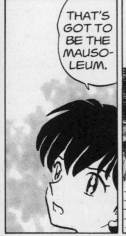

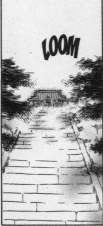

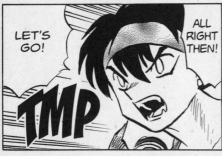

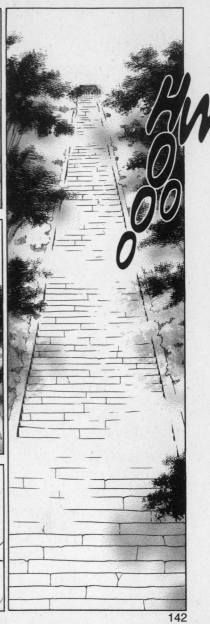

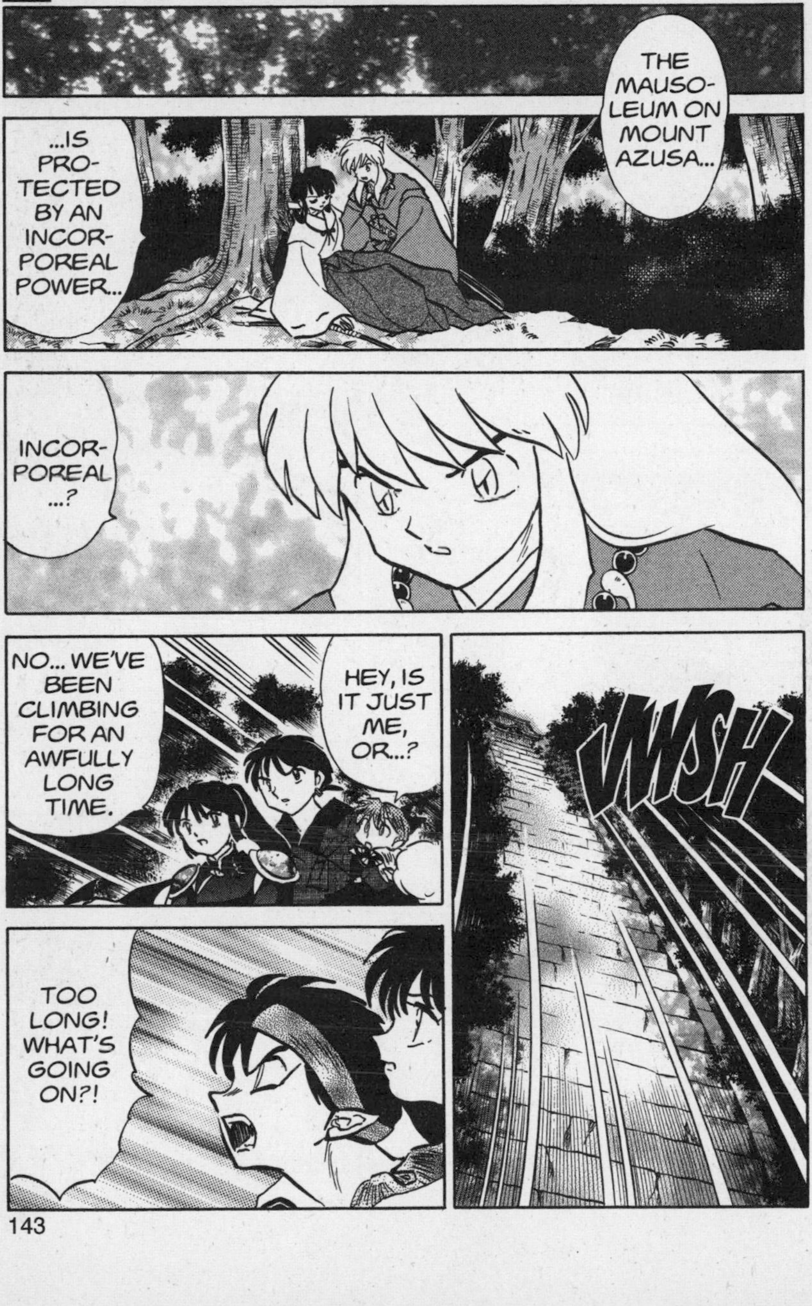
THE MAUSOLEUM ON MOUNT AZUSA...
...IS PROTECTED BY AN INCORPOREAL POWER...
INCORPOREAL...?
VWISH
HEY, IS IT JUST ME, OR...?
NO... WE'VE BEEN CLIMBING FOR AN AWFULLY LONG TIME.
TOO LONG! WHAT'S GOING ON?!

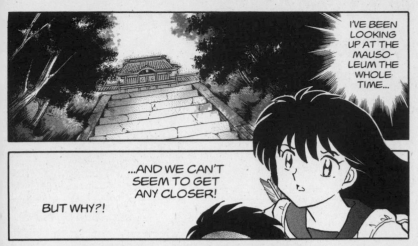

I'VE BEEN LOOKING UP AT THE MAUSOLEUM THE WHOLE TIME...
...AND WE CAN'T SEEM TO GET ANY CLOSER!
BUT WHY?!
...IF YOU DO NOT TRULY WISH TO HEAL ME...
!
IS IT...*MY* FAULT?!
AM I WAVERING? UNSURE?
I MEAN, OF COURSE MY FEELINGS HAVE BEEN HURT...
...AND I'VE GOTTEN MAD AT HER...
...BUT ISN'T THAT NORMAL?!
I'M NOT A SAINT!

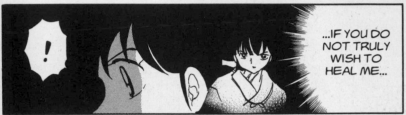

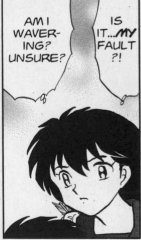

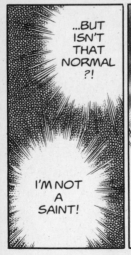

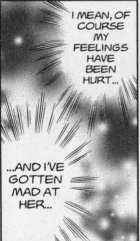

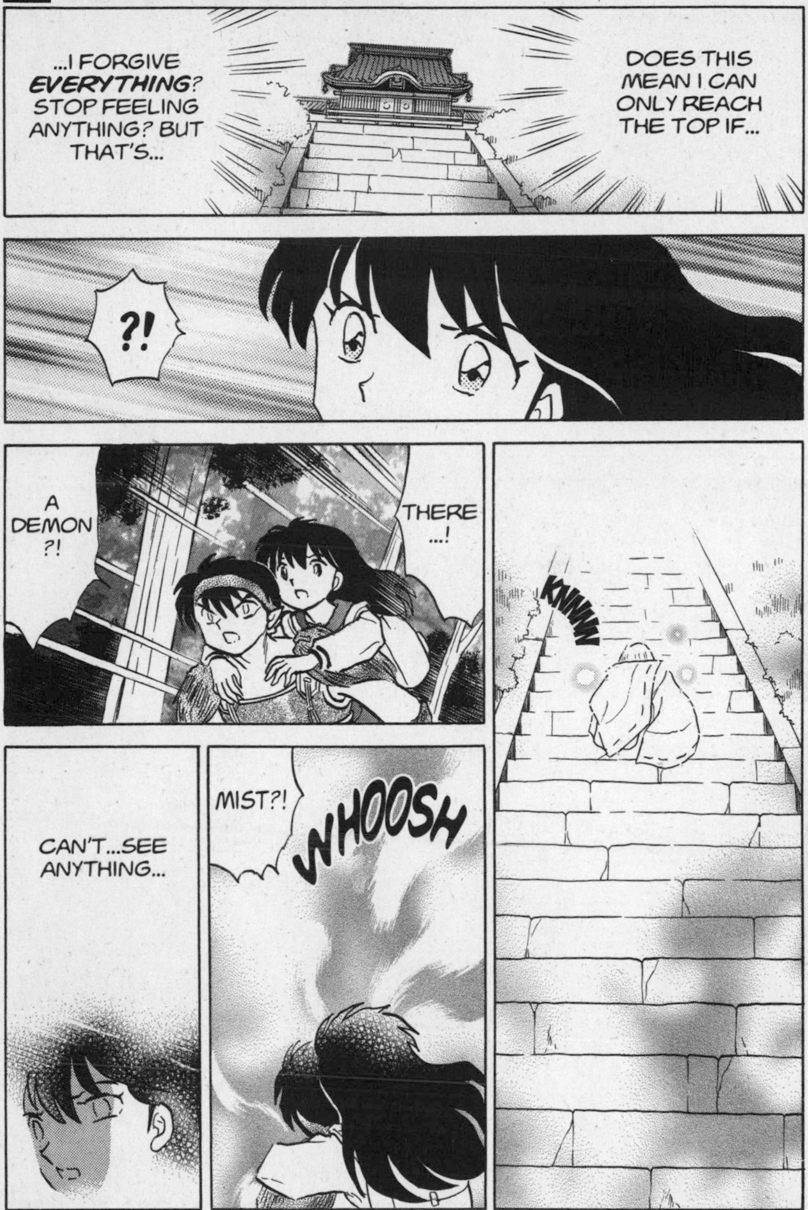
DOES THIS MEAN I CAN ONLY REACH THE TOP IF...
...I FORGIVE *EVERYTHING*? STOP FEELING ANYTHING? BUT THAT'S...
?!
KNNWW
THERE ...!
A DEMON ?!
MIST?!
WHOOSH
CAN'T...SEE ANYTHING...

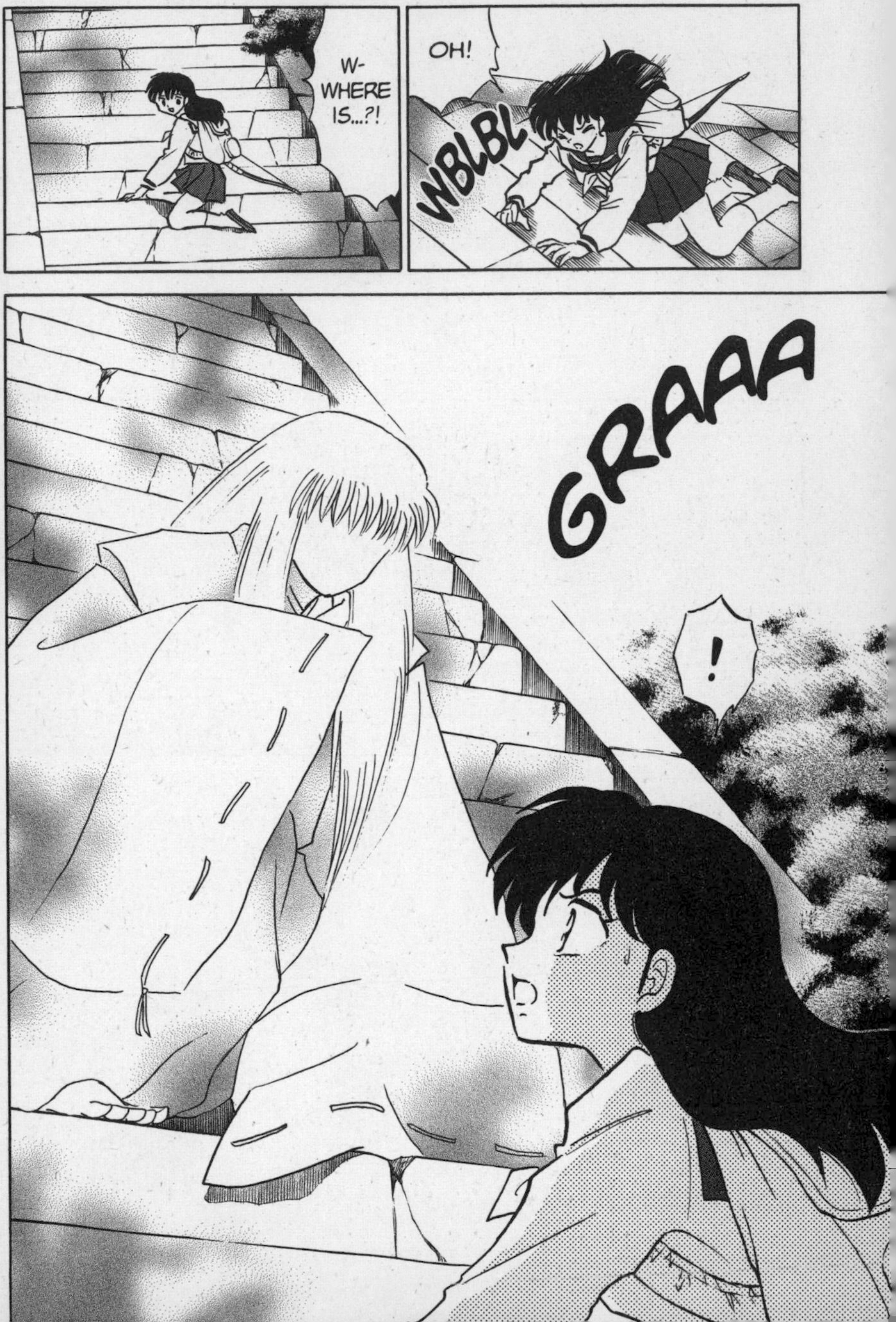
OH!
WBLBL
W-
WHERE
IS...?!
GRAAA
!

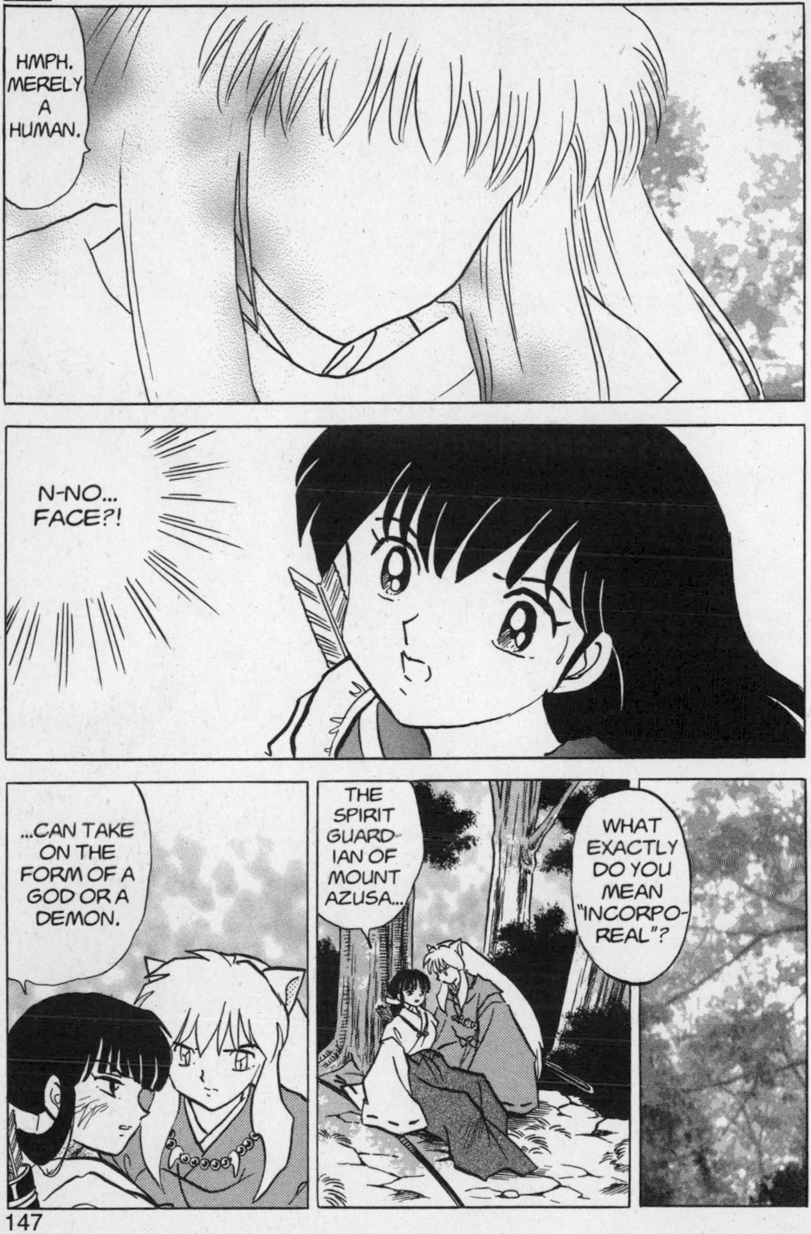
HMPH. MERELY A HUMAN.
N-NO... FACE?!
WHAT EXACTLY DO YOU MEAN "INCORPOREAL"?
THE SPIRIT GUARDIAN OF MOUNT AZUSA...
...CAN TAKE ON THE FORM OF A GOD OR A DEMON.

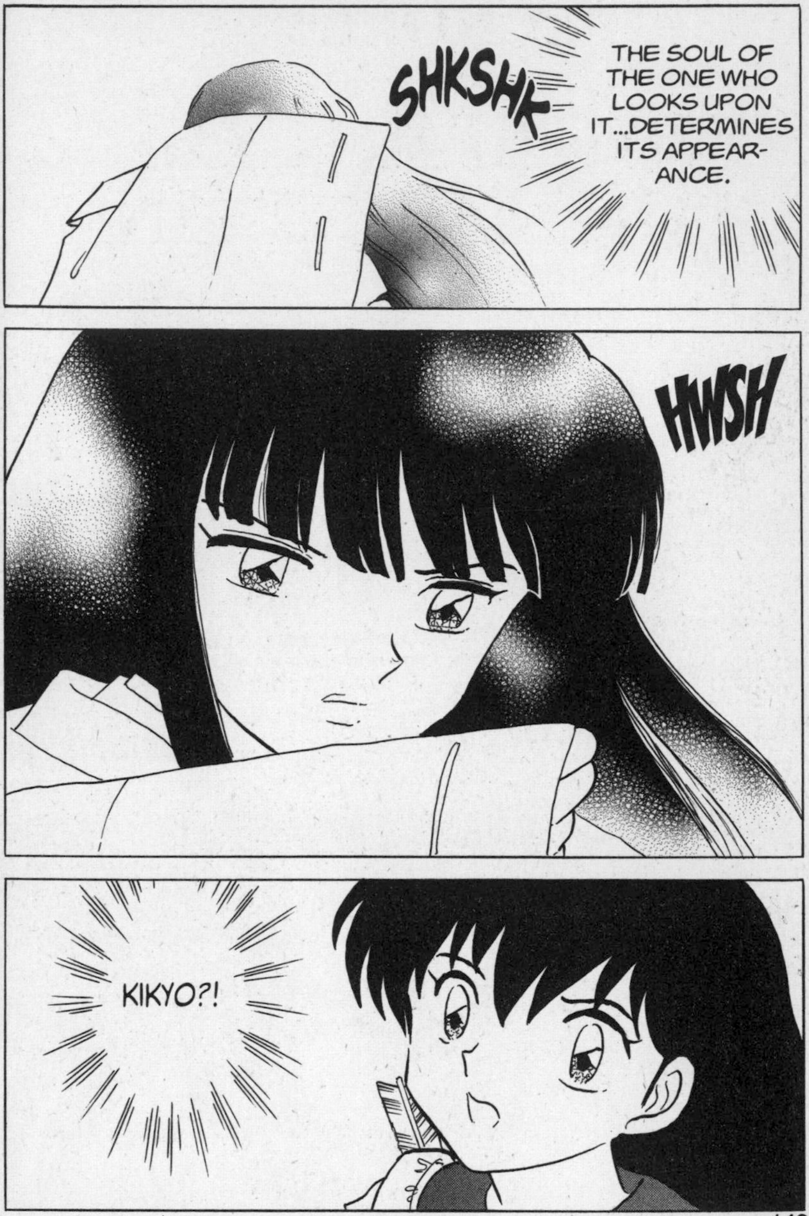
SHKSHK
THE SOUL OF THE ONE WHO LOOKS UPON IT...DETERMINES ITS APPEAR-ANCE.
HWSH
KIKYO?!

SCROLL 9

THE SPIRIT OF THE MOUNTAIN

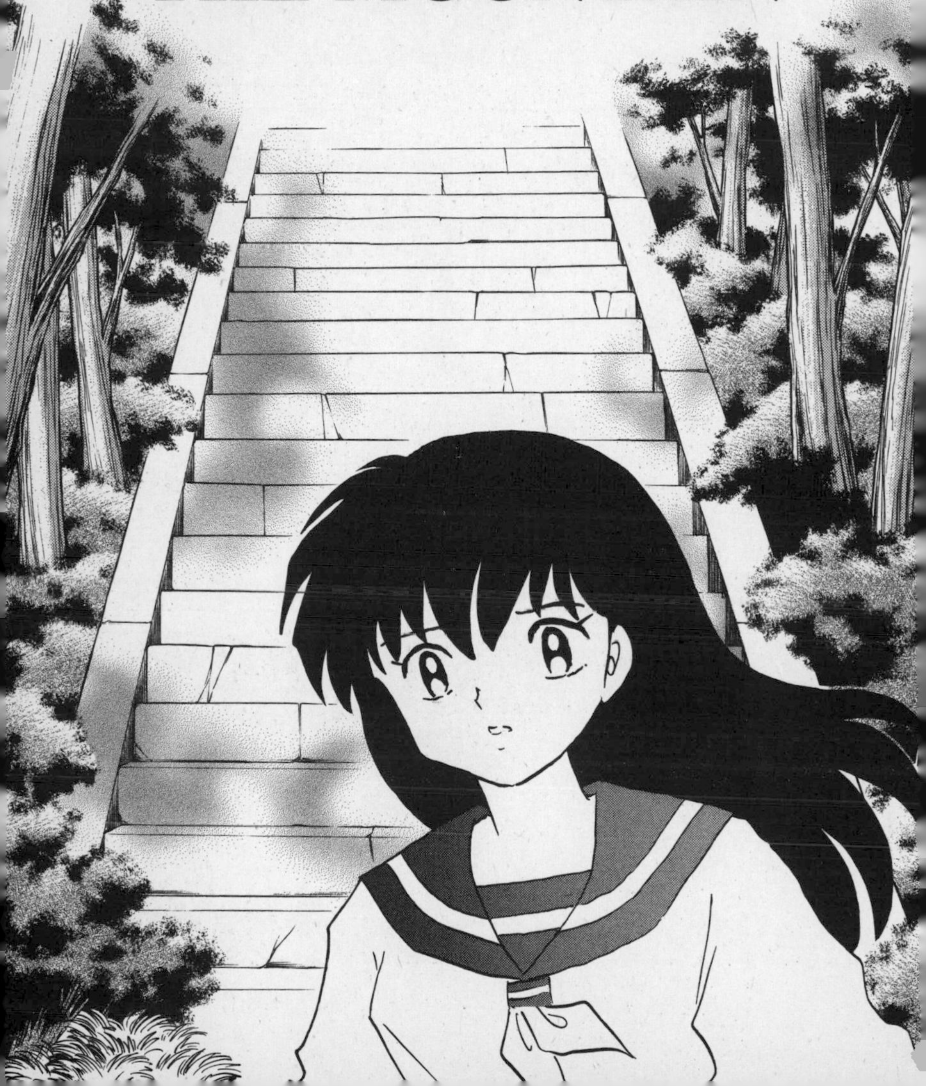

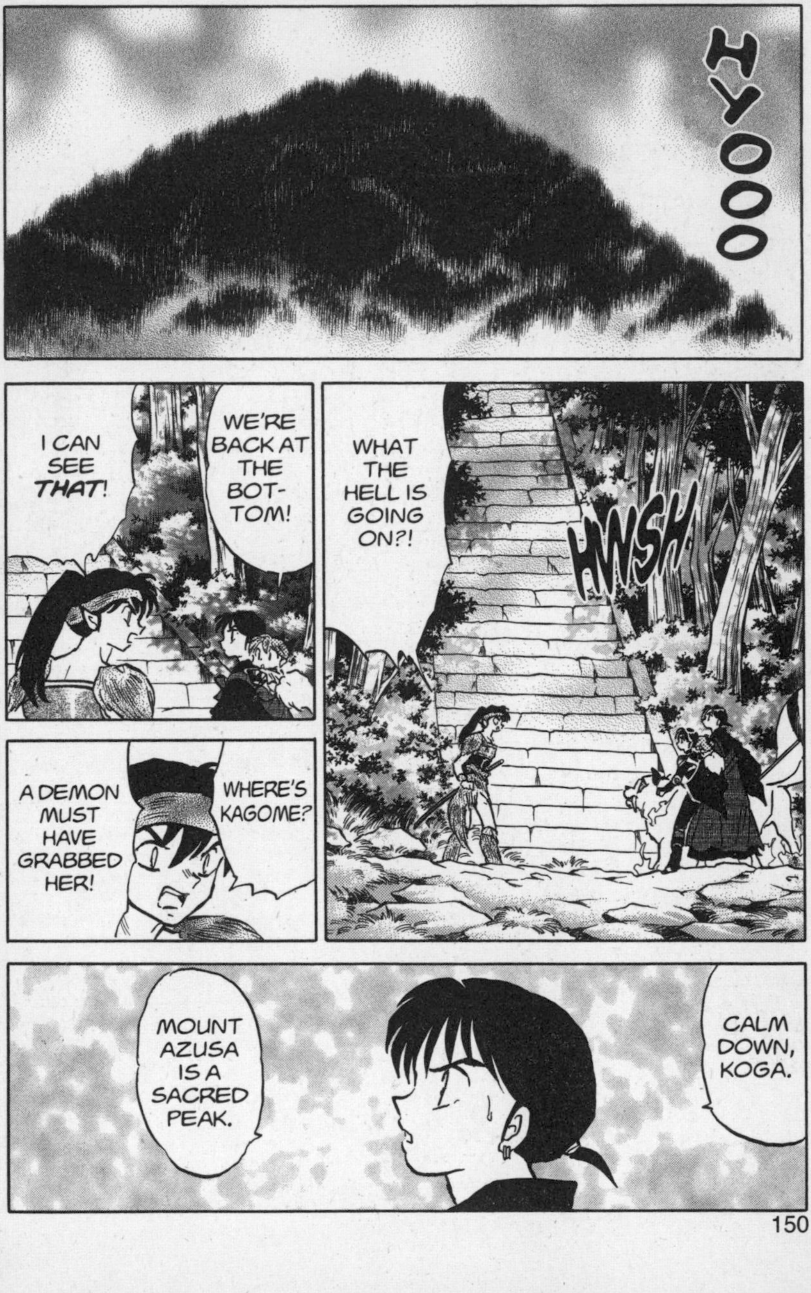
HYOOO
WHAT THE HELL IS GOING ON?!
HWSH
WE'RE BACK AT THE BOT-TOM!
I CAN SEE *THAT*!
WHERE'S KAGOME?
A DEMON MUST HAVE GRABBED HER!
CALM DOWN, KOGA.
MOUNT AZUSA IS A SACRED PEAK.

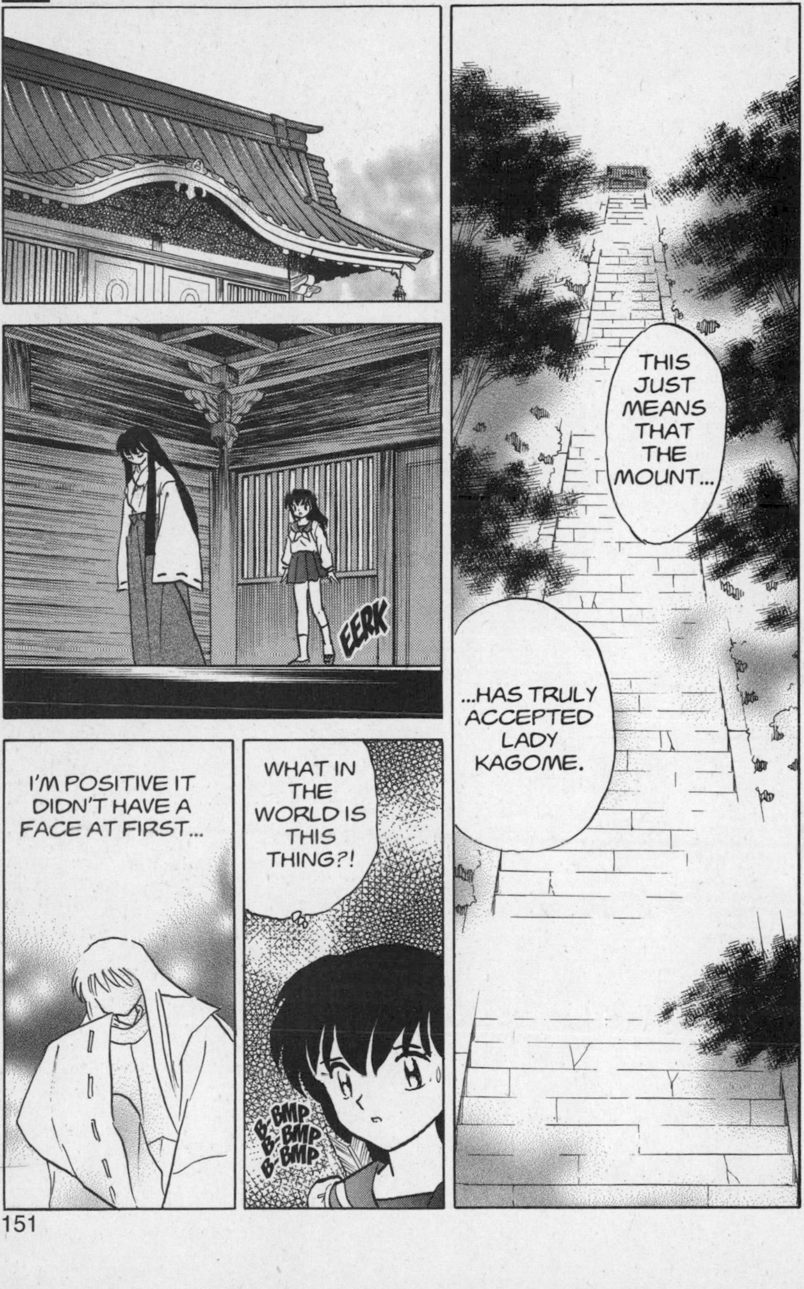
THIS JUST MEANS THAT THE MOUNT...
...HAS TRULY ACCEPTED LADY KAGOME.
EERK
WHAT IN THE WORLD IS THIS THING?!
B-BMP B-BMP B-BMP
I'M POSITIVE IT DIDN'T HAVE A FACE AT FIRST...

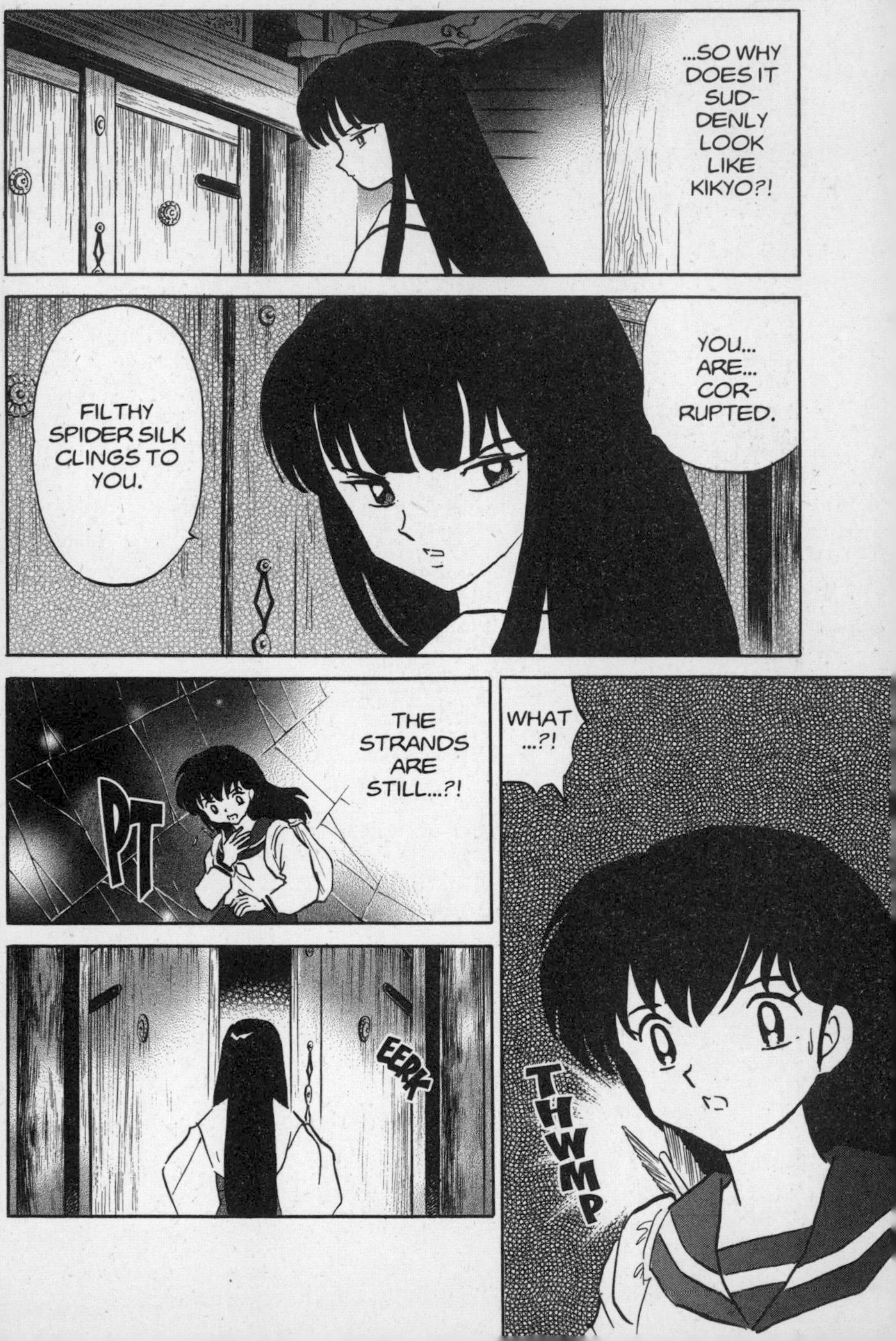
...SO WHY DOES IT SUD-DENLY LOOK LIKE KIKYO?!
YOU... ARE... COR-RUPTED.
FILTHY SPIDER SILK CLINGS TO YOU.
WHAT ...?!
THWMP
THE STRANDS ARE STILL...?!
PT
EERK

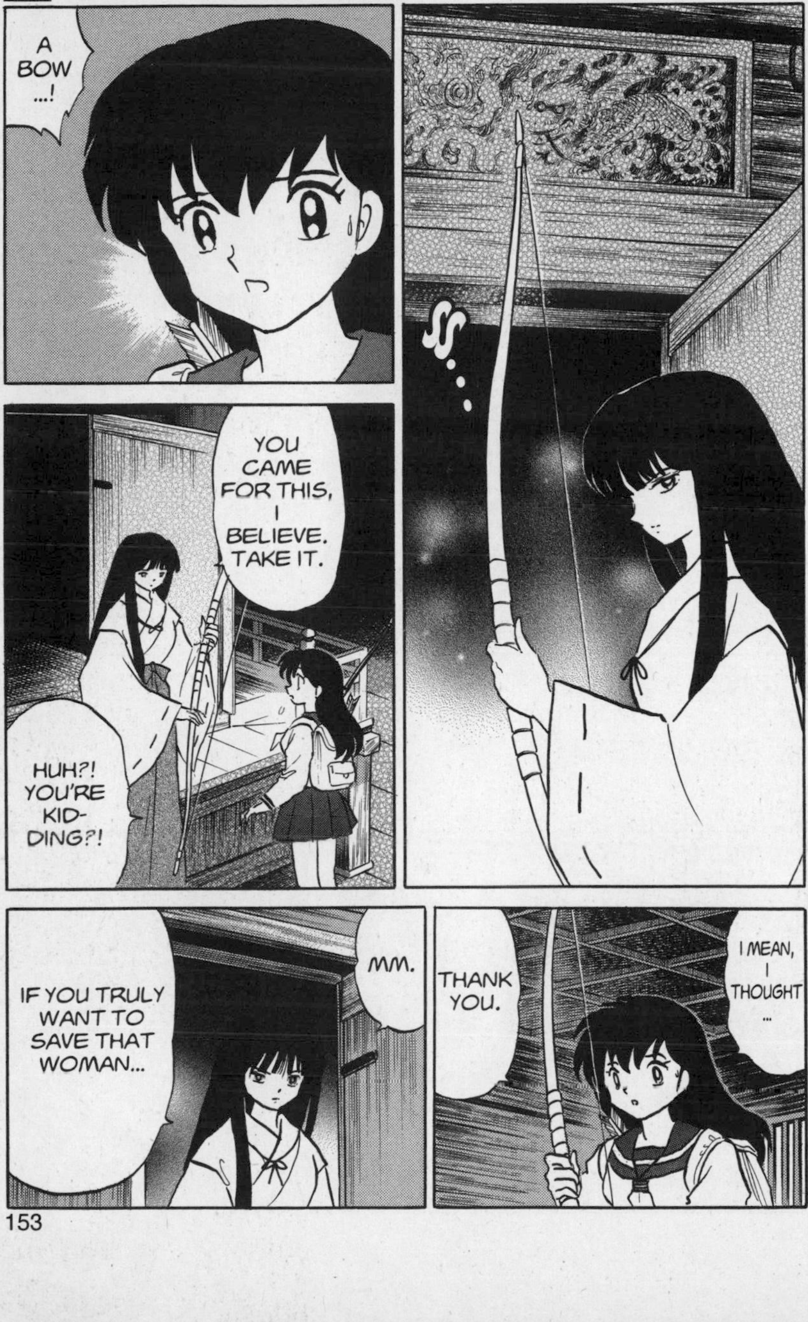
A BOW ...!
YOU CAME FOR THIS, I BELIEVE. TAKE IT.
HUH?! YOU'RE KID-DING?!
I MEAN, I THOUGHT ...
THANK YOU.
MM.
IF YOU TRULY WANT TO SAVE THAT WOMAN...

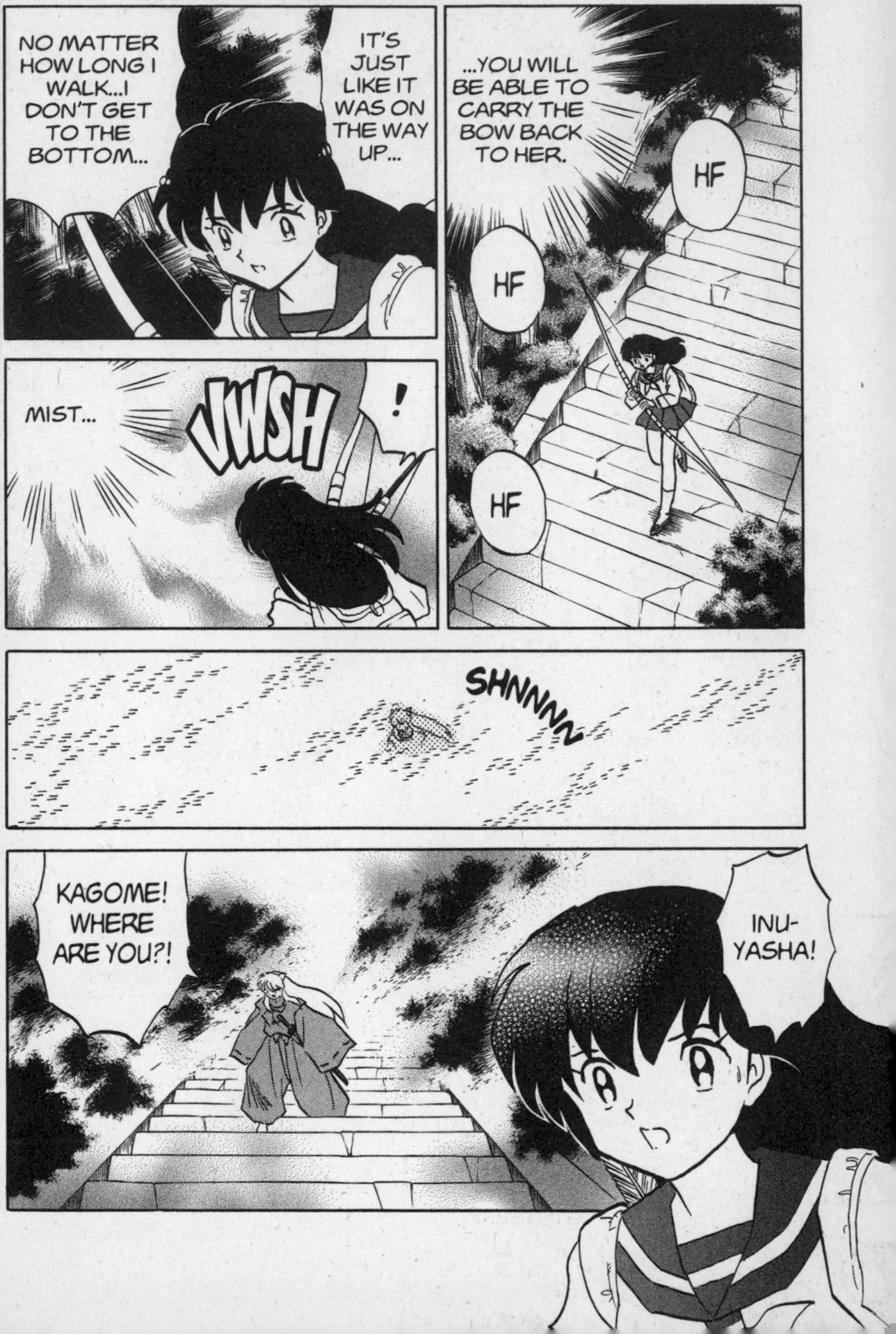
...YOU WILL BE ABLE TO CARRY THE BOW BACK TO HER.
HF
HF
HF
IT'S JUST LIKE IT WAS ON THE WAY UP...
NO MATTER HOW LONG I WALK...I DON'T GET TO THE BOTTOM...
!
JWSH
MIST...
SHNNNN
INU-YASHA!
KAGOME! WHERE ARE YOU?!

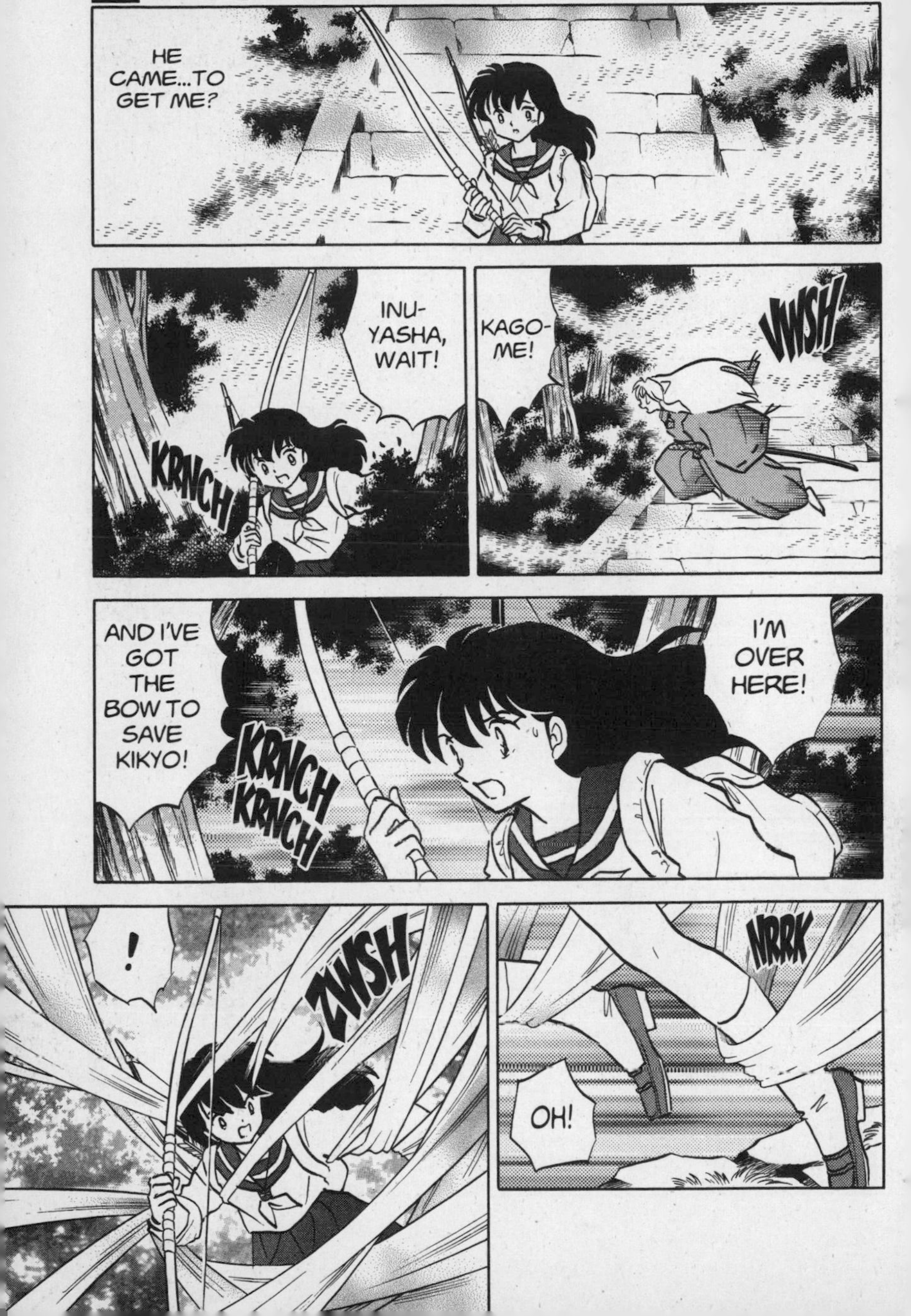
HE CAME...TO GET ME?
VWSH
KAGO-ME!
INU-YASHA, WAIT!
KRNCH
I'M OVER HERE!
AND I'VE GOT THE BOW TO SAVE KIKYO!
KRNCH KRNCH
NRRK
OH!
!
ZWSH

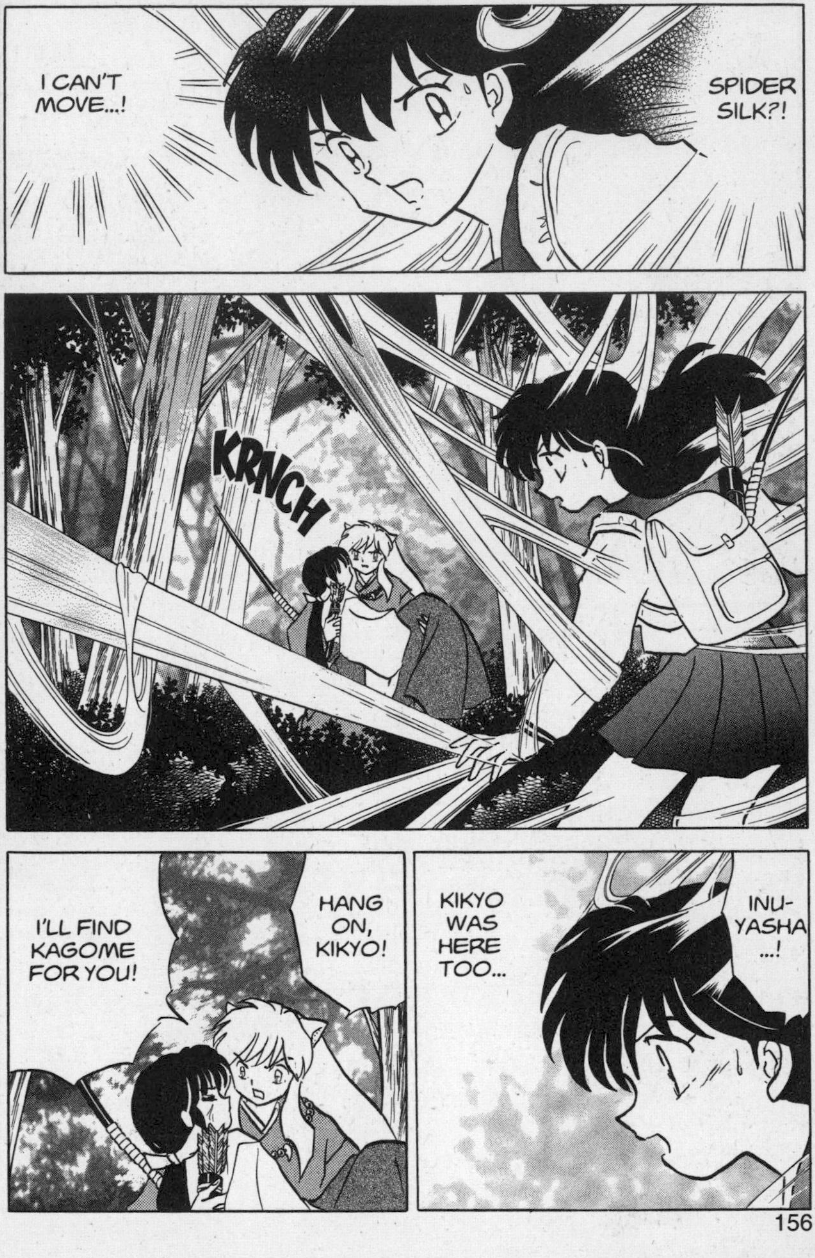
SPIDER SILK?!
I CAN'T MOVE...!
KRNCH
INU-YASHA...!
KIKYO WAS HERE TOO...
HANG ON, KIKYO!
I'LL FIND KAGOME FOR YOU!

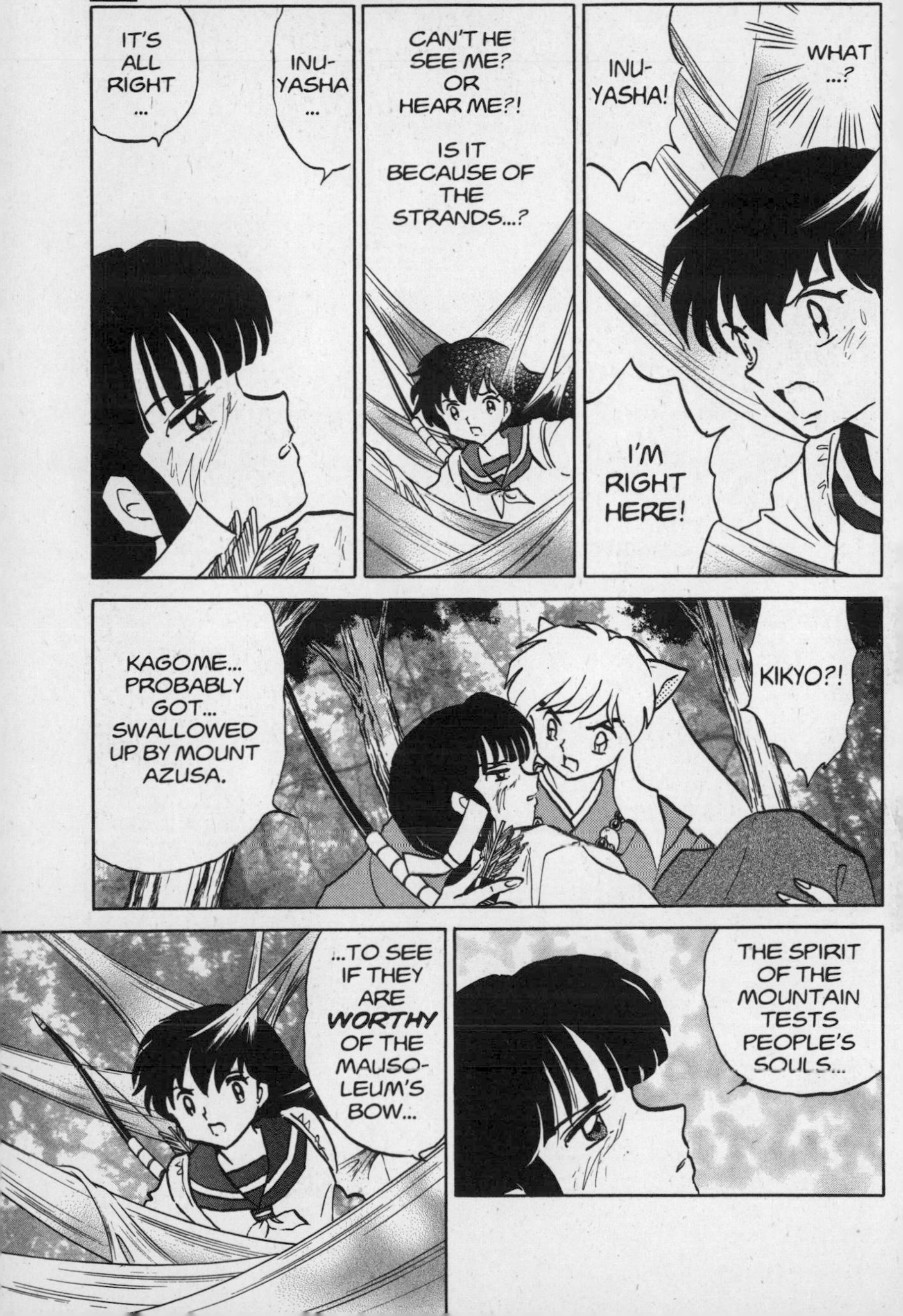
WHAT ...?
INU-YASHA!
I'M RIGHT HERE!
CAN'T HE SEE ME? OR HEAR ME?!
IS IT BECAUSE OF THE STRANDS...?
INU-YASHA ...
IT'S ALL RIGHT ...
KIKYO?!
KAGOME... PROBABLY GOT... SWALLOWED UP BY MOUNT AZUSA.
THE SPIRIT OF THE MOUNTAIN TESTS PEOPLE'S SOULS...
...TO SEE IF THEY ARE *WORTHY* OF THE MAUSOLEUM'S BOW...

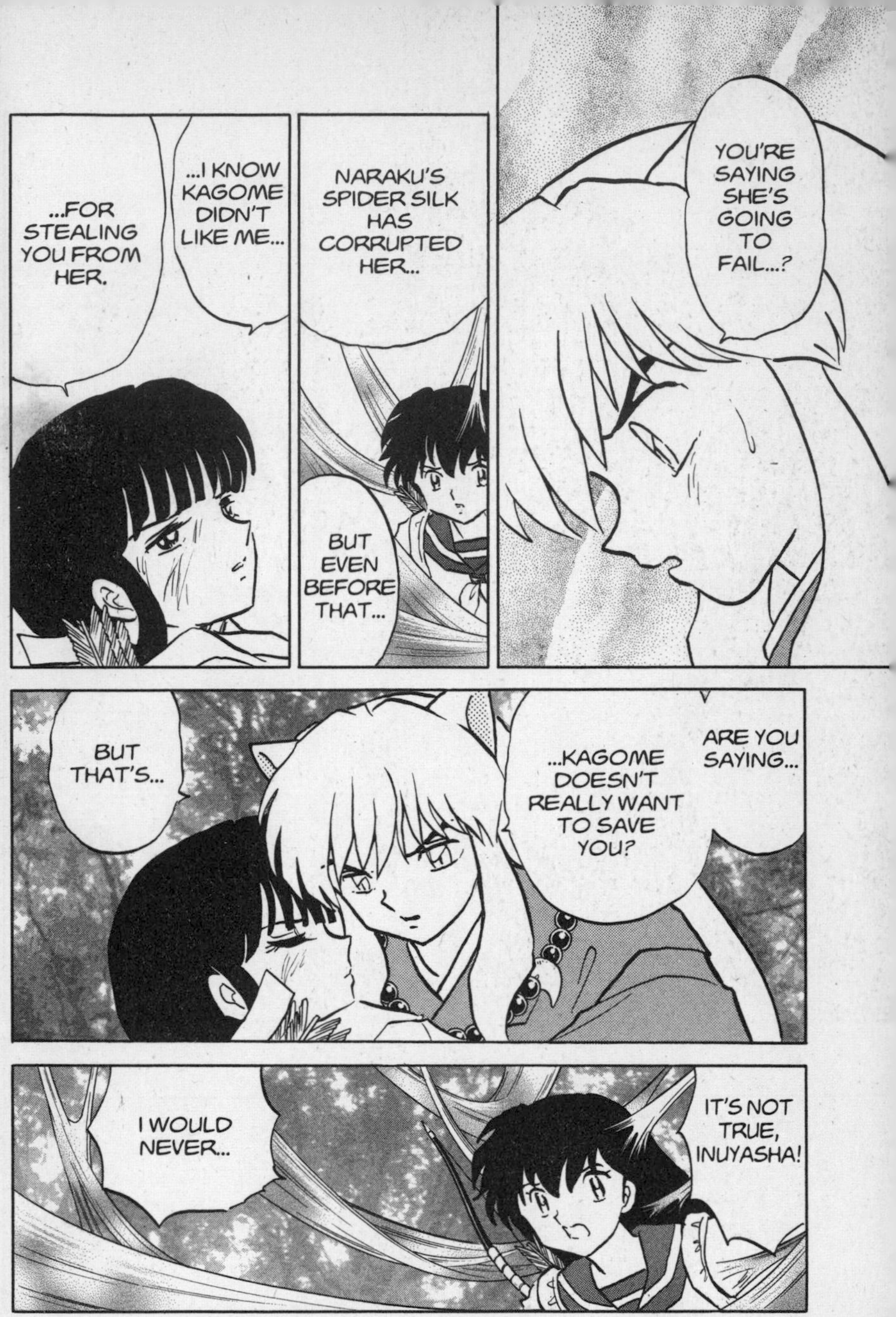
YOU'RE SAYING SHE'S GOING TO FAIL...?
NARAKU'S SPIDER SILK HAS CORRUPTED HER...
BUT EVEN BEFORE THAT...
...I KNOW KAGOME DIDN'T LIKE ME...
...FOR STEALING YOU FROM HER.
ARE YOU SAYING...
...KAGOME DOESN'T REALLY WANT TO SAVE YOU?
BUT THAT'S...
IT'S NOT TRUE, INUYASHA!
I WOULD NEVER...

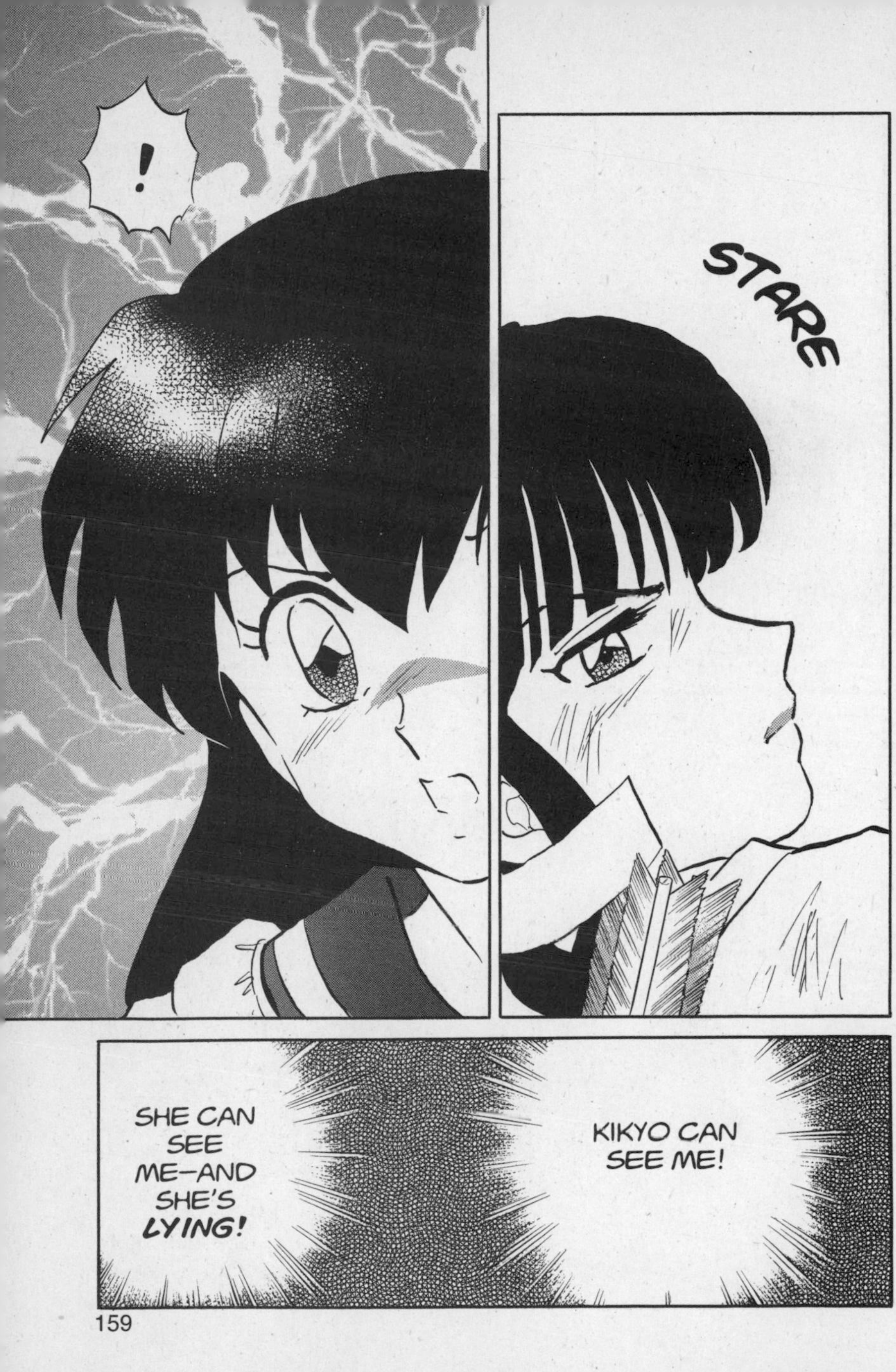
STARE
!
KIKYO CAN SEE ME!
SHE CAN SEE ME—AND SHE'S *LYING!*

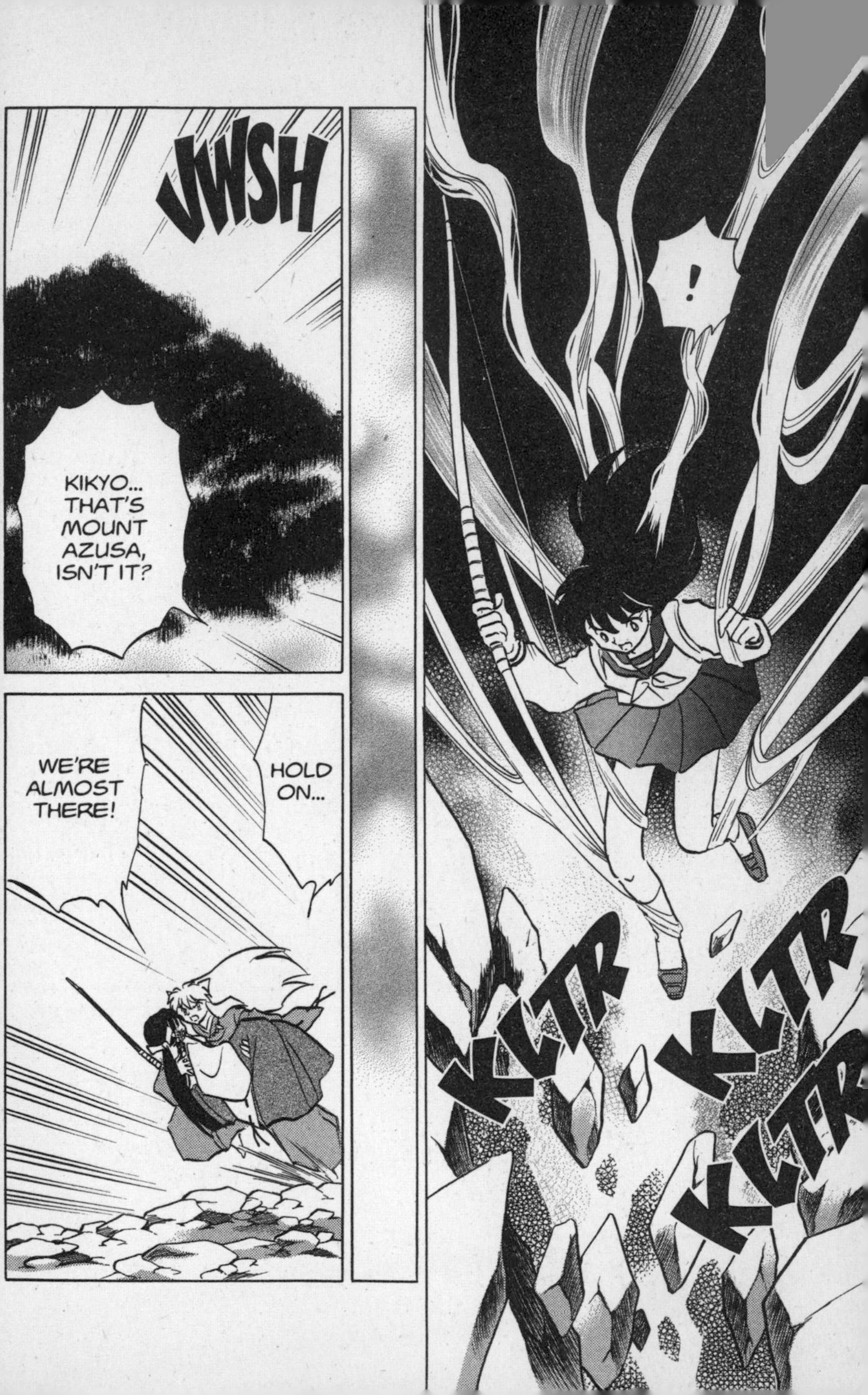
!
KLTR
KLTR
KLTR
VWSH
KIKYO... THAT'S MOUNT AZUSA, ISN'T IT?
HOLD ON...
WE'RE ALMOST THERE!

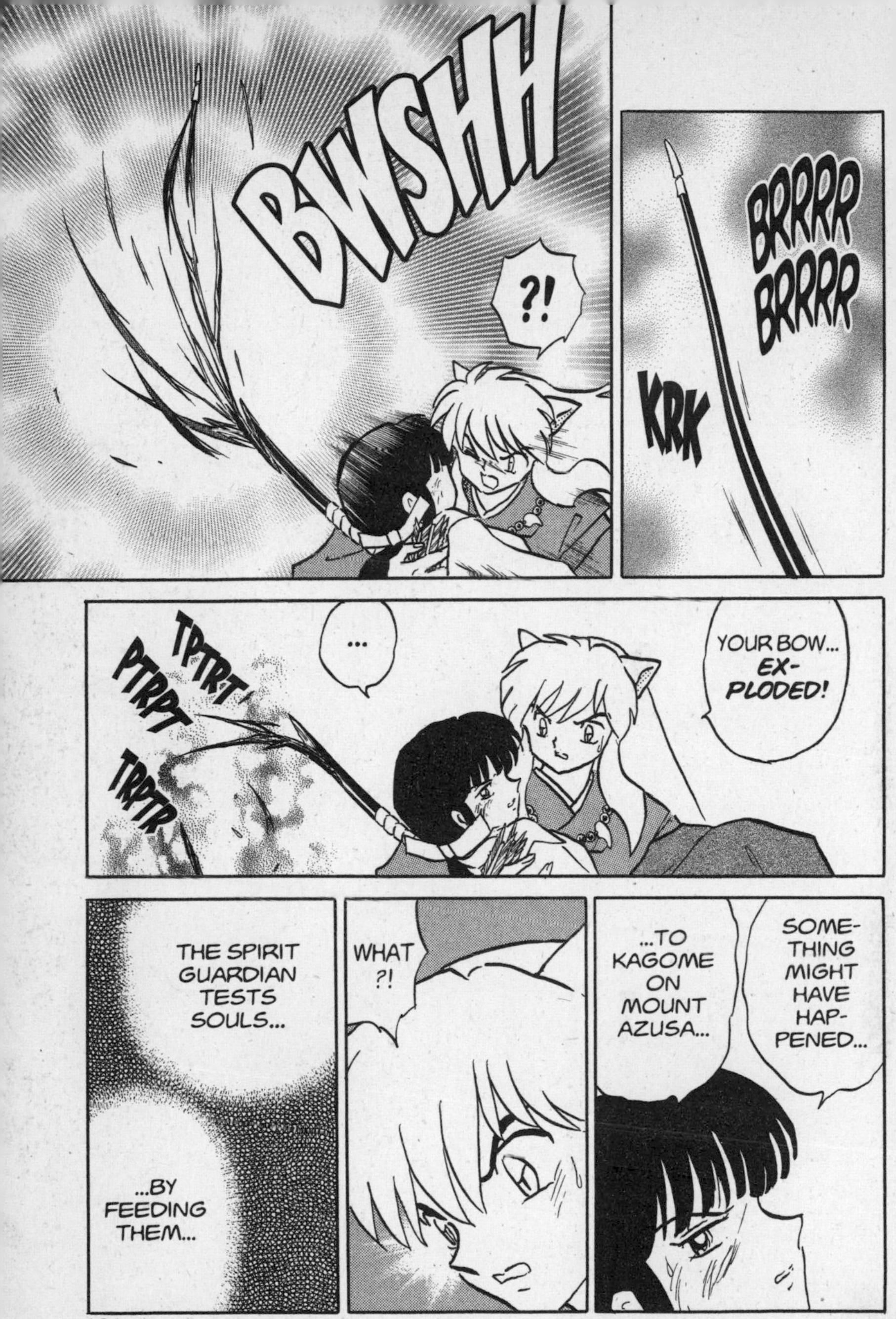
BRRRR BRRRR
KRK
BWSHH
?!
YOUR BOW... EX-PLODED!
...
TPTRT
PTRPT
TRPTR
SOME-THING MIGHT HAVE HAP-PENED...
...TO KAGOME ON MOUNT AZUSA...
WHAT?!
THE SPIRIT GUARDIAN TESTS SOULS...
...BY FEEDING THEM...

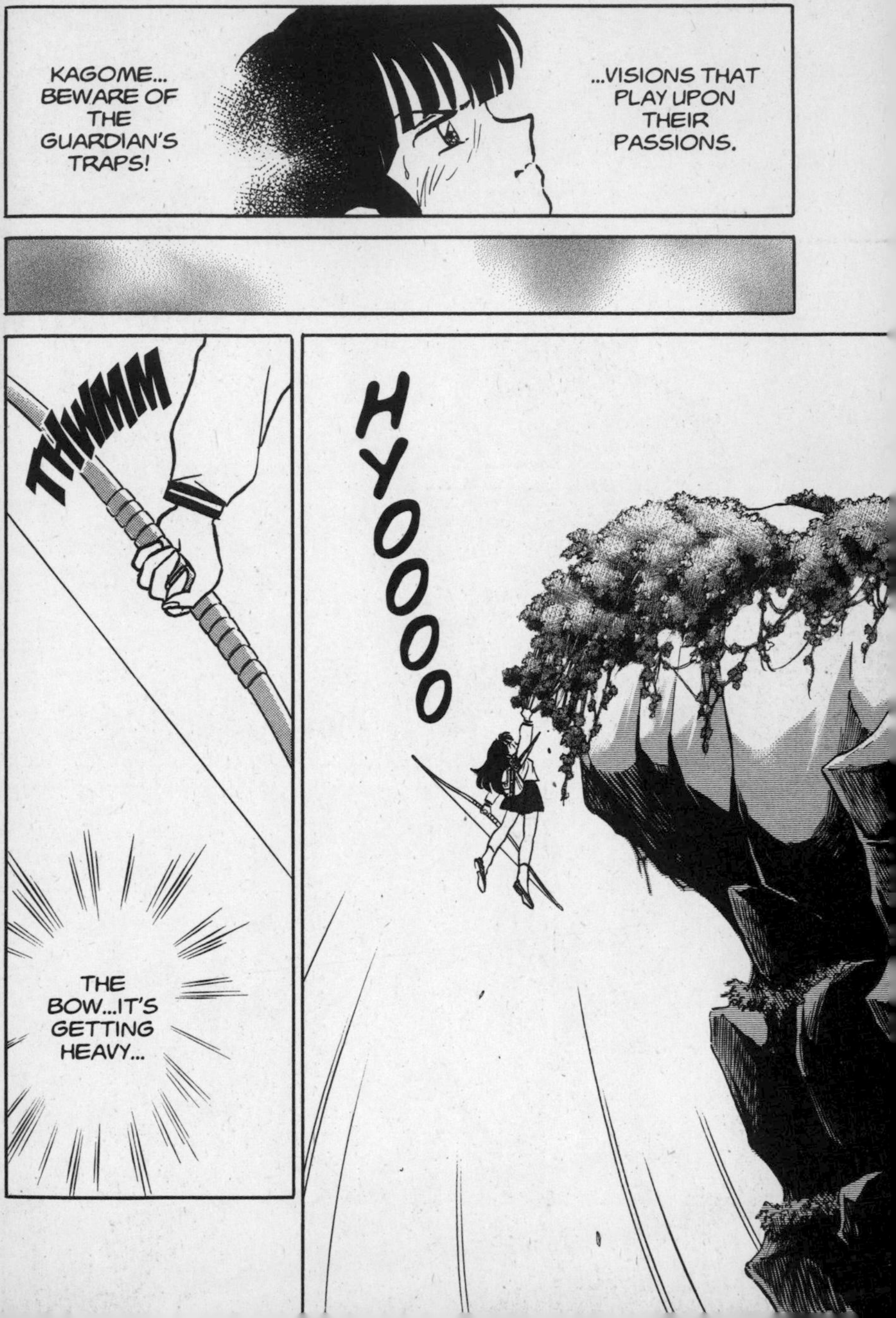
...VISIONS THAT PLAY UPON THEIR PASSIONS.
KAGOME... BEWARE OF THE GUARDIAN'S TRAPS!
HYOOOO
THWMM
THE BOW...IT'S GETTING HEAVY...

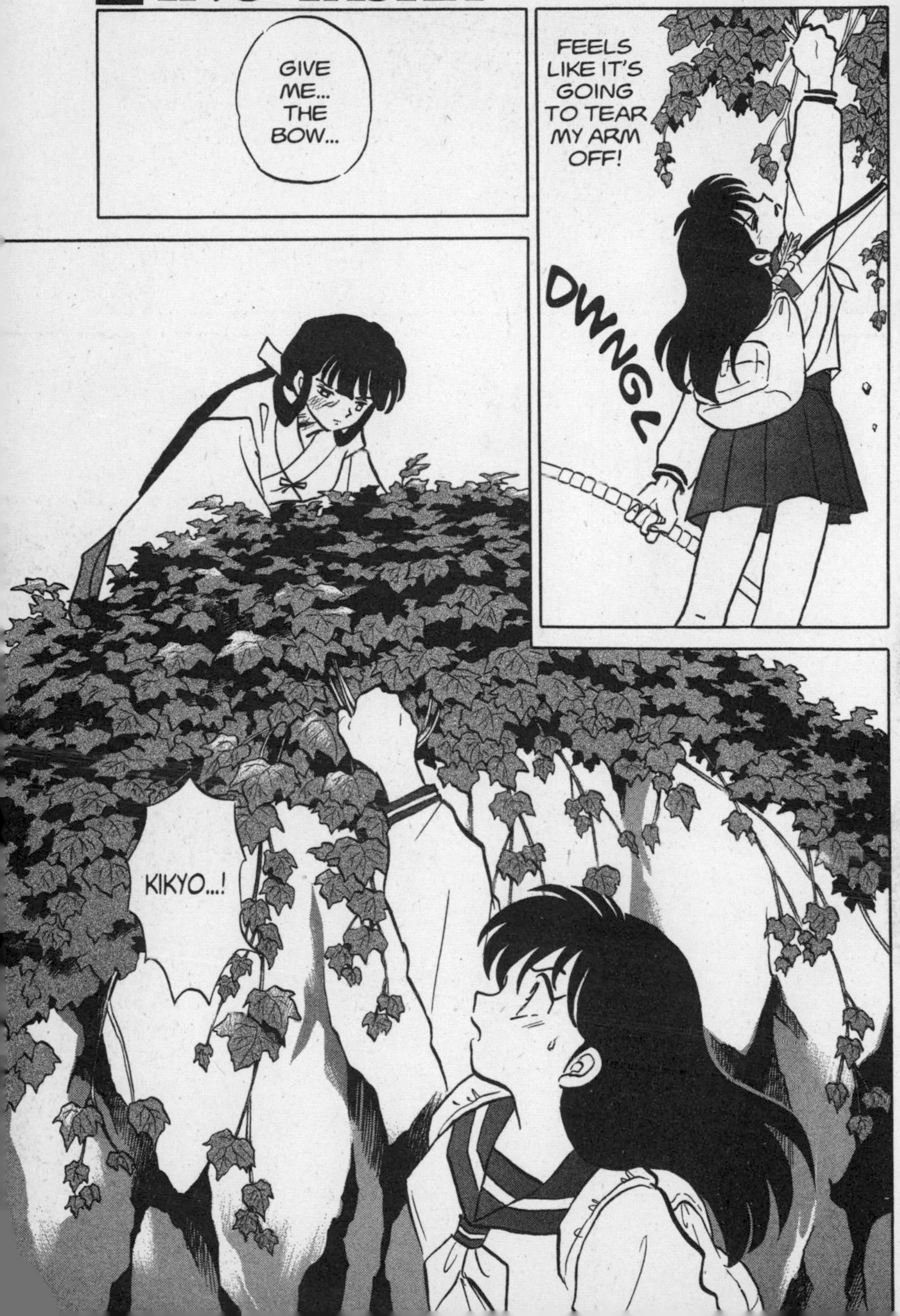
FEELS LIKE IT'S GOING TO TEAR MY ARM OFF!
DWNG!
GIVE ME... THE BOW...
KIKYO...!

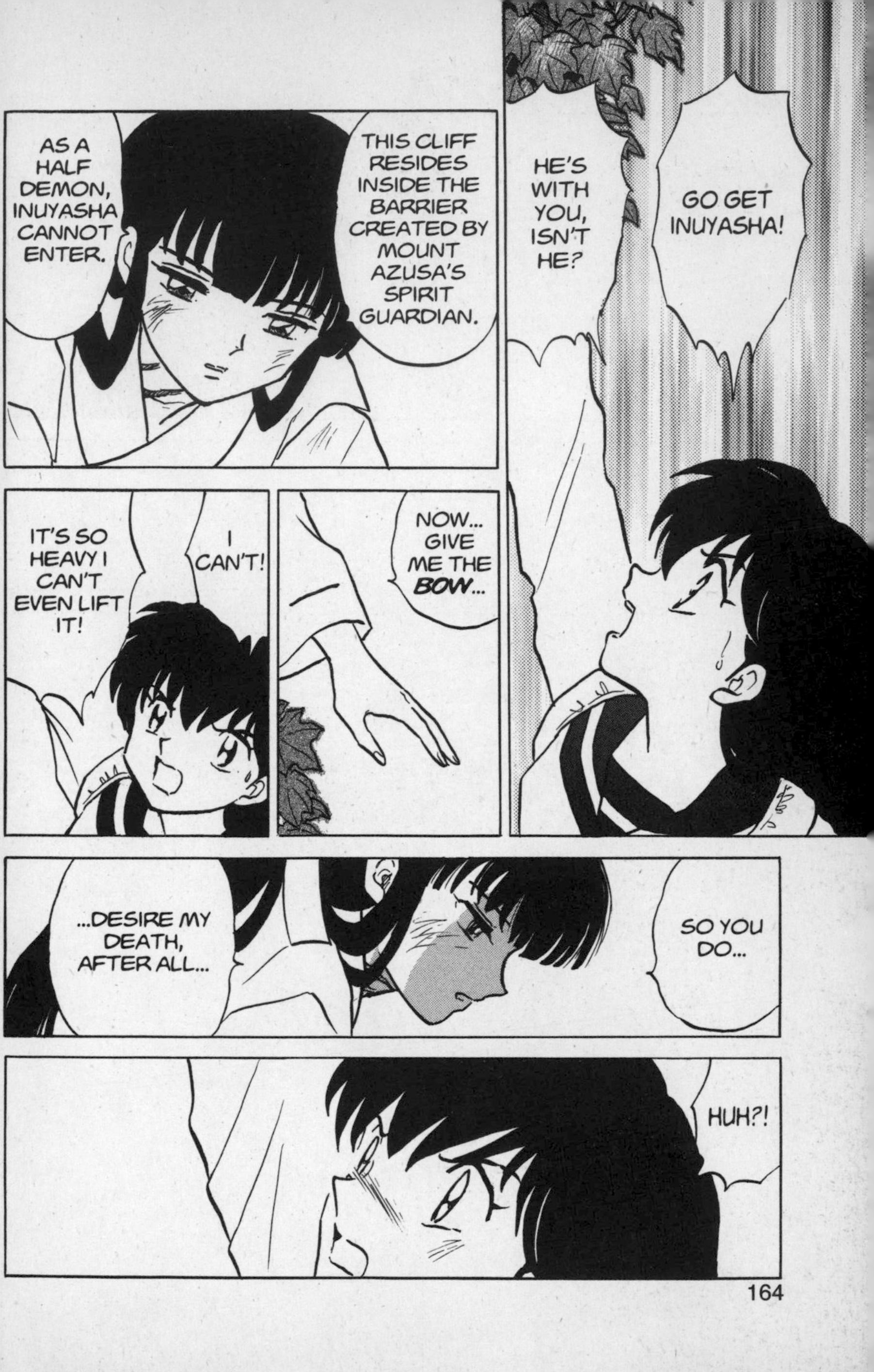
GO GET INUYASHA!
HE'S WITH YOU, ISN'T HE?
THIS CLIFF RESIDES INSIDE THE BARRIER CREATED BY MOUNT AZUSA'S SPIRIT GUARDIAN.
AS A HALF DEMON, INUYASHA CANNOT ENTER.
NOW... GIVE ME THE *BOW*...
I CAN'T!
IT'S SO HEAVY I CAN'T EVEN LIFT IT!
SO YOU DO...
...DESIRE MY DEATH, AFTER ALL...
HUH?!

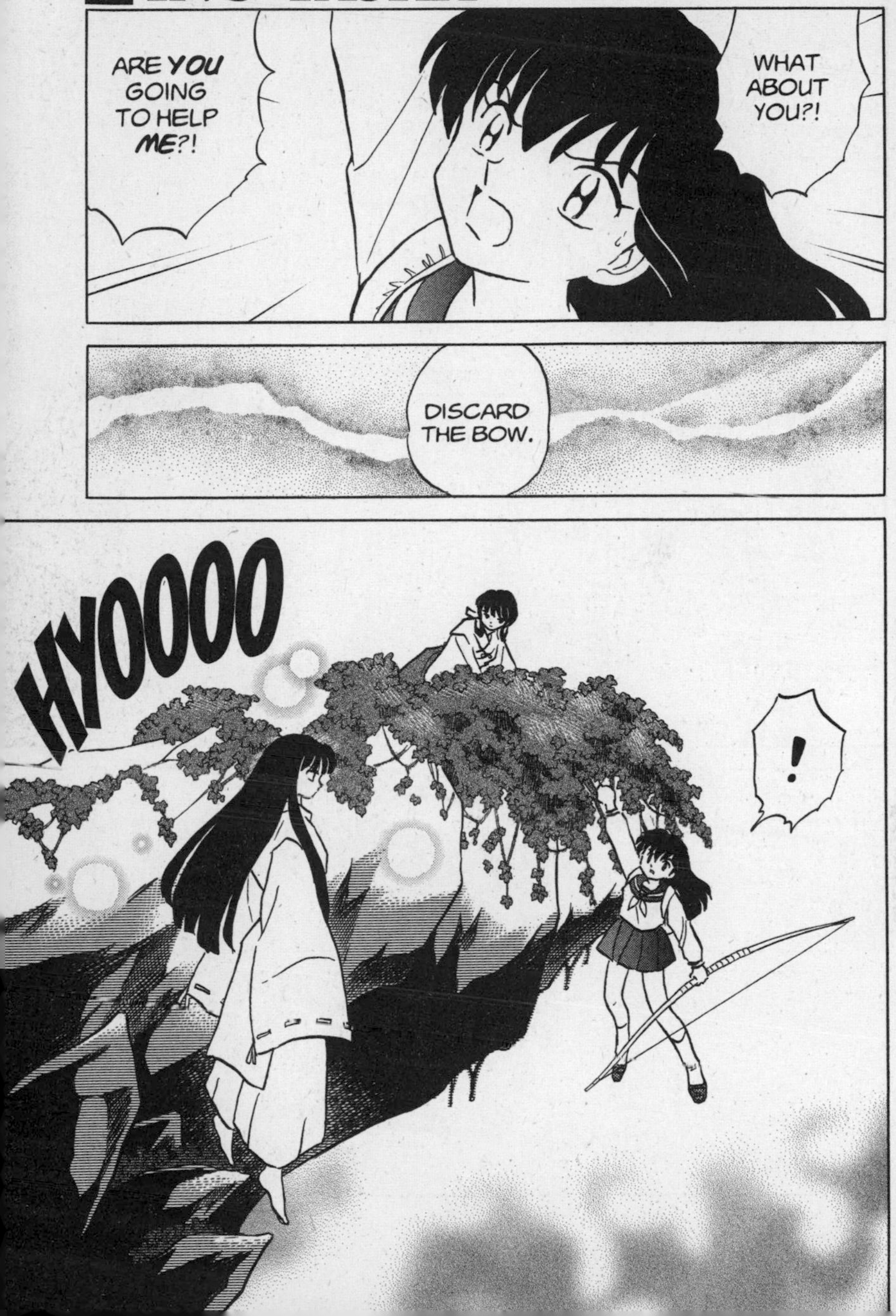
WHAT ABOUT YOU?!
ARE YOU GOING TO HELP ME?!
DISCARD THE BOW.
HYOOOO
!

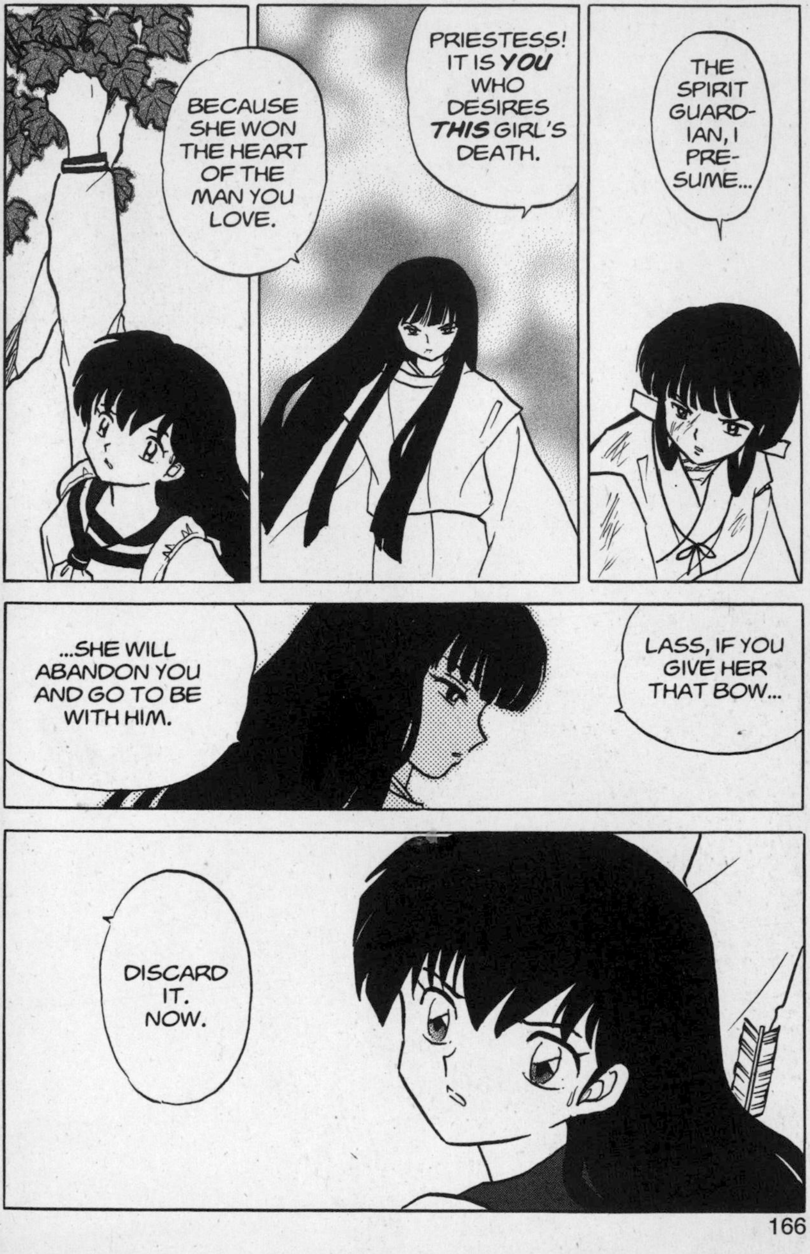
THE SPIRIT GUARDIAN, I PRESUME...
PRIESTESS! IT IS YOU WHO DESIRES THIS GIRL'S DEATH.
BECAUSE SHE WON THE HEART OF THE MAN YOU LOVE.
LASS, IF YOU GIVE HER THAT BOW...
...SHE WILL ABANDON YOU AND GO TO BE WITH HIM.
DISCARD IT. NOW.

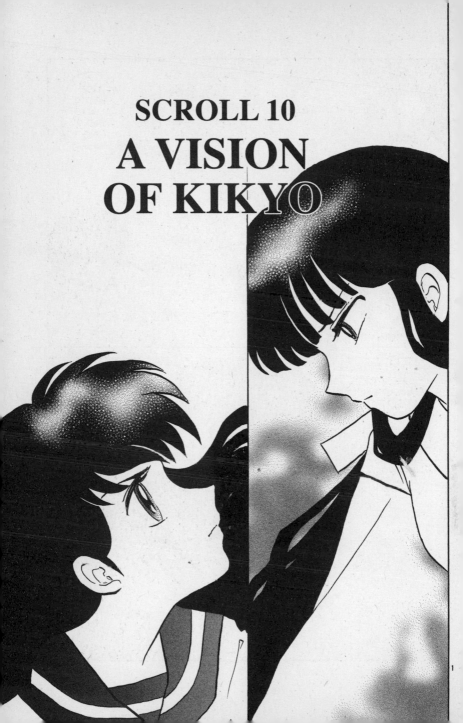

SCROLL 10
A VISION OF KIKYO

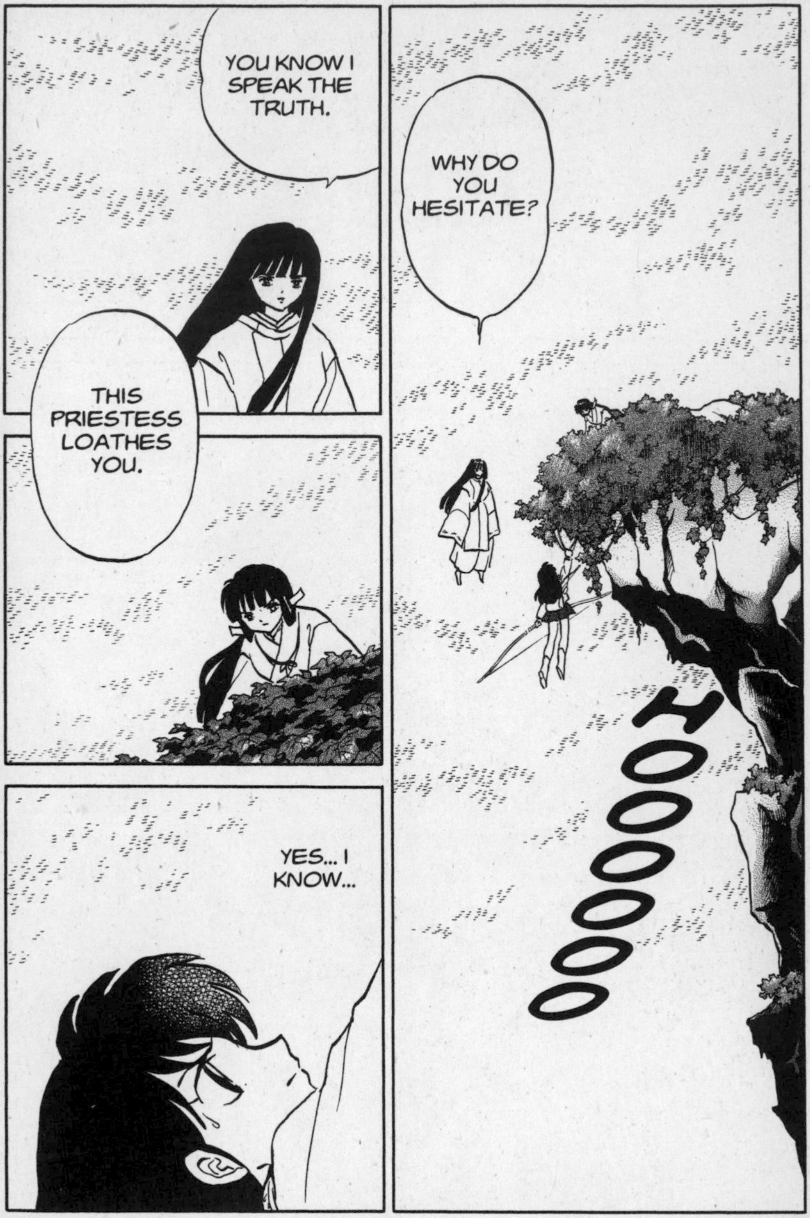
WHY DO YOU HESITATE?
HOOOOOOO
YOU KNOW I SPEAK THE TRUTH.
THIS PRIESTESS LOATHES YOU.
YES... I KNOW...

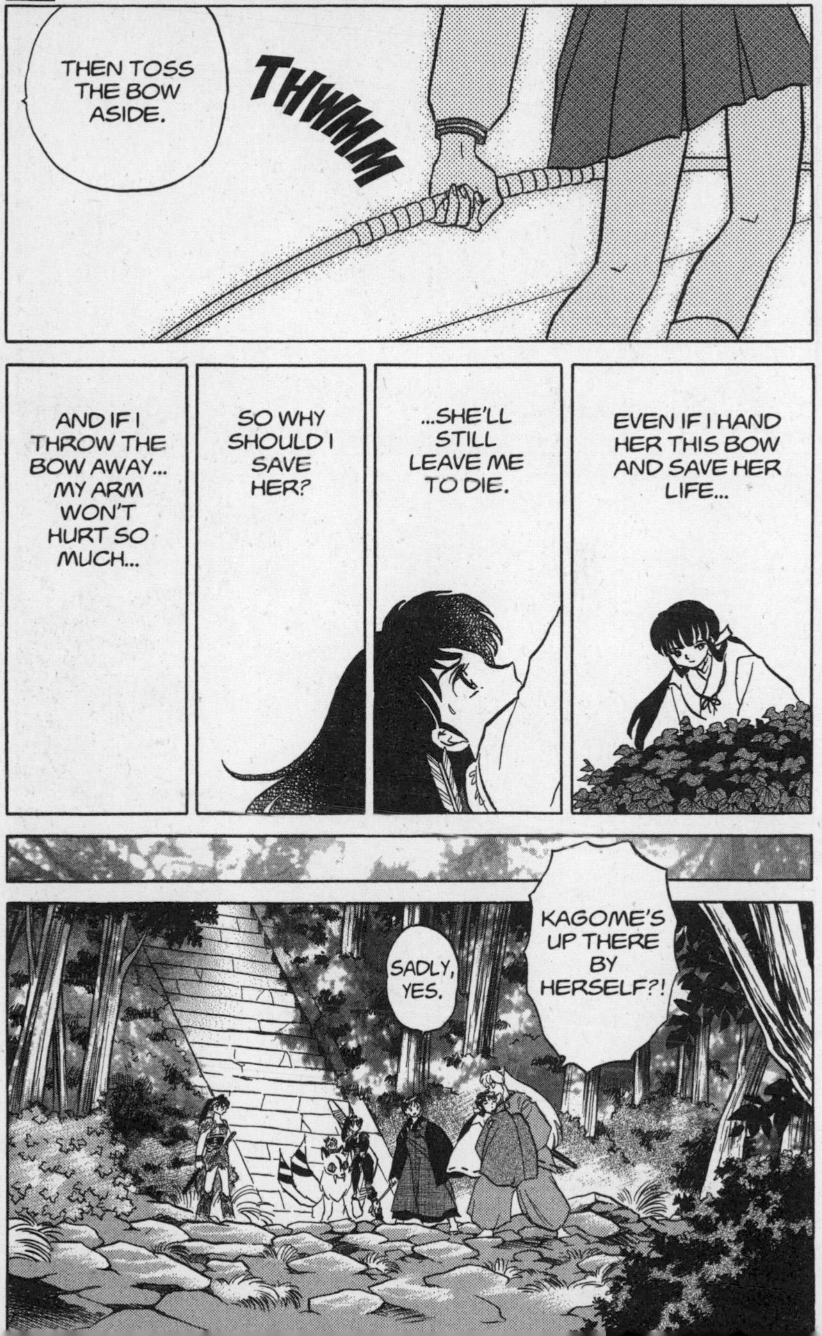
THEN TOSS THE BOW ASIDE.
THWMMM
EVEN IF I HAND HER THIS BOW AND SAVE HER LIFE...
...SHE'LL STILL LEAVE ME TO DIE.
SO WHY SHOULD I SAVE HER?
AND IF I THROW THE BOW AWAY... MY ARM WON'T HURT SO MUCH...
KAGOME'S UP THERE BY HERSELF?!
SADLY, YES.

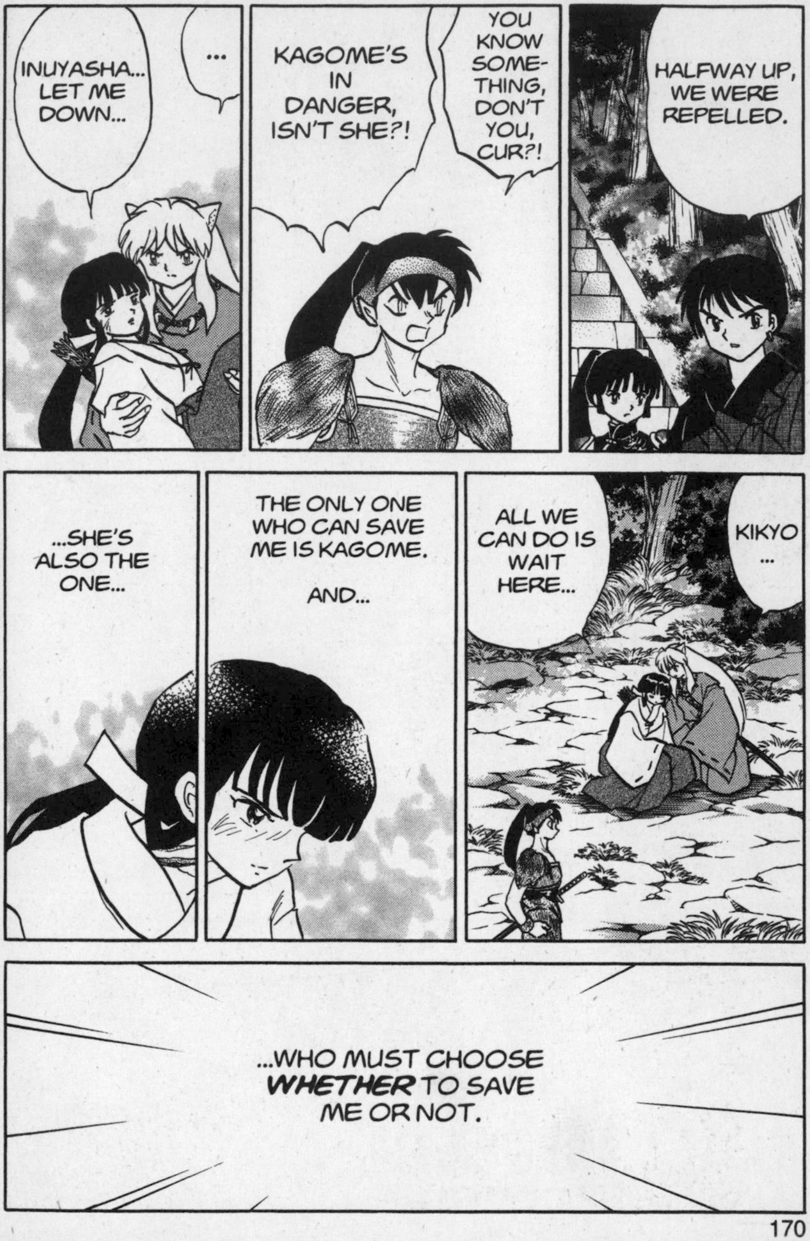
HALFWAY UP, WE WERE REPELLED.
YOU KNOW SOME-THING, DON'T YOU, CUR?!
KAGOME'S IN DANGER, ISN'T SHE?!
...
INUYASHA... LET ME DOWN...
KIKYO ...
ALL WE CAN DO IS WAIT HERE...
THE ONLY ONE WHO CAN SAVE ME IS KAGOME.
AND...
...SHE'S ALSO THE ONE...
...WHO MUST CHOOSE ***WHETHER*** TO SAVE ME OR NOT.

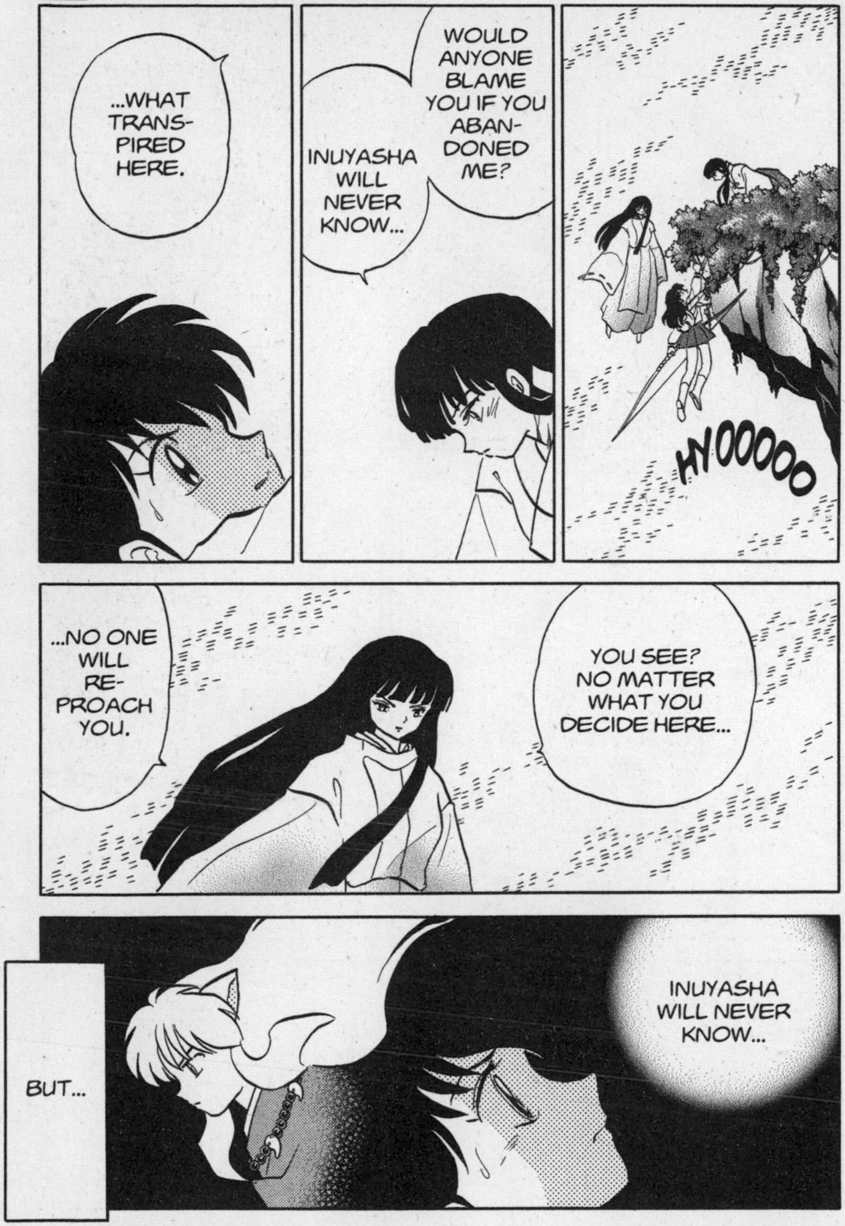
HYOOOOO
WOULD ANYONE BLAME YOU IF YOU ABAN-DONED ME?
INUYASHA WILL NEVER KNOW...
...WHAT TRANS-PIRED HERE.
YOU SEE? NO MATTER WHAT YOU DECIDE HERE...
...NO ONE WILL RE-PROACH YOU.
INUYASHA WILL NEVER KNOW...
BUT...

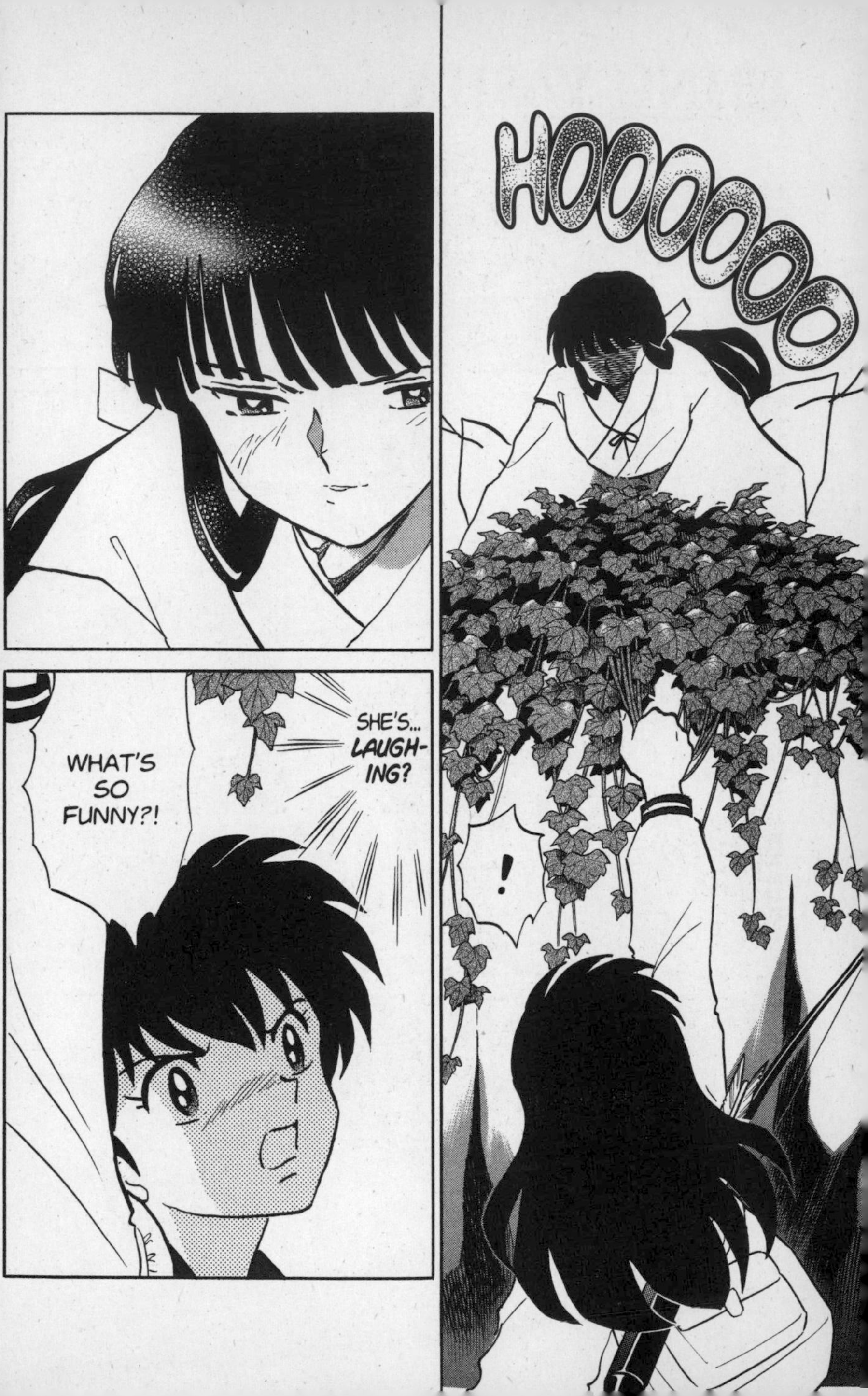
HOOOOOOO
!
SHE'S... LAUGHING?
WHAT'S SO FUNNY?!

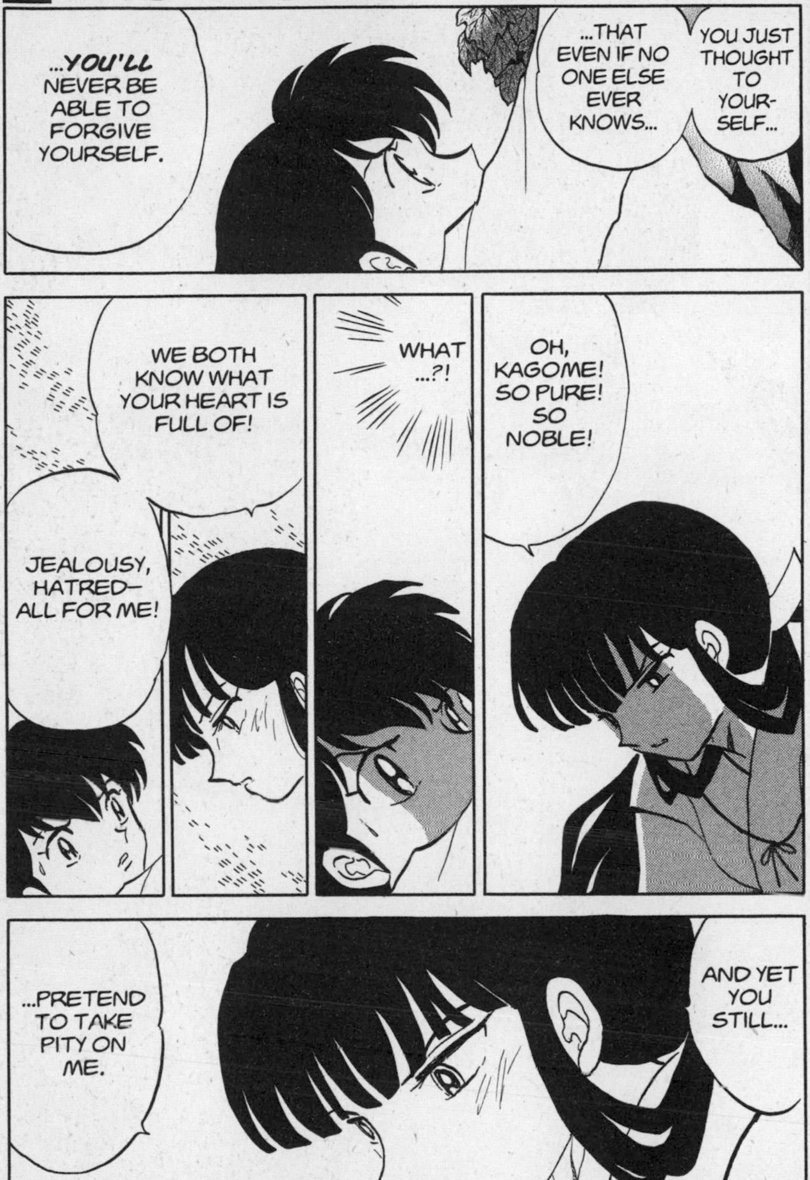
YOU JUST THOUGHT TO YOURSELF...
...THAT EVEN IF NO ONE ELSE EVER KNOWS...
...*YOU'LL* NEVER BE ABLE TO FORGIVE YOURSELF.
OH, KAGOME! SO PURE! SO NOBLE!
WHAT ...?!
WE BOTH KNOW WHAT YOUR HEART IS FULL OF!
JEALOUSY, HATRED— ALL FOR ME!
AND YET YOU STILL...
...PRETEND TO TAKE PITY ON ME.

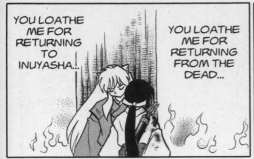

PRETEND TO TAKE PITY...?
WHAT ARE YOU TALKING ABOUT?!
YOU LOATHE ME FOR RETURNING FROM THE DEAD...
YOU LOATHE ME FOR RETURNING TO INUYASHA...
YOU BEHAVE AS IF HE ANNOYS YOU...
...WHILE DREAMING OF HAVING HIM ALL TO YOURSELF.
AND YET YOU EXTEND YOUR HAND TO ME WITH FEIGNED SYMPATHY.
DO YOU REALLY THINK I CAN BE DECEIVED ...
...BY SUCH PITIFUL LIES?!
Y...
YOU...!

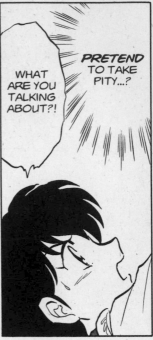

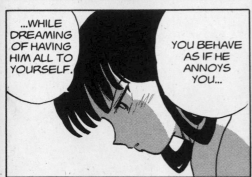

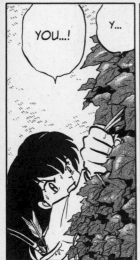

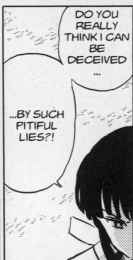

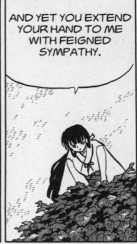

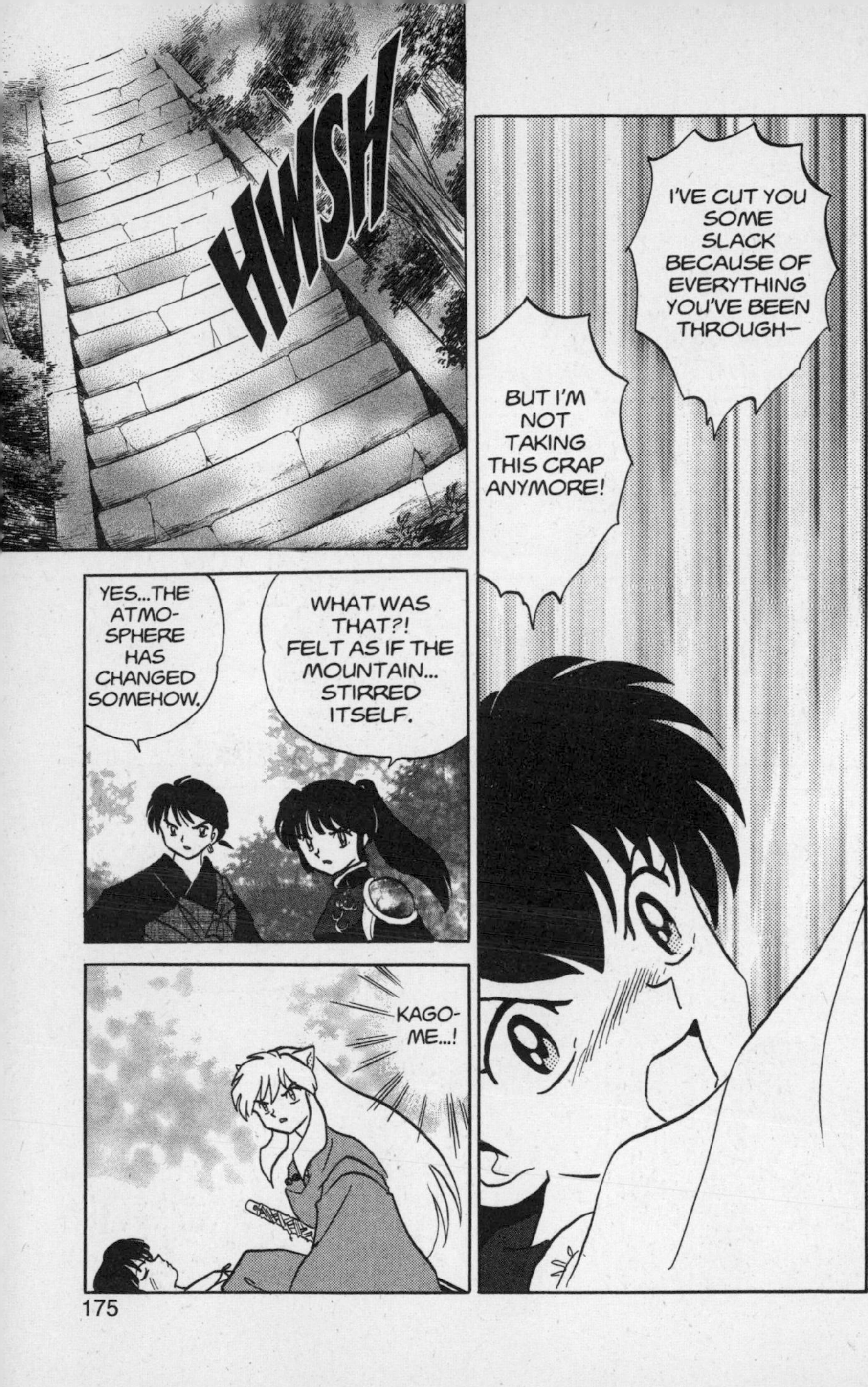
I'VE CUT YOU SOME SLACK BECAUSE OF EVERYTHING YOU'VE BEEN THROUGH—
BUT I'M NOT TAKING THIS CRAP ANYMORE!
HWSH
WHAT WAS THAT?! FELT AS IF THE MOUNTAIN... STIRRED ITSELF.
YES...THE ATMO-SPHERE HAS CHANGED SOMEHOW.
KAGO-ME...!

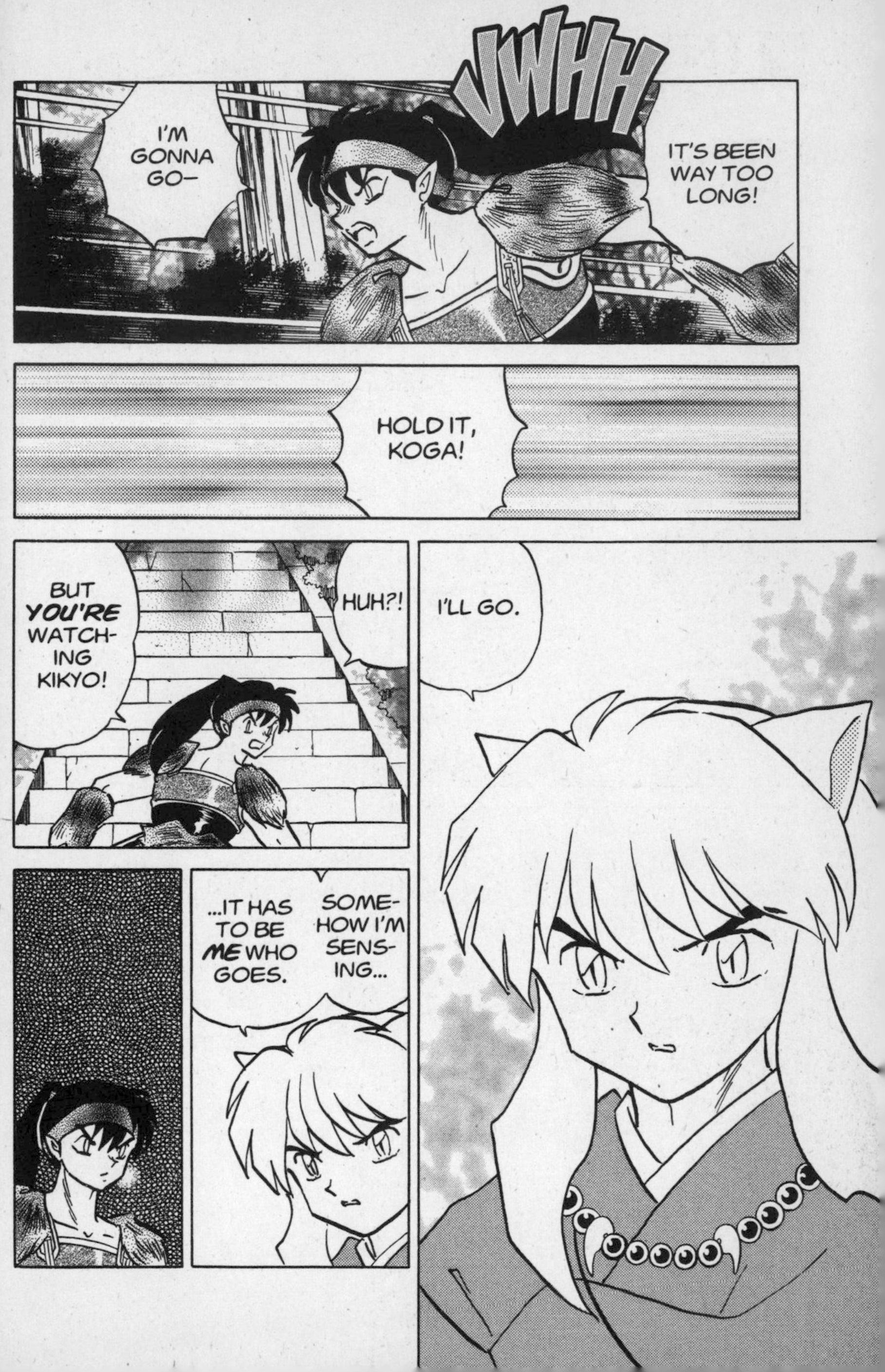
JWHH
IT'S BEEN WAY TOO LONG!
I'M GONNA GO—
HOLD IT, KOGA!
I'LL GO.
HUH?!
BUT ***YOU'RE*** WATCHING KIKYO!
SOMEHOW I'M SENSING...
...IT HAS TO BE ***ME*** WHO GOES.

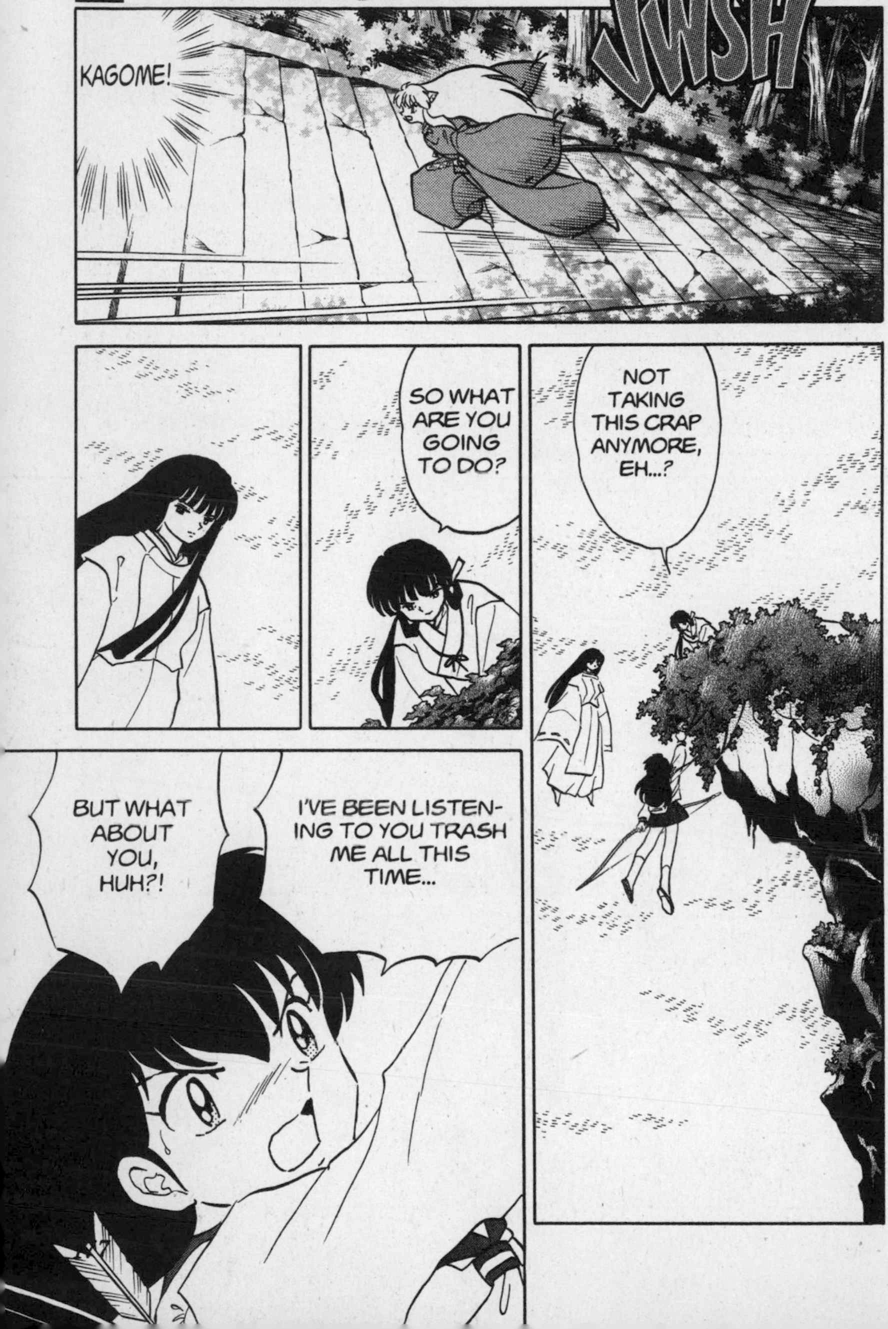
JWSH
KAGOME!
NOT TAKING THIS CRAP ANYMORE, EH...?
SO WHAT ARE YOU GOING TO DO?
I'VE BEEN LISTENING TO YOU TRASH ME ALL THIS TIME...
BUT WHAT ABOUT YOU, HUH?!

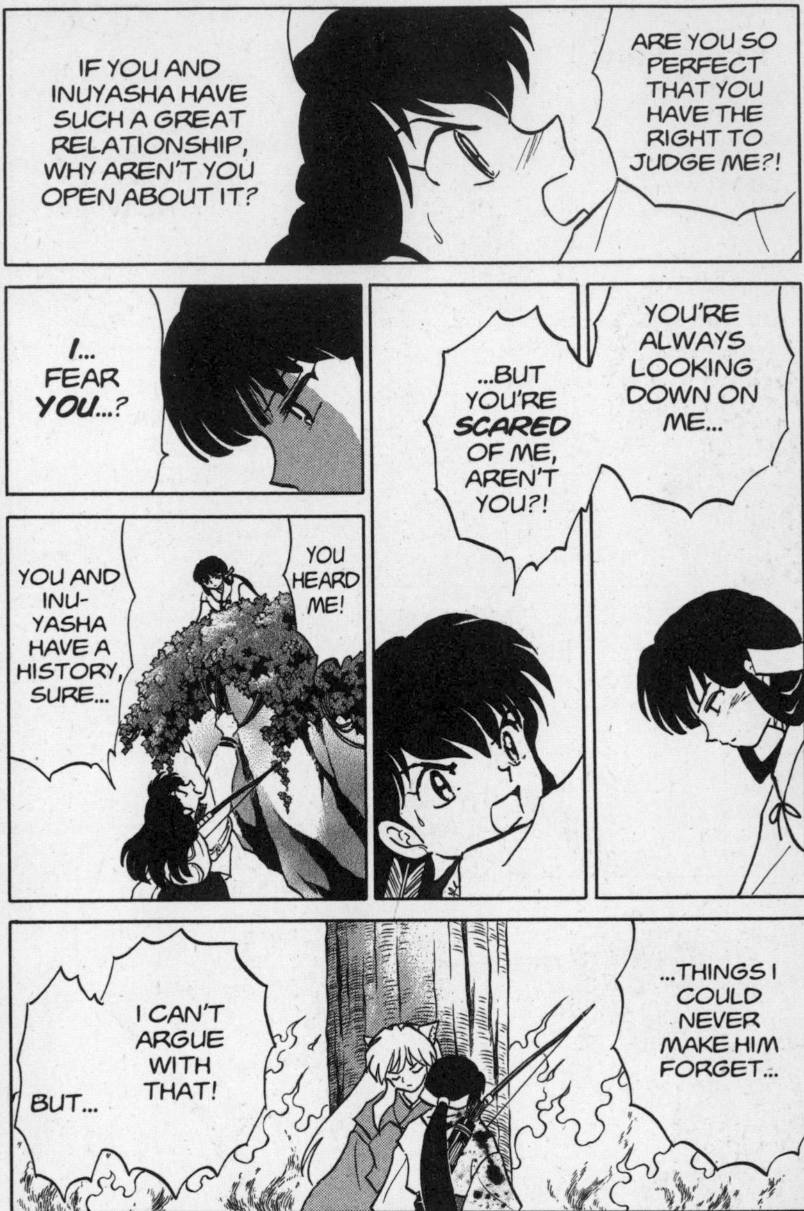
ARE YOU SO PERFECT THAT YOU HAVE THE RIGHT TO JUDGE ME?!
IF YOU AND INUYASHA HAVE SUCH A GREAT RELATIONSHIP, WHY AREN'T YOU OPEN ABOUT IT?
YOU'RE ALWAYS LOOKING DOWN ON ME...
...BUT YOU'RE *SCARED* OF ME, AREN'T YOU?!
I... FEAR *YOU*...?
YOU HEARD ME!
YOU AND INU-YASHA HAVE A HISTORY, SURE...
...THINGS I COULD NEVER MAKE HIM FORGET...
I CAN'T ARGUE WITH THAT!
BUT...

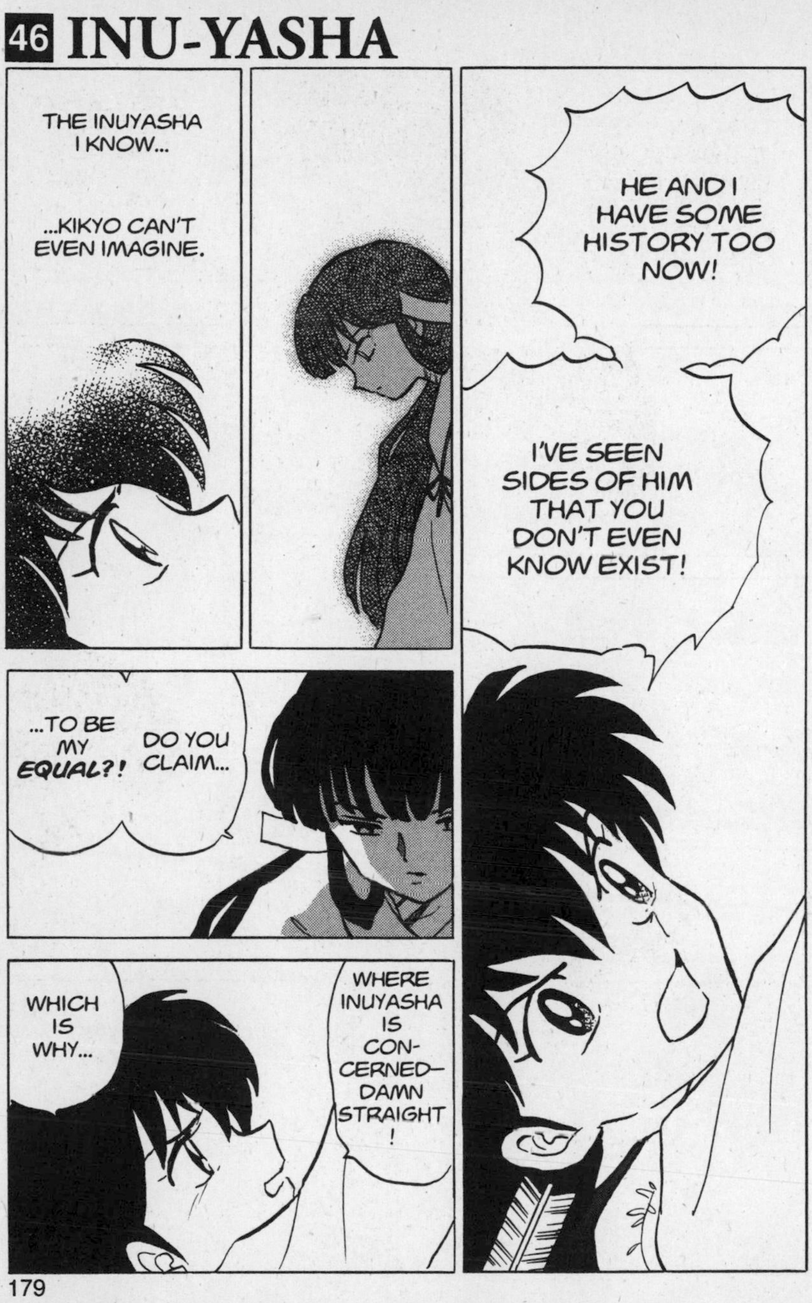
HE AND I HAVE SOME HISTORY TOO NOW!
I'VE SEEN SIDES OF HIM THAT YOU DON'T EVEN KNOW EXIST!
THE INUYASHA I KNOW...
...KIKYO CAN'T EVEN IMAGINE.
DO YOU CLAIM...
...TO BE MY EQUAL?!
WHERE INUYASHA IS CON-CERNED-DAMN STRAIGHT!
WHICH IS WHY...

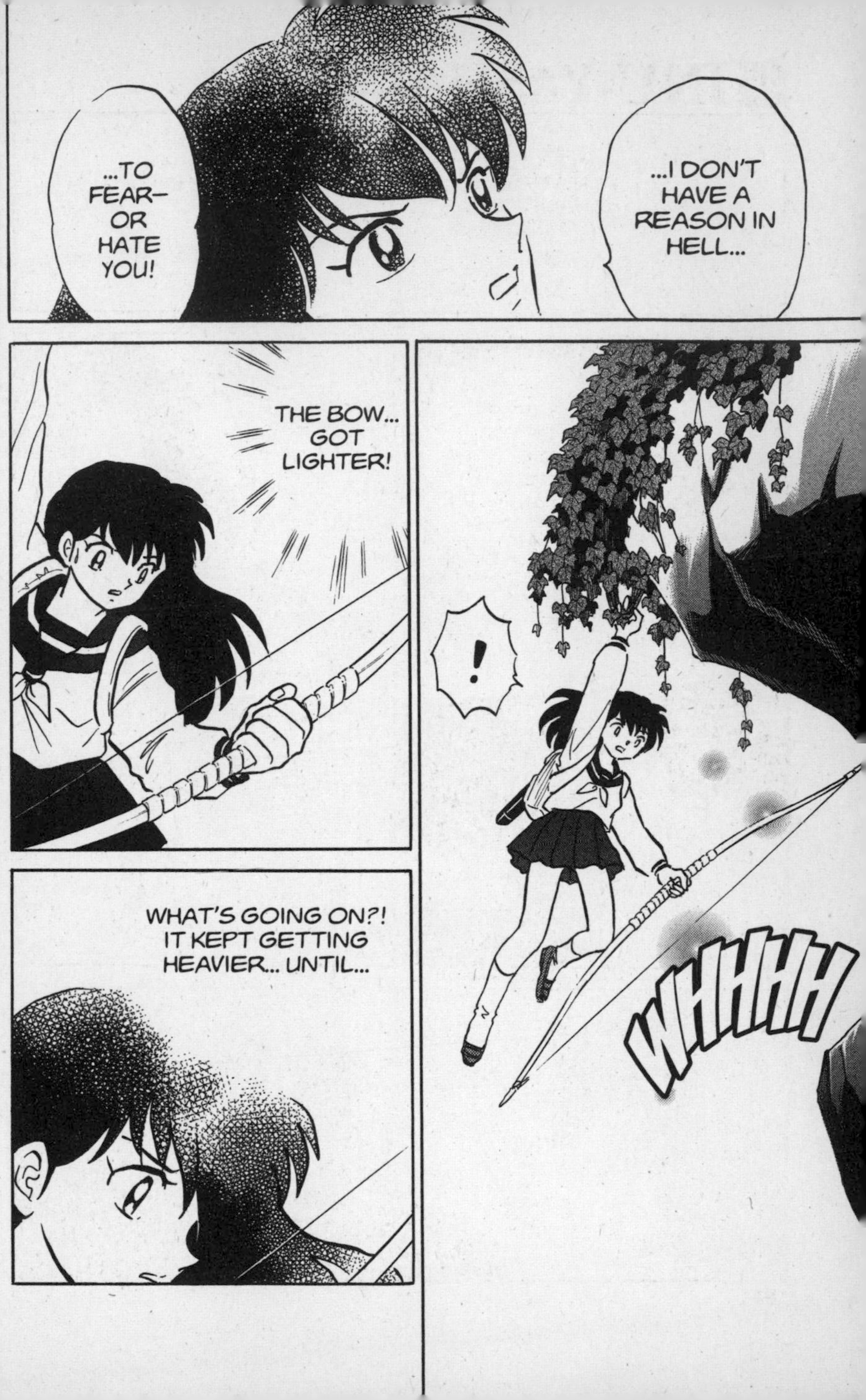
...I DON'T HAVE A REASON IN HELL...
...TO FEAR— OR HATE YOU!
!
WHHHHH
THE BOW... GOT LIGHTER!
WHAT'S GOING ON?! IT KEPT GETTING HEAVIER... UNTIL...

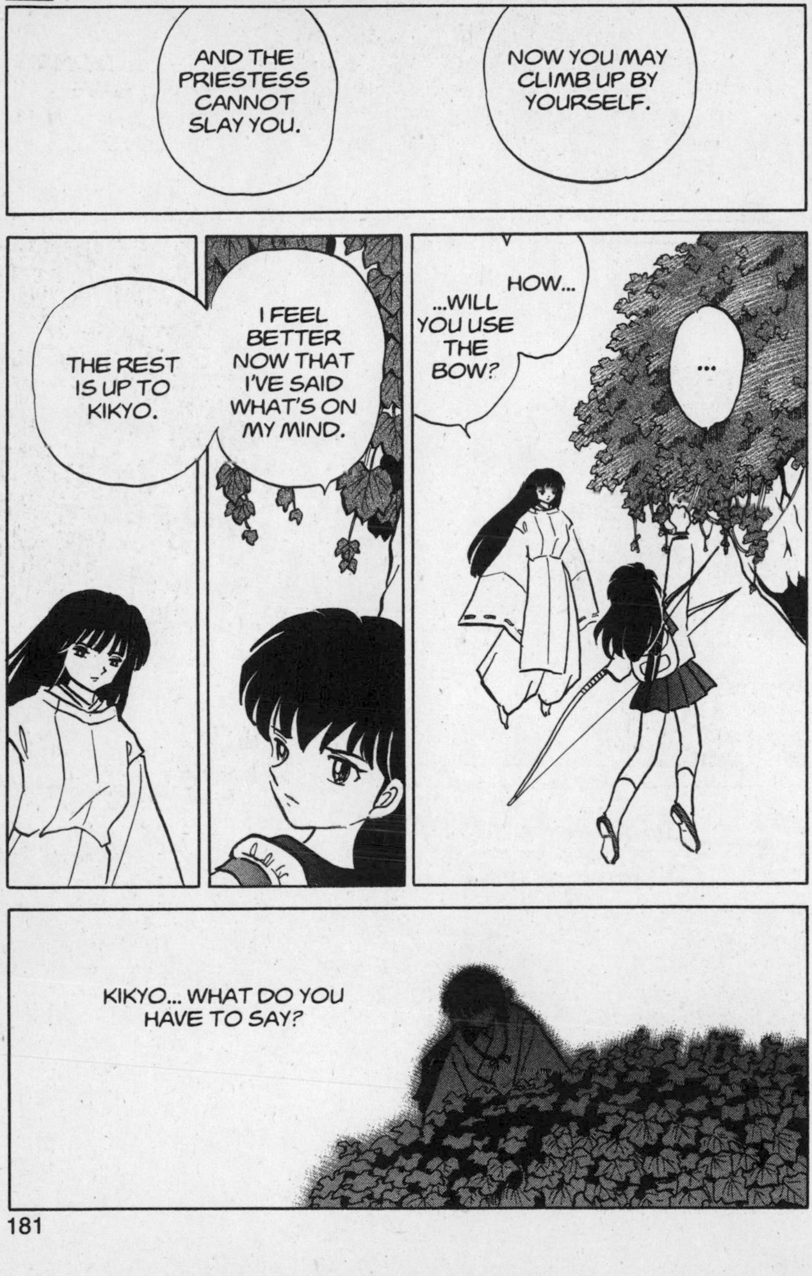
NOW YOU MAY CLIMB UP BY YOURSELF.
AND THE PRIESTESS CANNOT SLAY YOU.
...
HOW... ...WILL YOU USE THE BOW?
I FEEL BETTER NOW THAT I'VE SAID WHAT'S ON MY MIND.
THE REST IS UP TO KIKYO.
KIKYO... WHAT DO YOU HAVE TO SAY?

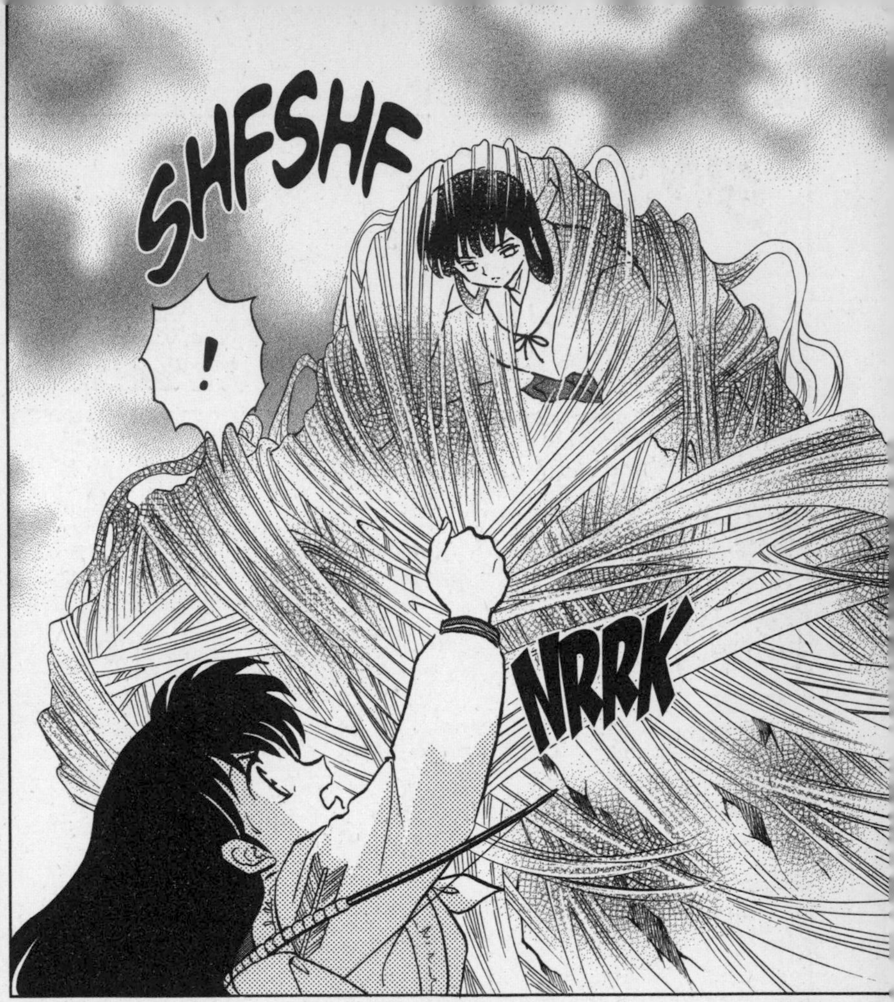
SHFSHF
!
NRRK

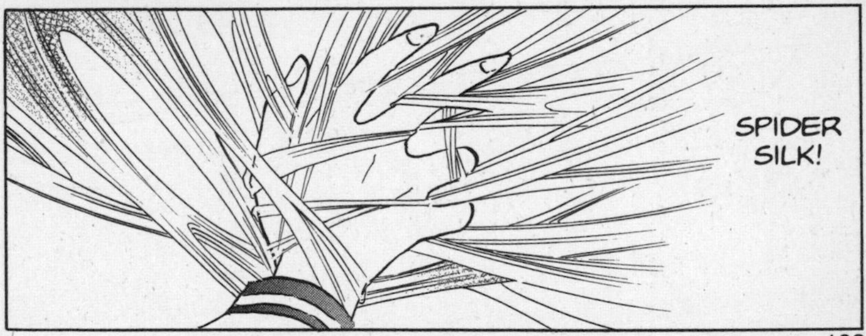
SPIDER SILK!

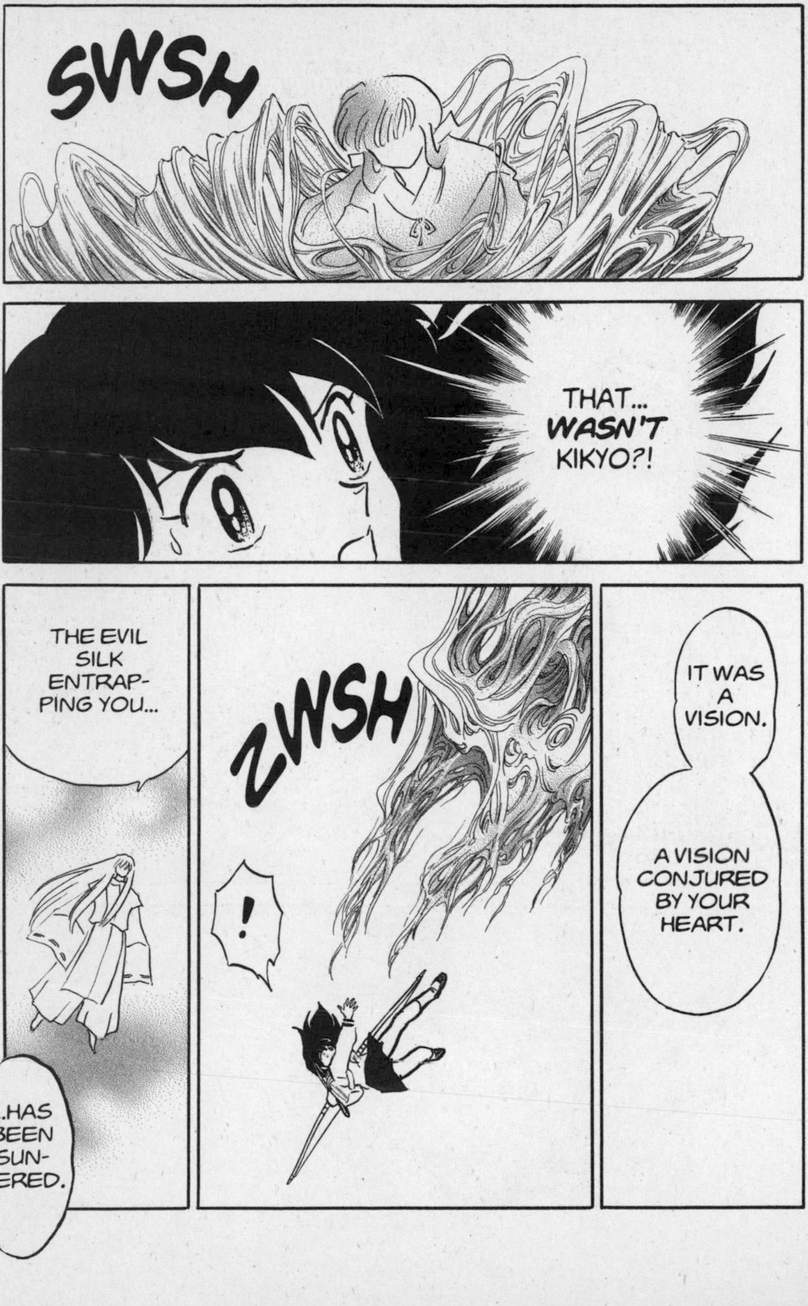
SWSH
THAT... WASN'T KIKYO?!
IT WAS A VISION.
A VISION CONJURED BY YOUR HEART.
ZWSH
!
THE EVIL SILK ENTRAPPING YOU...
...HAS BEEN SUNDERED.

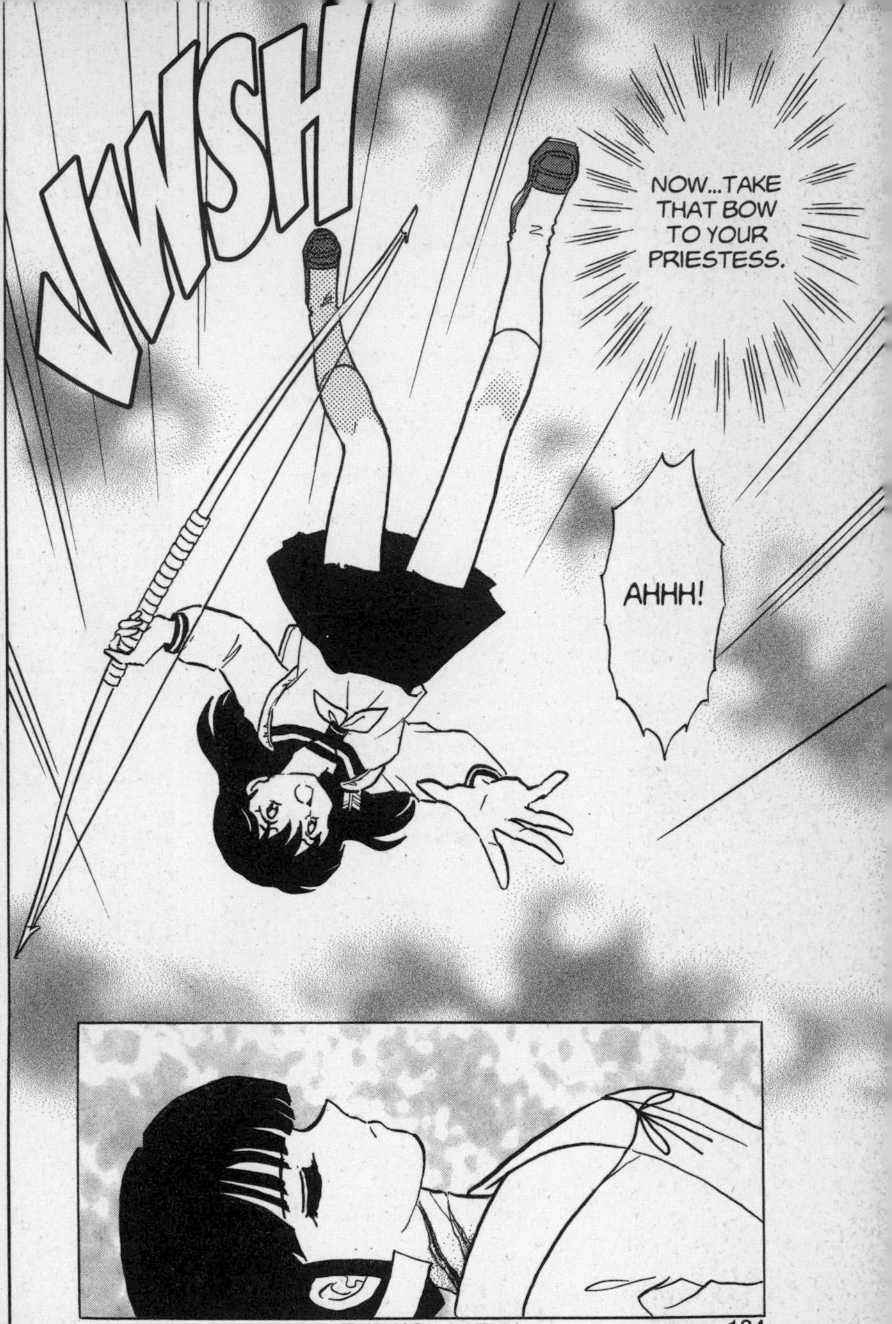
VWSH
NOW...TAKE THAT BOW TO YOUR PRIESTESS.
AHHH!

END VOLUME 46.

INUYASHA

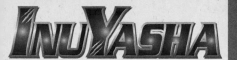

INUYASHA
VOL. 46
Shonen Sunday Edition

Story and Art by
RUMIKO TAKAHASHI

English Adaptation by Gerard Jones

Translation/Mari Morimoto
Touch-up Art & Lettering/Bill Schuch
Cover & Interior Graphic Design/Yuki Ameda
Editor/Annette Roman

VP, Production/Alvin Lu
VP, Sales & Product Marketing/Gonzalo Ferreyra
VP, Creative/Linda Espinosa
Publisher/Hyoe Narita

Printed in the U.S.A.

Published by VIZ Media, LLC
P.O. Box 77010
San Francisco, CA 94107

10 9 8 7 6 5 4 3 2 1
First printing, March 2010

RATED T+ FOR OLDER TEEN

PARENTAL ADVISORY
INUYASHA is rated T+ for Older Teen and is recommended for ages 16 and up. This volume contains violence.

ratings.viz.com

www.viz.com

WWW.SHONENSUNDAY.COM

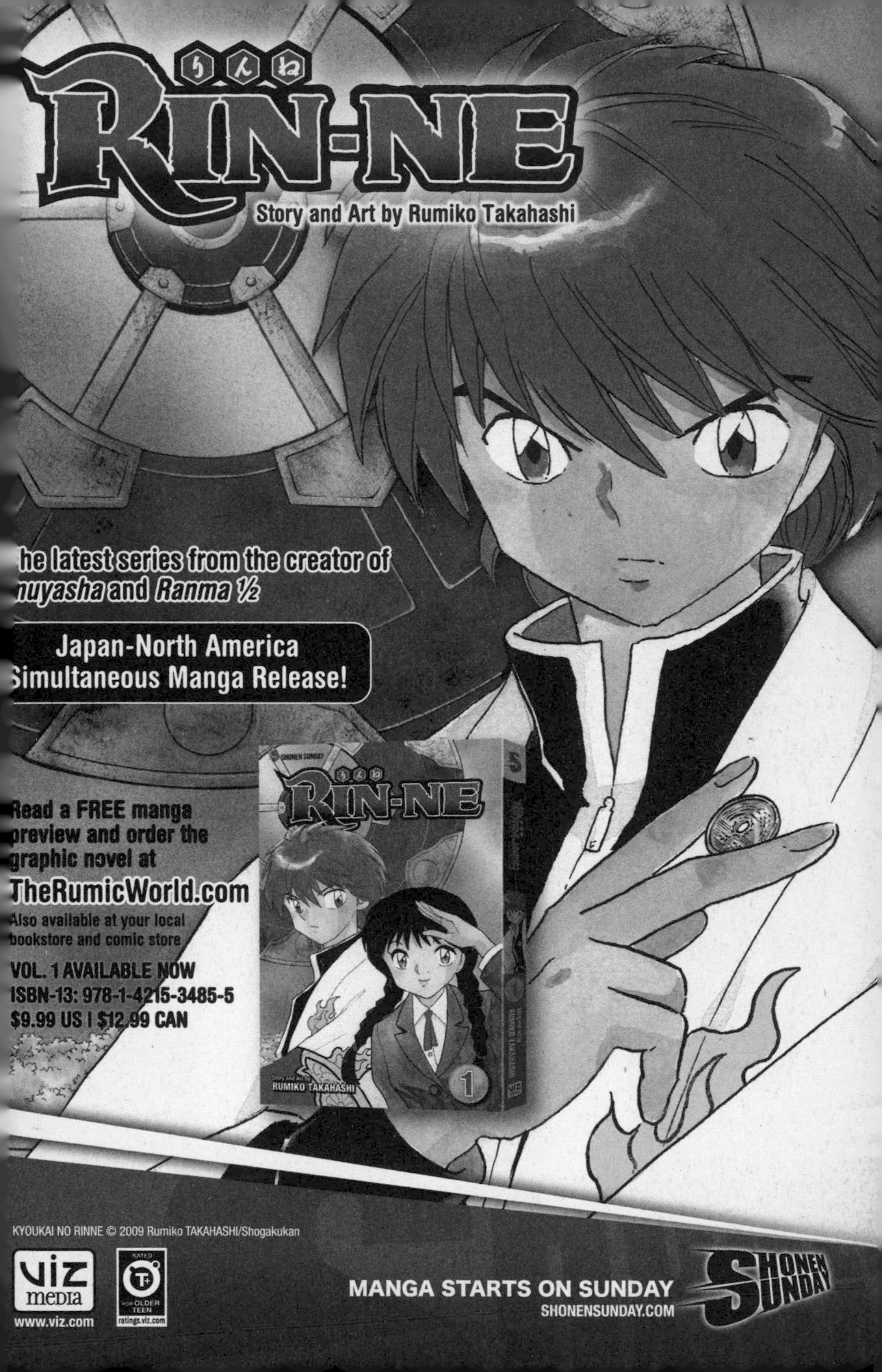
りんね
RIN-NE
Story and Art by Rumiko Takahashi
he latest series from the creator of
nuyasha and Ranma ½
Japan-North America
Simultaneous Manga Release!
Read a FREE manga
preview and order the
graphic novel at
TheRumicWorld.com
Also available at your local
bookstore and comic store
VOL. 1 AVAILABLE NOW
ISBN-13: 978-1-4215-3485-5
$9.99 US | $12.99 CAN
SHONEN SUNDAY
RIN-NE
Story and Art by
RUMIKO TAKAHASHI
1
KYOUKAI NO RINNE © 2009 Rumiko TAKAHASHI/Shogakukan
VIZ media
www.viz.com
RATED T+ FOR OLDER TEEN
ratings.viz.com
MANGA STARTS ON SUNDAY
SHONENSUNDAY.COM
SHONEN SUNDAY

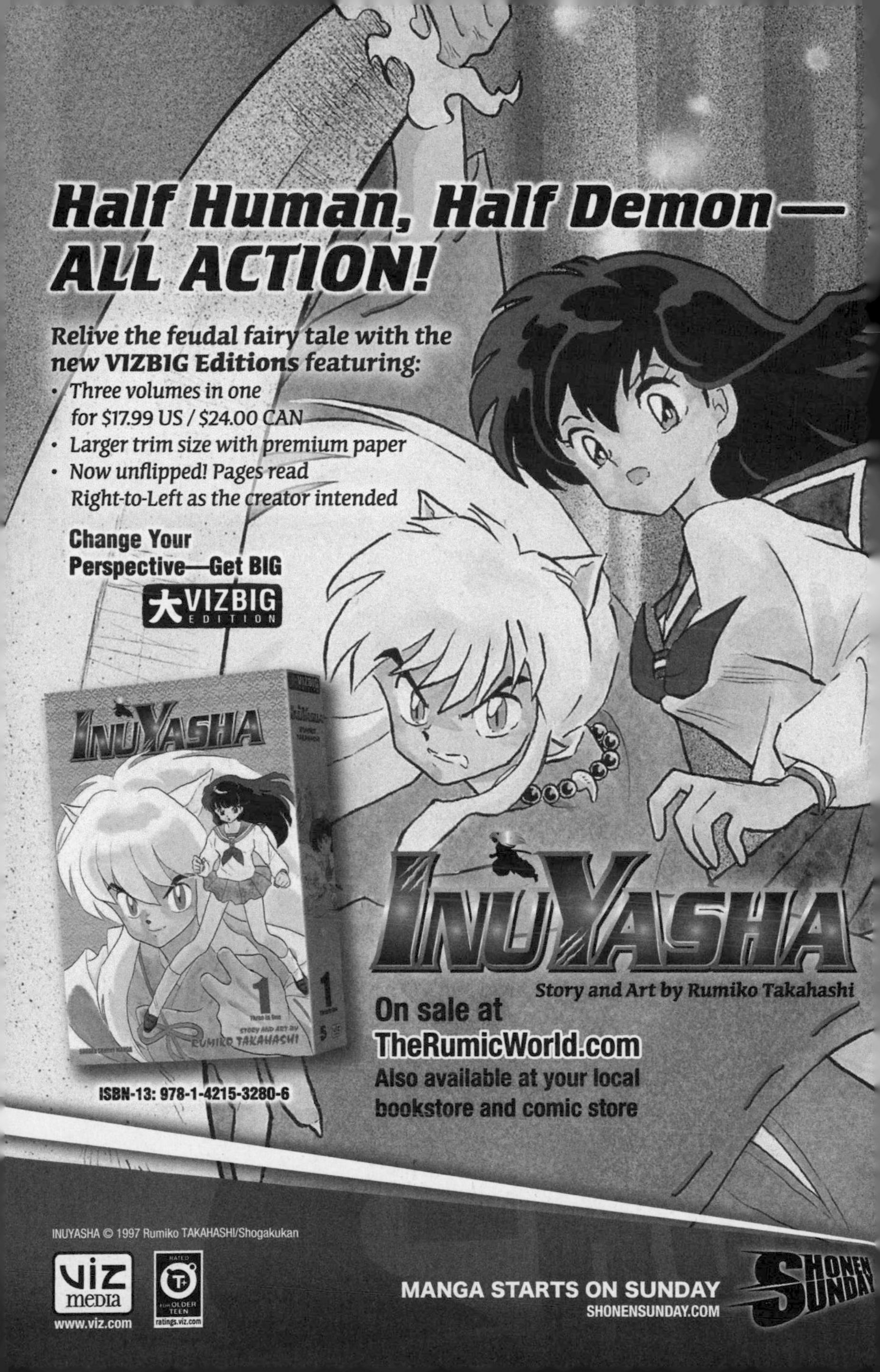
Half Human, Half Demon—
ALL ACTION!
Relive the feudal fairy tale with the new VIZBIG Editions featuring:
• Three volumes in one for $17.99 US / $24.00 CAN
• Larger trim size with premium paper
• Now unflipped! Pages read Right-to-Left as the creator intended
Change Your Perspective—Get BIG
大 VIZBIG EDITION
INUYASHA
1
STORY AND ART BY RUMIKO TAKAHASHI
ISBN-13: 978-1-4215-3280-6
INUYASHA
Story and Art by Rumiko Takahashi
On sale at
TheRumicWorld.com
Also available at your local bookstore and comic store
INUYASHA © 1997 Rumiko TAKAHASHI/Shogakukan
viz media
www.viz.com
RATED T+ FOR OLDER TEEN
ratings.viz.com
MANGA STARTS ON SUNDAY
SHONENSUNDAY.COM
SHONEN SUNDAY

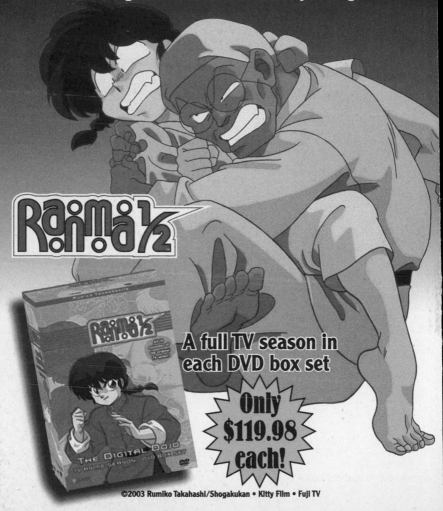

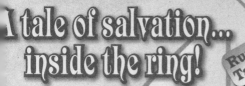

A tale of salvation... inside the ring!

Rumiko Takahashi's One-Pound Gospel

From the creator of *Inuyasha*, *Ranma 1/2* and *Maison Ikkoku*

Kosaku is a professional boxer whose inability to abstain from hearty food is the bane of his coach's existence. Sister Angela is a young, dedicated and fairly naive nun who catches Kosaku's eye. Can her faith redeem his gluttony?

Find out in the *One Pound Gospel* manga series— buy yours today!

At Your Indentured Service

Hayate's parents are bad with money, so they sell his organs to pay their debts. Hayate doesn't like this plan, so he comes up with a new one—kidnap and ransom a girl from a wealthy family. Solid plan… so how did he end up as her butler?

Find out in *Hayate the Combat Butler*— buy the manga at store.viz.com!

Hayate the Combat Butler

Renjiro Hata

WITHDRAWN